6.75

MOUNTAINEERING

The Freedom of the Hills

SECOND EDITION

SECOND EDITION

MOUNTAINEERING
THE FREEDOM *of the* HILLS

The Climbing Committee of The Mountaineers

HARVEY MANNING, *Chairman of Editors*

Editorial Committee: JOHN R. HAZLE, CARL HENRIKSON, NANCY BICKFORD MILLER, THOMAS MILLER, FRANZ MOHLING, ROWLAND TABOR, LESLEY STARK TABOR

Illustrations:

DONNA BALCH COOK *and* ROBERT CRAM

THE MOUNTAINEERS *Seattle, Washington*

THE MOUNTAINEERS

Organized 1906

To explore and study the mountains, forests, and watercourses of the Northwest;

To gather into permanent form the history and traditions of this region;

To preserve by the encouragement of protective legislation or otherwise the natural beauty of Northwest America;

To make expeditions into these regions in fulfillment of the above purposes;

To encourage a spirit of good fellowship among all lovers of outdoor life.

First Edition, April 1960

Reprinted June 1961, June 1963

April 1965, December 1966

Second Edition, December 1967

Reprinted June 1969, December 1970

DESIGN BY JOHN WARNER

MANUFACTURED IN THE UNITED STATES OF AMERICA BY

THE VAIL-BALLOU PRESS, INC., BINGHAMTON, NEW YORK

LIBRARY OF CONGRESS CATALOG CARD NO. 67-29175

*

FOREWORD

To the small group of Puget Sounders who organized The Mountaineers in 1906, wilderness was no distant or uncommon thing; it surrounded their young cities and towns, lying everywhere near the ends of streetcar lines and close to saltwater beaches. They felt no need of specially praising *wilderness* mountaineering; for them there wasn't any other kind. The sport they and their successors evolved differed from that of the Alps in many ways, particularly in the fact most peaks then attempted were more troublesome in the approaches than the final ascents.

Three decades later, when more difficult climbs began to be made regularly, using more sophisticated equipment and technique, wilderness remained dominant except here and there. And though the wilderness line had been driven back from tidewater into the mountain fronts, few thought the back-country could ever be civilized.

Three decades later still, it has become apparent the explosions of technology and population—amplified by ignorance, greed, and simple bad taste—can easily overwhelm the enclaves of wildness left in the Northwest. A climber, as climber, may not be concerned, may even cheer the growing ease of access by highway, logging road, and scooter track, the proposals for comfortable meadowland chalets offering soft beds and hot meals, if his interests are purely "Alpine."

However, after a generations-long tradition of battling brush and bad trails, dank forests and wild rivers, the true-bred Northwest climber, seeing the objects of his wry complaints disappearing, finds that he *likes* dank forests and evil brush, heavy packs and rough trails or no trails, or to be more precise, he likes mountains whose inner battlements of rock and snow are ringed around with strong outer defenses of tangled greenery. His sport is *wilderness mountaineering*, not simple "climbing", and that's the way he wants it.

This book is about wild mountains. But there won't *be* any a generation or two from now unless those who value the way of life here described help preserve wildlands sufficient for coming decades, coming generations.

We know what is happening in our home hills, the Cascades and Olympics. We also know from our travels, and from reports received through the mountain network, that all of North America and indeed every continent of the earth are similarly threatened—with the possible exception of Antarctica, and even there the population has risen phenomenally in the past several years.

A most interesting publishing project would be an annual international summary called *The Wilderness World*. This year—and any year in the past, and maybe for years in the future—such a volume would tell only partial and tentative conservation victories. Perhaps a regular tabulation of the steady losses on a worldwide scale is needed to shake the complacency of escapists who shrug off the taming of their local hills by saying the reservoir of wildness is so enormous there will always be someplace to go.

Earth is a small planet. What happens to the North Cascades matters in Norway and Japan. What happens to the New Zealand Alps and the Andes matters in Seattle. In a real sense, British Columbia belongs to the people of California, and Kenya to the people of Switzerland, and vice versa. Wild it may be, but lacking rain forests and blowdowns, slide alder, devils club, and beaver marshes, climbing will never be as good a sport on the moon.

A concerned individual should maximize his efforts by joining a group of like-minded people. In virtually every population center there are now mountain clubs inviting general membership; increasingly these are assuming leadership in protecting the natural scene. In addition there are organizations with broad national interests; in the United States the Sierra Club is preeminent, with chapters in every region and fighting conservation wars on every front in close alliance with local clubs.

The Mountaineers, with members throughout the Puget Sound region and others across the nation, invite all to join who sympathize with the purposes of the organization and wish to share, directly or vicariously, in its efforts to preserve the natural beauty of Northwest

America, and in its many activities, which include the Climbing Course presented annually since 1935 and a year-round program of hiking, camping, ski-mountaineering, and snowshoeing; hundreds of outings are scheduled each year, lasting a single day or several weeks, ranging from ocean beaches to high summits. For information on how to join, write The Mountaineers, P.O. Box 122, Seattle, Washington 98111.

HARVEY MANNING

December 1967

*

PREFACE

TO SECOND EDITION

When the first edition of this book was published in 1960, estimates of the year when the initial printing of 5000 copies would be exhausted ranged from 1963 to 1967, with some opinion they never would all be sold before the paper crumbled into dust. What could not have been predicted was that mountaineering would soon become comparatively popular in America—the sport of thousands rather than hundreds. The 25,000 copies of the first edition (plus another 3000 in the Japanese translation) are one measure of what has happened; another is the growing number of climbing schools presented by mountain clubs and increasingly by colleges and universities; and another is the crowds (again, relatively speaking, and surely nowhere resembling the Matterhorn queue) in some of the more famous climbing centers.

As the years went along, and it became apparent *Freedom* had been accepted not only by the Climbing Course of The Mountaineers but by students elsewhere in North America and the world, the Climbing Committee began planning a revised edition to embody changes since 1960 in equipment and technique and attitude. Individual members of the Climbing Committee (and also those of the Climbing Committees of the branches in Everett, Olympia, and Tacoma, sponsoring independent but parallel Climbing Courses) restudied the text and made suggestions. All these were placed in a file, together with those received from other climbers, in the club and out, from near and very far.

In the fall of 1965, by which time much rewriting was underway, Climbing Chairman John M. Davis appointed a *Freedom* Committee to carry the job to completion: Tom Hallstaff, Max Hollenbeck, Jim Mitchell, Roger Neubauer, Howard Stansbury, and as chairman, John M. Davis. Each member was assigned a number of chapters and appendices and made responsible for analyzing comments, consulting experts, assembling recommendations, reviewing new copy submitted, doing any further writing or research required, and leading discussions through the full committee to policy decisions. Those of the original editorial committee who were available—John R. Hazle, Tom and Nancy Miller, Franz Mohling, and Rowland Tabor—participated in commentary and/or discussion, with the others giving moral support.

The people listed below contributed major amounts of new writing or particularly-extensive critical comments. (*Freedom* Committee members are not named except where they acted as principal writers in addition to above-noted editorial duties.) "Equipment": rewritten by Tom Hallstaff. "Alpine Cuisine": much new material, and the whole revised, by Joan Firey. "Navigation in the Hills": map section rewritten by John Pollock, Rowland Tabor, and Dwight Crowder. "Roped Climbing": ropes and knots updated by Jim Mitchell. "Pitoncraft and Rappels": almost completely new, by Eric Bjornstad and Alex Bertullis, with comments by Fred Beckey, Jim Stuart, and John Armitage. "Ice": also nearly all new, written by Dave McBrayer, aided by his wife Alyce, based on a thorough preliminary review by himself and Pete Schoening, with comments from Hans Zogg and Jim Whittaker. "Arrests and Belays": updated by Roger Neubauer, with comments from Tom Nicolino. "First Aid": revised by Drs. John Lucas and John Stewart. "Alpine Rescue": revised in part by Roger Neubauer and Everett Lasher. "Mountain Geology": rewritten by the original author, Rowland Tabor, harrassed by Dwight Crowder. "The Cycle of Snow": new data and sections added by the sole author, Ed LaChapelle. "Mountain Weather": the new lightning section written by Bartlett Burns, the remainder revised with comments by Roger Wilcox and Neal Barr. "Food Requirements of the Climber": new statistics provided by Marian Arlin and Max Hollenbeck. "Meals for Semi-Expeditions": new in this edition, by Joan Firey. "Supplementary Reading": also new, compiled by Max Hollenbeck. The index was prepared by Susan Warner.

The others who helped with comments—on the above chapters or on the remainder, which were thoroughly reviewed but changed to a lesser degree—are too numerous to list or even remember. Countless Mountaineers sent useful notes, and also countless mountaineers from throughout America and Canada, and South America, Europe, Africa, and Asia, and from as far away (in distance though not in spirit) as New Zealand and Australia. May the criticisms and suggestions, from everywhere, keep coming; continuing revision of the book is planned.

The original artists, Bob Cram and Donna Cook, revised their drawings as needed and added new ones. Ed Hansen provided new illustrations for "Mountain Geology."

The editors were once more fortunate to have the invaluable services of John Warner as designer, and of Peggy Ferber as manuscript typist.

Thanks must be given the Literary Fund Committee, which now directs the editing, production, and distribution of Mountaineer books. By action of the Trustees of The Mountaineers, proceeds from sales of *Freedom*, over and above those required for its reprinting and revision, are entirely devoted to publishing similar educational materials; elsewhere in this book is a list of those currently available.

The second edition of *Mountaineering: The Freedom of the Hills* is offered, as was the first, with the hope it may make new friends for the mountain wilderness.

H.M.

December 1967

*

PREFACE

TO FIRST EDITION

In 1935, when The Mountaineers presented their first Climbing Course, the lack of a suitable textbook was immediately felt. Commonplace though it is that mountaineering can be learned only in the mountains, the high country season is so short that lectures and home studies in winter are desirable if students are to make most efficient use of field practices in spring and experience climbs in summer. The manuals available to the pioneer faculty had some value, for though their basis was mainly the Alps, that range after all was not only the birthplace of alpinism but until quite recently supplied most of its techniques and tools. However, in western America, far from networks of huts and trails and corps of guides and porters, the pure form of alpinism had by necessity evolved into the considerably different sport of wilderness mountaineering. Two generations of scrambles in the Cascades and Olympics had provided a good deal of local wisdom, little of it in print. At first The Mountaineers employed published manuals to their limits, supplementing them with mimeographed outlines based on lecture notes. Eventually these were fleshed out and lithographed as the paperbound *Climbers' Notebook*, issued in 1948, with some revision, by Superior Publishing Company of Seattle as the hardbound *Mountaineers Handbook*.

So swiftly were equipment and methods improving in the years after World War II that on publication the text was already passing into obsolescence. In 1949 The Mountaineers Climbing Committee began planning a revised second edition, but soon realized the changes were so sweeping as to entail a book entirely new. Furthermore, the character of the school itself had adjusted to the greatly enlarged postwar student body. In the early days, when every instructor knew every student, a concise summary was sufficient for classroom purposes. With increased enrollment a more explicit work seemed better suited to the steady decentralization of instruction.

In September of 1955 those who had served most recently as Climbing Committee chairmen planned a tentative chapter outline and working policy. These chairmen were Cameron Beckwith, Victor Josendal, Frank Doleshy, Harvey Manning, Ward Irwin, John R. Hazle, Roy Wessel, Maurice Muzzy, and Varnel Denhem. The chairmen during preparation of the manuscript and its publication were Harold Blinn, Alden Crittenden, Robert Latz, and Frank Fickeisen.

Membership of the editorial committee that assumed direction of the project fluctuated over the following 5 years. Those who served the entire term or a major part were Nancy Bickford, John R. Hazle, Carl Henrikson, Thomas Miller, Franz Mohling, Rowland Tabor, and Lesley Stark Tabor. Making essential contributions though over a shorter period were Peter McLellan, Robert and Louise Beckman, Robert Latz, and Ira Spring. Most of those named not only wrote and edited chapters but supervised the efforts of others. More important, at innumerable meetings of the full committee and in countless telephone and campfire conversations the group debated and decided editorial policy, production tactics, and in fact every detail down to subtleties of equipment design and technique.

It is not possible to assign credit for authorship with the exception of Chapter 21, "The Cycle of Snow," entirely the creation of Edward LaChapelle, with the critical help of Mark F. Meier and Richard C. Hubley. In every other case the general procedure was to assign a chapter to a writer, send his draft to a number of readers for criticisms, discuss these in editorial conference, and reassign the chapter, ordinarily to a fresh writer for the sake of a new viewpoint. Over the years each chapter was completely redrafted as many as seven times, so that in the final versions the outline may be the work of one person, the style that of another, with large units of the content supplied by several others. As is frequently the custom in such group efforts the editors sought to balance an overall structural uniformity with maximum retention of individual feeling and tone. The editors hope that any loss of smoothness in reading owing to variations in style from chapter to chapter is compensated for by this steady reminder that many climbers with many attitudes participated. The occasional inaccuracies and internal contradictions that doubtless have escaped editorial notice will serve as object lessons to the student that mountaineering is still an inexact amateur sport, not yet another division of professional engineering.

Those who contributed drafts of one or more chapters, or particularly extensive critical reviews, are Neal Barr, Phillip Bartow, Wolf Bauer, Theodore and Ruth Beck, Fred Beckey, Robert and Louise Beckman, Cameron Beckwith, George Bloom, Robert Brooks, William Campbell, Kenneth Carpenter, Nicholas Clinch, Alden Crittenden, Stan Curtis, William and Stella Degenhardt, Eugene Dodson, Frank Doleshy, John and Pauline Dyer, Sharon Fairley, Eugene Faure, Joseph Fiery, Ralph Goshorn, Robert Grant, Michael Hane, David Harrah, John R. Hazle, Carl Henrikson, Irving Herrigstad, Ryland Hill, Ward and Lois Irwin, Victor Josendal, Erick Karlsson, Neva Karrick, Tim Kelley, Dale Kunz, Everett Lasher, Robert Latz, Richard MacGowan, Peter McLellan, Harvey and Betty Manning, Genevieve Marcoux, Carol Marston, George Martin, Richard and Joan Merritt, Thomas and Nancy Miller, Robert Milnor, Franz Mohling, Dee Molenaar, Maurice Muzzy, John Osseward, Verl Rogers, Richard Savery, Peter Schoening, Robert Sipe, David Soules, Warren Spickard, Thomas Steinburn, Jean Stillwell, Rowland Tabor, Mary Kay Tarver, William and Joleen Unsoeld, Harriet Walker, Roy Wessel, and Stanley Worswick. In addition, hundreds of reviewers read manuscript early and late, adding the weight of their experience.

The illustrations were supervised from beginning to end by Nancy Bickford Miller. Innumerable preliminary sketches were contributed by Beverly Beck, Mary Jane Brockman, Charles Doan, Sylvia Duryea, Jo Anne Feringer, Honor Fernalld, and Robert Milnor, not to forget such double-threat writer-artists as Ed LaChapelle and Thomas Miller. Special mention is due Dee Molenaar, who took time from his classic series of drawings for the revised *Climber's Guide to the Cascades and Olympics* to prepare the important contour-map sequence in "Navigation in the Hills."

Two artists, however, have most reason to remember the long evolution of the manuscript titled *Hillwalking: The Lowdown on How to Get High* into the present book. From the start the editors felt illustrations would be a most distinctive value of the text. Every drawing was separately considered in committee, over and over again, in rough sketch, in semifinal pencil, in final ink, and time after time sent back to the drawing board. The fortitude and sweep temper of these two were remarkable; the reader can judge for himself their other talents. The division of labor will be easily evident: the equipment and scenery by Donna Balch Cook; the busy little men, sometimes sorely tried but frequently indomitable, by Robert Cram.

The photographs were assembled under the direction of Bob and Ira Spring. Scores of mountaineers assisted by submitting prints and many excellent ones were regretfully rejected. The attempt to suggest in a mere 16 scenes the essence of western American mountaineering drew the committee into rather nebulous areas of personal metaphysics, and the final choice can accurately be called arbitrary.

Under the system of multiple-review of every draft of every chapter, manuscript typing was an immense task, and without swift, intelligent help the editors would have been swamped. Lesley Stark Tabor coordinated the typing, and those whose labors were completely beyond reason were Stella Degenhardt, Maxine Denhem, Peggy Eaton Ferber, Margaret Kershaw, Marilyn Kinney, Martha, Jan, and Pat Millegan, and Alexandra Pye. The later and equally important burden of proofreading fell upon Grace Kent and Betty Manning, with the invaluable assistance of Raelynn Cole, Glenna Cox, Gayle Donahue, Wayne Gaskill, Peter Maloney, Martha Millegan, Ruth Partridge, and Alan Southern.

Without the advice and encouragement of Cameron Beckwith at every stage from first planning to final publication the book would never have been undertaken, much less come to press. As the manuscript was approaching full development, Jeannette Clark played an invaluable role by style-editing a number of the chapters. Though most of these returned into the mill of draft and redraft, her professional competence provided a model to be emulated, if not duplicated. The patience and courtesy of John Phillips of Vail-Ballou Press were a marvel to the editors, and deeply appreciated.

The debt to John Warner is beyond moderate expression. That he designed the book scarcely reflects his contribution, for from a very early period the committee depended heavily on his guidance not only in technical matters but in those of fundamental policy. Many decisions normally reserved for editors were entrusted to his judgment.

The Mountaineers being far from a wealthy organization, the manuscript would have lain forever in limbo without the faith of the numerous individuals who lent money to the club secured only and merely by prospective sales. A committee consisting of Victor Josendal, chairman, Leo Gallagher, Paul Wiseman, John R. Hazle, Richard Merritt, and Joseph Buswell made an initial investigation into the financial feasibility of publication. The Book Promotion Committee, under chairmen E. Allen Robinson and Warren Wilson, with members Sarah Blumenthal, Ellen Brooker, Alton DuFlon, Eleanor Hisey, Leon Israel, Ralph Johnson, Lowell Livingstone, and Paul Wiseman expended enormous energy first in raising the necessary capital and then in planning and executing distribution. The editors wish also to express their obligation to the leadership of The Mountaineers, particularly the presidents during the years of composition and production, Paul Wiseman and John R. Hazle.

Though tailored specifically to The Mountaineers Climbing Course, for practical reasons the order of presentation in the text does not follow the schedule of instruction. The topical outline tends to move from basic to advanced, but portions even of the earliest chapters are beyond the ordinary needs of the novice, while portions of the final chapters are virtually the articles of his acceptance. Within the Climbing Course, then, reading assignments will be sharply selective. For example, though the first-year student in that school will be asked to study Chapters 7, 8, 9, and parts of 10, not until the second year will Chapters 6, 11, and the remainder of 10 be emphasized. Since most first-year students attend at least some of the second-year lectures and practices there is not in reality such a pure division, but the general reader should know this context of use. However helpful a mountaineering textbook may be, without accompanying practice trips and experience climbs of gradually ascending difficulty it can quite easily supply exactly enough information to lead a beginning climber to disaster.

The lack of a bibliography, or even a list of suggested readings, may seem a cavalier dismissal of any and all previous writings. In fact, when the editors found that the book was being written almost entirely from personal knowledge, assimilated though this may have been from many sources, no further encouragement was needed to shirk preparation of a proper reading list. Whether or not the debt is expressly acknowledged, the local tradition of wilderness mountaineering, and thus the present work, owe much to mountaineers from other regions, continents, and times.

The beginning student should certainly read as widely in the literature as leisure and interest allow. The mountain world is large, and there is room for many varieties of experience and attitude. In any one book there is an inevitable emphasis on the climbing "style" of a particular region and group—or perhaps a particular editorial committee. Even within The Mountaineers there is no such uniformity of style as a textbook tends to suggest, and other places, other times exhibit styles either slightly or radically different, but not necessarily better or worse. The student seeking the deeper values of mountaineering does well to understand the experience and style of generations and regions other than his own.

Mountaincraft, by Geoffrey Winthrop Young, Methuen, London,

1949, is universally and properly credited as the classic of its kind. The writings of every superior mountaineer are worth reading, from Moses, Petrarch, and Wordsworth to Whymper, Smythe, and Rebuffat. Climbing journals report new expeditions and gather old history. Those of the American Alpine Club and the Alpine Club of Canada, taken together, summarize North American and world mountaineering. Regional annals add local depth, nor should one neglect the fascinating counterpoint of such foreign journals as that of the New Zealand Alpine Club. The catalogues of American and European firms specializing in mountaineering outfit are indispensable guides to the newest advances in equipment, and by implication, technique.

Publications of the Sierra Club have immense value for all who travel western ranges. Full acknowledgment of debt to the large and expanding Sierra Club list of conservation books, journals, and newsletters must await the future. Other debts of other kinds to articles and pamphlets are noted within this text.

Reading about mountains is a pleasure, and there is something to be learned from any book or journal. But for the apprentice and veteran alike, words are at best a poor substitute for peaks. The hope behind this book is that it will allow students to more quickly and safely become, on whatever level they choose, wilderness mountaineers.

H.M.

April 1960

Other Books from The Mountaineers

The North Cascades

The home hills of *Freedom* photographed by a climber, Tom Miller. 68 scenes of walls and glaciers, forests and meadows, displayed on large-format 10 × 12-inch pages. 10 maps by Dee Molenaar. Text by Harvey Manning calls for a North Cascades National Park. $10.

Across the Olympic Mountains: the 1889–90 Press Expedition

By Robert L. Wood. Published jointly with the University of Washington Press. 232 pages, 24 photos, 9 maps. $5.95.

Mountain Rescue Techniques

By Wastl Mariner. Translated and published in cooperation with the Oesterreichischer Alpenverein and the Mountain Rescue Council. The official manual of IKAR, the International Commission for Alpine Rescue. 200 pages, 117 drawings, paperbound. $3.50.

Medicine for Mountaineering

Written by climber-physicians with experience ranging from the Cascades to the West Ridge of Everest, edited by James A. Wilkerson, M.D. The first American manual of medical treatment, as distinguished from first aid. 300 pages, 75 drawings, $7.50.

Routes and Rocks: Hiker's Guide to the North Cascades from Glacier Peak to Lake Chelan

Trails and off-trail high routes, plus notes on geology. 240 pages, 96 drawings and maps, 9 photos, and three 13 × 22-inch U.S.G.S. maps with special overprints. By D. F. Crowder and R. W. Tabor of the U.S. Geological Survey. $5.

100 Hikes in Western Washington

Each of the 100 trips, recommended by The Mountaineers, is presented in a convenient two-page unit with text by Louise Marshall telling why to go and how, a sketch map, and a full-page photograph by Bob and Ira Spring. 240 pages, 110 photos, 102 maps. $4.95.

Trips and Trails: Camps, Short Hikes, and Viewpoints in the North Cascades and Olympics

Text by E. M. Sterling, photos by Bob and Ira Spring. 240 pages, 120 photos, 100 maps. $4.95. (A companion volume, *Central and South Cascades*, is scheduled for 1968).

Northwest Ski Trails

The principal tow-hill ski areas from Garibaldi Park in British Columbia to Bachelor's Butte in Oregon, and the ski tours available from each, together with others from undeveloped starting points. Chapters on equipment and technique. Text by Ted Mueller, photos by Bob and Ira Spring. 240 pages, 100 photos, 100 maps. $4.95.

Guide to Leavenworth Rock-Climbing Areas

By Fred Beckey and Eric Bjornstad. 88 pages, 10 sketches, 2 maps, paperbound. $2.50.

30 Hikes in Alaska: Western Chugach, Talkeetna, Kenai

Edited by William E. Hauser. Published jointly with the Mountaineering Club of Alaska. 80 pages, 6 photos, 31 maps, paperbound. $2.50.

Index to The Mountaineer

For the journal published annually since 1907, complete through 1966. $2.50.

*

CONTENTS

*

PLATES

PART ONE

Approaching the Peaks

1 *

EQUIPMENT

A MOUNTAINEER is, simply, one who seeks the freedom of the hills, full wilderness citizenship, with no barriers he cannot pass, no dangers he cannot avoid. Technique and equipment are inseparable components of freedom, and discussing one apart from the other is awkward at best. As a compromise, the present chapter focuses on the basic outfit of a climber, the gear he must have for nearly every trip, even the most elementary. Later chapters discuss further these basic tools—and also more specialized equipment—in the context of use.

The average apprentice goes through an initial period of confusion. He is likely to think the first technique he must master is rappelling and the first equipment he must buy is a coil of rope and a sack of iron. Moreover, however wisely he attempts to select his gear by reading catalogs, journals, and texts, by observing experienced mountaineers on climbs and asking them questions, he can easily be bewildered by the variety of tools used for any given purpose, some perhaps inferior, but many equally satisfactory. Hill-worn veterans assembled in a camp, costumed as if for a fashion parade of professional eccentrics, rigging shelters ranging from McKinley tents to plastic tarps, each cooking up his favorite hoosh, glop, blue-plate special, or son-of-a-gun stew, seem on the surface to have little in common but individualism.

Space is not available for a definitive encyclopedia of equipment in current favor, nor for an historical summary of what climbers used yesterday, nor predictions of where fashion trends will lead tomorrow. The following pages are not exhaustive, but rather are a brief summary of opinion designed to be useful in the difficult first months of assembling a basic outfit.

Freedom of the hills lies largely in the ability to cope with every problem of travel and living, and every emergency, with nothing more than what a party can carry conveniently on its shoulders. Equipment must be kept to the safe minimum, all frills and luxuries eliminated, and must be just as lightweight as is consistent with durability and versatility. Modern materials and methods of manufacture have made possible great saving in weight with no sacrifice of usefulness, most notably in sleeping bags and shelter; unfortunately, very often the lower the weight the higher the price.

Given unlimited funds a person can visit any mountaineering equipment shop and walk out an hour later fully and superbly outfitted for the high country. The novice of ordinary means must proceed more cautiously to avoid bankruptcy. However, if he has a background of hiking and camping many of the major expenditures lie behind him, and even the lifelong urbanite finds much in his closet, basement, and kitchen that can be converted to mountain use, though perhaps only as a stopgap.

The beginner need not bog down in either confusion or bankruptcy if he takes one trip at a time, one purchase at a time. Boots come first, necessary for even the simplest climb under alpine conditions, plus warm clothing and a litter of small and inexpensive essentials and a rucksack to carry them. For an overnight trip, shelter and kitchenware can be improvised at small cost, but the required packboard is a substantial investment and the indispensable sleeping bag a painful purchase; there is no economy in buying cheap. Before a person can venture onto steep snow he must have an ice ax. The climbing rope comes fairly late in the timetable since the novice will be—or should be— making his first roped climbs with an experienced companion who owns one.

The governing rule, then, is never to buy anything until the next climb demands it. By improvising, modifying, borrowing, and renting, the basic outfit can be budgeted over the entire first climbing season. In succeeding years stopgaps can be gradually replaced, all the more wisely for the delay, and specialized tools accumulated.

Boots: Foundation of the Climber

One day of climbing may involve travel through and over streams, mud, logs, brush, meadow, and scree, stepkicking in snow, and delicate balance on steep rock. A single pair of boots must usually suffice for all these conditions. A good climbing boot therefore represents a happy compromise between a number of conflicting requirements. It must be tough to withstand the scraping of rocks, stiff and solid for kicking steps in hard snow, yet light and flexible for rock. The upper must be high enough to support the ankles in rough walking, yet allow them to flex to the extreme angles required by cramponing and slabclimbing. The ideal sole should grip on both slippery logs and smooth rock. There must be room to wiggle the toes while wearing two pairs of heavy socks (the important thing to remember when trying on boots for size), but the fit must not be so loose that the foot can slip around

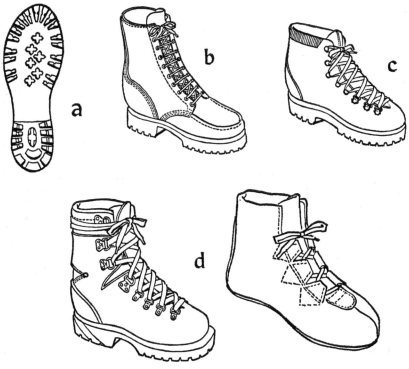

Fig. 1. Typical boots.
    a. Rubber lug sole.
    b. High boot.
    c. Low boot, with scree cuff.
    d. Cold-weather double boot. *Left,* outer boot.
        Right, inner boot.

inside, causing both blisters on trails and loss of control on small holds.

The compromise found best by most current climbers is a low-top (6-inch) boot with a lug sole of fairly-hard rubber. (Softer grades of rubber provide superior friction but wear rapidly.)

The added support of a slightly higher (8-inch) top may be desirable for climbers prone to ankle injuries. The extra inches of leather also keep the feet drier, but the same objective can be achieved by gaiters (see below) without the risk of ankle constriction.

The lug sole grips well on snow and provides excellent insulation from the cold. On all types of rock it is so satisfactory that special rock shoes are rarely needed. On the trail, jolts from stones are well-cushioned.

The principal objection to the lug-soled boot is that it is more treacherous on wet heather, brush, and footlogs than the once-universal tricouni-nailed boot, which also holds better on hard snow and ice. Nails, however, conduct heat from the foot and also are unsatisfactory for steep rock. Attempts have been made to combine the virtues of lugs and nails on a single boot, but the result has been to combine the vices instead. Neither nailed nor "half-breed" climbing boots are now in common use.

Dozens of boot styles are available which fall within the limits of the recommended compromise. Whichever is chosen must meet still further tests of acceptability. The welt should be narrow, lest it bend on small holds and cause a slip. The upper lacing should be with hooks rather than eyelets. The top should open wide so that even when the boot is wet or frozen it can be put on with minimum struggle by a climber wearing mittens; a loop sewn into the upper is very useful for heavy hauling, and almost mandatory for 8-inch boots. Double or triple layering in areas exposed to roughest wear adds to weight and expense, but also to durability and protection. (Inexpensive "trail shoes" which otherwise resemble climbing boots dispense with this layering.) Especially desirable is a hard toe to prevent rock bruises and uncomfortable compression by crampon straps, and to ease the task of stepkicking.

Water can enter the boot not only over the top but through the leather or seams. Boots of good-quality leather having a box tongue and being well-waterproofed, particularly at the seams, can exclude water for a long while, even when slopping around in wet snow (assuming none enters over the top). Poor leather ensures wet feet regardless of how much wax or grease is applied. Price is usually a fair measure of the leather quality.

A good pair of boots will, with periodic repair, last many years. Very inexpensive boots sometimes fall apart in a season or two. The period of usefulness can be considerably extended by proper care. To prevent mildew and rot, boots should be thoroughly dried after each climb, the mud first being washed off, paper stuffed inside, and a moderately-warm, perfectly-dry storage place chosen. High temperatures are almost as damaging to leather as to human skin, and the former lacks nerve endings to warn of harm being done; the boots seen roasting by the campfire are the same ones that mysteriously disintegrate on some future climb. Waterproofing is best done well before the next climb— say, immediately after the last climb—to allow a long period for the preservative to soak in. The type of preservative depends on how the leather was tanned (be sure to ask when buying): for chrome- or silicone-tanned leather, use a wax or silicone; for oil-tanned leather, use oil or grease.

SPECIAL-PURPOSE BOOTS

Various boots and footwear lacking in versatility are far superior for specific terrains. Though unnecessary for the beginner, they provide advantages on severe climbs which may mean the difference between success and failure, comfort and misery, safety and danger.

An inexpensive *cold-weather boot,* made of rubber and completely waterproof, was developed by the U.S. Army for the Korean War. Modified by the addition of a lug sole, it has been used successfully on Mt. McKinley and in the cold, wet, winter Cascades. More expensive, and the choice of many major Himalayan expeditions, is the "LOWA"-type double boot, consisting of a soft, insulated inner boot and a high, heavy outer; the inner may be removed for drying or for tent wear. Both Korean and double boots are so large that climbing on small holds is difficult. Also, crampons cannot be interchanged between them and regular boots.

Rock shoes are lightweight boots with uppers of soft leather or other material and a shallow lug sole. Rock shoes must fit tight; only one pair of socks should be worn.

Clothing

A climber's clothing is divided into three layers, each performing a specific task. Next to the skin is the *ventilating* layer, open-weave or fishnet underwear of absorbent material which allows some air circulation. Thus, perspiration can evaporate or be absorbed without soaking the *insulating* layer, which may consist of shirt, sweaters, or down clothing, depending on the severity of the weather, and whose value depends upon its ability to trap layers of stagnant air. The outer *protecting* layer shields the insulation from wind and rain, which greatly reduce its effectiveness.

Table 1 is a rough guide to the total thickness of insulation required for various situations, while Figure 2 illustrates the intense chilling effect of even a light breeze. For example, if the air temperature is 60°F and a 5-mile-per-hour wind is blowing, exposed flesh loses heat as rapidly as if the temperature were 20°F without wind.

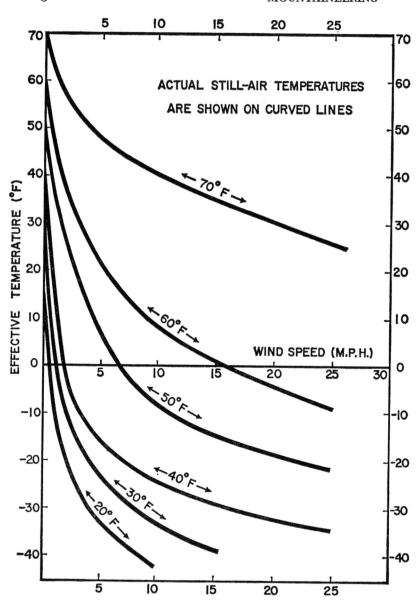

Fig. 2. Wind chill. To find effective temperature, read vertically from wind speed to actual still-air temperature, then read horizontally to the lefthand scale. For example, with a wind speed of 20 m.p.h. and an actual temperature of 70°F, the effective temperature is 30°F. (Based on data from U.S. Army Medical Research Laboratory, Fort Knox—February 1959.)

I. Mount Formidable, North Cascades. (Franz Mohling)

II. Ripsaw Ridge, North Cascades (Thomas Miller)

Table 1. Insulation Required for Various Situations.

Temperature	Total Thickness of Insulation (in inches)		
	Sleeping	*Light Work*	*Heavy Work*
40°F	1.5	.8	.2
0°F	2.5	1.3	.35
−40°F	3.5	1.9	.48

Table 1 and Figure 2 demonstrate several important requirements. Because of the rapid changes in temperature, wind, and exertion usually experienced, clothing must be versatile, quick and easy to put on or shed even under difficult conditions. The weight and bulk of woolen shirts and sweaters make them impractical as the sole source of insulation at very low temperatures; down becomes essential. Figure 2 shows the importance of windproof outer clothing.

Following paragraphs discuss in more detail the articles in a climber's wardrobe.

SOCKS

Wool socks are, in cold, wet mountains, the only kind worth wearing, for wool is the most efficient insulator of any wet fiber. A light, smoothly-woven pair is usually worn next to the skin and a heavy, roughly-woven pair outside these, plus a third pair for very cold weather or very large boots. Some climbers with tender feet prefer a light cotton or nylon sock next to the skin; this is in addition to the wool socks. The toes must always be free to wiggle; three tightly-packed pairs of socks give less protection from cold than two loose ones, since compression of fibers reduces the dead air space which is the chief source of insulation. Nylon reinforcement at toes and heel greatly extends the useful life of socks.

Insoles are often added to provide extra insulation and cushioning and for the sake of a snugger fit. The most common materials are felt, leather, and lambskin—all of which absorb moisture and must be taken out when drying the boot. Insoles of woven synthetic fiber are non-absorbent, do not become matted or damp, and have a loose structure that helps ventilate the foot.

The vapor-barrier principle can be employed to add insulating value. In one method the climber wears, from the foot out: (1) a light wool sock to absorb perspiration; (2) a plastic sock improvised from a polyethylene bag; (3) a heavier wool sock which—protected by the plastic from perspiration—forms a perpetually-dry wool insulator; (4) another plastic sock; (5) the boot.

TROUSERS

Climbing trousers ideally are warm, windproof, and water-repellent. Close-woven cotton satisfies the latter two requirements, but is miserably cold when wet. Wool is warmer, wind-resistant when closely woven, and sheds water when appropriately treated. Orlon is also good, being as warm as wool and drying more quickly. A hard-finish fabric is desirable for snow climbing, since fuzzy cloth collects snow particles which ultimately melt, soaking the pants. For easy motion, trousers should be cut full at the hips and knees but tapered at the ankles to reduce snagging by crampons and sharp rocks.

Fig. 3. Pants. *Left leg,* cuff closed with drawstring. *Right leg,* short gaiter.

The boundary between trousers and boots is the climber's most critical problem, particularly on snow. A satisfactory solution is cuffless pants with a drawstring in the bottom left open for ventilation during trail walking and drawn tight for snow. The ends of the drawstring may be tied under the boot to hold the pants down. Gaiters, described below, can be added to seal the gap completely.

Large pockets sewn onto the trouser thighs are useful for carrying small items in frequent demand. Buttoned flaps or zippers keep things from falling out and prevent snow getting in.

The life-expectancy of pants can be extended by reinforcing the seat and perhaps the knees with patches of leather, canvas, or plastic. Another school patches only—and with cloth—when the original trouser surface is completely breached and demands of comfort and modesty are urgent.

Excellent climbing pants and knickers are available commercially, but at a price. The average—which is to say impoverished—mountaineer chiefly uses old wool slacks become too shoddy for city wear, or ski pants, or Army surplus wool trousers. The cuffs are chopped off, drawstrings added if desired, pockets and patches sewed on, water-repelling compound applied. Patching continues to the point of no return and the garment is then burned, sometimes with considerable ceremony.

Wind pants made of light, tough, very closely-woven nylon, cut large enough to put on without removing boots, are designed to be worn over regular trousers when the weather is cold and windy. Though weighing only a few ounces and stuffing easily into a pocket, wind pants reduce heat loss considerably in a hard blow. As a fringe benefit, during sitting glissades they keep trousers dry and provide a fast running surface.

GAITERS

Short gaiters, 5 or 6 inches high, are sufficient for most summer climbing. They should be made of tough nylon, with elastic top and bottom to ensure a snug fit over pants and boot tops. A string tied under the instep holds the gaiters down; a full zipper allows them to be donned without removing boots. When deep snow is anticipated, longer (about 16 inches) gaiters are used, made in the form of a nylon tube large enough to admit the boot. Laces then permit the gaiter to be drawn close around the pants and boot top.

UNDERWEAR

An undershirt of open-weave material helps perspiration evaporate and traps an additional insulating layer of air. Cotton fishnet vests are popular, but like all cotton clothing, are cold when wet. Orlon fishnet is ideal but not available commercially. "Long Johns" are not usually necessary for summer climbing, though they may be carried as emergency gear.

SHIRTS AND SWEATERS

Shirts and sweaters provide insulation mainly by trapping air within and between themselves. Several light, loose-fitting layers are therefore more effective than one heavy garment, such as a logger's mackinaw.

The *layer system* is superbly adapted to the quick fluctuations of cold and heat typical of alpine regions. Layers are added or removed one by one to keep pace with changing conditions. At least one of the shirts should have a long tail so it will remain inside the pants and protect the midriff.

Shirts and sweaters should be entirely wool, slow to get wet and even then retaining much of its insulating value. Cotton sweatshirts absorb water like sponges and rapidly become worthless as insulation.

DOWN CLOTHING

Though two layers above underwear—a wool shirt and sweater—are sufficient in most climbing, Table 1 shows it is impractical to depend solely on conventional clothing at very low temperatures, because of the bulk and weight. Down has two properties—lightness and compressibility—which make it indispensable for these conditions. A down garment can be squeezed into an incredibly-small volume and yet quickly regain full bulk. Down must never be allowed to become wet since it absorbs a fantastic quantity of water and is almost impossible to dry while in the mountains.

Expeditionary climbers are frequently clothed in down from head to foot: hood, parka, pants or underwear, booties, and mitts. Down trousers should be cut full, or else have snap fasteners and a Velcro tape ("sticky tape") inner seam, so they can be put on easily while wearing boots.

During the summer in such ranges as the Cascades, down clothing is seldom worn while in motion, but many climbers carry a down parka or underwear as emergency clothing and for added comfort during the cold hours in camp. Down equipment also plays a vital role in planned bivouacs. A jacket weighing about 2 pounds is adequate for summer alpine use. Expeditionary conditions may require a thicker jacket weighing 3 pounds or more.

PARKAS

Insulation is the role of shirts, sweaters, or down clothing. Over these in foul weather comes the wind parka, whose function is to break the wind and shed water. A completely-waterproof parka is undesirable, since perspiration cannot evaporate and the climber is drenched even when sitting down in bright sunshine. Three materials are mainly used: cotton, nylon, and nylon coated with microporous rubber (for example, "Reevair").

Parkas of cotton or cotton reinforced with nylon are tough, wind-resistant, and repel water when properly treated. However, they are relatively bulky and heavy, weighing about 1½ pounds. Nylon parkas are tough, wind-resistant, light, and compact enough to stuff into a pocket, but have very little resistance to rain. They are excellent for high altitudes, where rain is not a problem. Additional raingear is desirable when using either cotton or nylon parkas.

Reevair-type material has much to recommend it, being a light nylon fabric coated with rubber containing microscopic pores which allow water vapor to pass out, but are too small to permit liquid water to enter. Thus, in theory, parkas of this material should be completely waterproof and yet free of condensation. In practice they are not perfectly waterproof, though better than treated cotton, and some condensation occurs, though much less than in a waterproof parka. Weight and bulk are only slightly greater than uncoated nylon. For a climber with a Reevair parka it becomes a reasonable gamble to dispense with additional raingear, though one can still get wet in heavy rain.

Fig. 4. Parkas. *Left,* for average conditions. *Right,* for more extreme conditions, loose-fitting to allow additional clothing inside, and with face tunnel. (Both have interior drawstrings at midriff.)

Essential in any parka are a hood with drawstring for fitting tightly around the face and full sleeves with buttons, elastic, or Velcro tape for closing around the wrists. The skirt should extend nearly to the knees, with a drawstring at the waist. Large slash pockets on the chest, with buttons or zippers, are useful for warming hands and storing mittens, goggles, and candy bars. A front zipper allows easy control of body temperature, but a zipper can jam, and a parka which cannot be closed will not give full protection when really needed; some climbers therefore prefer the pullover design.

A face tunnel and fur ruff help guard the face against freezing in very cold, windy weather. These should be on the wind parka rather than the down insulating parka; during hard work the down parka may be too warm, while the face, if unprotected, may freeze.

RAINGEAR

When hiking or climbing hard in the rain, the choice lies between getting wet quickly with cold rain or more slowly with warm perspiration inside an impervious parka. A variety of light, compact, and fairly-durable raingear is available; each presents the same problem in some degree.

Full-length ponchos shed all rain and allow considerable air circulation; their major fault lies in being so cumbersome as to be restricted to camps and open trails. A coated nylon poncho which can double as a tarp weighs about 1½ pounds. A fingertip-length rain cape and chaps —compact and weighing about 1 pound—are more suitable for active climbing. A close-fitting rain parka (about 8 ounces) allows less air circulation and causes more condensation, as do accompanying rain pants of similar weight.

At low altitudes, short pants carried for hot-weather hiking or dips in alpine lakes are also a form of raingear. By wearing shorts along the rainy trail, one can keep climbing pants dry in the pack for the next day's climb.

HEADGEAR

A cap with visor and earflaps shades the eyes and warms the ears but lessens visibility upward. Wool stocking caps give no shade but more warmth, fit under a parka hood, do not restrict field of view, and can be worn in the sleeping bag as a nightcap. A wool balaclava helmet or toque may be pulled down to cover the entire head and face when the weather turns cold. In severe conditions a down hood may be attached to the parka.

In hot sunshine a handkerchief knotted in its four corners shields the head and for additional cooling may be dipped periodically in water or covered with a topknot of snow.

HARD HATS

A very large proportion of mountaineering accidents involve head injuries, most of which, experience has shown, could have been prevented by properly-designed helmets.

Head injuries are generally caused by falling rock or by blows incurred when the climber himself falls. Thus, a hard hat must satisfy two primary requirements. First, it must protect against any likely impact. This requirement is not easy to define specifically; complete protection is not possible in a hat of reasonable dimensions. The best helmets suitable for climbing can stand up under a 6-pound rock falling from a height of 20 feet without serious injury to the head. Second, the hat must not be torn off during a fall; a snug fit and a sturdy chin strap are essential. A band across the back of the neck aids in resisting forward-thrusting forces.

In addition, it is desirable for the hat to be light, cool, and compact enough not to restrict vision or motion; the widebrim construction worker's hard hat is ill-adapted for mountaineering.

Two types of hard hat are in common use by climbers. The design offering most protection has a *fiberglass shell lined with crushable plastic foam*. These hats normally have no suspension and are not adjustable. They are available in graduated sizes so the vital snug fit can be obtained. Because of the close fit there is little air circulation, and many climbers find the heat intolerable. The second design— lighter, cooler, and cheaper, but affording much less protection—has an *unlined fiberglass shell held clear of the head by an adjustable suspension*. This type is more likely to be torn off in a fall and has less impact resistance, especially to lateral blows.

Each climber must make his own decision as to the degree of protection and comfort he desires. Any hard hat is better than none, but the finest helmet is useless at home in the closet.

MITTENS AND GLOVES

A single pair of heavy wool mittens suffices for most summer climbing, worn inside wind- and water-repellent overmitts when the situation demands. Where greater manual dexterity is necessary under cold conditions, such as during technical ice climbing, foam-insulated leather ski gloves are excellent. At very low temperatures (about 0°F), exposed fingers freeze to metal—in these circumstances light silk or nylon gloves are worn under down mitts; the gloves allow delicate tasks to be performed for short periods.

Fingerless gloves, which warm hands without hampering fingers, are good for cold rock. Flexible, unlined leather gloves are sometimes used on steep rock climbs, both for belaying and to protect the hands from the abrasion of prolonged ropehandling.

Packs

The climber usually owns two packs: a rucksack or summit pack just large enough to hold the necessities for a 1-day climb, and a packboard with a bag sufficient to carry camping gear and supplies for a week or more.

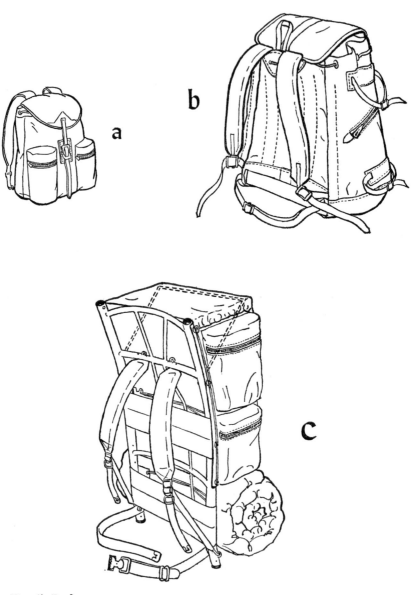

Fig. 5. Packs.
   a. Cloth rucksack ("pear-shaped").
   b. Frame rucksack ("wedge-shaped").
      (*Note:* A rucksack used for hauling up rock must have the pockets in-
         side to avoid snagging.)
   c. Packboard with contoured metal frame.

RUCKSACKS

Two types of rucksack are in common use. The oldest and most popular design is *pear-shaped,* closed at the top with a drawstring and flap, and with two or more external pockets. More modern designs are *wedge-shaped,* broad at the top and narrow at the bottom, often having no protruding outer pockets. This type of pack has advantages for high-angle climbing. The weight is carried high on the shoulders and close to the back; a slight forward lean brings the load directly over the feet so that balance is not disturbed.

Fig. 6. The importance of carrying weight high, close to the shoulders. *Left,* pack on hips, forcing a crouch. *Right,* pack allows comfortable upright stance.

In either design, a light flexible frame is an asset, helping to keep the back cool and enabling more weight to be carried in comfort; a rigid tubular frame should be avoided, however, since the rucksack often must be stowed inside the overnight pack. A waistband is essential to prevent unpredictable lurching about. Other useful accessories are an ice ax carrier, straps for attaching ropes and other gear, crampon attachments, and a sturdy hauling loop.

PACKBOARDS

For loads of 30 pounds or more, a packboard is desirable, consisting of a long, rigid frame of wood or metal, padded from the back by a taut piece of canvas or a network of strings or webbing. The frame allows the load to be carried high and shared among the shoulders, back, and hips. Well-padded shoulder straps and a wide waistband which can be drawn tight are essential. The waistband performs a vital function, controlling the distribution of load: a tight band places most of the weight upon the hips; a loose one loads the shoulders more heavily. The adjustment of shoulder straps and waistband has a major effect on comfort and carrying capacity, and therefore each climber should experiment to find the combination best for him.

The *wood-and-canvas* "Trapper Nelson" packboard, inexpensive and making an excellent mattress for snow camping, was the standard for many years. However, the modern *contoured aluminum frame*, though more expensive, is clearly superior. Both cotton and nylon bags are satisfactory, nylon being somewhat lighter and inevitably more costly.

On short trips the weight of the large pack bag can often be saved by attaching the rucksack directly to the frame. On expeditions the bag is also frequently eliminated by lashing directly to the frame articles of various sizes or shapes, such as oxygen tanks, ration boxes, or miscellaneous supplies stowed in a duffle bag or tarpaulin.

Shelters and Sleeping Bags

TARPS AND RAINFLYS

Some mountaineers prefer *plastic-coated nylon* as the material for tarps and rainflys; the 9- by 12-foot size, weighing about 2 pounds, is strong enough for hard wear and shelters two people easily and four intimately. Others depend on tarps of translucent *polyethylene* 3mm to 4mm thick, weighing about the same as coated nylon and much cheaper; though somewhat less durable than nylon, the cost is so small that frequent replacement is economically feasible. Polyethylene ribbed with nylon weighs and costs a bit more than plain poly, but is virtually indestructible as tarps go. An extremely light and compact tarp or rainfly can be made by reinforcing 1mm poly with Permacel-type fiberglass tape (the 9- by 9-foot size weighs about 8 ounces); beware of sharp twigs and carry a supply of tape (only fiberglass tape will stick) for emergency repairs.

Nylon tarps come with reinforced grommets sewn into sides and corners for easy rigging; poly tarps require the ingenious Visklamp, consisting of a small rubber ball and a dumbbell-shaped metal gadget, or—much simpler—permanently-attached loops of fiberglass tape. In either case rigging lines may be permanently attached or carried separately, as preferred. Tarp rigs are discussed in the next chapter.

TENTS

A tent is a profusion of compromises. Increases in comfort and roominess increase both weight and cost, as do special features to facilitate pitching or to improve protection from wind and insects. Worst problem of all is the dilemma of choosing between getting soaked by rain entering from outside or getting soaked by the condensation of vapor exhaled by human bodies on the inside. If the tent is made of completely-waterproof material and is not well ventilated, moisture exhaled by the occupants condenses on the cold walls and runs down to collect in puddles on the floor. In a single night the moisture breathed out by two sleepers can drench their sleeping bags. Water-repellent materials are porous enough to allow water vapor to escape, while surface tension keeps larger water droplets from entering, but heavy rain, wind, or physical contact destroys the fragile seal and water comes in. The problems of choosing a tent material are summarized in Table 2.

Table 2. Characteristics of Tent Materials.

Type	Example	Weight (ounces per square yard)	Tear Strength (pounds)	Rain Resistance	Condensation
Impervious coated nylon	Nylsurf	2⅝	3	Complete	Severe
Cotton	Element cloth	5¼	4	Fair	Slight
Cotton-nylon mixture	Nylon-pima	5	–	Fair	Slight
Nylon	Quanto Cloth	2½	8	Poor	Slight
Breathable coated nylon	Reevair	3½	7	Good	Moderate

A very light, completely-waterproof tent can be made from *impervious coated nylon,* but condensation is severe. Some success in control has been achieved by the use of several hooded vents to enhance air circulation. A *cotton* tent weighs almost twice as much; there is less condensation and rain resistance is sufficient for a large tent having steep sidewalls, such as the four-man "McKinley" type. In a two-man tent occupants and equipment invariably touch the walls, wicking in water; under these circumstances a rainfly is mandatory. *Nylon* makes the lightest tent of all, but rain resistance is so poor a fly is essential. *Nylon coated with microporous rubber* (Reevair, among other trade names) is a newcomer to the field and little experience with its use is

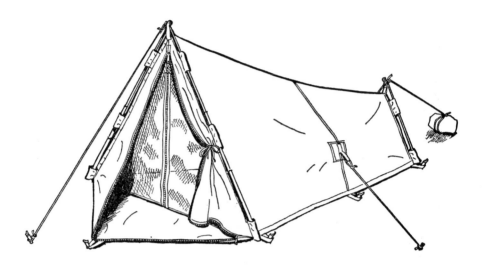

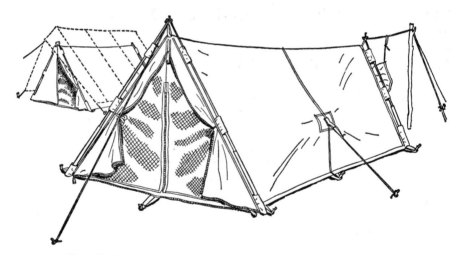

Fig. 7. Mountain tents.
  Upper. Two-man tent, low-ender style.
  Lower. Two-man tent, high-ender style. *Left,* with rain fly.
  Facing page. Four-man tent.

available. The material appears to be insufficiently porous to prevent condensation, but possible improvements, together with carefully-planned ventilation, might lead to a satisfactory design.

After more than a century, the perfect mountain tent has still not been built; the need continues for experiment and invention. At present, the most acceptable compromise seems to be a *nylon tent used with a fly* when rain is anticipated.

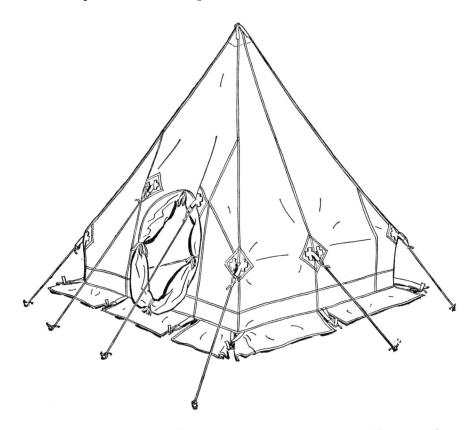

For the majority of alpine excursions, a two-man tent (big enough for three in a squeeze) is best, allowing more flexibility in campsite choice than larger tents, and a lower shelter weight per individual than one-man tents. Although a bit less versatile, the four-man McKinley type makes a happier home; the opportunity to stand, sit, and cook in comfort has a profound effect on morale during a long stormy spell.

SLEEPING BAGS

Warmest and lightest of all designs is the mummy bag tapering toward the feet, hooded to fit over the head, and with a small face opening that can be closed with drawstrings to exclude wind. The unfortunate few suffering from claustrophobia use a rectangular bag, despite its unnecessary extra weight and broad, breezy opening.

Zippers are the almost universal means of closure even though they sometimes snag the fabric or go off the trolley. Heat loss through the metal is prevented by backing up the zipper with a tube of insulating material.

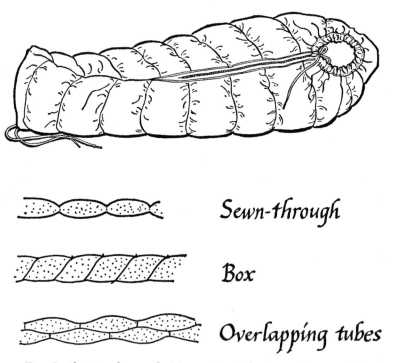

Fig. 8. Sleeping bag and cross-sections of construction methods.

The warmth, weight, and cost of a sleeping bag are chiefly functions of the kind and quantity of insulation—kapok, wool, Dacron, feathers, or down. Wool and kapok bags are inexpensive, but so heavy and bulky relative to warmth that neither merits consideration for alpine backpacking. Dacron is inexpensive and for equivalent weights about halfway between wool and down in warmth. Its great flaw is incompressibility, making for a very bulky roll. Feathers offer a much tighter roll and the same warmth at double the cost. The best insulation is down, the soft small underfeathers of aquatic fowls. Down bags are so expensive that down-and-feather mixtures are a frequent compromise, but for serious mountaineering pure down is the only insulation worth thinking about. With care, a good down bag lasts for years and repays its initial expense many times over. A cheap, heavy bag creates misery day and night.

Bags are made containing anywhere from less than 1 to more than 3 pounds of down. Those at the lower end of the scale are mainly intended to keep a person from freezing to death on a bivouac. Those at the higher and more expensive end give warmth unnecessary except in Arctic conditions. At alpine camps in western American mountains 2 pounds of down is about the average needed, though a person who "sleeps cold" may do well to buy a bag with more, or perhaps better, utilize the layer system by sleeping in a suit of down or Dacron underwear.

Included in total weight are other items besides insulation. A covering fabric too loosely woven allows loss of both insulation and warmth; too tightly woven or waterproofed it retains body moisture. Compromise is necessary. A removable washable inner liner adds a few ounces but saves drycleaning bills. A durable outer cover adds weight but also some insulation and moisture protection, and perhaps most important protects an expensive bag from abrasion.

The compressibility of down and feathers allows the bag to be rolled into a compact bundle that takes up little room in the pack. However, to restore its insulating qualities the bag should be briskly shaken before use and occasionally aired in the sun to restore pristine fluffiness. Since down is useless underneath the body, compressing flat and losing all insulating value, the bag should be held upside down when being fluffed so the filling comes to rest on top of the sleeper.

Three stitching methods are used to keep down uniformly distributed: tubular, box, and overlapping tube. In tubular construction the inner cover is stitched directly to the outer, a method simple and inexpensive but with substantial heat loss at the seams. Box construction is more expensive but the increase in warmth is equivalent to that gained by adding a pound of down to a tubular bag. The most efficient and expensive design has overlapping tubes, a third piece of cloth being sewn alternately to the inner and outer covers in a zigzag pattern.

Drycleaning may leave traces of toxic fluid absorbed into the bulk of a sleeping bag. Sickness and even death can occur if the bag is not well-aired before use.

Cooking and Eating Gear

STOVES

Solid fuels carried primarily as firestarters (see below) are light and cheap, but serve only for limited cooking. A stove with a pressure tank, burning kerosene, gasoline, or liquefied gas is needed for a normal amount of cookery, or if the only available water is melted snow.

A typical small gasoline stove weighs 1¼ pounds empty, burns for about an hour on ½ pint of fuel, and boils a quart of water in 6 or 7 minutes. Gasoline stoves generally do not have pumps: initial pressure is built up by burning a small splash of fuel on the tank; once ignited, pressure is maintained by heat from the burner. White gasoline is mandatory; leaded fuel clogs burner jets and emits toxic fumes.

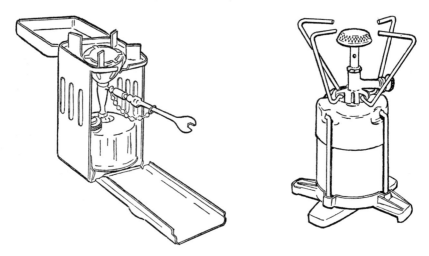

Fig. 9. Stoves. *Left,* gasoline. *Right,* pressurized gas.

Kerosene produces more heat per pound than gasoline, but being less volatile, stoves using it are usually pressurized with a pump, in addition to being primed with alcohol or gasoline. Kerosene stoves tend in consequence to be relatively heavy and tricky to light.

Stoves fueled with disposable cartridges of liquid gas are comparable to gasoline stoves in weight and heating capacity. They are much simpler to operate, a great advantage in a crowded tent during a storm.

Any stove must be shielded from the wind, since even a slight breeze makes performance highly erratic. Walls of snow and rocks are often necessary reinforcement for the combination shield and pot-supporter found on many models.

Extra fuel should be carried in a tightly-closed container, such as an aluminum bottle with a screw top backed up by a rubber gasket, double-wrapped in a plastic sack, plainly marked to avoid confusion, and stowed away in an outer pocket of the bag to avoid food contamination.

COOKING AND EATING UTENSILS

The least-expensive cooking utensils are tin cans in various sizes, junked (at home, *not* in the mountains) when rusty. Aluminum utensils cost a little more but are more durable. Bails are desirable for suspending pots over the fire, and lids to keep ashes out and steam in. Aluminum foil is versatile beyond description, under adept manipulation becoming a frying pan, oven for baking foods in a bed of coals, reflector oven for biscuits, and if need be even a cup or a pot.

For alpine eating some climbers carry two cups and a spoon; others a cup, aluminum-foil pie tin, and a spoon; others a set of nested plastic bowls and a spoon.

FOOD CONTAINERS

The Polyethylene Revolution has overturned the climb kitchen. Waterproof sheets of thin-ply poly, costing and weighing virtually nothing, are spread over food dumps to add sleeping space in the shelter. Transparent poly bags allow each article of food to be separately protected yet easily identified, and the commissary to be logically and conveniently grouped. Tough poly bottles and jars with screw-on or snap-on lids store any liquid or dry food, and being nearly inert chemically, rarely retain odors or flavors. Poly tea cups do not scorch the lips, as do aluminum, though it must be noted that with a stainless steel cup the tea can be drunk the same evening it's brewed. Aside from boot-stomping, about the only thing that damages poly is heat: above the temperature of boiling water it sags and bulges; left by a campfire or on a rock in the hot sun it becomes an interesting but useless blob.

High peaks are usually so bone-dry or snow-cluttered each climber must carry a canteen. A 1-pint capacity generally suffices in coastal mountains; a quart is not enough in more sun-blasted ranges. With a poly bottle, or a canteen of anodized aluminum, a climber can enjoy fruit juices untainted by the toxic metal salts generated in containers of steel or untreated aluminum.

Miscellaneous Equipment

A catalog of sometimes-useful miscellany could easily run to many volumes. The checklist at the end of this chapter suggests many items that need no elaboration. Others are discussed in later chapters. Some few things, however, not covered elsewhere, have been proven essential for every climber on every trip, not only by demands of convenience but by the recorded history of unnecessary tragedy.

FLASHLIGHTS AND HEADLAMPS

Climbs frequently begin before dawn and often end after dark. Every climber must therefore carry a flashlight or headlamp on every climb.

A hand-held flashlight is relatively light and fully satisfactory if the hands are free at all times. The headlamp has important advantages on glacier climbs where rope and ice ax place priority demands on the hands; in emergencies where the party must move over difficult terrain in the dark it can be a lifesaver.

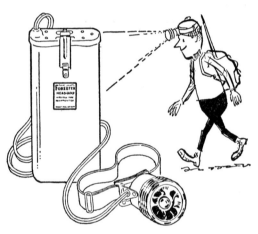

Fig. 10. Headlamp.

Most commercial headlamps are excessively heavy for any ordinary trip except a rescue—about 2 pounds for case and batteries, plus another ¾ pound for extra batteries. A much lighter and more practical alternative can be improvised from flashlight parts.

Alkaline batteries have a useful life, at room temperature, three- to four-times longer than the conventional lead-acid type. The advantage is even greater at low temperatures, becoming about 10:1 at 20°F. Low temperatures reduce considerably the useful life of both acid and alkaline batteries. At 70°F, for example, two size-D alkaline cells light an 0.3-ampere bulb continuously for more than 20 hours; at —20°F, only about 2 hours can be expected. In cold weather, therefore, batteries should be carried beneath the outer clothing to keep them warm.

An 0.3-ampere bulb provides sufficient light for most mountaineering purposes. More light can be obtained from a larger bulb, but at the cost of shorter battery life. In the example cited above, an 0.5-ampere bulb would reduce battery life from 20 hours to about 12.

A suggested safe minimum for most trips is a handlight or improvised headlamp with two size-D alkaline cells and an 0.3-ampere bulb, giving some 20 hours of useful light at room temperature; fresh cells inserted before the climb; an extra pair carried in the junkbag and also an extra bulb, perhaps stored inside a cube of sponge rubber behind the lamp reflector; on-off switch taped or a piece of cardboard placed between the cells to prevent light-wastage in the pack; total weight, a bit more than 1 pound.

FIRESTARTERS

An emergency supply of matches, waterproofed or stowed in a watertight container, must always be carried. A stub of plumber's candle or a bit of solid chemical fuel ("heat tabs," "canned heat," "fuel rations") is indispensable in igniting wet wood and starting a fire quickly in an emergency.

KNIFE

In food preparation, in firebuilding, in first aid, in high-angle rock climbing, and elsewhere in alpine life, a knife is so essential that every climber must carry one. The traditional Boy Scout knife with two folding blades, can opener, combination screwdriver and bottle opener, and sometimes an awl, is handiest and least expensive. For special purposes a hunting knife is superior, as are double-bitted axes, cavalry sabers, Gatling guns, and dynamite, but the modest mountaineer contents himself with a modest blade.

SUNBURN PREVENTATIVES

Sunlight at high altitudes has a burning capacity many times greater than at sealevel—so much greater, especially on snow, that it is a threat not only to comfort but health. Despite commercially-encouraged superstition, there is no way to get a suntan without getting a sunburn, for the two are inseparable parts of the same process. One can painlessly develop a tan only by controlling the length and intensity of exposure, and since the climber cannot avoid long exposure he must reduce the intensity of sunlight reaching his skin by the use of clothing wherever possible and sunburn preventatives where not possible.

Actors' grease paint (clown white) or zinc oxide pastes give virtually-complete protection, and a grease base ensures against their being washed off by perspiration. One application is good for the entire climb, except where fingers and equipment rub the skin bare. The major disadvantage is that cold cream is needed for easy removal.

Proprietary chemicals presented as "suntan" lotions should be avoided by the climber, being formulated for use on the seashore, usually from an alcohol base which quickly evaporates. Products aimed at the skier are likely to have an oil base and thus offer more protection.

Opinions on sunburn preventatives are equal in number to the census of experienced climbers. Individuals vary widely in natural pigmentation and thus in toleration to exposure and in degree of protection needed. There is only one rule: the penalty for underestimation is so severe that no amount of protection can be called excessive.

Tanned skin, whatever its cosmetic value, offers minor protection against the intense burning of high altitudes. More than one novice climber has gone along for weeks patiently building a tan, and on his first trip relying for protection solely on natural pigment found himself burned and blistered and peeled right back down to a winter white.

GLASSES—SUN AND PRESCRIPTION

Eyes are particularly vulnerable to the brilliance of mountain skies and if unprotected can quickly be painfully burned or even permanently damaged. It is essential for the climber to have sunglasses which greatly reduce the amount of both visible light and invisible ultraviolet and infrared rays striking the eyes; passage should be no more than 10 or 15 per cent. Any very dark lenses are adequate, whatever their color, but careful shopping is necessary, since about two-thirds of the sunglasses offered for sale on the American market have optical defects which at the least weary the eye, at the worst do harm. The design must be such as to keep light from entering at the sides and bottom, yet give adequate ventilation to prevent fogging. Extra pairs of goggles are worth carrying by any party venturing onto the blinding wastes of snowfield or glacier. In emergency a piece of cardboard with small slits can save the eye from damage, though providing minimal vision.

Climbers who need prescription glasses to obtain any clear view of their surroundings encounter special problems. A sound precaution to eliminate the possibility of splinters is having the lenses made of "safety glass," which costs only a trifle more than ordinary optical glass. Any climber so nearsighted as to have difficulty traveling treacherous terrain must always carry an extra pair in his rucksack. Fogging is increased by the double-baffle of prescription and sun glasses; the best combination in bright conditions is a pair of large, well-ventilated ski goggles worn loosely over prescription lenses.

INSECT REPELLENTS

The habits and avoidance of insects are described in the following chapter. When they must be lived with, as is all too frequently the case, various defenses may be employed. Complete coverage by clothing, including even gloves and head nets in extreme conditions, keeps out mosquitoes and flies but not no-see-ums or ticks. Insect repellents may be necessary, though until recently any strong enough to be effective was so disagreeable or toxic that climbers often chose to take their chances with the insects assisted only by active hands.

After a generation of research the Entomology Research Branch of the United States Department of Agriculture, in cooperation with the Army Medical Corps, announced *diethyl toluamide* to be the best chemical so far developed. In contrast to predecessors (many of which remain on the market, and should be avoided) it has the consistency of a light lotion, is not oily, has a pleasant odor, and rapidly dries to a thin film. One application to the skin is effective for 6 to 8 hours, to clothing for several days. Protection is nearly perfect against mosquitoes, and very good against flies, no-see-ums, chiggers, and ticks—the last previously virtually invulnerable. Diethyl toluamide in a 50 per cent alcohol solution is marketed commercially under several brand names, and is also available in stick form and as an aerosol spray.

REPAIR AND IMPROVISATION

All climbers through sad experience accumulate emergency kits composed of odd bits and pieces wonderfully versatile in times of trouble. An assortment of wire and nails and safety pins has obvious value in patching broken equipment. Needles, from blister-puncturing size up to sailors' awls for piercing leather, razor blades, yarn, squares of patching fabric, coils of nylon string—the list could be extended indefinitely. Generally a climber carries those items he wishes he had carried on some past climb. Though this may seem like locking the barn door after the horse is stolen, misfortunes do indeed tend to follow a pattern.

Ice Ax

The numerous uses of the ice ax are discussed in nine of the following chapters, a good measure of its importance.

The first requirements of an ax are that it have a strong *shaft*, securely attached to a *head* which is comfortable to grasp. These characteristics take precedence over all other features.

Particular attention should be given to the shaft, which undergoes the major strain. It may be made from ash, hickory, or epoxy-laminated wood; all are satisfactory, provided the grain is straight and free from knots. Ash is most common, though hickory is five times stronger. The lower 4 or 5 inches should be wrapped with adhesive tape or plastic electrical tape to prevent abrasion by rocks. Occasional rubbing with boiled linseed oil helps protect the wood against moisture, but varnishing makes the surface slippery and is not recommended.

At the bottom of the shaft is the *spike,* a metal point 2 or 3 inches long, set into the wood and held there by a metal band or *ferrule.* A streamlined juncture eases the thrust into snow.

The head of the ax has an *adze* about 2 inches wide and 4 inches long and a *pick* some 7 or 8 inches long. The adze may be flat or convex; neither is clearly superior. The bottom of the pick may have saw-like teeth which are thought by some to help prevent the pick from slipping when driven into ice; to be of value, such teeth should extend all the way to the end of the pick. Other features, such as carabiner holes, belaying notches, and stacking slits, have specialized uses.

For snow climbing and most glaciers, the adze, pick, and spike should be blunted to reduce the possibility of injury. Ice climbing, however, requires a sharp ax; special-alloy steels are sometimes used to ensure a light, tough head and sharp cutting edges and points.

If the ax is to be used at very low temperatures, the area contacted by the hand should be wrapped with adhesive tape to reduce heat absorption and prevent loss of skin, which can happen when cold metal is touched with bare flesh.

Loss of the ax is prevented by a *wrist loop* attached to a *glide ring* that rotates and slides freely on the shaft, limited about 8 inches from the spike by a stout screw, or *stop.*

Choosing an ax is no mysterious or difficult matter. Whatever the individual details and frills, every design offered by reputable climbing outfitters is adequate, and one is about as good as another. The more expensive axes may be a bit lighter for the same strength and have prettier workmanship. The important criterion is *solid construction,* and one need never have seen an ax to judge this competently before purchase, checking each detail methodically. Selecting the *shaft length* is a novice's main worry, and unnecessarily. The proper length depends simply on the climber's height and the terrain for which the ax is intended. For all-around climbing, the ax should reach easily and comfortably from the heel of the hand to the ground, with the arm hanging loose, and this is the obvious choice for the beginner. A somewhat shorter length is customary for ice climbing. A longer ax

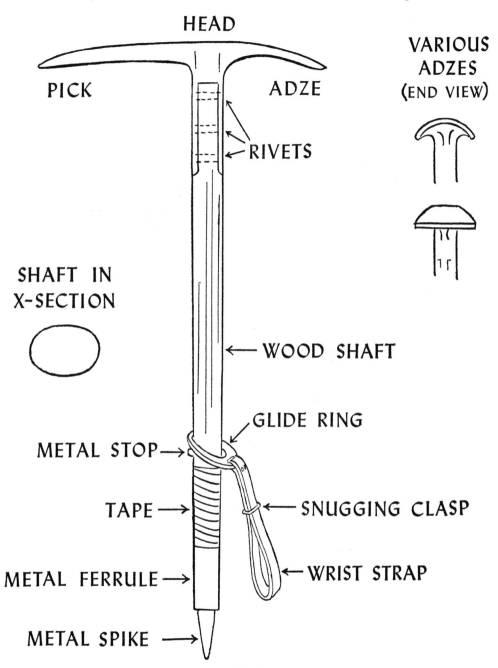

HEAD

PICK   ADZE

VARIOUS
ADZES
(END VIEW)

RIVETS

SHAFT IN
X-SECTION

WOOD SHAFT

GLIDE RING

METAL STOP →

TAPE →   ← SNUGGING CLASP

METAL FERRULE →   ← WRIST STRAP

METAL SPIKE →

Fig. 11. Ice ax.

has advantages on some kinds of snow, but can be very troublesome on mixed rock and snow.

Equipment Checklist

It is difficult on journey's eve to remember everything that may be needed. During the season most climbers leave their rucksacks permanently assembled, replenishing supplies as depleted. Much paraphernalia, particularly that of an emergency nature which is always carried but seldom used, is stowed in a waterproof "junk bag" to reduce the litter of small miscellany. It is customary to reserve in basement or garage a climbing corner where all the gear is stored, saving last-minute hectic scurrying all about the house. A checklist based on private experience and tacked on the wall and systematically consulted reduces mental strain and the overlooking of critical items. The following example is representative but by no means either universal or complete. *Starred items are essential for every person on every climb short or long.* Those in parentheses are optional depending on personal preference and the nature of the trip.

PERSONAL EQUIPMENT

Clothing
- *Boots
- *Socks
- *Underwear
- *Pants
- *Shirts and sweaters
- *Parka
- *Hat
- Hard hat
- Gaiters
- (Wind pants)
- (Short pants)
- (White cotton shirt)

In the Pockets
- *Pocket knife
- *Compass
- Altimeter
- (Matches, non-emergency)
- (Folding cup)

(Handkerchief)
(Chapstick)
(Cheap watch)
In the Pack
  *Flashlight or headlamp
  *Map
  *Mittens
  *Sunglasses
  *Extra food
  *Extra clothing
  *Rucksack
  Sleeping bag
  Canteen
  Sunburn preventative
  Toilet paper
  Extra socks
  Cooking kit:
    Metal grate
    Pots
    Cup and pie tin or two cups
    Spoon
    Matches
    Scouring pad
    Soap or detergent
  (Towel, toothbrush, etc.)
  (Camera and film)
  (Extra cord or tent line)
  (Insect repellent)
  (Poncho or other raingear)
  (Binoculars)
  (Air mattress or foam sheet)
  (Pliers for pot-lifting and general repair)
  *Junk bag containing:
    *Emergency matches in waterproof container
    *Firestarter or candle
    *Extra flashlight bulb and batteries
    Boot laces

Emergency sunglasses
(Wire)
(Sailmaker's needle)
(Heavy thread)
(Fish line)
(Nails)
(Razor blade)
(Safety pins)
(Paper and pencil)
*First aid kit

In the Car
(Change of clothes)
(Cold cream and cleansing tissues)
(Spare keys hidden on or near car)
(Succulent foods)
(Cold drinks hidden in nearby creek)

GROUP EQUIPMENT

Food
Large pots
Stove and fuel
Can opener
Tarpaulins or tents
(Ground cloth)
Extra first aid materials
Tent lines
(Solid chemical fuel)
(Collapsible saw)
(Snow shovel)

CLIMBING EQUIPMENT

Rock Climb
Climbing rope
Sling ropes
Pitons
Piton hammer
Carabiners

(Rock shoes)
(Bolt kit)
(Brake bar)
(Stirrups)
(Rappel seat sling)
(Descending rings)
(Swami belt)

Snow Climb

Rope
Ice ax
Crampons
Slings
Carabiners
(Pulleys)
(Wands)
(Ice screws)
(Ice hammer)
(Avalanche cord)
(Snowshoes)
(Skis, ski climbers, waxes, and ski boots)

Add for Cold Weather

(Down clothing)
(Extra socks)
(Heavy mittens and liners)
(Silk or nylon gloves)
(Insoles)
(Long underwear)
(Balaclava helmet or toque)
(Scarf)
(Anti-fog for goggles)

2 *

CAMPING AND SLEEPING

A CLIMBING camp is not a semipermanent base for enjoyment of the scenery but merely a pause in the upward progress to the peak, a rest stop prolonged overnight. Camps with wood, water, and shelter are preferred, but fuel and water can be carried and shelter improvised. The cosiest alpine corner doesn't merit a second glance if an hour too distant from tomorrow's summit; the way to gain an extra hour for the climb is to camp an hour higher on the mountain. Proximity to the summit, then, is the determining factor. Another basic requirement is simplicity. Camping gear must be quick to put up and take down, if need be in total darkness and raging storm.

How to Sleep

THE DRY BED

In Northwest America the weather is untrustworthy and huts scarce and therefore climbers always carry portable shelter. Tents and tarps both have virtues and vices and each for some conditions is unquestionably superior. Since a party can carry one or the other but usually not both, the question is much argued in alpine circles as to which is best for all-around use. Certainly a tent is the only shelter worthy of the name at high altitudes, very low temperatures, or in strong winds. Of prime importance, being a self-contained unit it can be erected almost anywhere. The main criticism is that tents are either heavy or expensive; no climber can afford the burden of a cheap, heavy tent, and the limited-budget climber cannot afford the expense of a light-

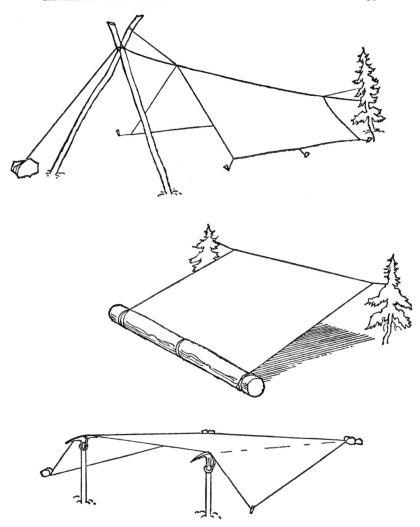

Fig. 12. Tarp rigs. *Upper,* A-tent with bipod at one end (can be used at both ends). *Middle,* shed roof. *Lower,* high-meadow, low-profile design.

weight one. A tarp is both light in weight and low in cost and offers adequate shelter from all but extreme weather. It gives less protection than a tent from heat loss and wind but allows more convenient study of natural science and scenic splendor. On the debit side a tarp demands human ingenuity and some cooperation from the landscape and is worthless in a hard blow.

Erecting any common design of mountain tent is simplicity itself, though it is well to learn the routine by practice elsewhere than on a high hill during a stormy night. Possibly the only aspect of installation not perfectly obvious is relationship to wind. The natural instinct is to face the opening leeward, but in this position alternations in air pressure cause the tent to flap and crack and generally raise hob with sleep. Pitched with the wind blowing directly in the open end, the tent distends like a balloon and remains relatively quiet, high interior air pressure acting as a buffer.

Rigging a tarpaulin shelter is an art using only a few basic designs but unlimited variations; the architect needs imagination and experience to become a master. Simplest and crudest method of all is wrapping up in the tarp as if it were a *large blanket,* a use particularly suited to weary climbers making camp late at night, but also most effective in gales. Protection from wind and rain is complete but in warm weather the sleeping bag becomes rather damp from perspiration by morning —which, of course, doesn't matter on a weekend trip.

The *A-tent* design resembles a true tent, the tarp being draped over a line stretched between two supports, its edges fastened down on either side. Trees or large boulders can be employed as end supports, but if these are lacking either one or two bipods can be improvised, as shown in the illustration. Maximum protection is gained by staking the edges flush with the ground, then heaping logs or packboards and other gear at the windward entrance. In calm weather the edges may be raised some distance in the air for spacious and gracious living.

The *shed roof* with the four corners tied to anything handy covers more floor area than the A-tent; though of no value in high wind it is ideal in mild weather or gently-falling rain. For the high corners trees are ideal tie points, large boulders are good, and if worse comes to worst ice axes can be used, though providing very little headroom. In quiet air the low edge can be raised but in wind it should be flush to the ground, anchored by a large log, stones, or a ridge of snow.

Whatever the design, a tarp must be rigged with tight lines to reduce flapping in the wind and to provide proper roof drainage. Tarp campers customarily carry a considerable quantity of strong, light nylon cord to enable them to use any conceivable kind of anchor points. By adjusting tension in stays and adding secondary anchor lines the roof pattern can be infinitely varied. If it is raining, drainage ditches may be needed. If not raining, climbers with a proper respect for the natural scene prefer to leave the vegetation undisturbed and fall out at night with ice axes if rivulets invade the sleeping area. It goes without saying that if ditches are dug they should be carefully filled, and the ground cover reconstructed, when breaking camp.

Tarps come in many dimensions and are so inexpensive a climber can afford to own several, ranging from a 6- by 8-foot single occupancy to a 12-foot-square family style. The most versatile size is about 9 feet by 12, providing luxurious living room for two people and their gear and adequate for three, or even four if they are small people or very good friends. In larger sizes weight and difficulty of rigging become objectionable. In smaller sizes the usable space approaches the vanishing point, since the outer margins of tarp-covered ground are usually only half-protected, if that. When terrain allows two tarps to be pitched together, the waste area is much decreased, whether the two be overlapped at or along the ridge in a giant A-tent or side by side in a shed. With such "circus tents" vast regions of meadow may be covered so that even a prolonged rain or drizzle can be outwaited in comparative freedom and comfort.

Equipment as well as climbers needs shelter. Whenever space is cramped within tent or tarp it is well to carry a number of large sacks and sheets of plastic for dry storage outside. In wet mountains the few extra ounces are worth the weight.

THE SOFT BED

The bed need not be kingly in dimensions nor feathery soft nor completely level but it should be reasonably satisfactory in each respect. A natural site can be improved by excavating roots and stones, though to a certain extent the sleeping posture can be adjusted around them. Hip and shoulder holes contribute some comfort. Before proceeding very far with construction it is well to test a bedstead by lying in several positions. Those that seem most promising can then be further improved by prying out the most obnoxious rocks, filling and scooping and grading to fit the frame.

Such engineering may suffice for an old stoic climber or a young limber one but most individuals require a yielding undersurface, such as is perfectly but infrequently provided by heather meadows and soft-carpeted forests. *Air mattresses* have become increasingly popular in recent years both for comfort and saving of fuss and effort. A shoulders-to-buttocks length is enough if supplemented by boughs or equipment; such a mattress constructed of proper materials can be very durable and weigh little more than a pound. Mattresses often give a chill sleep on snow due to interior convection currents, and with age they develop leaks that let the sleeper down in the middle of the night. Convection can be reduced by inserting a few ounces of down; in this case a filter is needed on the inlet and the mattress must *not* be blown up by mouth because of the moisture thus introduced. Sheets of *foam plastic* are superior in every respect except their incompressibility and consequent bulkiness. A 2- by 4-foot pad of ¼-inch-thick Ensolite foam (with closed cells, thus not absorbing water) weighs 1 pound; a polyethylene pad the same size weighs 7 ounces. These thin pads provide fair insulation but little softness; on expeditions when long periods will be spent on snow a full-length, 1½-inch-thick pad is worth its weight.

A mattress improvised from pack frames, ropes, and miscellaneous gear has been used to perfect satisfaction even on Yukon icefields. A wooden packboard is ideal since it conveniently carries the weight of shoulders and hips. A climbing rope can be spread at one end for the legs, boots and sweaters at the other for a pillow, or any other equipment substituted.

Fig. 13. Sleeping on packboard and gear.

On snow or wet ground in a forested area it may be worthwhile to build a *bough bed*. In national parks cutting boughs is quite properly forbidden and in any heavily-traveled area is an execrable practice even if legal. In remote regions a climber can abide with the spirit of conservation and still have a comfortable bed by taking only a few branches from any one tree and by using windfall as much as possible. On damp ground a very few boughs are sufficient but in mud or snow a great deal of time and a great many boughs are needed. The first layer consists of heavy, springy branches, thick as a thumb or even larger, laid crosswise from head to foot, heavy ends alternated. The next layer of padding boughs, no thicker than the small finger, are then "shingled" into the bed starting at the head and working down to the foot. The lazy or impatient camper merely heaps up boughs and then contorts his frame to avoid prodding by sharp sticks. Boughs should be scattered or burned after use; the ruins of ancient beds are unsightly.

THE WARM BED

Since a cold bed is poor for sleeping, body heat must be conserved by insulation, always attempting to gain maximum benefit from the limited amount that can be carried. The sleeping bag must be thoroughly fluffed out before use to loosen up the down and thus entrap dead air. Dry clothing should be worn to bed or placed underneath the body but not left wasted in the packsack. A wool stocking cap does wonders for the ears and dry socks for the feet—these extremities being invariably the first chilled. Heat loss from exhalation can be

III. Mount Fury, in the Picket Range of the North Cascades. (Thomas Miller)

IV. Bugaboos. (Erick Karlsson)

reduced by a "snorkel," a large wool sock, preferably clean, pulled over the face. On cold nights the sleeping bag should be kept tightly closed with just a chink for the nose.

On wet ground or snow, conduction of heat from the sleeper's underside is very rapid and mattresses and boughs are more important in their prevention of such loss than as cushions. Furthermore, all insulators lose efficiency when wet. On a long trip a sleeping bag, once soaked, means not merely one shivering night but many, unless it can somehow be dried. The difficulty of doing so is a good reason for making every effort to keep the bag dry. On the trail a bag can be hung loosely over the packboard and dried somewhat en route. A campfire will never do the job except with long patient hours. A day of sunshine usually is effective, though in unsettled weather the advisability of going off on a climb with bags draped in the meadows may be questioned.

It is a moot point whether wet clothing should be worn to bed. Certainly some drying can be thus accomplished—but perhaps at the expense of a cold sleep. It should be kept in mind that in good weather clothing will dry more comfortably next day while traveling and that in bad weather it will in any event get wet again very quickly. The amount of interior drying undertaken should therefore be kept at a minimum. In very cold conditions, however, damp clothing such as mittens, socks, and inner liners of high-altitude boots should be taken into the bag to keep them from freezing.

Least obvious of the many thieves of heat is radiation to the open sky. (For discussion in another context see Chapter 21.) Whenever two opposing surfaces differ in temperature the warmer radiates heat to the colder. Since the human body is usually warmer than the night sky, exposed portions of the body or sleeping bag radiate heat and grow cold. Any shelter at all serves as a baffle. A climber sacked out under a tree may sleep cozy and warm while his companion a few feet away shivers under the stars. Absurdly enough, shelter is often more necessary on a clear night than a cloudy one. Clouds often reflect heat back to earth and thus have the effect of a huge tarp between sleeper and sky; the clear nights are the cold ones.

Another and less subtle thief is cold air, which fortunately can often by avoided simply by remembering that it is heavier than warm air and in settled weather flows downward like water, following valleys and collecting in depressions. Thus there is often a chill breeze down a creek or a dry wash and a pool of cold air in a basin, whether or not it contains a lake.

Wind—discussed in some detail in Chapter 22—is the most active cooling agent and its capricious alpine behavior can be quite exasperating. Patterns of flow are often highly localized, with a full gale blasting one patch of meadow while a few yards away the flowers droop in still and sultry air. Also they are instantaneously reversible without warning so that a tarp strung as a windbreak in afternoon may become a balloon after sunset. One consolation of foul weather is that storm winds are fairly consistent.

A useful study is that of *microclimates,* weather on the scale of inches. Knowing that all the laws governing behavior of air masses on the global scale (see Chapter 22) apply also on the inch scale, often a perceptive climber can, by moving his bed a few feet, gain a sleep many degrees warmer. Microclimates demand micro-investigation. The grass of a dried-up alpine pool may be temptingly soft but perhaps in stable air the adjacent rocky knoll several feet high is 10 degrees warmer. A dry gulch may appear to offer superb wind protection but in fact be the channel of a roaring air river only 4 feet deep and 8 feet wide. The heather may be as thick and as dry below a snowpatch as above but be bathed in the night by icy air dribbling downward. A smattering of botanical knowledge is of value; if one observes in a little cranny flora characteristic of lower elevations it can be deduced that this is a warm little cranny, an admirable spot for a bed. Similarly one can study size and location of snowpatches and sleep where the snow is doing poorly.

BUGS

Wilderness is the occasional home of man and the constant home of insects. Bugs are a nuisance at any hour but never so intolerable as when engaged in destroying sleep; thus they are discussed in the present context rather than any of a dozen others relevant.

There are no recorded cases of malaria or yellow fever contracted from alpine *mosquitoes* and except in sub-Arctic ranges little danger of being bitten to death. The bite is painless and the itching an irritation at worst so that the hazard is chiefly mental—a statement that can also be made about the Chinese water torture. The larvae hatch in water but even mud or moist humus will suffice, so that mosquitoes inhabit all but the most scorched mountains. They are stimulated by warmth, arriving with spring and thriving until repeated fall frosts. Fortunately even a summer night is often cold enough to send them to bed; in the Cascades and Olympics elevations above 4000 feet usually become instantaneously and blessedly quiet at sunset.

Exactly what attracts mosquitoes is not fully known. They can be observed patiently probing tree bark and stones in exploration that seems purely random. However, experiments have shown their interest and appetite are excited by carbon dioxide, by warm, moist surfaces, especially those dark in color, and by motion. When awake a traveler can minimize his personal court of mosquitoes by fast walking and steady slapping but when asleep his best defense is a tent guarded by netting at every orifice. Lacking a tent, complex baffles of tarps and sweaters can be arranged about the sleeping bag opening, though if the night is warm enough for mosquitoes such baffles are uncomfortably warm. The ideal remedy for mosquitoes and every other flying bug is a steady breeze. Given a choice between insect hunger and a cold wind most climbers will take the latter.

Smallest of the fly family is the *no-see-um*, usually found in the Northwest no higher than 2500 feet and almost exclusively in dank river bottoms. Though invisible except in the dusk with the light behind it, this tiny insect gets off a most amazingly painful chew, the more unpleasant because one cannot see the creature to punish him. Wherever there is one no-see-um there are billions, every one of which can find its way into the most tightly-sealed tent.

The *deer fly*, which resembles an ordinary house fly, and the large, obscene *horse fly* especially infest lush meadows, though in sultry weather they can be found deep in the forests and high on the rocks. Needing warmth for propagation they arrive with summer and vanish with fall. A heavy rain seems to settle the flies, giving a few hours or even a day of relief. Being more sensitive than mosquitoes to wind and cold, even a small breeze or shadow diminishes their numbers. On the other hand flies have good vision and cannot be avoided by fast walking. Indeed, they will follow a climbing party onto rocks and ice far from their normal habitat and the only way to be rid of them is to stop and slap until every last one is dead.

Ticks do not live at alpine elevations but on approach marches in western ranges are a nuisance if not also a serious health menace, as discussed in Chapter 18. They are most abundant in the springtime of dry lands—a condition that varies with latitude and altitude but is easily recognized. When grass is coming up fresh and green, animal hosts are plentiful and ticks are at their prime. The Puget Sound country is too wet for them to thrive except in the Olympic rain shadow, where they are fairly common in March and April. On the east slopes of the Cascades, in the 2000–3000-foot grassy foothills, May and June are ordinarily their best months. In portions of Idaho, Montana, and eastern Oregon ticks are so numerous that there are far too many in every season except winter. Local inquiry is advisable.

The hallowed superstition that ticks drop down from tree branches is false. Ticks do not fly or climb or parachute. They creep along the ground, venturing sometimes 18 inches upward in search of a meal, rarely any higher except when they have found a host worth exploration. The hiker who spends a great deal of time sitting down is an obvious target. Fields of low grass and brush, and roads and trails much used and littered by animals, often support hordes of ticks. The majority can be thwarted merely by fastening the pants tight around the boots and then watching for little climbers on pants legs. Smooth dark fabrics are easiest to scan. Since ticks spend an average of 3 hours scouting a body before choosing a drill site and cannot, even if infected with disease, transmit germs for several more hours, travelers even in land of numerous infected ticks can gain almost complete protection if they pair off morning, noon, and night, strip to the skin, and inspect each other thoroughly. Formerly there was no alternative, but diethyl toluamide, discussed in Chapter 1, is the first feasible repellent found that discourages ticks. Probably a thorough application to trousers would eliminate the need for frequent inspection.

Ticks do not "screw in" and there is no merit whatsoever to the old wives' method of "unscrewing" ticks, clockwise or counterclockwise, even though it continues to be recommended by people who should know better. Another of the traditional methods, making a tick pull out by himself by touching his tail with kerosene or a flame, is also rarely effective. An application of sunburn cream or insect repellent sometimes works. A tick discovered during his preliminary prospecting will leave the country at a touch, being a nervous little beast. Even after an hour or so of serious drilling a gentle straightforward pull may still bring it entirely out into the open. Once deeply imbedded only surgery by razor blade or physician will do the trick. It may be less painful to take antibiotics and leave the head in the flesh like a thorn to fester and come out a few days later. All procedures connected with ticks are so loathsome that after camping in infested areas it is well to inspect not only bodies but clothing, sleeping bags, tents, packs, and other equipment. Ticks can meander about a long while seeking a host and may be encountered hours or days distant from their proper home.

Where to Sleep

SPOTTING CAMPSITES FROM A DISTANCE

To climb a certain peak it may be necessary to camp on a certain ridge. On this ridge there may be only one water supply, a little trickle from a dwindling snowpatch hidden away on an obscure hillside bench. This bench may be difficult to find, particularly if the search is made after dark. However, during the approach march the snowpatch may be clearly visible and bearings taken then on prominent nearby features greatly simplify later search. Similarly, if terrain is predominantly vertical the party possibly can avoid a night draped around trees by spying a snug little shelf, perhaps in the angle where two glacial moraines intersect. Clumps of trees amid seas of brush often stand out distinctly at a distance, or little patches of green meadow in a valley of boulders. The elements of geology presented in Chapter 20 are surprisingly valuable in deciphering from a distance the landscape in terms of campsites.

FOREST AND MEADOW

Forests ordinarily provide easy and excellent camps with plentiful firewood, soft undercover, ample water, and natural shelter. However, the deep forest gloom is often damp, especially early in the season when there is a lingering residue of snow. Additional debits are bugs and "widowmakers"—large dead limbs or trees waiting only the proper gust of wind before plunging to the ground. In gales thorough examination of the overhead prospect takes high priority.

Meadows above timberline are superbly situated and landscaped in the esthetic sense and offer surpassingly-comfortable camps when heather and trees and rocks and rivulets are properly arranged. However, meadows are often lacking in fuel, shelter, water, and convenient trees for rigging tarps, and are frequently windy and cold. Choosing a meadow camp therefore requires careful thought, making the most of distant views and paying close attention to microclimatology. Frequently one must decide between a high camp close to the peak and superbly scenic but windy and waterless, and a lower one that has less view and requires an earlier start but has more of the amenities that make for a decent sleep.

SNOW

In theory a snow camp can be as warm and comfortable as any other. In fact the extra effort required to bring a snow camp to practical as well as theoretical equality with other camps is best saved for the climb. However, for winter or expeditionary mountaineers frequently, and for all others occasionally, there is no alternative. Every person who goes into the mountains must be able to provide himself with the minimum conditions for a comfortable night on snow—or at the very least for survival.

In no other camp is insulation so important or shelter so essential. A bough bed, air mattress, climbing rope, ice axes, packboards, old newspapers, climbing boots, and anything else available should be interposed between sleeper and frost—better a lumpy bed than a cold one. The simplest and best shelter is a tent installed on a stamped-out platform slightly larger than the floor, with drainage ditches if rain is in prospect, and perhaps heaped snow for a windbreak, though in a heavy snowstorm such enclosures collect drifts that will collapse the tent unless periodically shoveled away during the night.

In forests the finest natural shelter is a *tree cave*, the conical depression in the snow formed around a tree trunk. Commonly there is a heavy screen of branches over the cave, giving perfect protection from blizzards when tarps and tents pitched in the open are collapsing right and left. A tarp to supplement the walls of snow and roof of branches makes a snug hideaway in the hardest blow or heaviest rainstorm. Before rigging the tarp the walls and floor and entrance stairway should be scooped and stamped, then small ledges gouged for equipment storage and kitchen duty. Since the chief objection to a tree cave is that in calm weather it collects cold air, frequently it is desirable to use a two-level design with an upper sleeping area connected to a lower living level. The latter should have enough headroom for convenient dressing and cooking, and with proper ventilation can even contain a cheerful wood fire surrounded by benches carved from the snow. In the absence of trees a similar shelter can be improvised by digging a trench some 4 to 6 feet deep and large enough to accommodate the party, then stretching a tarp over the top, perhaps gaining a slight pitch by anchoring one side to a ridge of snow. Though excellent in windy or rainy weather, a heavy snowfall can easily and disastrously collapse a roof so nearly flat.

A *snow cave* requires more time than can usually be justified merely to provide overnight comfort. A base camp that will be occupied for several days may be worth the effort, particularly if the party is waiting out a storm; there is absolutely no comparison between the comfort of a calm, quiet cave and a gale-swept tent. In emergencies snow caves have in the past so often meant survival that winter mountaineers consider knowledge of the construction technique mandatory. To build a cave all that is necessary is fairly firm snow of a minimum depth of about 6 feet, and a sidehill, such as along a river bank or snowdrift. The first step is to tunnel into the slope, excavating sufficient space for the party, removing loose snow on a tarp or ground sheet through a large construction tunnel, which is then plugged with blocks or balls of snow. Next is dug an entrance tunnel about 3 feet in length sloping downward to the outside to prevent escape of warm air, a tarp draped over the entrance to keep out breezes. To avoid asphyxiation a small ventilation hole is pushed to the outside with an ice ax and enlarged as needed if the interior becomes excessively warm. Though a cave can be dug by hand, a lightweight shovel blade that slips over the ice ax shaft can easily be made of sheet aluminum alloy. With it a cave for four can be dug in an hour or so depending on snow conditions.

There are simpler designs. A one-man cave can be scooped in soft snow by hand in a few minutes, the opening blocked by additional snow as the person burrows further in; such shelter requires no equipment and is an important emergency technique, for even in so rude a cave body warmth soon raises air temperature to survival level.

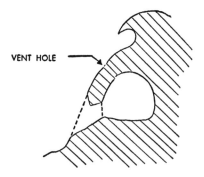

VENT HOLE

Fig. 14. Snow cave, cross section.

ABOVE TIMBERLINE

When a summit lies more than a reasonable day's journey from timberline, intermediate camps must be made in the mineral zone. There are few useful generalizations about such camps, which may be located in sheltered rock piles or on exposed glacier plains. The chief thing to remember is that even in generally-stable weather gale winds are almost the normal condition at high altitudes, and the temperature range may be such as to cause heat prostration by day and frozen feet at night. High camps often present safety problems of the type encountered on the climb itself—ice and rockfall and avalanches, not to mention minor annoyances such as the sandblasting by pumice endemic on Cascade volcanoes. The site may be selected to take advantage of natural protection such as partially-filled crevasses, rock walls, fallen seracs, or the moat between glacier edge and rock cliff, but often the climber must build a windbreak of rocks or snow. A well-pitched tent may be the best shelter, though one poorly pitched will merely keep the entire party awake with its cannonlike cracks. For a one-night stand when retreat to timberline can be made even in the worst of weather it is usually best simply to wrap up in a tarp.

BIVOUACS

In American terminology a bivouac is a camp made in the course of a climb using only the materials that can easily be carried in a rucksack. For long and difficult ascents bivouacs often are planned and their rigors lessened by a light sleeping bag, a special bivouac sack, or perhaps merely a tarp and extra clothing. Since a planned bivouac ordinarily occurs only on a difficult climb the weight of special equipment must be kept small, but a pound or two extra per man is worthwhile where it might prevent death from exposure. Especially useful is the *bivouac sack*, a large tent-like envelope of tightly-woven fabric, just large enough to accommodate one or two climbers, needing no poles or stakes but equipped with strong loops for anchoring to rocks or pitons. A good combination for the individual is a *half-length down bag*, weight about 1 pound, *used with a down jacket*. Another alternative is fitting a plastic *bivouac sleeve* inside the pack; the climber puts his feet in the pack and pulls the sleeve up over his legs and hips, protecting his upper torso and extremities with a roomy parka of coated nylon. On extreme rock climbs where the terrain is vertical or even overhanging, a light nylon hammock suspended from pitons is sometimes used.

More common is the bivouac forced by such unanticipated delays as an accident or loss of route. At low altitude with plentiful boughs under and over the sleepers and wood for a roaring fire there is no discomfort. At high altitudes in reasonably-good weather a bivouac is a memorable experience, the physical miseries more than repaid by a sky that reveals a wealth of unsuspected stars. In bad weather a high bivouac can be dangerous in itself and leave the party seriously debilitated by morning.

The harshness of most bivouacs results from failure to find an appropriate site. Search absolutely and categorically must commence while ample daylight remains, rather than straggling on until last strength and last light vanish together, and the night must be spent crouched on a narrow ledge or contorted around a projecting rock or hung from pitons in a stance that would have been considered cruel even in medieval dungeons. The first consideration is safety, and surrounding terrain should be minutely scanned; during the night there is small chance of avoiding falling rock or avalanches. Next in priority are shelter from wind and weather and level space for comfortable sitting. For warmth the entire party should huddle up together rather than going off to shiver separately.

In organizing a bivouac anything or anyone liable to fall—packs, bivouac sack, and climbers—is anchored. Body heat is conserved by brushing snow from clothing, exchanging damp garments for dry, removing wet boots (and anchoring them with care), placing feet in the rucksack. Pockets are emptied, belts and other items of clothing that impede circulation loosened, and a snorkel sock slipped over the nose and mouth.

The bivouac is the most rudimentary and rarest and least desirable of camps, yet in a sense it is the optimum camp for a climber, perfectly embodying his austere ideals. A bivouac can be made anyplace with minimum equipment and time and extracts the maximum possible comfort from terrain and weather and materials available. Every climber in planning every camp should begin thinking in terms of a bivouac, very cautiously and only grudgingly adding items to this skeleton.

3 *

ALPINE CUISINE

THE climber eats primarily to provide fuel for reaching summits. In theory, therefore, some standard menu could be devised, such as cube sugar, margarine, chipped beef, powdered milk, prunes, and vitamin tablets, which would serve every excursion short or long. It is even possible that these ingredients or their chemical equivalents could be homogenized and pressed into compact, durable bars imprinted with the recommended daily dosage.

However, the mountain experience is considerably more complex than a track meet, and includes not only victories on peaks but such small joys as a nice cup of tea. Good food gives a festive touch to summit celebrations, improves the scenery, and keeps up spirits during days of storm and fog. Bad food makes trails steeper, beds lumpier, sunsets paler, and friends harder to get along with.

Nonetheless, few people go into wilderness primarily to eat. The greatest pleasure consistent with time and energy available—this is the *second* aim of alpine cuisine. Quickly and simply fueling the body is the first.

The Fire

At some point in the last several tens of thousands of years man developed a liking for hot food. Little or no physiological basis has been found for the addiction, but psychologically the habit is hard to kick for much more than a weekend. Most climbers therefore heat some of their food, usually with a stove, sometimes with a wood fire;

the third option is no fire at all, often a forced choice but one preferred on short trips by many a lazy old sandwich-eating peakbagger.

Aside from the role of fire in cooking, in a survival situation the warmth of flames or hot food can be lifesaving. The Complete Wilderness Man is always prepared for every eventuality. He carries adequate clothing, knows heat-conserving survival techniques, and has a reserve of foods that need no fire at all. But he also has a canny ability to make wood burn, and is never caught without dry matches and an emergency supply of chemical fuel; if lost in a forest or timberline meadow, a wood fire may save his life, as may chemical fire when he is trapped on glacier or cliff by weather, darkness, or accident.

STOVES

Above timberline and on glaciers there is no wood; in the meadow camps of popular climbing areas all the easy fuel is long gone and what remains is scenery and should be left unmolested; even in a forest a party may not have the time or desire to gather damp sticks and nurse a flame. Typically, therefore, the contemporary climber cooks his meals over chemical fire, gaining the advantages of speed and simplicity at the cost of a relatively-small amount of extra weight in the pack.

Solid fuels (see Chapter 1) are normally carried for such emergencies as kindling a wood fire or providing hot drinks on a bivouac, and may also do for a limited amount of other cookery. However, when chemical fuel must be relied upon for any considerable number of meals, a stove is indispensable. The investment in weight, and the problems of learning to use the stove and keeping the fuel from contaminating food, are minor alongside the dependability (once the stove is mastered) and the extra time allowed for climbing, sleeping, and other mountain activities more enjoyable than cooking.

A number of ingenious, inexpensive, and lightweight stoves are available. (See Chapter 1.) Each has advantages, each has special tricks. The climber should make first acquaintance with his stove in the city, and then escalate the relationship through steadily less ideal conditions.

On a long trip when fuel must be conserved, stove-cookery requires careful preplanning before a meal is begun to ensure that something is always on the flame. Pot lids, rarely used in wood-fire cookery, save heat. When the stove is set on snow it must be insulated to prevent tank pressure from falling.

The chief enemy of any stove is wind. Placement in a sheltered nook helps, but often the flame must be kept roaring to combat the wind—very wasteful of fuel. A stove works best in a tent, where the flame can be closed down to an efficient cooking level. In cold weather stoves are harder to get started, requiring more care and patience in priming.

WOOD FIRE

The bough bed and the wood fire are both becoming obsolete in alpine regions, replaced by the mattress and stove. Within valley forests the prodigality of nature is such that any and all dead wood can be used with an easy conscience, and similarly in high basins where winter avalanches regularly prune the cliffs, bringing down a fresh supply of fuel for the following summer. But one should *never* take from the country without questioning, first, whether the country can afford the loss, and one should *never* set out on a trip into an unfamiliar area irrevocably committed to cooking with wood in or above the timberline zone.

The dead wood produced by a struggling alpine ecosystem, perhaps over a half-century or more, may tempt even the pure in heart to haul silver logs and snags to the kitchen, or erode off branches with a folding saw, but if a log or snag is worth a photograph or even an admiring glance it is too valuable to be used for firewood. In the case of *every* alpine fire the burden falls on the camper to prove to himself that the fire is really needed, and that it will not damage the view.

Still, a wood fire is the only variety suitable for sitting around and drying socks, warming cold bones, and singing folk songs; opportunities for evening seminars are not common on trips with an intensive climbing schedule, but often linger in the memory of philosophers beyond the more dramatic events of the day. Another advantage is that the fuel is gathered on the spot rather than carried on the back. Also, any extensive amount of cooking is faster than on a stove—once the fire is going. For esthetic and social and practical reasons, therefore, a wood fire is often the preferred alternative in forests and on long trips. The emergency values for misfortunate mountaineers scarcely need emphasis.

Building a Fire

In dry, calm weather firebuilding is often so easy that even a spent cigarette tossed into the brush starts a splendid blaze and burns whole sections of timber. In a howling rainstorm the combined concentration of several experienced woodsmen, applied for hours, may achieve nothing better than an occasional wisp of smoke. In heavy timber a persistent craftsman can almost always succeed; in high meadows the only solution may be a bolt of lightning.

The primary requirement is a plentiful supply of dry matches carried in a waterproof container. (Some "waterproof" matches tend also to be fireproof.) Solid chemical fuels provide steady flame beneath kindling, and in wet conditions often make the difference between painless combustion and the fruitless expenditure of matches by the gross. The paper in food packages must be burned in any event, and should not be overlooked through any qualm that its use is unsportsmanlike; unfortunately, though, most food-industry paper has a mysterious tendency to be incombustible in the mountains.

When the situation is at all difficult, the secret of success lies in the extended search for good wood; it may be pointless to attempt to start a fire until an hour or more has been spent assembling proper materials in sufficient quantity to sustain a chain reaction. "Squaw wood" is gathered with no tools but the hands and perhaps a pocket knife. A folding saw is sometimes useful in pruning tough, dead underbranches from alpine trees, but should not be considered a license to desecrate silver snags. Hatchets are principally used by inexperienced high-country travelers to mutilate living trees, and have no place in the gear of a wilderness citizen. Neither do the double-bitted axes and chainsaws carried by some regiments of the heavy cavalry.

The first need is tinder, which in wet weather must be gathered by the bushel. The dead lower branches of standing trees, protected by the canopy of live cover, are the most dependable source, though seasoned twigs under large logs, or the flaking undersides of decaying logs, are often better. Larger dry twigs or slabs can be slivered with a knife. Much searching may be necessary to find the driest of the dry—under a rock ledge or a peculiar bend of a tree. The traveler in any one mountain range soon finds that some of the native species burn better than others, and some don't burn at all, however dry; it is well to observe the characteristics of the local woods, and learn to recognize them (by look if not by name) for future reference.

Once enough tinder is gathered (and carefully sheltered), armloads of larger material must be obtained—all the dry that can be found, but also great quantities of the wet. With fuel assembled and sorted in several piles ranging from tinder through little kindling to big stuff, the firebuilder commences, nourishing the fire from small to large, taking care never to stifle a hesitant flame with excess fuel, never sparing the bellows of the human lungs, and providing shelter from gusts of wind.

Once the fire is definitely going and becoming large enough to be useful, there remains the decision of how large it should be allowed to grow. For cooking, a bed of hot coals is most efficient, and therefore the fire is kept small during meal preparation. The general rule among climbers is that the fire then goes out immediately, either because it's time for bed or because scarce fuel must be conserved for future campers. When a seminar or drying-out seems in order, the fire may be expanded, but only when the ecosystem can tolerate exorbitant wastage of resources.

Cooking Setups

The easiest and wisest way to cook on a wood fire is with a *wire grate* weighing 8 ounces or less, propped up on rocks or logs. Since a single grate serves half a dozen or more people, the added load per person is insignificant.

Of the more complex devices traditional to woods lore, the *dingle-stick* is most worthy of serious consideration, but only when the party lacks a grate. The *crossbar* is tedious to erect, but may be worth the effort for large parties or semipermanent camps; in popular areas one may be found already installed.

A pot set on a flat rock beside the flames can absorb sufficient heat to boil its contents though only a fraction of its bottom plus one side are exposed to fire. This method is often used to supplement a grate or dingle or crossbar, the serious cooking being directly over the flames while other pots set on rocks keep the soup simmering and the dish-water warming.

Housekeeping

KITCHEN ORGANIZATION

Organization of a climbing kitchen properly begins long before packs are shouldered: months before in the case of expeditions; at home for 1- to 2-week "semi-expeditions"; at the trailhead for weekend outings. Utensils are planned so that there are sufficient, but no superfluous, cooking and storage pots. For long trips with many meals, foods are packed in logical groupings to save time and trouble in camp; for shorter trips they are merely divided among the party for carrying and the components of each meal assembled as needed.

Each mountain kitchen has its own requirements, dictated by the location, the fuel, the menu, the number of people, the weather, the schedule, and other factors. A typical situation involving three climbers cooking with wood (obviously a far more complicated affair than where a stove is employed) may be described to express the spirit of the thing. Upon arrival, one person chooses a site for the kitchen, rigs a grate or dinglestick, and builds the fire; a second gathers enough wood to keep the fire going through the meal; the third gathers pots and hauls water, finds the meal components, and begins preparation. Since too many cooks not only spoil the broth but kick over too many pots, one agreed-upon chef (for that meal, if not the trip) stirs the pots and stokes the fire; his companions stay out of the way except to bring more wood or water or to stir such pots or prepare such side-dishes as he suggests. In a small party of longtime companions, the division of responsibilities usually just happens without discussion. The larger the party, and the shorter their personal acquaintance, the more formal organization is needed—assignment of duties by a leader if there is one, or otherwise by the commune.

In another situation, where rather large numbers of relative strangers are climbing together, each person cooks by himself, for himself— doing a bit more work but free of organizational tensions.

FRUSTRATING ANIMALS

Placing edibles deep in the packsack usually protects them against animal appetites during the night or a single day away from camp. Longer absences require greater caution. The ideal container for a cache is a large metal tin with a tight lid—on some trips in some areas worth the weight. When metal is impractical, heavy-duty plastic bags or sheets may be used.

For a *ground cache* vulnerable foods are wrapped tightly in a water-proof plastic sheet, placed in a well-drained area, and anchored by rocks—heavily around the sides, lightly but tightly on top. For a *tree cache* the food sack is suspended from a branch higher from the ground and farther from the trunk than any local bear can reach. The upper surface of the sack must slant smoothly and steeply lest little creatures scamper along the branch, drop onto the top, and gnaw an entrance.

In areas frequented only by climbers, such devices are quite dependable, but they are of little value in country traveled by campers who "live off the land." Here, the main consideration is skillfully concealing the cache. A note left with the cache, explaining its importance, may shame some thieves into stealing only the tasty and expensive foods, but will only delight the deliberate vandal. Most people who go into the mountains, whether to climb, hike, fish, hunt, or whatever, respect the country and their fellow outdoorsmen, but in heavily-populated alpine land the only sure way to protect a cache is to sit on it.

DISHWASHING

On weekend climbs it is easiest to carry the dishes and pots home dirty; the city kitchen quickly disposes of a chore that is rarely better than inconvenient in the hills. On longer trips where utensils are used more than once they must be kept reasonably clean. Cooking pots should be filled with water as soon as emptied and left to soak. Food particles in pots and dishes can be eroded away with sand or gravel, or—more efficiently—with a pad of woven metal or plastic, or a commercially-available paper towel impregnated with detergent. After scraping, utensils are swirled with cold water or snow to remove solids, then with hot water (perhaps supplemented by a bit of soap or detergent) to cut the grease.

Especially in warm weather, the repeated use of dirty utensils may lead to digestive disturbances. However, very often dishwashing must be put off until the next morning, or the next evening, or until the blizzard stops. No harm is necessarily done in such case if the facts of bacterial growth are kept in mind. The heat of the fire sterilizes cooking pots; as for eating utensils, the climber merely avoids eating all the way down to the germ cultures at the bottom of the plate.

FIRE AND GARBAGE CONTROL

The true mountaineer—climber, hillwalker, or river-watcher—walks softly through the wilderness, seeking to leave not the slightest trace of his passage. He has at all times a proper respect for nature and for the rights of visitors following him.

Fire

The respectful traveler rarely builds wood fires in alpine terrain, and only when he can do so without robbing the landscape of fuel that also happens to be beautiful. He always prefers to use an established firepit rather than starting a new one, and never leaves a fire without drowning it with water or snow until the last ash is cold to the fingers. When he has by necessity used a virgin fireplace in forest or meadow, he guards against later underground creep (since an apparently-dead fire may be smoldering beneath the surface) by digging a circular trench with the ice ax; if the humus is so much as warm within this trench, he digs others with increasing diameter until the limit of creep is found, and then stirs and saturates every inch of enclosed soil. Finally, he covers the ashes with humus and soil, and perhaps even transplants clumps of grass to the site, seeking to re-create the semblance of virginity. Where such precautions are unnecessary, as in sand or gravel, he still scatters ashes and charred sticks.

Garbage

The respectful traveler has a garbage sack in his automobile for banana peels and sandwich wrappers. On the trail or peak he stows every particle of paper, glass, plastic, and metal in his pack for later disposal.

Camp garbage is more troublesome, and on this point the wilderness world is in a state of transition. The old rule, which remains valid in remote areas, is "burn bash and bury." Burn all paper; also burn all aluminum foil and cans, since a hot fire can largely oxidize them to an ash and melt the remainder to small ingots; also burn all "tin cans," since the fire not only burns away aromas that lead bears and other nosy animals to excavate buried garbage, but also consumes paper labels, burns off the coating of lacquer or tin, and begins oxidation of the iron. In a wet climate, an unburned can may remain intact for a generation, while a scorched one may be reduced to soil within a few years. (In a dry climate, however, experiments conducted in the High Sierra suggest that even thoroughly-burned cans may remain intact for a century.) Finally, after all garbage has been burned, the cans are stamped flat, the ashes raked and re-raked for bits of aluminum foil and other metal, and the total package is carried to a place where a hole can be dug without wrecking the groundcover and is buried as deep as possible—and once again, the ground surface is reconstructed.

This old rule served very well, when observed, until the population explosion began. Then mountaineers began to find that in popular areas wherever they tried to bury garbage they were merely digging up garbage.

And so came the new rule: *if you can carry it into the wilderness full, you can carry it out empty.* The rule applies universally to trips lasting one day or several; the garbage, burned or unburned, is carried home in a heavy-duty plastic bag brought along for the purpose. In many parts of the world, including virtually all National Parks in America and the entire State of California, the new rule applies even for much longer trips; unless the Forest Service or Park Service or other land-manager has provided on-site facilities for garbage disposal, the mountaineer cannot decently do else but transport the junk to a city trash can.

In recent years many a mountaineer has developed the habit or hobby of not only making his own passage invisible but of spending extra effort to obliterate evidence of his predecessors—most of whom were just ignorant and thoughtless. This mountaineer-garbageman cleans trails as he walks them, impaling bits of paper with his ice ax. In established camps he spends his spare time burning decayed boots, yellowed magazines, rotten mattresses, punctured liferafts, and plastic tarps, and burning not only his own cans but those nearby, burying all together along with shards of glass and bits of aluminum foil and cartridge casings and beer can pull-tabs and infinite further artifacts left by people who enjoy the wildlands with the innocence of reckless childhood but have not yet learned the responsibilities of maturity.

Leaving a clean camp, and cleaning up a filthy camp, may have the effect of stimulating subsequent visitors to think it over before tossing cans into the brush. In theory, at least, many a person who will leave garbage where he finds existing garbage will not initiate the desecration of a field of clean flowers.

In the High Sierra of California and the Cascades and Olympics of Washington, hillwalkers have begun to send volunteer reclamation teams to salvage meadows and lakes wrecked by a previous thoughtless generation, spending a weekend or even longer gathering cans and other debris from the flowers, from lake bottoms, and packing pounds or tons of metal and glass out of the hills. More such efforts will be required in the future to supplement the clean-up efforts of federal and state managers of public lands.

WATER POLLUTION

Not long ago, travelers of wilderness mountains (contrasted to the Himalaya and Alps) drank any and all water found along the way with no more thought about its safety than a glance around to see what the animals might have been up to. Nowadays, however, with the growing back-country population, the traditionally-inviolate springs and rills are not always to be trusted, particularly in camps favored by the cavalry, but also wherever walkers are numerous, not to mention areas undergoing "multiple-use" by herds of sheep or cattle.

Some preliminary research results suggest that much supposedly-virgin wilderness water, however clear and cold, may be so contaminated by thoughtless humans and their uncontrolled domestic animals that it could be as dangerous as any city sewer.

For personal protection, therefore, each traveler must now and increasingly in future inspect carefully the water he proposes to use, and when in doubt give it preliminary treatment (see Chapter 18) as if it came from the Hudson or Ganges.

Additionally, each good wilderness citizen must take special pains not to be guilty of "RE" (random elimination), seeking instead to satisfy his needs at some distance from water channels.

Short-Haul Eating: Weekends

On trips of 2 or 3 days, or even longer if basecamp is close to the road, weight is not a factor in planning meals. Any food on the grocery-store shelves, tinned, fresh, or frozen, is a candidate for consideration; the modern abundance of processed foods leaves great scope for the imagination.

SUPPER

When it is known in advance that time will be plentiful, gourmets (and exhibitionists) plan sensational suppers, such as: a tossed salad of fresh lettuce, tomatoes, and cucumbers, imported egg drop soup, corn on the cob, broiled sirloin steaks with fresh mushrooms and onions, a shortcake made of hot brown-and-serve biscuits and frozen straw-berries, and for beverages, fresh milk, or perhaps liebfraumilch, followed by coffee, liqueur, and cigars. However, the climber fre-quently arrives in camp at 6 or 7 p.m. and must be in bed by 8 if he is to be cheerfully away at 3 a.m. or earlier. Remembering the old adage that "though the food is cold, the inner man is hot," he often contents himself with a supper of sandwiches and fruit juice.

Between menus of steak and salad on one hand and sandwiches and juice on the other lie many meals both nourishing and delicious yet easily and rapidly prepared. The *supermarket stew* is concocted from various cans selected by intuition or at random. A pedestrian but safe example is a can of beef and gravy mixed with a can of kernel corn. More daring but quite edible are chow mein and shrimp, ravioli and turkey, beans and chopped ham. In any combination a dash of grated cheese or a chunk of margarine may enormously improve things. Bread, a hot drink, and a dessert of pastry or instant pudding round out a satisfying meal. Another simple supper is built around *hot sandwiches*: hamburgers, hot dogs, or minute steaks fried or broiled, combined with salad greens or relish, supplemented by drinks and dessert.

Cup cookery is particularly suitable for one-man meals, especially in cold and windy camps. Having at hand chemical fuel, two large cups, and a pot of water, the climber crawls into his sleeping bag and heats each course in sequence. A cup of soup, next a cup of meatballs eaten with bread and butter, finally a nice cup of tea and a Danish and off to sleep.

BREAKFAST

If the climb begins in the middle of the night, breakfast is merely the first installment of lunch. A tiny can of fruit cocktail, or a doughnut and a swallow of milk, are typical menus. Some climbers are convinced their legs won't work without hot food; their neurosis can be quickly pampered with instant cereal or cocoa cooked by chemical fire.

LUNCH

As soon as breakfast is completed the climber commences lunch, which he continues to eat as long as he is awake, stopping briefly for supper. He has food in his rucksack and knick-knacks in his pockets, main courses for the summit lunch, nibbles for rest-stops, and sweets to suck while walking.

Few climbs are conducted so austerely that one cannot eat for pleasure as well as physiological efficiency. The confirmed athlete may go solely on glucose tablets, but the average climber eats whatever delicacies he is clever enough to carry. Small lunches are the rule, since a feast followed by violent exertion sets up a competition between the digestive and muscular functions of the blood that leads to indigestion or weakness or both.

The menus of short-haul lunches frequently are very much like those of semi-expedition lunches (discussed in the following section); many efficient foods, such as cashew nuts, also taste good.

However, the range of alternatives is much greater. Sandwiches made before leaving town, wrapped first in plastic and then in foil, remain fresh and tasty through a weekend. Apples, oranges, bananas, grapes, cherry tomatoes, cucumbers, celery—fresh fruits and vegetables in general—are never quite so delicious as high on a hot, dry cliff. The choice, actually, is limited only by imagination and financial resources, and the time available before the trip for browsing through supermarkets and delicacy shops. A sound rule for short trips is to carry a variety of foods, even if this means carrying home a surplus; the appetite often becomes tricky in a quick transition from city life and the beginner may not be able to predict in advance what will appeal to him during the climb, when he must take nourishment but may not be in the mood.

WATER

The notion lingers that because it is a pleasure to drink when thirsty it must be harmful, and therefore one should resist the devil by sucking a stone, or perhaps a prune pit. Punishing the flesh through deliberate dehydration is an excellent way to prepare for a mystic experience, but a bad way to climb mountains. Water is as vital to life as oxygen; the body can lose as much as a gallon of water without lasting physical damage, but efficiency is substantially lowered well before this point. Authorities recommend an average intake of 2 quarts of water a day during active exertion—4 quarts in hot weather. (It must be noted that the system apparently can adapt over a period of time to a far smaller amount without critical loss in efficiency; certainly the 5-day ascents of hot walls in Yosemite Valley have been made with less than 20 quarts—roughly 40 pounds—per man.)

The old superstition has some basis in fact; as beginners frequently learn the hard way, even when water is plentiful thirst should be slaked in moderation. Tossing a pound or so of liquid into the stomach slows a man down; if he is very hot and the water is very cold it can even knock him out. Drink little, drink often is the rule, and to this end climbers often carry loaded canteens even when they could, strictly speaking, survive from one creek to the next.

Plain water is always acceptable to the thirsty, and is the best drink in the world when it comes from a snowfield stream of white froth, but for summits and other dry spots doctored-up water goes down better and also provides instant energy from simple sugars. A canteen supply of pure water should always be available in the party for first-aid purposes, but citric powders can be used to mix lemonade in a cup, or one may carry cans of juice, or for a rare treat, cans of pop.

The same subterranean tradition that recommends sucking stones forbids eating snow. In contrary evidence, if all the tons of snow consumed by climbers over the years were heaped in a pile, the Greenland icecap would appear by comparison merely a heavy frost. The only caution is to learn moderation, melting snow in the mouth before swallowing, just as a small child learns to lick rather than chew an ice cream cone.

Long-Haul Eating: The Semi-Expedition

The "semi-expedition" is an extended outing with all food and equipment hauled on the climbers' backs. The limit is about 2 weeks, since few people are capable of carrying, at any one time, the loads necessary for more than that. Longer trips become, logistically at least, true expeditions requiring relay-packing, porters, or airplane drops. The climber on a short vacation and a shorter budget may not be able to afford the expense of hired transport or the time of relay-packing, and in such case plans the duration of his excursion to correspond to his carrying capacity.

Though even today there are wildernesses in Alaska, Canada, and the Antarctic large enough to require true expeditions, in Western America, where only relatively-small enclaves of primitive nature remain, the semi-expedition is the most characteristic wilderness experience. One goal of contemporary preservationists can be defined as seeking to save for present and future generations the opportunity for semi-expeditions. For this reason roads, airplanes, air drops, helicopters, scooters, and all other mechanized devices are barred from lands included in the National Wilderness Preservation System of the United States.

The success of a semi-expedition depends on menu planning. Too much food means too much weight and too few peaks. Too little or improper food means not enough stamina and too few peaks. Unpalatable food in any quantity means low morale and unpleasant memories.

PLANNING AND PACKAGING

Dividing the Group

Since meals are social events, many parties plan all food in common. However, on other occasions tastes are so divergent that breakfast and lunch are left to the individual and only supper, the most complicated meal of the day, is a group effort.

The size of cooking units should rarely exceed six. Beyond that number the efficiency of group preparation is outweighed by complications of large fires, large pots, and hungry mobs milling about in discontent. Though a party of eight may possibly still cook better as a single unit, ten climbers usually are best split up. Many factors influence the decision, such as closeness of social ties, type of fuel available, and the intensity of the climbing schedule.

Selecting the Menu

Packs are not significantly heavier on short hauls if food quantities are estimated high, since excess weight may be only one or several pounds; also, if vital ingredients are overlooked there is no real hardship, since anyone can get by for a weekend without sugar in his oatmeal. Semi-expeditions, on the other hand, demand precise planning, both to save the unnecessary ounces that pyramid to staggering pounds and to ensure that right down to the last meal there is salt for the potatoes. The climber who groans as he shoulders an 80-pound pack on Day One feels justifiable bitterness when he arrives back at the road on Day Fourteen carrying an unused pound of margarine. And the climber who must endure bland tea night after night can never forgive the blundering fool who forgot the lemon crystals.

Meals are sometimes planned by the group sitting in committee, sometimes by an elected individual. In either case the same procedure is followed. First, menus are written down for each meal. From this is compiled an ingredients list with estimated quantities, and from this the shopping list. Estimation comes easily for the experienced semi-expeditioner who knows that a certain amount of a certain ingredient is just about right for so many companions of long-expressed tastes. The less experienced can benefit from study of Appendices 1 and 2.

The dietician must first of all decide how much food the particular party can reasonably carry for the trip in question and must then, at all costs, plan meals to remain within the maximum load limit. A commonly-accepted rule of thumb is 2 pounds of food per man per day, enough to fuel an active climber and to feed him quite well if currently-available dehydrated products are used. Actually, a very careful planner can provide enough calories with less than 2 pounds, and a careless planner can easily exceed 2 pounds without providing enough calories. Many climbers, particularly in Europe and America, have enough emergency food around their waists and hips to survive without eating for days or weeks, and therefore it is often possible to plan meals well below the 2-pound allotment, leaving enough leeway so that after all the essentials have been included there is room for a luxury tin of jam or peanut butter, or some other frivolity. It is much easier to plan on the low side and add extras than to think big and be forced to subtract a soup here, a dessert there.

Packaging

The elaborate packages of commercial foods are often too bulky and heavy for the strained back of the semi-expeditioner; a supermarket cart piled high with cardboard-enclosed air can be, and must be, reduced to utilitarian containers.

After all foods have been gathered, they are repacked for carrying —a considerable but worthwhile chore. Many types of plastic sacks and sheets are available for the purpose, including some that offer airtight seals, but the average semi-expeditioner gets by with freezer-type sacks of various sizes, tied or rubber-banded at the mouth. For finely-powdered items, such as powdered potatoes or jello, double-sacking is wise and adds insignificant weight. Plastics have an odor that can permeate dehydrated foods, particularly dairy products, and make them unpalatable, but the effect is not noticeable until well after 2 weeks. Items such as honey and mustard can be safely stowed in plastic refillable tubes or flexible freezer containers with tight lids.

Though requiring considerable work at home, the greatest ease in camp comes from packaging individual meals before packs are ever hoisted. By doing so one can avoid the problems of too much rice at some meals and hardly enough for the last—as can happen when one has a single "rice sack" for the entire trip. A labeling system is also to the cook's advantage (felt pens mark efficiently on plastic). Smaller packages can be placed in larger ones of heavier-ply plastic, and lumped (and labeled) as "Breakfast," "Supper," "Drinks," "Desserts," "Soups," "Spices," "Candy," and so on. When planning is not so critical from the standpoint of weight, it may still be useful to gather foods into logical groupings.

LUNCH

For the climber, unlike mountain travelers with more relaxed schedules, lunch is a critically-important meal, beginning early and continuing late—and in the case of a bivouac, replacing suppers and breakfasts. Frequently, therefore, nearly half the daily 2-pound ration is allotted to lunch.

Lunching and munching preferences vary so widely that it is

prudent for every party member to share in the planning; those who love their kippered herring or Italian salami may not be able to abide blue cheese and provoloni. A popular stable is "glorp," or "squirrel food," a mixture of nuts, candy, raisins, and other dehydrated fruits: one handful makes a snack, several make a meal; fastidious eaters may prefer the constituents served separately. The menu shown in Table 3 takes a bit more trouble to plan but usually pleases most palates day after day. The protein constituents should be included in every lunch; one or more of the others can be deleted on easy days. The "special delights" are a matter of personal taste. Appendix 2 suggests a variety of foods within each category.

Table 3. Basic Semi-Expedition Lunch.

Category	Amounts (Ounces per man-day)
Meat	2
Cheese	2
Nuts or peanut butter	2
Dried fruit	2
Bread or crackers	3
Chocolate or candy bars	2
Hard candy	1
Drinks and special delights	2
Total	16

SUPPER

Main Course

With 1 pound of the man-day ration allotted to lunch, half to two-thirds of the other pound is devoted to supper, which consists largely of rehydrated foods. Commercially-packaged freeze-dried dinners, complete in one box, offer tempting meals—beef stew, chili con carne, and others—at luxury prices. A packaged pre-cooked bean dinner provides a welcome change of pace from the menus described below.

In every climbing area of the world, parallel evolution has produced the same magnificent meal, variously called "one-pot-supper," "mulligan," "hoosh," or "glop." By any name its virtues are extraordinary. A large number of compatible ingredients are cooked in a single pot with a saving of equipment, time, and fuel. The blended components have a flavor greater than the sum of the parts; the result is a complete, satisfying, and memorable meal.

Every glop involves an act of unique creation and no two are ever exactly the same; the master chef steers by dead reckoning and insight. Most glops have a simple-quick and a complex-long form, and thus can be adapted to the time available. For example, one that has proved lastingly popular requires in its simple form only warm water, instant potatoes, and Goteborg sausage and is ready to eat within minutes. In the complex form spices and dehydrated vegetables and margarine are added and the mixture is allowed to simmer and blend.

The complete glop begins with a base of spicy flavor provided by a dehydrated soup, placed in the pot along with the water. At appropriate later times, depending on the meal, starches and meats and various other things are added. Appendix 2 suggests some basic glops that offer unlimited opportunity for adaptation by individual imagination. Table 4 and Table 5 (page 66) give the principal alternatives available in meats and starches, and the amounts in each category.

Table 4. Meats for Semi-Expedition Glops.

Category	Amount (Ounces per man-serving)

Tinned
  Chicken (boneless)
  Chopped meat ("spam")
  Corned beef
  Ham
  Roast beef (avoid gravy)
  Salmon
  Tuna
	4

Sausage	**4**
Chipped beef	2

Dried, compressed
  Meat bars
  Bacon bars
	1½–2

Vacuum-dried	1–2

Freeze-dried
  Meat
  Shrimp
  Ham
	1⅓–1½
	½–1
	½–⅔

Soups and Side-Dishes

A cup of soup is always a welcome prelude to the main course, and should be planned whenever considerations of time, weight, and fuel allow—always remembering, though, that whatever weight and fuel are expended on soup may be at the expense of the glop. Europe provides dozens of delicious dehydrated soups; America, not many. One package stretched with water (better a thin soup than a thick) serves a party of three or four; with the addition of a bouillon cube, four or five.

Table 5. Starches for Semi-Expedition Glops.

Category	Amount (Ounces per man-serving)	Amount (Dry measure in cups)
Rice		
Pre-cooked (5-minute soak type)	2⅓	⅔
Quick-cooking (10–15-minute cooking type)	2	¼
Potatoes		
Mashed, powdered	2	¼
Mashed flakes (bulkier, easier mixing)	2	1, shaken down
Sliced, diced, cubed (slow cooking, may be soaked)	2	—
Wheat, processed ("Ala." Slow cooking—15 minutes. Good change of pace.)	2	⅓
Pasta (macaroni, spaghetti, noodles. To go with meat. Choose thin varieties cooking in 7 minutes or less.)	2	—
Macaroni (to go with cheese)	3	—

If the weight of a genuine soup cannot be afforded, bouillon is an old favorite, made from little cubes that weigh nothing at all and have virtually no food value but are helpful in replacing water and salt, warming cold bodies, and stimulating the appetites of exhausted climbers.

Though bulky, dehydrated vegetables weigh little and cost little and become amazingly appealing to some people after a few days of potatoes and sausage. Spinach and carrots taste most like fresh. Freeze-dried and vacuum-dried vegetables and fruits are even better but too expensive for frequent use. The food value of all these is mostly psychological, but it is not a bad plan to slip in a side-dish of vegetables once very several days; often they are greeted more enthusiastically than dessert.

Bread or biscuit can rarely be planned for supper on a semi-expedition, but scraps left over from lunch are welcome.

Drinks and Desserts

Drinks and/or desserts are also added according to the weight allotment available. The total of 2 pounds per man-day usually does not allow soup, vegetable side-dish, drink, and dessert for every supper. Planning one or two trimmings for each day provides a good balance; not all, and maybe none, are wanted after a long, hard climb, and the extras can accumulate for the light days and rest days, including storm days when there is nothing to do but eat and sleep.

After a dry day on the peak a cold flavorful drink is immensely delightful, and ideally the first order of business on reaching camp is mixing a pot of punch—lemonade, orange juice, grape juice, or whatever—from concentrated fruit bases or from citric powders and sugar. However, the weight of these usually means going without a hot drink or soup. The artificially-sweetened drinks are inferior but are so light they can be used more liberally.

Tea is another no-weight item that can be planned for every supper, allowing one bag a man per day, or carrying bulk tea if preferred. Instant coffee can also be carried to allow addicts to maintain their habit. Where the weight mounts up in these drinks is in the addition of sugar. Before the trip, count the members of the party who use sugar in their tea or coffee and figure about ½-⅓ ounce (a heaping teaspoon) per serving; on the trip, watch the sugar-users to make sure they don't consume the entire supply in a couple of days. Tea drinking can be varied by use of spiced varieties or a bit of dried mint or some lemon crystals; tea with brown sugar or honey is an abomination to purists but ambrosia to others. A powdered cream product should be included for those who can't endure black coffee, or even coffee with milk. Plain cocoa, and also coffee-cocoa, a half-and-half mixture of instant powders of the two, are as much desserts as they are drinks. The same is true of hot jello.

Full-scale desserts—pudding being the standard—are usually planned only once every several days. The time and fuel required by cooked puddings have made them rather a rarity in mountain camps. Instants are tricky and seem to demand a special flare; one cook may follow every direction faithfully and still end up with slop while another tosses the ingredients in the pot, shakes them around, and gets a beautiful set. Some new varieties of instant, notably a "whip-and-chill" brand, are highly dependable and have a flavor equal or superior to the best of the cooked puddings. On a cold day when climbers are chilly, any pudding—even instant—may be more appreciated served hot.

Ice cream can be made at any camp where snow is available plus 6–8 ounces of extra salt and an hour of extra time. A package of powdered ice cream mix is thoroughly whipped up in a pot with the recommended amount of liquid; cream is always specified, but a double-strength mixture of powdered whole milk does the job. In a nearby snow bank, dig a circular hole with a diameter 4 inches greater

than the pot and depth 3 inches deeper than the pot. Line the bottom
and sides of this hole with plastic bags. Spread the bottom with an inch
or so of snow and sprinkle heavily with salt. Place the pot in the hole. Fill
the space between the pot and the plastic with alternating layers of
snow and salt, tamped down and stirred with a stick. Cover the pot
with a lid and leave it alone for 15 minutes. Then, every 10 minutes or
so, for a total of three or four times, stir the thickening mixture within
the pot and add layers of snow and salt outside the pot. Finally,
go away for 15 minutes. If a lot of salt is available, production is
easy; with care and experience, a pot of hard-frozen ice cream can be
made (serving four–six) with as little as 6 ounces of salt, a pot of "milk
shake" with half that amount. Serve with a topping of jam or fresh
blueberries.

Staples and Seasonings

Sugar comes in two colors, one merely sweet, one also tasty. There
are those who prefer the brown (as crude as available) in everything,
including tea and coffee; for finicky groups it is safer to carry some of
the white as well.

Powdered milk used to be a trial, since the whole variety was difficult to mix without lumps and the easy-mixing non-fat variety was
bland. Easy-mixing whole milk is now available and is the only kind to
carry.

Margarine (preferred to butter on long trips for its keeping qualities) makes every other food taste better—bread, potatoes, glops,
oatmeal, even cocoa. It also has the most calories per pound of any
food in the climbing larder; when weight is extremely critical and a
party is trying to shave a few ounces from the 2-pound ration, the
margarine allotment can be raised at the expense of other items.

Salt is essential to the body as well as the palate. Cooked cereals are
virtually inedible without it, and individuals may want to salt their
glop to taste. Relatively little is needed, since other foods (such as soup
mix used as a base for glops) supply most of the physiological requirements.

As for spices—packages of dehydrated onions, tomatoes, peppers,
and soups and shakers of pepper and garlic salt and mixed condiments
—their total weight is insignificant beside that of a piton but they can
transform survival rations into banquets.

BREAKFAST

Breakfasts are a major semi-expedition problem. Cold-and-fast meals
save time and fuel but are heavy and bulky; mush-and-cocoa meals
take time but slip down easily in a freezing pre-dawn. The usual
procedure is to plan fast breakfasts for the long days, hot for the
medium days, roughly half-and-half, and add one or two luxury

breakfasts for layover days of rain or recuperation. Another aspect of the problem is that most parties include a mixture of farm-type hearty-breakfasters and urbanized late-starters who can barely tolerate the thought of solid nourishment until the sun is high. The amounts suggested in the sample menus of Appendix 2 will strike the former as starvation and the latter as nausea; when there is any argument the farmers must give way in the interests of group efficiency, consoling themselves with the thought that lunch will begin shortly.

For the fast start, many climbers prepackage a standard meal before the trip, measuring a prepared cereal (grape nuts, crushed corn flakes), sugar, raisins or other fruit, and powdered milk into a "breakfast bag." Stir in water—cold for a cold meal, hot for a hot—and breakfast is ready.

A hot drink is a pleasant addition to a cold meal and a standard element of a hot one. Cocoa, plain or chocolate ovaltine, coffee-cocoa, plain or chocolate malted milk, and just plain milk are common choices.

Mush—oat meal, farina, wheatena, or whatever—is the standard hot climbing breakfast; the instant or quick varieties don't really take any time at all beyond heating water. Sugar, milk, and margarine can be mixed into the cooking pot or added by the individual to taste. Wheat germ can be added to the mush—or to cold cereals—for additional protein and vitamin B.

Fruits, dried by sun or vacuum, can be soaked or cooked the previous night for quick reheating in the morning, then eaten separately or combined with the cooked mush. A powdered citrus drink, often warmed for a predawn start, adds variety; so, also, do the luscious freeze-dried fruits, which volume-for-volume are the equivalent of eating pure money.

Into almost every rat-race a day of rain must fall and with it opportunity for the luxury breakfast—which actually need not weigh a great deal, the luxury lying in the time of preparation. Hotcakes can be delicious or execrable and should never be counted on as truly luxurious unless the cook is experienced. A small, lightweight skillet that can double as someone's eating dish or a pot lid (as in some cooking sets) is almost a necessity; a small spatula is helpful. Syrup can be made from brown sugar, or lunch jam can be used. Powdered eggs can be mixed up with milk and cheese and scrambled; much better are the packaged omelets now available—add water, fry, and ham and eggs miraculously appear. A teflon-coated pan is best for omelet cookery. Bacon is an old favorite with either hotcakes or scrambled eggs; canned sausages or spam are magnificent. Whatever the main course, the ideal luxury breakfast includes cold orange juice for a start, stewed fruit, hot beverage, and bread or biscuit spread with margarine and jam or honey. When all this is eaten, it is noon or nearly so and time to take a short walk before lunch.

High-Altitude Eating

WATER

Far above timberline water is often at a premium. As soon as the campsite is located one or more members of the party begin collecting a reservoir, since at sundown the high mountains generally freeze tight. Sometimes a tongue of snow dribbles a stream, but more often only dampens the rock or makes mud. In the latter case a depression may be dredged, the water allowed to clear, and the resulting spring channeled into a pot by a piton or tent stake. Another common source of water is overhanging eaves of snow. Their drips vary in volume; a number of pots under a number of drips may be required to fill party needs.

In the absence of streams or drips, "water machines" can be devised if the sun is shining or has been recently. A dark tarp spread thin with snow makes great pools of water with little effort. Plastic bags filled with snow are slow but steady. A warm rock with a flat, tilted surface is fast but tedious. If there is no sunshine the only source of water is snow melted by chemical fire, always the last resort since the process is time-consuming and costly of fuel and the resulting liquid should not be called water but by its proper name, "melted snow," suitable for cooking and hot beverages but a nauseous beverage taken straight. When a single night is to be spent at high camp and prospects for sunshine are poor it is best to carry a large canteen supply from lower altitudes. In long stays at high altitude, dehydration is the major problem faced by the climber, who must work constantly at melting and drinking water to avoid serious debilitation.

The climber's last thoughts before bed are to protect his precious water supply from freezing, usually by storage next to or in the sleeping bag. There is no more cheerless beginning for a climb than a canteen of ice.

FOOD

In the gales characteristic of high camps cooking is difficult if not impossible. The most suitable foods are those that require only warming or may be eaten cold if worse comes to worst. Fuel must always be carried and its weight is another argument for simplicity. Boil-cookery is out of the question. For every 10-degree drop in boiling temperature, cooking time is approximately doubled; Table 6 shows the drastically-inverse ratio between boiling point and altitude.

Table 6. Boiling Point of Water.

Altitude (Feet)	Degrees (Fahrenheit)	Cooking Time (Sealevel = 1)
Sealevel	212	1
5,000	203	1.9
10,000	193	3.8
15,000	184	7.2
20,000	176	13.0

At low altitude a climber can make flagrant errors in diet without catastrophe; the same is not true at high altitude. The problems of prolonged stays in rarified air, specifically in the Himalaya and to some extent in the Andes, have received much study in the last few years, but lie beyond the scope of the treatment here. Short visits to high altitude are documented by more than a century of experience. A typical quick gain in elevation is the weekend ascent of Mount Rainier in the Cascades, where climbers normally spend Friday night near sealevel, Saturday night at 10,000 feet, and perhaps only 20 hours after leaving tidewater reach the 14,410-foot summit. A majority feel symptoms of mountain sickness ranging from a slight malaise to violent vomiting. The eating habits proved successful on Rainier by past generations are obviously valuable in all less-demanding situations, and apply up to approximately the 20,000-foot level.

In the abrupt ascent to high altitude there is not time for physiological acclimatization and the entire circulatory system is laboring merely to supply oxygen to the body. Large meals and foods difficult to digest demand attention the system simply cannot spare and illness results. The climber therefore eats light and often, never loading his stomach with a heavy meal. The menu stresses carbohydrates, which are easiest to digest, and scants fats and proteins, which are most difficult— though a good (*not* excessive) meal of fat and protein the night before the ascent is helpful in stoking the body later on.

Only trial and error can teach a person what foods his body can tolerate at high altitude. Some individuals seem unaffected and with great relish eat smoked oysters and pepperoni on the summit of Rainier—partly, no doubt, for the benefit of their green companions. The climber in doubt should depend chiefly on carbohydrates, but at all costs and at whatever effort must continue to eat, lest the loss of energy reinforce the debilitating effect of oxygen lack; even when thoroughly ill, nourishment can often be taken in the form of fruit juice.

4 *

WILDERNESS TRAVEL

MANY mountains of the world have been closely surrounded by civilization for centuries. Armies and elephants have crossed the Alps and the Himalaya is protected from approach more by politics than nature. In such ranges it is possible to be purely a climber, trusting a native guide or railway conductor to lead the way to the first rocks or ice.

There is another sort of mountain range that lies deep in wilderness. When the climbing party parks its automobiles at the end of a road in a Cascade valley or is dumped on the beach of a British Columbia fjord it faces long hours or days of wilderness travel before enjoying alpine pleasures. The technique of muddling through brush is not so glamorous as Class Five rock climbing but many a peak has been lost in thickets of slide alder. Indeed, frequently the major defenses of a wilderness mountain lie below snowline and the final scramble to the summit is an anticlimax after the epic approach.

Routes in Wilderness

There is no one set of immutable laws governing choice of wilderness route, for each range has its own peculiarities of geology and climate. The Canadian Rockies mountaineer accustomed to broad, meadowed valleys and open forests is horrified when he encounters the narrow canyons in the Coast Range totally occupied by jungles and cataracts. The Cascade mountaineer used to deep snow in June everywhere above 4000 feet feels parched when he visits the Sierra Nevada

V. Dome Peak from White Rock Lake, North Cascades. (Bob and Ira Spring)

VI. Sledging up the Seward Glacier, St. Elias Range. (Thomas Miller)

and must climb thousands of feet higher to find more than scraps of snow.

Prolonged mountaineering in a single range fills one with the lore of routefinding in that range, but even the wiliest traveler should enter each new range humble in spirit. He is not utterly ignorant for in knowing any mountain well he knows something of all mountains. This knowledge can be extrapolated, and supplemented by information from guidebooks, journals, maps, and acquaintances. None of these is a substitute for firsthand experience but all at least prepare him to be a good student.

Climate and geology make mountains what they are. Knowing that the west slope of the Olympics receives in excess of 150 inches of annual precipitation with a frost level that extends in winter to sea-level prepares the experienced mountaineer for dense brush and a low snowline and miserable weather. Knowing that the Tetons are arid and hot prepares him for a relative absence of brush, snow, water, and weather unfit for climbing. Knowing that the Olympics are composed mostly of weak sediments leads him to anticipate wearisome scree and easy ridge-running. Knowing that the Sir Donald group of the Selkirks is quartzite gives advance confidence in the soundness of the rock however steep. The mountaineer who knows the major outlines of a range's climate and geology can learn a great deal more by map study. Indeed, from a good map the informed reader can work backwards and describe the climate and geology.

TRAILS

A trail by definition is not wilderness even though it be a corridor of civilization barely a foot wide. Usually there is something of a trail between the roadhead and terra incognita, a track that starts bravely and dwindles to nothing. In many a present wilderness the traveler comes upon useful artifacts of a past penetration by civilization, fragmentary trails of long-vanished miners or trappers.

Even in ranges with heavy traffic and thus well-posted with signs a moderate degree of alertness is required to find and keep the trail. The beginning may be obliterated by logging operations or highway construction. Parties often stagnate mentally on a long monotonous walk and miss their proper turnoff. A good many more, awaiting an intersection with a prominent sign that has been flattened by winter snows or carried off by a souvenir hunter, find themselves at nightfall far up the wrong creek. Signs are poor substitutes for the methods of orientation discussed in the next chapter.

The climber needs to keep clearly in mind that very few trails were engineered for him. Miners build trails to the ore, fishermen to the high

lakes, trappers along valleys, and pioneers over passes. Frequently the
mine or the lake or the pass is a splendid basecamp. Moreover, any old
remnant of track is worth following if it goes reasonably near the right
destination. Inevitably, however, there comes the painful moment
when a pleasant trail must be abandoned because it goes to a lake or a
prospect hole many miles up the wrong valley.

A human trail is almost always blazed in forests and marked above
timberline by rock cairns. Following a marked trail requires some skill
and much care. The tree with the critical blaze grows old and topples,
an avalanche carries away a cairn. Also, many marks are made by lost
mountaineers who scrape trees and pile rocks while getting more
thoroughly lost.

An important principle in choosing off-trail routes is always to follow
the course that a trail would follow if there were one. Trail builders
generally find the easiest going; by studying their work one can more
quickly and wisely navigate the pure wilderness.

BRUSH

The commonest variety of brush is a mixture of hardy deciduous
species such as vine maple, slide alder, and willow. Wherever there is
running water and/or sliding snow, brush thrives. The classic example
is a low-altitude gully swept by avalanches in winter and a torrent in
summer. Coniferous trees cannot mature but conditions are perfect for
supple shrubs which flourish during the short summer season, usually
bend undamaged under the snow, and even if stripped to the ground
quickly sprout again from the roots. Mature coniferous forests reach
high and steal all the sunlight, eventually throttling deciduous trees.
Along river banks brush keeps a window on the sun and builds a narrow dense thicket. A river that changes course frequently prevents
conifers from gaining control and has a wide belt of alder bottom. At
subalpine elevations the entire valley floor may be a tangle, winter
avalanche snow lasting late into summer and thus forbidding forests
but encouraging brush.

There are some plants that flourish even in the deepest shadow providing there is sufficient moisture. Preeminent in horror is the poison-
spiked devil's club habitual to swamps and boggy creeks, passage of
which sometimes makes gloves a necessity.

Large conifers are on the side of justice and the traveler but small
ones are poor friends. The second-growth timber that springs densely
up after a fire or windstorm or logging is at its worst when about 20
feet high, the branches completely filling the space between trees, the
overhead cover not yet so thick that lack of sunlight has caused these
lower limbs to die and fall away. Moreover, at this age deciduous

brush is still very much in the contest. Even more difficult to negotiate are blowdowns, avalanche fans, and logging shows where the jumble of trash is so chaotic that frequently a quarter-mile an hour is an heroic velocity. A single such obstacle only a few hundred feet wide justifies major modifications of route and schedule.

Another variety of brush is the scrub growth at timberline where wind forces conifers to huddle next to the ground. Usually such wind-sculpted shrubs stand alone or in small clumps but occasionally they form a continuous belt between forests and meadows.

If a skirmish with brush must be accepted there is no technique at all. Brushfighting is not a diversion for civilized, gentle folk. One cannot afford charity toward slide alder or devil's club; one must hate and punish and kill when possible. Yet withal one must have the fortitude for a long campaign and contain fury within a pace that can be maintained. Sometimes one can or must walk atop the brush, balancing on limber holds and bouncing lightly from alder to maple like a circus aerialist. Sometimes the best tactic is one of pure weight, falling forward against the tangle and then pulling the branches apart to bring the legs through. Sometimes it is necessary to rush like a bull at the thicket hoping to unravel its twinings by a savage onslaught. Sometimes a party will be utterly defeated unless armed with a machete. Generally there is no subtlety to fighting brush. Only strength will do the job. It is not unusual to spend all of a long day from first light to dark making 2 miles up a jungle valley in the North Cascades.

Brush is not without its dangers. Downhill-slanting vine maple or alder gives slippery footing and if one is bouncing along many feet from the ground a lost hold can cause a bad fall. Brush obscures cliffs, boulders, and ravines and more than once has led a traveler to mischief.

The best policy of all is to avoid brush. So bald a statement seems much like forthrightly condemning Hell, yet even in ranges where brush is a frightful menace an alert traveler often can thread an easy path. The following rules are helpful:

1. Use trails as much as possible. Five miles of trail are less work than one mile of brush.
2. Travel above the brush on early-season snowcover. Some valleys are easy going in May when the party walks on 10 feet of snow but are almost impossible in July when the party must burrow under 10 feet of brush.
3. In summer avoid avalanche tracks. When following a long valley this means the best route (in the northern hemisphere) is on slopes with a south or west exposure where the snow does not avalanche so ferociously as on the opposite exposures. (See Chapter 20.)

When climbing a valley wall it means sticking to the "timber cones" between avalanche paths.

4. Always aim for the heaviest timber.

5. In summer avoid all water. Even in heavily-drenched coastal ranges the ridge spurs between creeks and the valley walls above rivers may be dry and brushless while the creek bottoms and valley floors are nightmares.

6. As a final alternative consider going right into the channel of the stream. Gravel and boulder beds may provide a clear tunnel through the brush, though wading may be the price of freedom. Streams flowing in deep canyons, however, are usually either choked with fallen timber or interrupted by waterfalls.

7. If the valley bottoms are hopeless and the valley sides scarred by myriad avalanche tracks, climb as directly as possible to timberline and take a high route above vegetation. The difficulties of the rocks and ice must of course be weighed against those of the green valley.

8. In alpine valleys travel on scree and remnants of snow rather than the adjacent gardens of alder.

9. Seek game trails. Animals dislike brush as much as man. Their intelligence is less than human but their experience greater.

TALUS

The rocks of the peaks constantly crumble and tumble and pile up in the valley as talus. Most of the rubble emerges from gullies and spreads below them in fan-shaped cones. Commonly these cones merge into one another, forming between valley greenery and precipice rockery a broad band of talus. Just as commonly the talus fans alternate with timber cones.

In hard-rock mountains such as the southern Selkirks talus is built solidly over the ages. At the bottom, soil has filled the interstices between boulders, making level pathways. Higher are dependable rockpiles where the climber can leap about lightly, guarding against the occasional teetering stone by his very momentum. Still higher the slopes of small fragments, called *scree,* are so secure and so well-anchored by flowers that they can be treated like snow and negotiated by stepkicking.

In soft-rock mountains such as the Olympics and portions of the Canadian Rockies talus can be dangerous. Since disintegration of the peaks is rapid even huge boulders may be delicately balanced and the traveler must always be ready to skip nimbly aside when his foothold suddenly sinks. Rarely but occasionally a talus slope is so insecure that kicking loose one key stone will destroy the precarious equilibrium and set off a disastrous rock avalanche. The scree may be loose as sand, requiring great patience and energy to climb. In the lower talus moss is usually a good indication of solid boulder placement. In the upper reaches grass and flowers mark scree with some degree of stability.

The most careful person on the stablest scree cannot avoid kicking loose many a pebble and boulder and therefore routes are preferred which allow each climber to walk freely, letting the rocks fall where they may. When the choice of route is restricted, as in a narrow gully, each member must tread gently and instantaneously give a warning shout should he start a stone rolling. Frequently it is essential for the party to travel closely bunched-up so that rocks cannot attain dangerous momentum between members.

In descent loose scree is sometimes sought rather than avoided, for the sport of "screeing." The object is to start a minor slide of pebbles and then ride it down, shuffling the feet adroitly to keep them on the surface, avoiding large leg-breaker rocks, stepping to the side if things get out of hand.

SNOW

The techniques of snow climbing discussed in Chapter 12 are properly used whether the snow lies on a high spire or in the deep woods. If slopes are at all long and steep, safeguards such as ax and rope should be employed even if the party is walking along a trail—a trail buried under a dozen feet of snow. Indeed, during low-altitude travel the climber often is burdened with a heavy pack which magnifies every difficulty.

Not to be overlooked are the advantages of snow in cross-country travel. Talus, brush, and logging slash are paved highways when covered by a consolidated snow and for this reason many a peak is best climbed early in the season. During the same season snow bridges may provide quick passage over rushing streams, remembering that crossing bridges over streams is often much like crossing bridges over crevasses, described in Chapter 14. As spring merges into summer and obstacles emerge, the route along a valley floor may be quite erratic, taking advantage of every remaining snow patch for the few yards or steps of easy walking it provides.

STREAM CROSSINGS

When a party enters wilderness without trail or bridge, water becomes a major impediment. In the Canadian Coast Range climbers frequently spend more time and energy crossing a perilous river than on their ultimate objective, the mountain.

Making the Crossing

Frequently it is possible to cross a stream by hopping from one boulder to another. The sequence should be closely studied beforehand and every stride and leap rehearsed mentally. Often safety lies in smooth and steady progress, the stones being too unsteady and slippery to allow balance for more than a moment in transit to the next.

Downed trees provide superb bridges and always are the first hope when the stream is deep and swift. At low altitude footlogs are relatively plentiful and require a second thought only when awkwardly thin or steeply inclined. In deep forest a party may find easy passage over even the widest river on a semipermanent log jam wedged together during some past flood. Higher in the mountains footlogs are harder to come by, particularly when the river changes course periodically, preventing the growth of large timber near its channel. Footlogs of thin and limber alpine firs or riverbottom alder are quite formidable.

The efforts of a wilderness traveler are directed toward finding a dry crossing by stone or log but the wet crossing must often be accepted. One sound bit of not entirely-obvious advice is to seek always the widest part of a river. The narrows of a watercourse, though seemingly offering shortest duration of suffering, are the deepest and the swiftest.

The greatest evil of wading, or fording, often is wet clothes and feet. If the water is placid and the stones rounded, spartan climbers carry boots and lower garments dry in the pack. In more severe conditions an excellent plan is to remove socks before wading and wear boots alone in the water. On the far side the boots can be drained and dry socks replaced.

The force of moving water is usually underestimated. A swift stream flowing only shin-deep boils up against the knees. Knee-deep water may boil above the waist and give the traveler a disconcerting sensation of buoyancy. Whenever water boils above the knee it is dangerous—the rocks underfoot are also buoyant and easily dislodged and one false step turns the brave climber into a frightened swimmer bouncing in white water from boulder to boulder, dragged down by boots and pack. It is well to remember that frothy water contains so much air that though wet enough to drown it may not be dense enough to float the human body. Water milky from glacier-milled rock flour presents the added difficulty that one cannot see the bottom but must probe blindly with the feet.

Fording a torrent is chancy work. Usually it is best to face upstream on the crossing, leaning into the current and stabbing the ice ax or a stout pole upstream for a third point of suspension. The leading foot probes for solid placement on the shifting bottom, the following foot advances, and then the ax or pole is thrust into a new position. Sometimes the crossing is best made in pairs, one person bracing the other while he advances to a secure stance.

On a very hazardous crossing it is only common sense for the leader to be belayed. A study of Chapter 10 is useful, supplemented by visualization of a body caught in stream flow. Obviously it is best for the belay to be placed as far above the crossing as possible, for in a "fall" the leader will pendulum in the current to the near bank. The higher upstream the belay, the shorter the fall. Rescuers poised on the bank at the end of the pendulum swing can often save a life by swift action. Once the leader has attained the far shore his companions can be safeguarded by an anchored handline, but rope has so much stretch it is little help in maintaining footing. When there is any doubt every member should be belayed.

Some rivers are quite perfectly impassable. If the headwaters are fed by snow, early morning is usually the time of minimum flow and a party may camp overnight awaiting low water. Sometimes it is necessary to hike hours or days seeking a vulnerable point. Very rarely a Tyrolean traverse (see Chapter 11) can be rigged if one member is capable of swimming or wading the flood to fix a line on the far bank. One of the few justifications for contaminating mountains with horses is the relative ease with which they wade swift water. For the widest and deepest rivers, rafts are the only alternative short of hiking to the headwaters—which in the case of the Columbia would make a very long outing indeed.

Finding the Crossing

Whenever the peak lies beyond a respectable river the crossing is a major factor in route. A distant view—perhaps from a ridge before descending into the valley—is sometimes better than a hundred close views from a riverbank. When a distant view is unavailable or unhelpful it is desirable to intersect a stream before crossing is absolutely necessary. Intersecting at the theoretically-ideal point usually results in having to send upstream and downstream search parties who at reunion debate to madness the merits of their discoveries. The party must balance one against the other the merits of going along close to the bank for the sake of finding a footlog or log jam, at the expense of suffering riverbottom brush, and walking high on open ridge slopes, then striking directly for the river.

Efficient Walking

In generations past, walking was so necessary a human activity that nearly everyone was expert. Nowadays, with the advance of mechanized transportation, walking has become so rare an art that usually a person taking up the sport of wilderness mountaineering must first learn to walk before he can climb. Though the technique is not at all complicated and can be performed in a rough and ready fashion even by infants, a little study and practice are needed to become proficient.

PREPARING TO WALK

Conditioning

Any physical activity is most easily performed by a body in good condition from frequent exercise. Through a sustained high level of muscular exertion the capacity for exertion is increased, as discussed in Appendix 1. However, mountaineering being predominantly a sport of those with sedentary occupations, most climbers must undergo the annual agonies of "getting in condition." On an extended trip conditioning comes naturally and easily. During the first days the heart pounds and the lungs gasp and the muscles ache but the system steadily adjusts and after a week or less reaches that splendid and exhilarating state when extraordinary feats are possible and enjoyable. Weekend climbing is frustrating. The body "tunes up" during the weekend and on Monday (back in the office) is ready for marvelous things. By Thursday, disappointed, it begins to relax. Generally the early part of a climbing season requires a gradual increase in ambition, for it takes several months of weekend outings to attain the physical fitness gained in one good week of hard walking. A schedule of training exercises helps immensely in developing endurance. Chapter 7 discusses the value of pushups, jogging around the block, and so forth.

Going Light

If the fault of overloading were not so universal it would be banal to declare that one can walk faster with a light pack. Most novices quickly learn to do without pajamas, parasols, and cast-iron skillets but even experienced climbers sometimes fail to thoroughly analyze their gear. Each item should be considered individually. Is it absolutely necessary? Was it used on the previous trip? Is there any lighter substitute? Ruthless paring of ounces—always reserving climbing and safety essentials—saves pounds of weight and adds miles to the hiking range.

Etiquette

Walking is more often than not a social sport and demands a regard for certain social amenities, a trail etiquette which is really no more than commonsense thoughtfulness. On the trail the man ahead is allowed enough room so that he doesn't feel pressed. It is very bad form to bend back the branches of a tree like a catapult and loose them full in the face of a following companion. If one wishes to tie a shoelace or take a slower pace it is simple courtesy to step aside and not block traffic. Quite evidently, these and other instances of trail etiquette do not depend on an elaborate code but on simple consideration. Wilderness is characterized by a small population density and ill-will fostered by stumbling over one another is decidedly unnecessary.

THE ACT OF WALKING: PACE

It is one thing to walk from the doorstep to the family automobile or from the subway to the theater. On such short journeys it is not essential to walk efficiently. It is quite another matter to walk many miles through rough wilderness carrying heavy loads. The maximum capacity varies with individuals. A 90-pound girl cannot carry a 90-pound pack nearly so easily as can a 200-pound athlete. The first-of-the-season climber lethargic from a winter at a desk cannot walk 20 trail miles or thrash through a blowdown so easily as the perfectly-conditioned end-of-the-season climber. However, whatever the maximum capacity may be of a particular individual at a particular moment, it cannot be realized without careful attention to practices of good walking. Just as expert drivers can get many more miles to the gallon from their automobiles, so can expert walkers get many more pound-miles-per-day from their bodies.

The proper pace is a complex equation between the body's strength, the load it is carrying, the distance to be traveled, and the time available. It is silly to specify 3 miles per hour as good average speed, or 1000 feet of altitude per hour, or 15 miles per day. There is too wide a range between flat trail and coastal jungle, between 10-pound rucksack loads and 100-pound expeditionary loads, for any average to be meaningful. There are several aspects to pace: first, the speed, or number of steps taken during an hour; second, the manner in which these steps should be taken to conserve energy; third, how frequently the party should cease taking steps—that is, rest.

Speed

The commonest mistake of the beginner is walking too fast, thinking desperately of the great distance to be covered. It is pointless to travel 1 mile in 4 minutes—or 15 minutes—if the result is such utter exhaustion that the remaining 9 miles to basecamp are impossible. Nor do mountaineers keep books listing the "best time from Swamp Camp to Blowdown Camp as 3 hours 47 minutes 12.5 seconds." Sometimes it may be necessary to make all possible haste from Swamp Camp to Blowdown Camp, as when being pursued by a forest fire. If an entire day is available for the journey it is far more meritorious to arrive relaxed at Blowdown with memories and photographs of the flora, fauna, and geology en route.

There is a simple test by which any individual at any time can determine if his pace is proper: if it cannot be sustained hour after hour it is too fast. Two departments of the body have separate control. A person can walk only as fast as his legs will allow: when it becomes a mighty effort to drag the foot forward the pace is too fast. A person can walk only as fast as his lungs will allow: when the lungs are desperately gasping for air the pace is too fast. Either symptom requires a slowdown. Along a flat trail the legs complain while the lungs are still content. At high altitude the lungs are starving for air while the legs are growing stiff from lack of exercise.

Ambition and vanity usually ensure males against going slower than possible. Some hikers, particularly wives, place excessive emphasis on the rule that a pace should be comfortable. The body complains long before it is hurt. The muscles may ache but still have 10 miles left in them; the lungs may gasp but be able to continue gasping another 3 hours. Indeed, the body improves its efficiency most rapidly when driven close to its limits of performance. A reasonable degree of suffering is inevitable if one is to become a good walker.

Speed fluctuates during the day. At the beginning of a walk, especially in the morning, it is well to go along slowly to let the body become gradually aware of the demands that will be made. With so courteous a start it will be more enthusiastic about gearing up to full power. The phenomenon of "second wind" is familiar. After an initial period during which willpower must be exerted to keep going, suddenly the hiker finds himself striding along happy and strong, free to observe with pleasure the flowers growing by the way. Physiologically this means the heart has taken a faster tempo, the blood is circulating more rapidly, the muscles have loosened.

Since the trail is never uniform the climber must constantly adjust his pace. On a steep hill he plods slowly and methodically but as the grade lessens his speed increases until on a decline he may fairly be flying along. Late in the day speed decreases, for though adrenalin secretions allow short bursts of explosive exertion there is no second wind. The body has already done its utmost and the accumulating poisons of fatigue steadily lower efficiency.

Rest Step

If one mountaineering technique had to be singled out as most important of all, honors would go to the rest step, used on snow, rock, brush, and trail whenever expenditure of energy is so great that either legs or lungs need an interval of recuperation between steps. The pace is slow, since for every step there is an alternating rest. This is the pattern:

1. One foot advances to a new position.
2. The *unweighted* advanced leg rests, the body entirely supported on the rear leg.
3. Rear foot advances.

When air is thin it is the lungs that need a pause, sometimes for two or three or five breaths to each step. At lower altitude it is leg muscles that need extra time to accumulate energy. An important element of the rest step is mental composure. When the summit seems to remain constantly distant for hours on end the individual must trust the rest step to slowly but steadily chew up the miles. When monotony impairs morale he must draw on his inner resources, his ability to lose time and place in reflection.

Rest Stops

A reasonable speed, with the rest step when needed, eliminates nearly all the collapsing-type rests of the novice hiker, who will sag in a heap at the slightest provocation. Still, some rests are required by the most expert walkers. Formulas are frequently proposed for the allowable number of rests per hour and their optimum duration. All such formulas presume uniform human beings with uniform packs walking along uniform trails and therefore they are all nonsense. Their one germ of truth is that "to rest is not to conquer." A party sprawled in the meadows is not getting any closer to its objectives. It is simple logic to ask always whether a rest is really necessary, and if not whether there is time for luxury. A party holding to a tight schedule will not rest nearly so often as members would like. If there is no hurry it will rest whenever the mood seizes.

Mandatory for a large party and desirable for any is a *shakedown* rest during the first hour of the day. Bootlaces become untied, packstraps need adjustment, body chemistry demands attention.

During the early part of a day, while the body is fresh, rests should be infrequent and short: for climbers in average condition with packs of average weight, about every 45 minutes and lasting 2 or 3 minutes. For such *breathers* it is best to rest in a standing or semi-reclining position, leaning against a tree or hillside to remove packweight from the shoulders, taking deep breaths and a bite to eat.

Later on the body demands more complete relaxation and about every hour or two the party staggers into a *sackout* rest. When it is nearing time for a stop members begin watching for some point with special advantages, such as convenient slopes for unslinging packs, a water supply, a view, or pretty flowers. It is all too easy to prolong such moments, but when the camp or summit is still far away climbers should remember how agonizing is the resumption of a march once muscles become cold and stiff.

Experienced walkers, knowing the day's itinerary and whether it is easy or rough, automatically include the proper number of breathers and sackouts. They know moreover that at the tag end of a hard haul the body, despite all reason and rest-stepping, begins to defy will and demand the *collapse* rest, toppling into snow or mud and lying there utterly inert and content.

Downhill and Sidehill

Downhill walking is nowhere near so fatiguing as uphill walking but the blessings of gravity are not unmixed. It is on the downtrail that blisters are raised and knee cartilage displaced, for weight drops abruptly and roughly on legs and feet. The entire body is so shocked and jarred that after a long descent the very head may begin to ache. Far sooner the hiker feels his knees coming loose at the hinges and expects them to begin working both ways like those of a rag doll. Even more serious, at every step the toes jam forward in the boot and hot spots develop on the feet.

The first preparation for the downtrail is to stuff the boots full of socks and tie the laces up tight to reduce motion of foot within boot. The downhill pace is kept much more moderate than the one urged by gravity. The leg lands on each step with bent knee to cushion the jar and the feet are placed as lightly as possible, as if they were already sore. Such restraint is extremely tiring to muscles of the upper leg and in loose soil or needles or scree a stiff-legged glissade provides welcome relief. Rests on the downtrail are just as essential as on the uptrail.

Sidehill-gouging is one of the very bad things in the mountain world; when it cannot be avoided there is nothing for it but to suffer the agonies of bent ankles and contorted hips. If there is a choice between struggling along a sidehill and dropping into a flat valley the altitude loss is often more than compensated for by the saving of legs and ankles. Similarly, if the top of the ridge is rounded the walking may be much easier in the long run even though there are many ups and downs. On a long sidehill-gouge it may be possible to switchback occasionally to alternate muscle strain.

The Ice Ax

On open trails many climbers stow the ax in the pack, head down with shaft protruding. In rough country the ax is so useful in the hands, and in the pack snags so frequently on brush and tree limbs, it is better brought out into the open.

When the ax is carried in the hand on good trail the shaft is grasped at the balance point, the spike forward and the head to the rear with the pick down. Thus the man behind is safeguarded against accidentally running into the spike and the pick can do the owner no harm in a stumble for it rams harmlessly into the ground. Alternately the ax may be carried with the shaft in the armpit, the spike again forward, the pick against the arm and pointing out from the body. When a climber is weary or footing is poor he can use the ax for a cane grasped by the head with the pick forward. However, he must not carry over ax-handling habits acquired on trails to the very different conditions of steep snow, where the ax must always be held ready for the self-arrest described in Chapter 15.

Fig. 15. Ice ax carry, in hand.

Fig. 16. Ice ax carry, as cane.

On steep slippery ground, whether mud, needles, or grass, the shaft is reversed and carried with the head forward and the pick down for quick gouging of a foothold or for quick jamming-in of the pick to stop a slip.

On any terrain other than a flat and beaten trail the climber discovers numerous unsuspected virtues of the ax. In stream-fording it provides a third leg among the slippery shifting stones. When hopping over talus it gives many a slight touch-and-go balance point. On steep hillsides, just as on steep snow (see Chapter 12), the ax held horizontally across the body, spike touching the slope, helps hold a stable, vertical stance. Moreover, though the ice ax self-arrest is treated in Chapter 15 as a technique for snow, many a climber has been most happy to use it to stop himself in steep meadows and forest.

5 *

NAVIGATION

IN THE HILLS

NAVIGATION is the technique of precisely determining one's present location, the location of the objective, and the direction of travel connecting these two points. On the high seas or in the air calculation is simplified by mathematical formulas and accurate instruments. When good maps are available, mountain navigation can be even easier and more exact; without good maps, it often takes on something of the character of a black art. Skill is very largely a function of experience, though the basic tools and procedures can quickly be mastered.

Direction-Finders: The Compass

Nature offers more or less useful direction indicators. In the latitude of Washington State the summer sun rises somewhere between northeast and east, is due south at noon, and sets between west and northwest. South slopes are sunnier and thus drier than north, with vegetation sparser or of an entirely different type. North slopes are snowier and because of more intense glaciation in past ages often are steeper. A person stranded in the wilderness without equipment may be completely dependent on such information. However, so long a climber is connected to his rucksack he can simplify orientation by always carrying among his personal gear an artificial direction-finder.

A compass is a magnetized needle mounted freely so that it can respond to the earth's magnetism. It is by far the quickest and most accurate means of establishing direction since the needle always points to the same place on the surface of the earth—almost always, that is. Large ore bodies and some rocks struck by lightning may deflect the earth's magnetic field. In addition many items in the climber's outfit are slightly magnetized, such as ice axes, knives, exposure meters, pitons, and other ironware; the compass must be kept clear from these distractions during use.

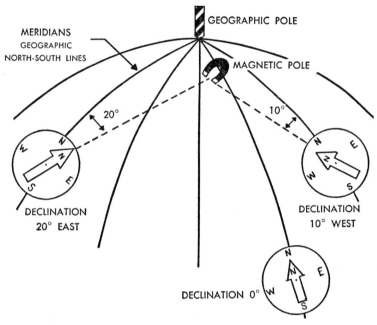

Fig. 17. Compass declination.

The compass needle does not point to the geographic north pole near the center of the Arctic Ocean, but to the magnetic north pole about a thousand miles to the south in Canada. The angle of difference between true north and magnetic north, the *magnetic declination,* is stated on most maps. Declination changes a trifle from year to year but mountain navigation is never so precise as to be affected by the shift. Indeed, ordinarily a climber need only remember whether declination is east or west, small or large.

A simple, rugged, inexpensive compass is perfectly adequate for most wilderness purposes. The north end of the needle must be distinctively marked and the marking memorized, since confusing north with south produces gross errors. A locking device is useful both to stabilize oscillations of the needle during use and to protect it from excessive battering while being carried. A dampened compass eliminates excessive oscillations.

A circumference showing cardinal directions suffices for ordinary travel but calibration in degrees is better adapted to precise navigation. Instruments designed for professional use have various elaborations and minutely-superior accuracy but for climbing the added expense is rarely justified.

On a sunny day a rough and ready compass can be improvised from a watch. Turning the timepiece so that the hour hand points at the sun, true south then lies halfway between the hour hand and 12. In such fogbound ranges as those of the Northwest this handy relationship, reversed, allows the sun-starved climber possessing both a compass and watch at least to locate the position of the sun behind the clouds.

Terrain Descriptions: Maps

Navigation is aided by verbal descriptions of an area gained in conversation or correspondence with previous visitors, or from published sources such as alpine journals and route guides. The value of photographs, especially those taken from airplanes, is obvious, though compared to the human eye a camera lens gives at best a distorted view of the world. Aerial photographs—even when available—are bulky, expensive, difficult to interpret, and difficult to keep in good condition, but are well worth the trouble and expense when extremely-precise knowledge of the terrain is needed. For some regions, such as portions of the British Columbia Coast Range, there are aerial photographs but no detailed maps. Generally a climber depends chiefly for terrain description on a map, a symbolic picture of an area that by convenient shorthand conveys a wealth of information in a form easily carried and easily understood.

MAP ACCURACY

Early maps were largely works of the imagination, compilations of travelers' tales and rumors plus a heavy measure of conjecture, trustworthy in proportion to the information, integrity, and skill of the geographer. In modern times cartography has developed such refinements of technique that a map is usually just as accurate as it states itself to be. Until quite recently maps were prepared entirely by ground survey, walking over the terrain taking compass bearings and elevation angles, measuring distances by rod and chain. Nowadays surveyors need walk over only enough of the ground to establish a few key distances and elevations. Complex machines combine this information with aerial photographs and automatically produce maps which are nearly perfect representations of the face of the land.

A mountaineer uses maps produced by each of the three historical methods. Perhaps he has only a sketch made by a friend or published in a journal, more or less primitive and conjectural. Perhaps the map is issued by a public agency, based on painstaking ground surveys—or perhaps on a quick walk-through 50 years ago. Maps derived from aerial photographs are often incredibly precise, but even these are only as good as the work on the ground and on the drafting board.

A map is judged first by reputation of the producer, secondly by the date, since even trusted suppliers have improved their methods with the years, and because time itself changes the terrain, particularly in regard to the works of man. Most significant of all is the *map scale*, the ratio between a distance on the earth's surface and its representation on the map. For example, a map identified as 1/125000, or 1:125000, uses one inch on the map to picture 125,000 inches on the ground. Obviously the smaller the denominator of the fraction the more room there is for detail. Indeed, usually the scale directly reflects the amount of information gathered by the mapmakers.

CLIMBING MAPS

Highway maps published by oil companies and other commercial concerns are either free or inexpensive and contain the most current information on primary and secondary highways. Good as these are for approaching the mountain range, rarely are forest roads shown to any extent.

Forest Service maps and comparable ones issued by other government agencies are invaluable. The comprehensive "Forest Maps," and the "Ranger District Maps" covering sections of the former, are revised periodically in the light of news brought in by rangers walking over the country. Forest Service maps are the best guides to the current state of roads, trails, shelters, and other works of man. Drainage patterns and divides are carefully traced and some elevations are given, though nothing is shown about the vertical shape of the terrain. The maps can be obtained free of charge by writing to headquarters offices of the various National Forests or picked up at any ranger station. Similar maps transcribed more or less carefully from Forest Service and other sources are produced commercially for some areas. These are commonly called "county" or "sportsman" maps and are sold in stores catering to hunters and fishermen.

Hunters' maps distributed prior to each hunting season by several of the larger timber companies are revised yearly and are excellent for finding passable routes through the growing maze of logging roads. Careful perusal frequently reveals a new or shorter approach than those described in guide books or shown on other maps.

Pictorial relief maps covering parts of the Cascades and Olympics have their specific purposes and limitations. These are commercially produced, compiled from topographic and Forest Service maps, and represent a somewhat happy medium between the two. In essence, an oblique, full-color view of the terrain is shown as it would be viewed

Fig. 18. A mountain area seen visually.

from an extreme altitude. Though not three-dimensional, the illusion is given, but only in direct relation to the skill of the illustrator. Such maps are intended for general planning purposes and provide the trail mileages not shown on government maps. They cannot be used for

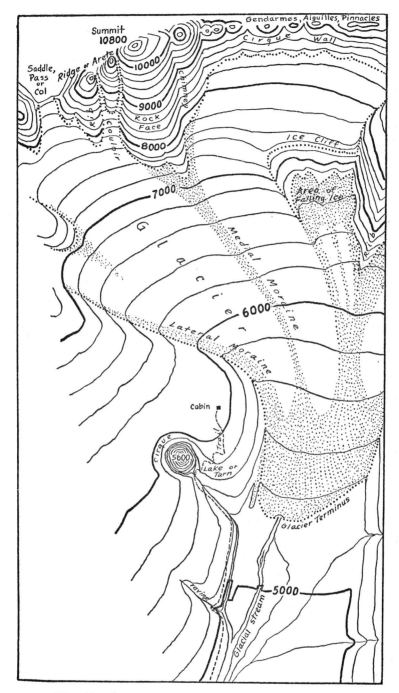

Fig. 19. The same mountain seen on a contour map.

compass navigation and in the back country must be employed solely as supplements to topographic maps. It should be emphasized at this point that no one map tells the whole story, and that all sources should be thoroughly studied before entering unknown territory.

Topographic maps give symbolically an actual picture of the land. For many years the United States Geological Survey has been engaged in mapping the entire nation with the highest feasible degree of accuracy. For instance, until recently most of its maps of the North Cascades were based on laborious foot-and-horseback reconnaissances made around 1900; they contain hilarious errors (often not funny when discovered in the field), but are remarkable in that they were made at all in those days. Mapping by aerial photography began in the 1930s; by the 1960s the technique had become a wonder of painstaking accuracy. The map date, then, is a primary consideration. Any map predating the 1930s must be used with reservation until given a thorough field check. For positive proof of highest quality, one should look on the sheet for the identifying phrase, "Topography from aerial photographs by multiplex methods."

Geological Survey maps are published in four scales referred to as "series." Maps on a *scale of 1:250000, the United States series,* are issued for all states including Alaska, for some portions of which they are the only maps. The scale, about ¼ inch to 1 mile, is of small use to the mountaineer afoot. However, these "quarter-million" sheets are superb for broad orientation, superior to highway maps in that with just a bit of practice one can soon name and describe hills and dales better than most local residents; from a summit they allow identification of peaks and ranges in the haze far beyond the boundaries of localized maps. Many are offered in three-dimensional molded-plastic editions, splendid for home study of mountain range structure and drainage patterns.

The oldest maps, some of which are still in print for remote regions, were published on a *scale of 1:125000* (roughly ½ inch to the mile) in the *30-minute series,* each sheet covering an area of 30 minutes or ½ degree of longitude and latitude, a ground distance in the northern United States of about 25 miles east and west and about 35 miles north and south. A few mountain areas are not yet surveyed in any greater detail, but the maps are always many years old and usually interest the historian more than the climber.

Newer maps have enough detail for a *scale of 1:62500* (roughly 1 inch to the mile) in the *15-minute series,* each covering about 12 by 18 miles in the northern United States. For the mountaineer this series is the ideal, giving sufficient topographic information for route selection, and each sheet including enough country to make orientation easy.

Unfortunately, all new mapping in the conterminous United States, and eventually much old mapping, is planned for a *scale of 1:24000* (2½ inches to the mile) in the *7½-minute series,* each sheet covering an area 6 miles by 9. The "7½'s" offer almost too much detail, delineating virtually every short switchback on a trail. The average hiker walks through one of these maps in a few hours, so that several must be carried if the trip is of any distance. And even when atop a summit in the center of the sheet, features more than a few miles away in any direction are off the edge. Not many passes or summits are large and flat enough for spreading out all the sheets necessary for orientation and for identification of local features, much less distant— even assuming the wind makes feasible so gorgeous a display of cartographic art, anchored with rocks, pitons, and ice axes. Though magnificent for home study, in the field 7½'s are confounded nuisances.

Topographic maps of areas west of the Mississippi River can be purchased at mountain shops or ordered directly from the U.S. Geological Survey, Federal Center, Denver, Colorado 80225. For the east, maps should be ordered from the U.S. Geological Survey, Washington D.C. 20242. Index maps for each state are free on request.

Similar topographic maps are available for much of Canada. Indexes to maps published by the federal government are free on request from the Map Distribution Office, 615 Booth Street, Ottawa, Ontario. Indexes to maps issued by the individual provinces may be obtained, at no cost, by writing the appropriate government office in each provincial capital. For British Columbia, write to the Surveys and Mapping Branch, Department of Lands, Forests, and Water Resources, Victoria, B.C.

INTERPRETATION OF TOPOGRAPHIC MAPS

Topographic maps show the shape of the terrain with *contour lines,* imaginary lines drawn on the surface of the land, each one at a constant elevation above sealevel.

The interval between contour lines is always an even number of feet and generally ranges from 20 to 250, depending on the scale of the map. Maps of steep terrain have a larger contour interval than equivalent-scale maps of flat terrain. For convenient reading, usually each fifth contour line is heavier and its elevation printed periodically along its length. Interpretation of contour maps is quite simple. Widely-spaced lines indicate a gentle slope; lines that run together, a cliff. A valley makes a pattern of V's pointing upstream. A ridge appears as downhill-pointing V's or U's depending on sharpness of the crest.

Closed circles or loops indicate summits. Contour maps offer much information about the landscape but do not tell all. In the older reconnaissance surveys contour lines were sketched more or less freehand. Even with modern maps it must be remembered that a 50-foot cliff will not show at all if the interval is 100 feet.

MAP PROTECTION AND MODIFICATION

Inexpensive, easily-replaced maps are expendable, but not during the climb. Enclosure in a clear plastic bag is not only adequate protection but allows use without damage even in wet weather. Weight and trouble can be saved by transcribing Forest Service information and personal experience onto a topographic map, marking new roads and trails or routes, mileage and time between various points. When a popular climbing area is split between two or more maps it is worthwhile to prepare a composite, trimming margins and assembling the parts with flexible paper tape. Some topographic maps are confusing even to an expert. It is helpful to outline the ridge structure with pencil lines along the main crests. More laborious but even more valuable is shading a map to simulate shadows cast when the sun is low in the northwest. Such techniques speed development of the stereoscopic vision characteristic of a practiced reader.

Orientation

By orientation a climber finds where he is. If a quick look around doesn't do the job, he spreads his map flat with open compass on top, lines up map-true-north (the top of map, if not otherwise indicated) with compass-dial-north, and turns map and compass as a unit until dial-north and needle-north (magnetic) are separated by the proper declination. The map is now oriented.

With *point-position known* (summit, pass, lake outlet, river forks), any visible feature can be identified from the map, any feature shown on the map can be located. Assume the climber discovers from the summit register he is atop Mount Majestic. To identify an unknown peak, he orients the map, places a straightedge on map-Majestic, pivots it to point toward the peak, then inspects the map to see what peaks touch the straightedge. (The ice ax shaft, though far from ideal, is usually the longest, straightest edge handy.) To find Unsavory Spire, he places his shaft to intersect map-Majestic and map-Unsavory and sights along the shaft. He is now looking at Unsavory, among other peaks; by comparing terrain and map he sorts them out.

With *line-position known* (ridge, trail, river) and one visible feature recognized, point-position can be found. Assume the climber knows he is on Unsavory Ridge and in the distance recognizes Mount Majestic. He places the compass directly atop map-Majestic and orients the map. Now, with the compass center as pivot, he swings his shaft to point at Majestic. Where the shaft intersects map-Unsavory-Ridge, that is where the climber is, or close. (A more craftsmanlike method: hold compass at eyelevel in the palm, adjust for declination, sight along a pencil across compass center to Majestic, note where pencil intersects far circumference of dial; take this *bearing* and transfer to map, using the compass as a sort of protractor; since the map need not be oriented, and a smaller straightedge can be used, precision is greater.)

With only *area-position known,* at least two visible features must be recognized to find point-position. Assume the climber knows only he is in the Fantastic Crags. Again he takes a bearing on Majestic, and this time pencils the bearing line on the map. He also recognizes Unsavory Spire, takes a second bearing, draws a second line. Where the two lines intersect, that's where the climber is. However, if he happens to be on top of a ridge and the lines intersect in the Fantastic River, something is wrong. Perhaps he now recognizes Imposing Peak and the third bearing line intersects one of the others at a more reasonable location. (The closer to a right angle is the angle between any two bearing lines, the more precisely their intersection shows position.) If several bearings agree on a location with no similarity to the terrain, then the climber suspects it's a crazy old map, he has read the compass incorrectly, or maybe those peaks aren't Unsavory and Imposing after all.

With only area-position known and only one visible feature recognized, only line-position (along the bearing line) can be found. However, assume the climber remains certain of good old Majestic, and also feels sure he is on a ridge, not in a river. He therefore knows he is at or near one of the several points where the Majestic bearing line intersects a Fantastic ridge. Perhaps, from comparison of map and terrain, he finds only one that fits the facts.

Since mountains are not two-dimensional, as symbolized on the map, the *altimeter* is sometimes as helpful as the compass, particularly where accurate topographical maps are available. With *altitude known* point-position can often be found with only one visible feature recognized; in any other case, altitude provides a check against map and compass orientation. The altimeter measures atmospheric pressure, which varies not only with altitude but also with weather, as discussed in Chapter 22, and therefore must be adjusted frequently at known elevations, preferably every few hours.

Navigation

By navigation a climber gets where he wants to go. Even while pounding a trail or following a leader, the navigator, unlike the passenger, does not orient purely by trail signs and summit registers, or navigate entirely by boot heels. At every step the look of the country changes a bit; at every step the navigator with his sharp and roving eye updates his last certain fix. At a pass, or around a bulge in the ridge, or through a sudden break in the clouds, whenever many new peaks and valleys appear, he pauses to connect them to the map.

The navigator knows how amazingly different the country looks backside from frontside. While the eager apprentice gazes to the summit, the sad old navigator constantly glances over his shoulder to camp, not so much because he wishes he'd never left as because he hopes to get back. Particularly at critical turns he fixes in his mind the *over-the-shoulder shape of the route,* such as: opposite a waterfall, at a moraine with an iron-stained boulder perched on the crest, the route busts through a cedar thicket and down a mossy slab to a gnarled snag.

When the route is complex, and especially when a late return is anticipated, the navigator finds a small *notebook* valuable for entering times, elevations, landmarks, and compass courses, as well as for writing his memoirs in later years.

When landmarks are lacking or obscured by fog or night, or may be on the return, the *route is marked.* On snow and glaciers wands are used, as described in Chapter 14. On complex cliffs some climbers carry a bright crayon for quick scribbling; those who go about with pressurized paint cans would be better employed splashing spiritual guidance along highways. The best marker for most terrain is bright-colored crepe paper in thin rolls, durable enough not to disintegrate in the first rain or wind, as does toilet paper, but perishable enough to vanish without a trace over the winter. Hikers who wound every passing tree with their little hatchets, filling the forest with lost-man blazes, deserve all the consideration accorded a gypo logger caught moonlighting in a National Park. Unless he can, and does, remove them during the return, the climber who decorates the hills with bright plastic strips should in all justice spend eternity, or at least that large portion thereof until the plastic is destroyed by nature, in the company of those condemned to haunt forever the alpine garbage dumps they spent their earthly vacations so energetically building.

In home hills or foreign, the navigator at all times keeps firmly in mind which way to go if completely baffled—the compass direction to some long unmistakable line, such as a highway or trail or lake or ridge, that forms one boundary of his climbing area. He knows the *baseline* always lies in the same compass direction wherever he is in the area, and whether or not it is a quick way out, it at least means an ultimate way out.

Navigators of ocean and air often travel great distances entirely by instrument to an exact destination. Mountain navigators also occasionally travel great distances blind, and sometimes even get where they want to go. Except when the objective is a baseline, a *compass course* cannot be set without an initial exact orientation. Once a course is set, a navigator can in clear weather hold to it visually, pointing his nose either at the objective or some intervening point on the bearing line. Assume a navigator on a broad glacier has been caught napping by a cloud, and just manages to whip out his compass for a bearing on Mount Scimitar before it vanishes. If Scimitar is the goal, the one bearing is enough; he doesn't know where he is but he knows which way to go. Since it is impossible to hold a blind course following his nose, the navigator extends a rope team along the bearing, then travels somewhat to the rear with open compass in hand, calling yaw corrections forward.

Assume Incredible is the goal. Having oriented his map and penciled in the Scimitar bearing, the navigator can usually set a course within the proper quadrant. That is, if Scimitar lies an estimated mile due north, and the map shows Incredible a mile due west of Scimitar, the navigator steers northwest; his estimate may be wrong and Incredible lie closer to north or west, but unless the map is lousy certainly it is not northeast or south. If he manages a bearing on Gasper as well as Scimitar, then he can perhaps set an accurate course to Incredible without ever seeing it.

Assume there are numerous crevasses which forbid a straightline course. By one method, the navigator first judges the end-to-end length of his lead rope team, then has the team leader scrape a mark in the snow on signal from the last man, who gives the signal each time he comes up to the previous mark; thus the navigator, with a running tally, measures distance traveled. For each zig and zag he jots in his notebook the bearing and the number of ropelengths. Periodically, such as when a major route decision is required, he plots the zigs and zags on the map and from the new estimated position resets his course. By this simple method he can steer blind many hours with a somewhat better than random chance of finding Incredible.

The altimeter is particularly invaluable in blind navigation. Descending a ridge in a foul, black night, the navigator may be happy indeed to have noted, in the bright dawn, the exact altitude at which the route emerged onto the ridge from a chimney. Or perhaps to reach the easy backside of Incredible a 7000-foot snow col must be crossed. When the altimeter reads 7500 feet and steep snow still rises into the fog, the navigator deduces he has missed the col and is now making a new route on the frontside of Incredible, or possibly the first ascent of some nearby peak.

Lost

A good navigator is never lost, but having learned humility, he always carries enough food and clothing to survive hours or days of confusion. Moreover, his first act as an apprentice navigator is to master techniques for minimizing confusion.

The first rule is, *stop*. Exactly when caution is most vital, on the weary descent with night near, temptation is strongest to plunge hopefully forward, increasing any error with every step. If orientation cannot be quickly regained, but was certain a short time earlier, retrace the route to the known point; an hour groaning upward may save a bitter night out. If the last certain orientation is hours away, and the present position can be approximately determined, it may be best to move cautiously ahead, alert for landmarks. On the other hand, the probable position may be so hopelessly off course it is time to bivouac. The final recourse, possibly delayed until morning, is the baseline.

Climbing history reveals the significant fact that a party of two or more, though the greenest novices or most complacent passengers, rarely gets dangerously lost. It is the lone human, abruptly aware how small and fragile he is, how immense and powerful the wilderness, who throws away his life. Terror in the face of nature is no sign of cowardice, but rather is the sane reaction; it is entirely proper, when alone, to treat every step as a life-or-death matter. However, it is essential not to try to take all the steps at once, in a hurry. Terror must be overcome by reason or it can kill.

Stop. Look around. Listen. Shout, and listen for answering shouts, but don't chase imaginary shouts. Instead, sit down, calm down. Look at the map. Look around. Resist panic, resist wishful thinking. Relax. Once cool and collected, though still confused, mark the present position with a cairn or toilet paper. Scout in all directions, each time returning to the marked position. Well before dark, give up the scouting. Obtain water, collect firewood, if available. Find shelter from the weather, if bad. Spend the night keeping the fire going, and listening, and singing cheerful songs, and rehearsing out loud the funny story this will make someday.

If the lost climber behaves in this manner, and his companions are similarly sensible, they are invariably reunited in the morning. While he resumes his scouting, they are following the search methods described in Chapter 19. If they do not begin search next day, through some misunderstanding such as a divided party, the lost climber must once again fight down panic. He may decide, after a day or so, it is best to proceed cautiously to the baseline, but if the terrain is prohibitively dangerous for lone travel he concentrates on letting himself be found. It is easy to find a lost person who stays in one place out in the open, builds a fire, periodically shouts, or all of these. It is difficult to find a person who thrashes on in hysteric hope, steadily weakening. It is particularly difficult if he trusts the old, discredited rule of following a stream out of the wilderness. A stream may lead deeper into wilderness, and certainly will lead away from the search area and into dense timber.

Freedom of the Hills

Navigation in the high country is not a science, but an art. Some travelers have the gift and some don't, but all must learn the tools and all can improve with practice. Under its other name, routefinding, navigation is the subject of several following chapters. Indeed, it is essentially the subject of this entire book.

In medieval times the greatest honor a visitor could receive was the rights of a citizen, the freedom of the city. The alpine navigator seeks to wander at will through valley jungles, green meadows, steep cliffs, and broad glaciers, to earn the rights of citizen in an alien land, to be fully at home in the high country, a mountaineer with freedom of the hills.

PART TWO

Rock Climbing

6 *

ROUTEFINDING ON ROCK

Just as philosophy once included all the sciences, which one by one became separate disciplines as they were sufficiently refined, certain spectacular techniques of mountaineering have in recent years become separate sports. Downhill skiing is one of these and rock climbing is another. On scarps cut by river, ocean, or ancient glacier, on quarries, façades of College Gothic, and any other stone close to highway or trolley line, the skills described in some of the following chapters can be and are acquired by increasing numbers of people who may or may not have any interest in the mountains as mountains.

Cliff climbing is not only good fun but excellent training for rock mountaineering, since the better command a climber has of technique the freer is his mind for the larger problem of route and the wider his choice among alternatives. The cliff climber out for a day's exercise never suffers the frustration felt by a mountaineer when the puzzle of the route evades solution and the summit recedes into impossibility with the sun's westerly descent—nor the equally great satisfaction of discovering the key to the maze after prolonged physical and mental efforts. To the crafts of rock climbing, rock mountaineering adds routefinding—the most difficult and the most rewarding of alpine arts. The art is not mastered quickly. Many a person becomes highly skilled in climbing rock while still utterly ignorant about choosing the best rock to climb. Moreover, excellence in both is by no means always found in the same person. There are acrobats who must be led to the rock, their hands placed on the first holds, and their course constantly corrected as they move. There are rock mountaineers who are not superior technicians and include specialists in their party to handle the difficult leads. Part of the pleasure of rock mountaineering is that every season and every climb teaches a new lesson, poses a new problem requiring a new solution, and provides a new satisfaction.

On rock as elsewhere all routes are found by "climbing with the eyes." The eyes begin their work by examining a map and continue when the peak is approached by choosing first the gully, ridge, or face which will be the general line of attack and then the deviations within this general line. Finally the eyes select the individual holds for hands and feet.

Strategy: The Use of Geology

The first concern of the climber is the geologic history of the area in which his objective is located, for whether or not he understands the processes that have created the mountain he will be encountering their implications every step of the way. The type of rock, the mountain structure, the past and present glaciation all have important consequences. Often the geologic background can be studied beforehand in publications or maps but usually the climber waits until he is on the peak to gather data. Unless the evidence is understood, however, he cannot interpret what he sees. Chapter 20 briefly surveys the principles of mountain construction most important for the alpinist. There are many thousands of unique rocks and curious structures; some of the more common ones will be described here in their role as climbing terrain.

INTERNAL MOUNTAIN STRUCTURE

In 1865, after numerous unsuccessful attempts by himself and others on the Italian side of the Matterhorn, Edward Whymper led a party to the summit from the Swiss side with almost ridiculous ease. The victory was not from luck or skill but from tilted strata. On the Italian side climbers had been defeated by rocks downsloping like shingles; the uptilted rocks of the Swiss side formed a staircase. The conquest of the Matterhorn is but one example of the important effect of the *lay of the strata* in sedimentary structures. Flat-lying strata generally offer step-like irregularities easily ascended. If the strata are tilted downward into the peak the resulting *upslab* is so much the better; holds are abundant and even loose rocks tend to hold firmly in place. On *downslab* not only are the holds upside down from the climber's viewpoint but loose rocks tend to slide from position with little provocation.

The lay often leads to *ledge-running* routes, particularly common in certain parts of the Canadian Rockies. Some layers form good ledge systems while others form cliffs, and the party traverses along one

VII. Forbidden Peak, North Cascades. (Thomas Miller)

VIII. High camp on Ptarmigan Ridge, Mount Rainier. (Thomas Miller)

ledge seeking a break by which access may be gained to the next-higher ledge. If the strata are tilted, a single ledge may be followed on a long angling ascent, possibly all the way to the summit ridge. *Differential erosion* is the process responsible, strong bands of rock becoming cliffs while the weaker ones become ledges. The effect is very striking when the strata have wide variations in strength, as on the banded mountainsides of the Canadian Rockies where the ascent alternates between loose scree and steep cliffs. If the contrast between two strata is extreme the cliff is overhanging.

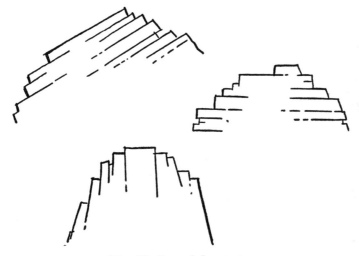

Fig. 20. Lay of the strata.

Another aspect of a mountain's internal structure which influences route selection is the *jointing* present to some extent in all rocks. Sometimes the jointing is so pronounced it produces a system of ledges and gullies similar to those of strata. Smaller joints lend themselves to various of the climbing techniques described in following chapters. *Faults* are of more questionable value since a fault zone usually consists of crushed and shattered fragments. When a fault plane is vertical it tends to be eroded into a deep gully of loose rock that is best avoided. If it is horizontal a very decent ledge may result. A *sill* or *dike* of igneous rock forms a cliff or a rib if stronger than the surrounding rocks, a ledge or gully if weaker. Effects of internal structure on route could be elaborated almost endlessly. From the few examples given here numerous others can be deduced from the analysis of mountain structure in Chapter 20.

EXTERNAL MOUNTAIN STRUCTURE

Obviously the inside of a mountain has a lot to do with its outside shape. However, the major features are usually due only secondarily to the inner nature and primarily to the forces of erosion which ultimately wear down all rocks, weak and strong alike. Whatever its internal constitution and whatever its past history of erosion, the mountain as it confronts the climber is composed of ridges, faces, and gullies.

The most obvious route is often a *gully* or *couloir*. These have several characteristic disadvantages. Not only are they the natural channels for stonefall but their very existence indicates a relatively weak or fractured rock. Snow remains the longest and when the snow melts there are waterfalls which dwindle to rock-slickening springs leaving moss and mud that may stay until the snow returns. Gullies are the wettest parts of the mountain and even when dry demonstrate the fact with water-smoothed downsloping ledges and holds. Finally, by presenting a lower angle than the enclosing cliffs gullies must often compensate for an easy lower portion by culminating above in a steep *cul de sac*, or dead end. Unless a gully can be seen to lead all the way to the crest of the ridge such an unwelcome surprise must be suspected. Despite all these objections gully routes are most common of all. Besides being obvious they have a second advantage: the *exposure*, or distance that a climber might fall, averages less than on either ridges or faces.

The experienced climber considers *ridge* or *arete* routes more sporting. Exposure is greater than in gullies, a trial to those with a tendency to vertigo, but to the seasoned alpinist ascents of sound ridges immersed in the huge ocean of atmosphere are exhilarating beyond compare. The rock is usually the soundest in the mountain, though strength may be highly relative. In a region of very weak rocks the ridges are impossibly fragile; even when rocks are sound, frost-wedging splits many crests into piles of delicately-balanced boulders awaiting only the climber's touch to crash into the valley. On ridges there is little danger of rock falling on the climber but considerable danger of the climber falling with the rocks. When it comes to comfort, ridges are the sunniest parts of the peak and soonest free of snow but also the windiest. Often of great importance is the fact that the best view of incoming weather is had from a ridge. Being the flying buttresses of the peak, ridges offer the lowest average angle from the base to summit, but when the crest is interrupted by numerous towers, or *gendarmes*, the average is no consolation. Still, even if the crest is difficult the climber can often follow one side or the other of the ridge, just as in a gully he may sometimes climb along the walls if stopped in the channel.

Finally there is the rock *face*, the steepest, most exposed, and subtlest of routes though not necessarily the most difficult. The rock is ordinarily about as strong as in the ridges and less severely riven by frost. Rockfall is scattered, tending to flow off the faces into the gullies. On the other hand stonefall down a face gives little warning; the climber's only consolation is that if he hears the shrill scream of an invisible missile it didn't hit him. The combination of exposure, relatively-solid holds, and freedom from rockfall gives face climbing its attraction. The challenge is provided by the absence of a clearly-defined line of progress, the wealth of options exercising imagination to the utmost.

Few routes are simply a gully or a ridge or a face. The outer defenses may be breached by a gully which leads to the crest of a ridge, which in turn is followed until it flattens out into a face. Any other sequence or alternation, once or many times, may occur on a single climb.

The concept of *primary and secondary features* is helpful. There are such things as faces on ridges and gullies in faces and so forth. The resulting climbing sequence, or *pitch*, combines the virtues and vices of the primary or dominant feature with those of the secondary or modifying one. When climbing a gully, short faces, *slabs*, are expected as a matter of course, and small ridges, *ribs*, are sought for their soundness and freedom from rockfall. When climbing ridges, gendarmes present short faces and these may be penetrated by means of gullies or their smaller relatives, *chimneys* and *cracks*. When climbing faces the alternation between ridges and gullies is constant. In all such complex routes the qualities of the larger primary feature are modified by those of the smaller secondary feature. Even in a stone-swept gully a rib may be safe; even on a steep face a chimney may offer an easy avenue through part of the precipice.

FAMILY HABITS OF ROCKS

Granitic Rock

Granite—with which may be grouped the higher grades of metamorphic rock—is in general both solid and rough-textured. Very high angles can be climbed since friction holds work very well; even the smallest knobs are usually trustworthy both for balance and counter-force, and ironware can be anchored firmly into cracks. Ordinarily there is ample jointing and thus extensive crack systems, often forming tiers of ledges. Rockfall is at a minimum.

Granitic rock has been the medium for the highest development and the greatest exploits of rock climbing, notably in such areas as the Mont Blanc Aiguilles, Yosemite Valley in the Sierra, and the Stuart Range of the Cascades.

Low-Grade Metamorphic Rock

A low degree of metamorphism provides inferior climbing. The myriad minute cracks are so closely spaced that all are undependable. Weathering is so rapid that surfaces are crumbling and rockfall steady. Peaks composed of such rocks have highly-broken faces, complex gully systems, and serrate ridges. Since high angles cannot be safely climbed the route generally follows debris-filled ledges and gullies. Some peaks of the Canadian Rockies and the Olympics just barely thrust summits through heaps of disheartening rubble.

Sedimentary Rock

The sedimentary family includes rocks ranging all the way from superb to rotten. Weathering reduces many to such low angles they are not mountaineering problems at all. When strong and weak layers are interbedded and eroded into steep faces—as in the Canadian Rockies —nature may be said to have created routes truly impregnable to any rational climber.

Among prominent members of the sedimentary family is shale, normally very loose and prohibitively dangerous when steep. Sandstone cemented by silica is relatively durable; when the cement is lime or iron the surface is usually covered with a layer of sand which makes footing treacherous. Limestone and its relatives are thoroughly untrustworthy in wet climates but in relatively-arid mountains such as the Italian Dolomites afford superb climbing, although piton cracks are scarce. The rating of conglomerate, like that of sandstone, depends on the cement. An example of a conglomerate which provides excellent sport is that of the Schawangunks of New York State.

In all sediments shearing and fracturing may have transformed an originally-sound rock into one loose and dangerous—also true of the lower-grade metamorphics and of the extrusive volcanics. When strata are thin, alternation in value is frequent. When strata are thick, or so poorly defined as to form a rather homogeneous mass, the entire route may be uniform.

Volcanic Rock

Volcanic rock seldom interests a climber. For instance, on the volcanoes of the Pacific Northwest where glaciers have plucked deeply into the mountain and then abruptly retreated, the steady rockfall gives fair warning of the temporary nature of the cliffs. Some volcanics are firm as granite, the columnar basalt of the Devil's Tower in Wyoming being an outstanding example. Another is the "pillow lava" of the Sawtooths in the Olympic Mountains, where hot fluid rock flowed into water and in cooling assumed a rounded form. The bond between the pillows is so strong and fracturing so infrequent that climbing is almost entirely on rounded regularly-spaced holds without cracks and without loose rock.

Vegetable Contamination

At high altitude rock is usually pure mineral. Below an elevation that varies with every range lichens modify the rock considerably. When dry they can be scuffed away or crushed by the boot, but when dampened by rain or fog form a slimy coating which ruins friction. In lower altitudes moss often obscures the rock and completely spoils climbing.

Even if the rock is not covered by vegetable growth the action of organic acids from surrounding plants tremendously accelerates weathering. Low-altitude cliffs in moist climates such as that of the Cascades offer little clean rock but a great deal of steep dirt, grass, and tough cedar trees. Such ascents can scarcely be called rock climbs, but several Cascade peaks, notably the North Peak of Index, offer so distinctive and difficult a challenge that the sport of dirt-and-cedar climbing has attained considerable—albeit evil—fame.

Tactics: Climbing with the Eyes

Knowing the rocks of a peak and its broad outlines the climber can plan his strategy of assault. He will know whether it is to be a sand scramble or an engineering project, whether he had best follow ridges or whether only gullies are feasible. In short, he will know in a general way what is possible and practical—perhaps without even having seen the peak in question. However, perfecting the grand strategy and formulating the step-by-step tactics of the climb usually require visual inspection.

THE DISTANT VIEW

A great deal of information can be gained from a distant view that will not be available on the close approach. Once within the maze of the peak the climber may crane his neck upward in vain attempting to see where a certain gully leads, or whether a ridge carries through to the summit, whereas from a distance such matters would have been perfectly obvious had he taken time to study and memorize. Sometimes a distant view during a momentary break in the mist may be the only one the party ever gets, the success of the climb depending on good use of that brief inspection.

Steepness of rock is difficult to judge; optical illusions are every-where present in the lines and planes of cliffs and ridges. Seen full face, cliffs always appear vertical; only a side view gives any idea of the true angle. Ridges and gullies may be indistinguishable from one viewpoint and stand out in clear relief from another. The more angles of view the better. *Shadows* tell a great deal about the surface structure. In early morning or late afternoon, or during cloudy weather with scattered shafts of light, prominent features are highlighted that are completely invisible when the entire mountain is uniformly flooded with sunshine or uniformly darkened by night or clouds. Shadows not only reveal the existence of ridges and gullies but indicate their relative size.

The most positive delineation of a mountain is that etched by *snow*. Early-season views or photographs showing residual snow from winter are best, but even a light summer flurry clearly marks the ledge systems. Snow cannot permanently cling to slopes over 40°—if the snow can stick on a slope the climber knows that he also will be able to stick there once the snow has melted. It is necessary, however, to distinguish between snow and ice and rime, since ice can plaster itself on nearly-vertical cliffs and rime clings even to overhangs. Snow can often be singled out by being whiter than ice and more uniform than rime. By studying the snow patterns the climber can determine how steep the climbing will be, where the ledges are and where they are interrupted, the continuity of the gullies, and the location of ridges and ribs. Avalanche fans must be noted; cliffs that in fall are many rope lengths high may be completely obscured in spring by an even slope of snow.

Reasoning from the visible to the invisible is one of the subtler skills of routefinding. For example, the angle of a face can be estimated by the depth of couloirs that still contain snow. If the couloirs are shallow the face cannot be much above 40° but if they are deeply incised it may be exceedingly steep. Frequently one can reason from large to small, the large details of a mountain tending to resemble the small details. If there are numerous visible ledges one can usually expect to find them connected by a network of smaller ones. If a ridge is fairly even in profile, without numerous towers and notches, one can reasonably hope for a moderate angle of climb. If under even the best viewing conditions there are no outstanding ridges and gullies one can expect a scarcity of holds and frequent need for hardware. If there is a bewildering variety of ridges and gullies one can foresee hazards of rotten rock. The rule needs thoughtful application, for the large details are often created by geologic processes that have no relation to the processes responsible for the small details.

THE CLOSE EXAMINATION

The distant examination is so important that a party often spends considerable time and effort obtaining useful data, gathering photographs taken from a variety of angles and at different seasons of the year, studying contour maps, and even making reconnaisance climbs near the proposed objective. While approaching the peak they take every opportunity to study it from every angle, perhaps even climbing out of the way to get new perspectives. Fieldglasses are useful, for example, in identifying the nature of the vegetation on a cliff; once it is known whether a certain green speck is a patch of grass or a clump of trees one can estimate the size of adjacent features.

Usually the puzzle cannot be completely solved from a distance, either because good views are not obtainable or because some of the mountain's secrets are too carefully hidden. There may be cliffs that hide in the shadows of gullies, ledges that appear suitable for finger traverses and turn out to be four-lane highways. The party may use trees for scale and find that what they had taken for scraggly bushes are in fact towering giants. The quality of the rock cannot always be determined accurately, yet the solidity and number of holds remain the critical factor in determining what angle can be climbed. Therefore the same methods that are used from a distance are constantly applied during the climb itself. In addition there are several other considerations that become important.

The effects of rain or snow frequently modify plans. Though an early start is ordinarily preferred the party may be wasting its time venturing onto rock made greasy by rain or glazed by an overnight snowstorm and would do better to enjoy a few extra hours of sleep, or even a rest day in camp, giving the sun a chance to dry the rock. Rough-surfaced or fractured rocks are least affected by moisture. Peaks with heavy growths of moss or lichen become treacherous even in fog, whatever the rock may be. Sometimes precipitation can be outsmarted. If the original plan was to climb the west side of the peak and the night brings a storm followed by a clear dawn, the party might do better to change to the east side, perhaps cleaned up by the morning sunshine while the west side continues icy or wet until late afternoon.

Rockfall is a constant preoccupation from first to last. The greatest hazard is usually not spontaneous disintegration of cliffs but the stuff kicked loose by people. On a rotten peak that allows several route variations the party should be divided into several groups. Sometimes a zigzag course is possible so that rarely is any climber below another. When only a single vertical line can be followed and hazard is extreme the party must keep ranks closed up, or alternatively have only one person at a time in motion with all others under safe cover.

"Climbing with the eyes" has further applications during the ascent. The route ahead is studied not only for technical difficulty but for belay points. Possible alternate routes should be studied just as carefully as the one in use so that if a retreat is necessary a new attempt can be made. Frequently, indeed, trial-and-error is the only way to storm the defenses of a baffling peak.

The descent is kept constantly in mind, *looking backward frequently* to become familiar with the way the route will look when climbing down. An excellent plan is conscious memorization of prominent features so that one can announce, for example, that at such and such a gendarme the party must leave the ridge via a particular gully, or that one of a series of ribs is the correct one, or that at a certain boulder it is essential to traverse out of a gully. Such key points may be worth marking with bright-colored crepe paper or chalk. Any other information that may prove useful on the descent, such as good rappel points or available bivouacs, should also be filed away.

7 *

BALANCE

Most mountain travel is nothing more than simple sidewalk-style walking adapted to precipitous and irregular terrain. In the process of adaptation it takes on the name of *balance climbing*, the technique of walking up and down even the steepest cliffs with weight over the feet, the hands used chiefly to steady the body in an upright position.

The Elements of Balance

WEIGHT OVER THE FEET

The upright posture places weight on the skeleton supported by the legs, a natural, relaxed stance which minimizes muscular tension, allows easy breathing, and thus increases endurance. The principle is simple: legs are stronger than arms; walking is less strenuous than doing pullups. The climber may feel more secure leaning in against the slope, clutching the mountain to his breast, but he is not. The close proximity of the cliff restricts his vision and hampers his motion. More important, body weight tends to push the feet outward, breaking off weak holds and reducing friction on slippery ones. At all times the upright position is more secure, compressing loose rock to keep it in place, and giving maximum friction.

THREE-POINT SUPPORT

In pure balance climbing body weight is always carried by the feet, but the hands have an important role as insurance against failure of footholds. On difficult rock the climber is always supported by three

holds and moves only one limb at a time. The remaining two hands
and a foot, or hand and two feet, form a stable tripod. If one hold fails
during movement there are still two points of support, normally
enough to allow recovery of balance. A climber who lunges upward
depending on two holds is in a bad way if one fails, leaving him teetering on one foot or dangling by one hand. Three-point support also
eliminates spreadeagling since the climber always has a continuous
sequence of holds he can retrace.

Fig. 21. Climber leaning in, unstable.

SMOOTH MOTION

The erect climber is physically relaxed. Supported by three points he
can relax mentally as well. Thus he can proceed to walk smoothly his
vertical way. The rest step, so useful for steep trails and steep snow, is
also the proper pace for steep rock, muscular effort and breathing coordinated so that there is always a good reserve of energy for
emergencies. In addition to relaxing *between* efforts the climber relaxes
during effort, moving smoothly and continuously from hold to hold, the
gradual transfer of weight minimizing stress on holds and giving better
control of friction. Lunging causes great momentary stresses which
tend either to destroy the hold or cause the foot to change position and
lose friction. Lunging also is tiring, leaving a person weakest at the
very moment he most needs to be strong—when his jerky motion has
left him hanging by one hand. The expert moves so smoothly he
appears to be exerting no effort at all, but to be flowing easily and
gracefully up the rock. The flow is not necessarily fast. The connois-
seur of style has much more admiration for the slow, smooth climber,
apparently nonchalant with everything always under complete control,

than for the speedy muscleman who jerks and hauls his way up the pitch in record time.

CLIMBING WITH THE EYES

Smoothness of motion demands careful preplanning of the route by climbing with the eyes. Generally the best views are obtained at a distance, but often other business distracts the climber and he arrives at the bottom of a cliff looking straight up the rock, from which position angles and distances are difficult to judge and holds impossible to evaluate. Before setting forth on a pitch the climber scans it carefully, seeking a complete sequence of holds all the way to the next stopping point. If no such sequence is apparent he examines possible alternatives to be kept in mind if the first experiment fails.

Once on the pitch visual examination continues of terrain well ahead, not only the immediate holds. Such short-range views often revise original plans, showing that some holds are not as feasible as they looked from a distance, also showing new holds previously hidden. It is this climbing ahead with the eyes that allows an expert to flow gracefully, not only constantly revising his route but planning in advance exactly how to use each hold. Spreadeagling, a most humiliating and dangerous posture, almost always results from climbing blind, hopefully lunging ahead without any clear idea of what comes next.

Footholds

The ideal foothold is a level platform that accommodates the entire foot, and the climber does not scorn such "buckets" when he can find them. Much more numerous, however, are small holds just large enough for the side of the boot or a portion of the toe, and these are the key to balance climbing. Even if buckets are liberally scattered over a pitch it is usually better to make intermediate steps on smaller holds; both for smooth motion and conservation of energy, holds should be close together. Long strides are tiring, break rhythm, and cause loss of footing. Generally each upward step should be no higher than the knee—somewhat less on very steep rock.

The holds that can be used depend on the type of footgear. (See Chapter 1.) With multiple-use climbing boots generally one prefers relatively large and/or rough-textured holds. For maximum choice, it is important that the boots be snug-fitting and have rigid soles and narrow welts. With special rock shoes, the range of possibility is extended to holds that may be invisible to the naked eye, and can only be found with the probing, testing foot.

Smoothness of applying force and attention to vertical position determine how small a hold a climber can trust. Many are of the "three-second" variety on which balance can be maintained only briefly. Before using so sketchy a step, or steps, one must always have clearly in view a substantial platform and move continuously until it is reached.

The side of the foot is preferred to the toe. Toeholds place greater strain on leg muscles, causing "sewing-machine leg." Also, both boots and feet have less rigidity when supported at the toe and may have

Fig. 22. Footholds.
a. Correct—close together.
b. Incorrect—too far apart.

enough give to let the foot slip. When the route is straight up, the climber can walk pigeon-toed, selecting holds at alternate sides of the body. This position allows the knee to bend without bumping into the cliff and keeps holds at all times directly under the body. When it is necessary or desirable to traverse and holds are too narrow to stride one foot past the other, the climber *shuffles,* bringing the rear foot up

Fig. 23. Traversing.
a. Correct—shuffling.
b. Incorrect—cross-legged.

to the front foot. Sometimes it is necessary to *hop-step* to exchange feet. Never being executed except with good handholds, this is not actually a free jump, which of course must always be avoided.

The *knee hold* is denounced by purists and certainly is overused by novices. However, on occasion upright posture and smooth motion are better preserved by use of the knee, such as when there is a good wide platform above, too high for a reasonable step yet without small intermediate holds below it. A climber should never get onto his knee unless positive there is room to arise—being trapped on one's knees is even more humiliating and dangerous than being spreadeagled.

SLAB

The term "slab" implies use of holds almost at the limit of friction. Actually the name is often misapplied to fairly-uniform slopes of rock which in fact are sprinkled with small niches and knobs. A true slab has no holds for the side or toe of the foot and friction of the flat sole is all that supports the climber.

Fig. 24. Slab climbing.

Footwork on slab requires the most refined and perfect balance— weight completely on the feet, motions always smooth and uniform. Usually it is neither possible nor desirable to have three-point support. Though the hands are often used for stability, with fingertips just touching the rock, for maximum friction weight is kept entirely on the feet, which must be flat against the surface even if this means flexing the ankles considerably. Pure slab is relatively rare and when very steep is to be avoided, but it provides excellent training; when a climber finds how steep a slab he can stick to on friction alone he can confidently extend his use of small, sloping holds.

Handholds

In balance climbing, weight is never suspended from hands, which rest securely but lightly on holds, ready to check a slip of the feet; the hands are chiefly important in keeping the climber in an upright position. Beginners are all too likely to put their faith in their hands, but tired arms are a disgrace in more sophisticated circles.

Just as "buckets" are preferred for the feet, so are "doorknob"-sized *cling holds* for the hands, and they are never disdained when available. Generally the climber must rely on smaller cling holds that perhaps accommodate only one or two fingertips. If properly placed even a single finger may be enough for balance, though somewhat deficient if called upon to hold most of the body weight. The *downpressure hold* is frequently better, the heel of the hand pressed against a flat or sloping surface for friction.

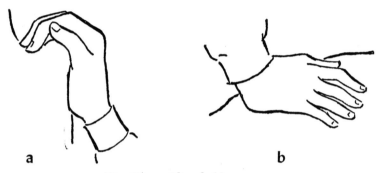

a   b

Fig. 25. a. Cling hold.
b. Downpressure hold.

The optimum location for a handhold in climbing up is between the waist and the head, or on the average about chest level. On low-angle slopes there may be tempting holds in the vicinity of the knees, but if a climber leans in to accept their invitation he must bend at the waist and lose his vertical stance. On steep slopes there is a tendency to reach high for inviting doorknobs; such long stretches tire the arms and lead one into doing pullups.

Actually the distinction between balance and counterforce (subject of the following chapter) is made for convenience of analysis rather than as a description of reality. The balance-climbing cling hold and downpressure hold both merge indistinguishably into holds which help raise or lower the body. Indeed, it is vanity to insist on keeping all the weight on the feet when a few pounds of pressure on a handhold will immensely simplify matters.

Testing Holds

The climber stakes his life on his holds, but not without investigation. A hold is never trusted unless tested as fully as circumstance allows. The first test is a general appraisal of the rock, as discussed in the previous chapter and elaborated in Chapter 20. The second is a visual inspection of the particular hold in question, its foundations and attachment to the mountain. Size is of no significance, for even a huge block may be precariously balanced and need only a touch to send it crashing down. Finally comes the physical test, by weight. In ascent most holds are encountered first by the hands, which test first with a gentle downward pull, a harder tug, and then rough pushes and pulls in all directions. In descent the feet must do the job, shoving, stamping, and kicking. The object is not to dislodge the hold, which may be loose in one line of push or pull but in another quite strong and dependable. Since application of force frequently changes as a climber passes over a hold it is necessary to know in which directions a hold is secure, insecure, or untested. Once limits have been found they are respected; if they cannot be investigated safely the climber warns his belayer.

Descending

Climbing down is in many ways more enjoyable than climbing up, the pleasure in graceful motion unalloyed with the labor of overcoming gravity. Too often a party throws away half the fun by descending from the summit on the easy "backside" or by employing the cheap spectacularity of rappels. Most pitches are about half again as difficult to descend as to ascend, partly because of late-afternoon weariness, partly from less experience in technique. However, most of the difference lies in the fact that on the way up a climber is first investigating terrain with his eyes and then his supple hands; on the way down he is feeling his way with blind clumsy feet. Also, though gravity eases labor it magnifies error.

When possible a climber *faces outward* for the best view and freest motion, having the option of proceeding straight down or to either side. He crouches to grasp handholds as far down as comfortable: the lower the hold the longer it can be used; the lower the center of gravity the more stable the stance. Balance often is neither so easy nor so desirable as in up-climbing. On broken terrain it may be faster and safer to swing the body down on solid handholds than to laboriously test footholds. Such "headfirst" descent is used sparingly; on a long route the arms tire quickly.

On steeper rock the climber *turns sideways*. With solid cling holds he can lean out into space and examine the terrain directly under. With more tenuous holds he traverses, zigzagging down to gain lateral views. On rock still steeper he must *face in*. Though the rucksack no longer scrapes against the cliff and greater dexterity is permitted limbs, visibility is poor to nonexistent. A climber may be able to examine the route ahead through his crotch or—first informing his belayer—lean out against the rope for an over-the-shoulder glance. Otherwise descent is made by blind foot-probing, trusting in the rope. The last man down, lacking an upper belay, depends on oral or manual guidance from his companions.

Fig. 26. Climbing down.
a. Facing out.
b. Facing sideways.
c. Facing in.

Practice

The best practice for rock climbing is rock climbing. However, for many climbers the season is too short or the peaks too distant to attain top form relying entirely on true alpine ascents. To gain maximum pleasure from a short vacation or the few weekends available for rock mountaineering, most dedicated climbers train themselves during winter and spring. Chief in importance is good physical condition, remembering that lungs and legs and abdomen are the primary tools of climbing; fingers and arms are secondary. Calisthenics are excellent if done regularly—a certain number of fingertip pushups each morning, chinnings on fences each evening, squeezes of a rubber ball, and so forth. Useful as these are in developing important muscles, the best exercise of all is distance running, at the fastest speed possible and preferably over hilly terrain.

A closer approach to mountains is provided by such city terrain as approximates rock conditions. The counterforce methods described in the following chapter can be used to climb telephone poles and trees and doorways. Balance is developed by walking railroad rails, traversing garden walls and the sides of brick buildings. On a nearby quarry or river scarp or glacial erratic there may be short pitches that offer practice in all rock technique. If the easiest way is too easy, sporting routes can be arbitrarily defined, certain holds ruled unusable, or a "no-hands" ascent specified. The climber keeps in mind that he is not trying to reach the top of the boulder or scarp but to train and coordinate various muscles and limbs.

Short pitches teach a person his limits—and pleasantly and easily, since he is risking not his life but only a drop of a few feet to the grass or until caught by his upper belay. The limit—the point of falling—should be relentlessly sought. Usually this point is far beyond what the climber initially thinks. It must be pointed out that excessive practice on short pitches is very bad, the climber becoming conditioned to short exertions followed by complete relaxation. Moreover, he comes to accept falls as a normal part of climbing, a poor habit indeed on true mountains. Long climbs are the only ones that give practice in rhythm, pace, and rope-handling. As soon as the snow melts away from lowland cliffs the climber begins long scrambles over perhaps elementary rock to improve rope-team coordination. Important ascents are, after all, party ascents, not solo ventures.

Exposure, the distance one might fall if holds fail, is of no concern to an experienced climber certain his holds will not fail. To him a mile of atmosphere beneath is no more impressive than a hundred feet of air, since both are about equally fatal in a fall. However, exposure must be assimilated gradually. It is harmful to force oneself into exposed positions on the old theory of tossing a child into water to make him swim; such forced exposure leads to vertigo, a psychological malady but nevertheless dangerous. If a person first develops his technique to a level of complete trustworthiness his tolerance for exposure increases rapidly.

8 *

COUNTERFORCE

BALANCE climbing is ordinary sidewalk- or staircase-style walking adapted to small and irregular steps. When terrain is utterly lacking in steps of any kind whatsoever, counterforce methods may often be employed. Taken together the two constitute a unified technique of "free" rock climbing. Balance is normally preferred, letting legs do the work and thus being least tiring, but it is not possible unless there are sufficient nearly-horizontal footholds. Counterforce methods produce stresses through the body that can be maintained only for short intervals. However, by their help a climber can use a greater variety of holds—upsidedown, vertical, or any which way. Even on an otherwise elementary ascent there may be one stride impossible in balance but easily passed with counterforce. On difficult rock the proportion of counterforce increases. Usually the two are thoroughly intermixed; the graceful climber continues his smooth and continuous flow now in balance, now moving naturally into a counterforce hold, now back into balance.

Due to the very nature of counterforce methods a climber running out of energy in midpitch may have an extremely difficult time stopping for a rest or returning into balance. The prodigious finger traverses, laybacks, and chimney stems of fiction are best kept there. Moreover, counterforce rarely has the security of three-point support; failure of holds is usually total and simultaneous. However, it is not true that balance is always safe and counterforce always dangerous. When holds are small and the rock steep often it is better to use a secure counterforce hold than continue in balance for the pure swank of it.

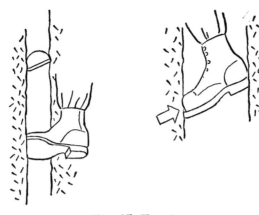

Fig. 27. Foot jams.

Unlike balance, where gravity alone attaches the climber to the mountain, in counterforce a tension is created in the human body along a line between two rock surfaces. This tension, or opposition of forces, supports the climber independently of gravity. There are several ways in which such tensions are created: (1) a portion of the body is *jammed* between surfaces; (2) a portion of the body is twisted or *rotated* between surfaces; (3) one portion of the body *pulls or pushes* against holds while an opposed portion does the same in an opposing direction. The pressure applied may be minor, merely a few pounds; in some techniques the entire body weight is supported.

Jams and Rotation

The simplest instance of counterforce is the *jam hold*, a portion of the body being thrust firmly into a crack. In a *foot jam* the boot is inserted, then twisted, friction of the welt being perhaps sufficient to easily support the entire body weight. In a *hand jam* the fingers are

Fig. 28. Elbow jam, view from above.

slipped in and a fist made, obviously a hold of limited capacity. Less commonly useful are jams of the knee, elbow, or the entire trunk—or at the other extreme, the fingers alone. Always implicit is the danger that jamming may be complete and permanent.

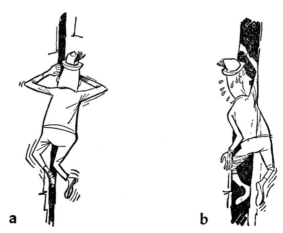

Fig. 29. Jam holds.
a. Foot. (With hands used in opposition to each other, pulling outward on edges of crack.)
b. Knee and forearm.

The next-longer extension of stress through the body is in a *rotation* hold, where tension derives from torque of various muscles in combination. In a common variety the twisting of shoulder and arm muscles maintains the push by elbow against that of the hand. Many jams depend to some extent on rotation—and the rotation hold itself is transitional to the next variety of counterforce.

Pushes and Pulls in Opposition

The previous chapter discussed the *cling hold* for balance; the identical hold can support weight and thus involve counterforce. In the simplest case the climber merely curls his fingers around the rock and clutches, the extreme case being the *finger traverse* where the entire body is held by the arms, feet dangling. In a narrow crack, fingers are curled around one side and thumb pressed against the other. The previously-mentioned *pressure hold* for balance is transformed into a counterforce hold by pushing with the arms to support weight. Using both hands with downpressure to hoist oneself onto a ledge is called *tabling*.

Fig. 30. Types of cling holds. *Left,* fingers opposing palm; *right,* fingers opposing thumb.

Opposing pressure of one hand against the other introduces additional possibilities. On a knob the climber can push down on the top with one hand and pull up on the bottom with the other; in a scoop, push up on the ceiling and push down on the floor; on a rib, push inward with both arms, the *bear hug*—or perhaps cross arms over chest and pull inward with both, a *cross-pressure hold.*

Fig. 31. a. Undercling hold.
b. Use of holds with force applied inward.

Hands can be opposed to feet. For instance, with good platforms for feet and only overhanging holds for hands, a climber can push down with feet while pulling or pushing up with hands, as in the *undercling hold.*

The *layback*—in its most obvious application—depends on tension of both arms pulling against one side of a crack while both feet push against the other. It is possible for a muscular person to ascend in an overhanging stance, body hanging from his hands. The climber of average strength can employ the technique only in the semi-upright stance illustrated, most of the weight on his feet, arms exerting just enough pull to give the feet traction. Too much emphasis is given the association of the layback with cracks. Far wider in application is the *partial layback*, a good exmple being when a climber can find one excellent platform foothold and one excellent cling hold, but nothing

Fig. 32. a. Layback.
b. Bear hug.

else except two vertical-sided roughnesses. These perhaps are the key to the pitch if he can push against one with a foot and pull against the other with a hand and from two useless bits of rock fashion one good layback step.

Stems

Most famous, most spectacular, and most common of complex counterforce techniques is chimney-stemming. Several very different stems are applicable to chimneys narrow, medium, and wide. Any chimney is climbed to the fullest possible extent by balance with holds on one wall or the other—shifting from side to side or combining holds on both walls. Between balance sequences may lie a short stretch that must be stemmed. Sometimes a long stem is necessary, perhaps an entire lead, but generally this is only possible if the chimney provides good ledges for periodic rest while balanced. Some stemming stances, such as opposition of hips against feet, are sufficiently comfortable to allow brief recuperative pauses, but even here weak knees introduce "sewing-machine" action. In every stem the major hazard is the tendency of feet to creep above the waist, the trunk then slipping down inside clothing to jam the body with feet high above head.

Fig. 33. Chimney-stemming.
        a. Wide chimney, hands and feet.
        b. Medium chimney, back, hands, and feet.
        c. Medium chimney, back and feet.
        d. Narrow chimney, back, knees, and feet.

Mixed Application

Counterforce begins with nothing more complicated than pushing down with hands, stuffing a foot in a crack, or dangling by the fingers, and progresses to applications so complex they can only be described by force diagrams and mathematical equations. Occasionally an entire pitch is counterforce. A long crack may be climbed all the way and perhaps even comfortably using jams for the feet and outward pulls by the hands. A somewhat-larger crack might make an occasional knee or body jam desirable. As the crack widens into a chimney the climber may enter, starting with a body jam and progressing to a full stem.

Possibilities of counterforce are limited only by individual strength, but such limits must be respected. Whenever joints are abnormally flexed or muscles excessively strained the limit has been found. When in balance, rest is perpetually available, but not so during counterforce, and therefore a person should not attempt any pure counterforce pitch unless certain he has the strength to finish. Better otherwise to start right out with the Class Six technique of Chapter 11, manufacturing with iron and rope the resting points omitted by nature.

9 *

ROPED CLIMBING

IF a climber could be certain his skill would never fail and luck would always be with him, that he would never slip or stumble even once in all his years of mountaineering, the only reason for climbing in groups would be sociability. However, no human is infallible and alpine terrain is treacherous. The most experienced climber can sometimes misjudge the difficulty of a route or be momentarily careless. Rock holds break away unexpectedly, snow is slippery, and glaciers are honeycombed with crevasses. The lone individual cannot reasonably stray far from well-beaten paths—nor does merely increasing the size of the party to three, or a dozen, or a hundred members make much difference since this may have the sole effect of providing 2, or 11, or 99 witnesses to an accident if it occurs.

More than any other item of equipment, the climbing rope clears the way to safe travel in the high world of steep rock and ice. It is not necessary to march against the peaks in single combat risking life and limb at every step; the rope ties individuals together and creates a larger entity, the rope team, with larger reserves of strength. If a member of the team slips he is not doomed, as he might be defended only by his own resources, for he has the help of his companions in stopping his fall. So basic a tool is the rope that along with boots and ice ax it is one of the universal symbols of mountaineering—or to be more specific, of safe and sane mountaineering.

The Climbing Rope

SELECTION

Several features are desirable in a climbing rope. It must be strong enough to hold a falling body yet light enough to be carried; tough enough to resist abrasion and cuts yet flexible enough to handle easily with a minimum of snarling even when frozen or wet; large enough to be gripped easily by the hands yet not so large as to be cumbersome; long enough to provide sufficient working space between climbers yet not so long as to be unnecessarily heavy. From experimentation dating back to pioneer days has evolved what is agreed by most contemporary climbers to be the best available all-purpose compromise—a rope of Mountain-Climbing Goldline, a synthetic fiber, $7/16$-inch in diameter, 120 feet long. Almost as good is Mountain Nylon. A very inferior second choice is a manila rope of the same dimensions. Table 7 statistically compares the three; for somewhat different data from another source, see Table 9 in Chapter 11. A rope of European manufacture, Perlon, is gaining acceptance for climbing in America, though little statistical data is available on its performance.

Table 7. Physical Properties of $7/16''$ Diameter Mountain-Climbing Ropes.

	Manila	Nylon	Goldline
(1) *Breaking Strength, Pounds* (Max. load at break; stretch rate 4 inches per minute)			
Dry Test Conditions	2500	4575	5025
Wet Test Conditions	2620	3900	4500
(2) *Elongation to Break* (The "stretch," expressed as a percentage of a free length under no load)			
Dry Test Conditions	12%	48%	62%
Wet Test Conditions	19%	49%	63%
(3) *Energy Absorption, Ft. Pounds per Ft.* (Computed capacity of rope to absorb kinetic energy)			
Dry Test Conditions	100	675	*
Wet Test Conditions	167	604	*
(4) *Abrasion over Rough Bar* (Per cent of original strength retained after 25 cycles of abrasion over a 1.3″ dia. cast-iron bar)	64%	71%	*

Table 7. Physical Properties of Mountain-Climbing Ropes. (*continued*)

	Manila	Nylon	Goldline
(5) *Strength over Carabiner, Pounds* (Breaking strength over ⅜″ dia. bar)	1250	2180	2796
(6) *Weathering* (Per cent of original strength retained after exposure for 186 days at Kure Beach, N. C.)	50%	75%	*
(7) *Water Absorption* (Percentage of weight gained after dry rope was soaked for 24 hours)	57%	29%	30%

* No comparable data available.
Source: Adapted from Leonard, Richard M. and Wexler, Arnold, Belaying the Leader, *Sierra Club, 1956, pp. 12–13. Data revised by Plymouth Cordage Company, Massachusetts, September 1958.*

Fiber

Numerous fibers have been used or suggested for climbing ropes—silk, linen, sisal, hemp, rayon, cotton, flax, jute, and others. During World War II, Mountain Nylon was developed for the U.S. Army, proved superior to predecessors, and would quickly have become the exclusive choice of climbers were it not rather expensive. Yachting Nylon is equally strong but has a softer lay that tends to allow the strands to separate, as well as making it more prone to kink and tangle. All other Nylon ropes—woven, braided, or otherwise manufactured—are weaker than Mountain Nylon and some have strikingly-small resistance to abrasion. The recent development of Mountain-Climbing Goldline has put Mountain Nylon in the shade. Though chemically similar and about the same in price, it has a clear margin of superiority in the properties useful to the mountaineer. Manila, though far inferior, is about one-fifth the price and is much stronger than any fiber of comparable cost.

Goldline, and to a lesser extent Nylon, is not only stronger than manila at holding a static load (see Tables 7 and 9) but its greater elongation before failure helps absorb the force of a fall and gives a tremendous superiority in energy absorption. Though all fibers deteriorate through abrasion, weather, and bending over a carabiner, the synthetics have such a good margin of safety that with proper care they can be trusted for ordinary use several climbing seasons, while a manila rope must be discarded after one season.

The lower cost of manila continues to give it a place in mountaineering, despite relative weakness, short life, and a tendency when new to form miserable messes of kinks. Though it should never be trusted in high-angle rock climbing where hard falls are possible, its strength is adequate for nearly all snow and glacier climbs, and many rock climbs as well; there is certainly no point in going to great expense to gain a safety margin far in excess of need.

Again, one specific variety of manila is recommended—three-strand "balloon rope" made from a high-grade manila abaca, with a dry breaking strength for $\frac{7}{16}$-inch diameter of 2500 pounds, compared to only 1750 pounds for common grade manila abaca, United States Government specification TR601A. Though the latter is commonly used by mountaineers it certainly cannot be given any considerable degree of trust.

Perlon climbing rope is a recent European development consisting of a woven sheath covering a core of parallel Nylon strands. Two types of Perlon are currently available. One ("Everest") has a tensile strength equivalent to Goldline, though less elongation (41 per cent compared to 62). The newer type ("Dynamic") has an elongation at rupture of up to 80 per cent; with a 176-pound test weight in a 15-foot fall, its impact strength is 2134 pounds. A direct comparison of the physical properties of Perlon with Goldline is difficult because of the difference in tests conducted by American and European manufacturers.

Diameter

The $\frac{7}{16}$-inch diameter of the climbing rope became customary before the advent of synthetics, any smaller diameter of manila being dangerously weak. The superior strength of synthetics would seem to allow an equal degree of protection with smaller diameters. However there is not as yet conclusive data with respect to the smaller-diameter ropes. For example, a given amount of abrasion obviously has a relatively-greater effect in weakening a $\frac{3}{8}$-inch rope than one of $\frac{7}{16}$-inch diameter. Also, along with better equipment has come in recent years increased safety consciousness, and climbers—taking into account the weakening of a rope by weathering, cuts, abrasion, knots, and sharp bends over carabiners—prefer a $\frac{7}{16}$-inch diameter even in synthetics for a larger safety margin. Perhaps most important is the factor of control. In a hard fall on rock even $\frac{7}{16}$-inch rope is hard to keep in grip; smaller diameters, virtually impossible. For snow and glacier and moderate rock, a $\frac{3}{8}$-inch synthetic rope which has suffered no abrasion or prior hard fall to weaken it has proved to be adequate in strength and large enough for the usual run of rope-handling.

Length

A climbing rope seems always to be either too short or too long, giving either too little space for maneuvering or an annoying excess of entangling line. Since few climbers can afford to purchase or carry a multitude of ropes, or predict beforehand the exact conditions of a climb, it is necessary to compromise, and 120 feet has proven best for all-around use. Three climbers can tie to such a line and still have enough working room for snow, glaciers, and easy rock. On difficult rock or ice, where it is often best to have a full 120 feet between members, a single rope serves for a two-man team, and if a three-man team is desired two ropes are used, the middleman tying into both.

Other lengths are sometimes better. For Class Five and Six rock 150 feet is standard. For a climb with only one short pitch, reached after a long backpacking trip, 60 feet may be preferred.

CARE OF THE ROPE

Over and over again during his career the life of a climber literally hangs by a rope, which must therefore be treated with appropriate care. Stepping on a climbing rope, particularly with crampons, is a mortal sin; the novice caught in the act may be shocked by the horrified reaction of his experienced companions, but not when he understands that each fiber cut is a particle of strength lost. Ropes can be cut by falling rocks or abraded by running over sharp edges, and though it is not always practical to eliminate such damage, every attempt should be made to keep it at a minimum. Campfire sparks are an obvious hazard, particularly since with a predawn start the burn may go unnoticed. Synthetic fiber is attacked by a number of organic compounds such as gasoline and oil and must never be carried in a dirty automobile trunk. Manila—and synthetic to a lesser extent—is subject to mold when stored in an airtight space while wet; any climbing rope should be air-dried after use and kept in a cool, dry place.

The life span of any rope is limited and frequent inspections must be made to determine whether it is still worthy of trust. It is well for a climber to be thrifty of life rather than dollars and examine his rope with a steely eye before, during, and after a climb, discarding it at the first indication of weakness or damage with a ruthless disregard for his mountaineering budget. Climbers become attached to items of their gear, companions through the years; sentiment may be indulged toward a favorite hat, but not a rope. Owners of synthetics are especially likely to think one rope is good for a climbing career; Table 7 shows that weathering alone, even without cuts or abrasion, lowers the strength of any fiber steadily and surely.

Once subjected to a severe strain a rope must be relegated to secondary uses, such as belay practice, and never again entrusted with lives. A hard fall, for instance, means the rope must be used with restraint through the remainder of the climb until it can be retired with honor. Sometimes in driving mountain roads automobiles bog down and the climbing rope is pressed into service as a towline; once so used it becomes a towline forever.

Binding the Ends and Marking the Middle

To prevent unraveling, the ends of the climbing rope should be bound. Wrapping with adhesive tape is simplest, the tape replaced from time to time. Manila with its short life deserves no greater effort but most owners of synthetic ropes prefer a more permanent method, such as fusing the end-fibers in a match flame, then whipping with heavy thread, finally coating the ends with tape, wax, or paint.

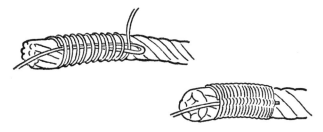

Fig. 34. Whipping a rope.

To expedite finding the middle of the rope a permanent marking is desirable. Whipping with bright thread is best; lazier climbers use colored tape. Definitely not recommended are paint or indelible ink which may chemically attack and thus weaken the fibers.

COILING THE ROPE

When not in use the rope should be coiled for easy carrying in a manner that will allow rapid uncoiling when needed. The climber needn't bother his head learning more than one of the many adequate techniques, but the one chosen must be learned to perfection.

The *mountaineer's coil* is convenient when the rope is to be carried for a long period of time or stored at home, though it does not allow rapid uncoiling when needed. To begin, the coiler sits down, picks up a bight of rope within several feet of the "starting end," and winds coil after coil neatly around his leg from boot instep to knee. (Especially with a new rope, the coil will tend to form a figure-8 rather than the neat oval illustrated; one should let the rope have its own way, since forcing it into neatness adds kinks.) When only several feet of rope remain in the "finishing end" it is joined to the "starting end" with a square knot. Each is then wound spirally around the circumference until they meet again. A square knot joins the ends and holds the coil together. Done properly the coil slings nicely over the shoulder or across the chest. However, if the rope must be carried any considerable distance it should be stowed in the pack both for protection and to avoid snagging on brush or rocks.

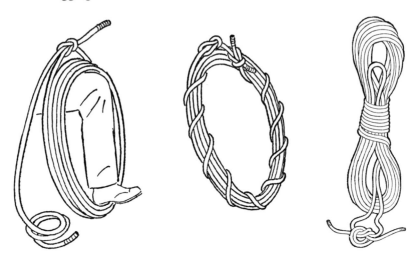

Fig. 35. Coiling a rope. *Left and center,* mountaineer's coil.
Right, skein coil.

A second method, the *skein coil,* is faster to do and undo and thus more convenient when the rope is used intermittently but frequently on a climb. Leaving 10-12 feet of each end free, hand coil the remainder of the doubled rope and wrap the coils three or four times with the free ends. (The coils can be of any diameter: wrap from the hand to elbow for short ones, from boot-instep to knee for longer ones.) Pass the ends through the upper loop. Use their remaining 6–8 feet each to sling the coil over the shoulders, or else stuff the entire rope in a rucksack. Coiled in this manner the rope is readily available for quick use since both ends and also the middle are instantly at hand.

Mountaineering Knots

The rope serves no useful purpose until tied to someone or something. Ninety per cent of mountaineering knot-tying falls in three categories: knots for the end of a rope; knots for the middle; knots for joining two ropes. For each use the climber must thoroughly master at least one knot and preferably several others for less-frequent but important occasions. Knots must be learned so well that each can be tied quickly and perfectly even in the middle of a roaring night when the mind is dull, the rope frozen, the fingers stiff; the novice can simulate typical mountain conditions at home by practicing his knots under a cold shower with his eyes closed. On long climbs every wasted minute adds to a pyramid of wasted hours that either lose the summit or force a bivouac; swiftness and sureness in tying and untying are characteristic of the experienced climber.

Knots must be inspected frequently, for with few exceptions all tend to loosen during use, particularly in synthetic fibers. The danger of trusting a knot that is no longer a knot is quite obvious, but more than one mountaineer has learned his lesson the hard way, discovering after a delicate passage that the rope was merely draped around his waist; after such a chilling experience one needs no encouragement to repeatedly check the status of his knot during a climb. Whenever possible, knots should be "backed up" with overhand knots, as shown in various of the illustrations, or less desirably with half-hitches; though the back-up knots also work loose they lengthen the life-expectancy of the knots they reinforce.

It is extremely important that the knot attaching a climber to the rope be tightly tied. A loose fit may be more comfortable but in a hard fall the climber can literally fall out of the rope, the waistloop riding up to the armpits, forcing the arms upward, and slipping off his body. Even if the loop does not slip over the arms it may still compress the chest, making breathing difficult for the fallen climber.

Indispensable as knots are they have a serious and unavoidable shortcoming. Any abrupt angle, such as a sharp bend over a carabiner, reduces the strength of a rope. No sharper angles can be conceived than those made by knots, which therefore are always points of weakness; *the breaking strength of a rope in use—which means a rope with knots in it—is a third to a half lower than stated in Table 7.* The weakening is not significant in new $\frac{7}{16}$-inch synthetic; even at the lowered breaking point it still is stronger than the human body, so that long before the knot fails the falling climber will have been torn apart by the force of the fall. However, $\frac{7}{16}$-inch manila and synthetic of smaller diameter have no such substantial reserve. The climber must always calculate the *useful* strength of a rope—that is, the strength when knotted.

KNOTS FOR THE END MAN

The best knot for tying into the end of a rope is the *bowline*, simple and strong, resistant to jamming, and easy to untie even when the rope is wet or frozen. The *single bowline* is economical of rope, but if a long fall is possible the *bowline-on-a-coil* is highly preferable, distributing shock over a much broader area and thus decreasing chances of cracked ribs or a broken back. Any number of coils may be used: several provide a good cushion for falls; when excessive line dragging between

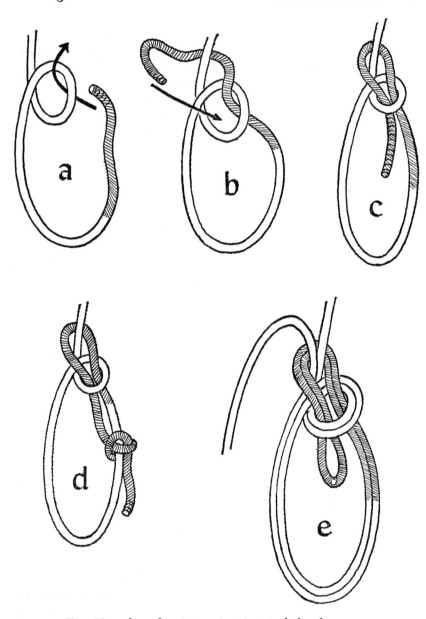

Fig. 36. a, b, and c. 3 steps in tying single bowline.
    d. Single bowline backed up with overhand knot.
    e. Double bowline.

IX. The Terrible Traverse on Mount Constance, Olympic Mountains. (Harvey Manning)

X. Serra Peaks, British Columbia Coast Range (Frank Fickeison)

climbers is a nuisance, any desired amount of rope can be coiled into knots. Half-hitches or preferably an overhand knot should be used without exception, for bowlines are especially prone to working loose. All bowlines have the same appearance, being the same knot; when tying, check for the "bowline look."

KNOTS FOR THE MIDDLEMAN

The middleman can tie in using the same knots as the end man, but with the rope doubled. The *double bowline* is simple to tie and distributes the shock of a fall. The *double bowline-on-a-coil* has the disadvantage of being uneconomical of rope. The *bowline-on-a-bight* requires less rope but is more difficult to learn and with one little mistake, easily made, or with great stress from both ends simultaneously, becomes a slip knot.

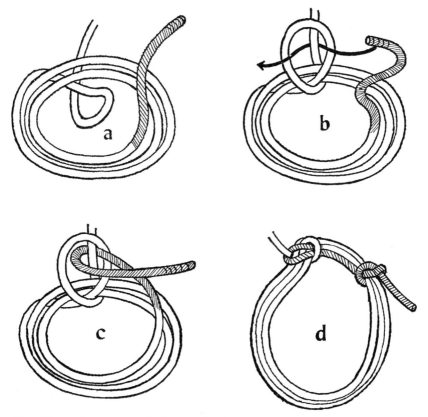

Fig. 37. Bowline on a coil. (Note: this knot can also be tied directly from step *a* to step *d* by using the method shown in Fig. 36.)

KNOTS FOR JOINING ROPES

The *fisherman's knot* is uncomplicated and easy to adjust; when backed up with an overhand knot it provides more security and is no bulkier. The *water knot,* or *ring bend* or *overhand bend,* holds very well on ropes of any kind and is the best way to tie ends of nylon webbing. (See Chapter 11.) The *Flemish bend,* perhaps the best joining knot of all, is tied similarly to the water knot except that it starts with a figure-eight rather than an overhand. *Sheet bends* serve admirably for ropes of different diameters, though mistakes in tying are frequent. Interlocking single bowlines can be used to join ropes of any diameter, the disadvantages being the sharp angles of bend and the bulkiness of the loops. The *square knot* is a poor means of linkage when a variable load will be applied, since under these circumstances it is extremely prone to loosening. All these knots should be tied with enough line left over to allow reinforcement by an overhand knot or half-hitches.

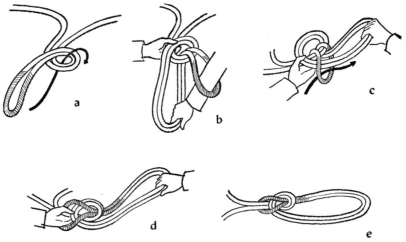

Fig. 38. Bowline-on-a-bight.

KNOTS FOR SPECIAL PURPOSES

Though a novice can get along with a repertoire of single bowline, double bowline, and square knot, he will not progress very far into more complex climbing situations before he must master several more—and certainly adeptness in rope-handling is facilitated by every additional knot well-learned.

Very frequently the climber needs a loop somewhere in the middle of a rope and the middleman's knots previously described may require

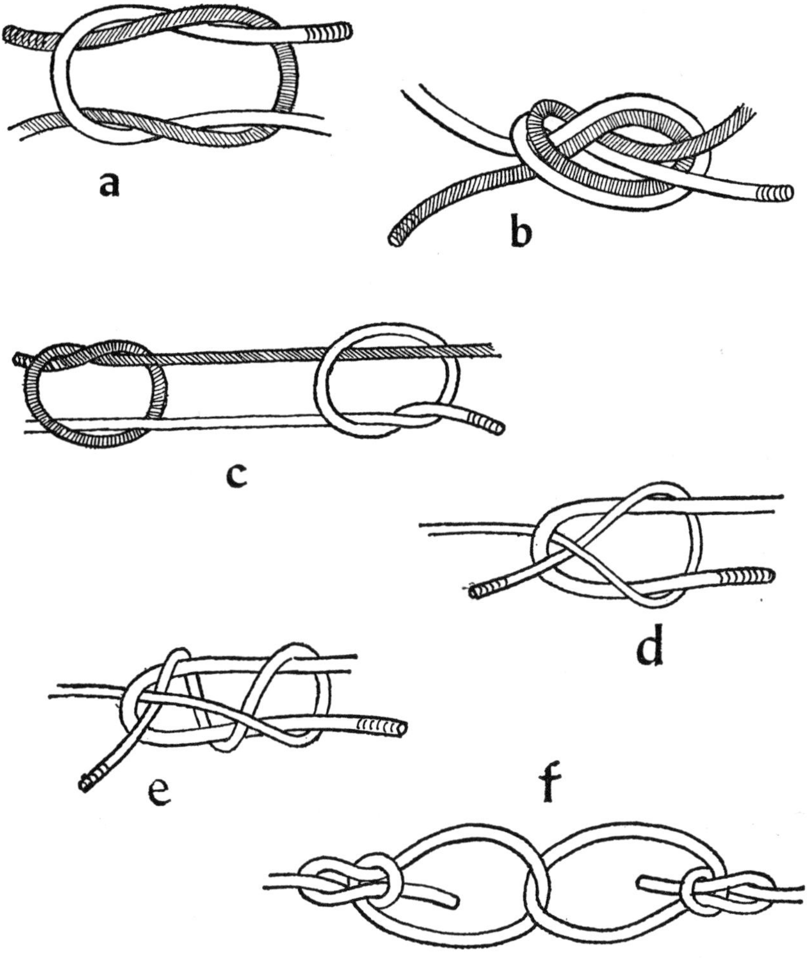

Fig. 39. Knots for joining ropes.

a. Square knot.	d. Sheet bend.
b. Water knot or ring bend.	e. Double sheet bend.
c. Fisherman's knot.	f. Two bowlines.

too much time; in most common cases of this sort a knot is desired that is very simple and very easy to adjust. The *overhand knot* satisfies both these requirements but jams under stress, unlike its variation, the *figure-eight*. The *belayer's hitch* is excellent on all counts except that when carelessly tied it degenerates into a slip knot.

Half-hitches have innumerable uses, not only in reinforcing other knots but for attaching any free rope end to a tree or carabiner, as in anchoring a belay or pitching a tarp. A bowline does the same job but is not so easily adjusted.

Fig. 40. Figure-8 knot. *Below,* used to tie a belayer to his anchor.

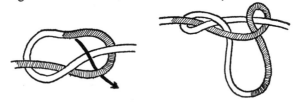

Fig. 41. Belayer's hitch.

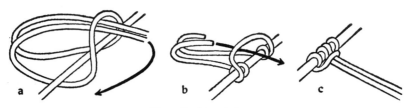

Fig. 42. Prusik knot.

The ingenious *prusik knot* is invaluable both in high-angle rock climbing and in rescue (see Chapters 11 and 19), having the distinctive characteristic of freezing one rope to another under tension, yet being easily moved to a new position when tension is released. Several similar knots are used for the same purpose. Since the prusik knot depends entirely on friction for its effectiveness, the rougher the ropes the better. The ropes may have such smooth surfaces that the knot will not hold with two turns of one rope around the other, as illustrated; one or more additional turns add the needed friction.

Though relatively difficult to learn and rather uncommonly used in mountaineering, rope splicing is a superb way to join permanently two ropes. A splice not only makes a smooth junction but lowers rope strength by only 10 per cent, giving a much stronger bond than any knot.

Rope Team Travel

Roped climbing requires—obviously—a rope. Equally apparent is the need for knots to attach the rope to various objects. The most common such objects are people, and as always the introduction of people into a static situation brings immense complications. For one thing people are different. For another they move—in the present case, as rope teams.

WHEN TO ROPE

The general rule is: a party ropes before entering any terrain where an individual probably could not check his own fall, and where a fall could lead to serious consequences. The rope is always and invariably worn on snow-covered glaciers (see Chapter 14) and steep, exposed snow (see Chapter 15).

On rock the time to rope is not always obvious. The policy is to rope whenever a fall would be dangerous—even if the climbing is easy and a slip very unlikely. Using this test one would ask on any pitch whether, if a climber fainted and fell unconscious from his holds, he would be seriously hurt. However, such a test is extreme. It is true that climbers have fainted and fallen and been badly hurt, but it is also true that people have fainted and fallen and been badly hurt while walking along a city street or standing up in a bathtub. Climbing is—overall— more hazardous than walking city streets or taking a bath, but danger cannot be completely eliminated from the world, particularly in the atomic age; some judgment must be used to maintain a uniform degree of safety in all of a person's activities.

When difficulty is combined with exposure, roping is mandatory for

everyone; when the climbing is easy, experienced and able climbers
may travel for short distances unroped despite the exposure. However,
judgment must always lean in the direction of caution; roping is not a
mark of inexperience or incompetence—rather the exact reverse. Moreover, the party should always rope in advance of need instead of
waiting until everyone is clinging precariously to the mountain. Furthermore, a request for the rope by any one member is binding,
without argument, on the entire team.

As a complicating factor, the value of the rope must sometimes be
balanced against the hazards of its use, such as on rubble slopes where
rope constantly sweeps down debris, or on unstable snow where in an
avalanche the rope hinders efforts of the individuals to extricate
themselves. Decision is difficult and each case must be separately
considered; statistics show that seasoned mountaineers guess better
than novices, but not so much better as to allow anyone, however
many years he has been climbing, to become overconfident.

ORDER OF ROPING

Each position on a rope team places quite different responsibilities
on the climber. The first man up a rock pitch, the leader, makes most
of the routefinding decisions and takes the greatest risk, since he has
the farthest to fall in case of a slip. The second man can help select the
route but his major task is providing the leader with a sound belay, as
discussed in the next chapter. On a three-man team the third climber
ordinarily has nothing to do but take care of himself, though sometimes
he may pay his way by carrying the heaviest rucksack or standing
watch for rockfall.

In descent the situation is somewhat different. The first man down
usually must find the route, guarded by a belay from above. The
second man down on a rope of three (or the first man on a rope of
two) must belay the last or uppermost climber, who again has the least
protection. On a traverse the end men both chance long falls, only the
middleman being held by belays from both sides.

When all members of a party are approximately equal in ability,
positions on the rope are chosen on a basis of personal preference, and
it is customary to rotate occasionally to distribute the workload. A rope
of two equals ordinarily uses the pleasant and rapid "leapfrog" method,
each climber alternately belaying and leading. Even in an experienced
party individuals usually differ in skill. One person may be more agile
and therefore leads the difficult pitches. Another may be the best
belayer and is entrusted with providing protection for the leader at the
most critical points.

When members are considerably different in skill and experience the order on ascent is best man first, second-best second, third-best third. On descent the best man remains in the uppermost and most exposed position, and thus is the last down. The second-best man ideally still should be second down to provide a sound belay, but if the route is obscure it may be necessary for him to go first to find the way; the least-skilled climber, ideally always at the bottom end of the team, in this case comes second. On a traverse the weakest member is given the most protected position, the middle of the rope. Such absolute distinctions between individuals are rather rare and special cases are innumerable. Sometimes position is determined on a basis of weight—the lightest man leading, the heaviest belaying. Sometimes one member is an avid photographer and requests the freedom of being third. Finally, weariness or illness change the situation. Rope order must be assigned always with careful consideration of the pitch just ahead and the current strength of team members and changed to meet changing conditions.

ROUTE CLASSIFICATION

The reader has doubtless observed in the preceding discussion a rather pussyfooted presentation of general rules about when and where to use such and such an item of equipment or to employ this or that technique; for every rule there has been a paragraph of qualifications. Confusion in communication has long troubled rock climbers, and methodical thinkers have attempted to solve the problem by devising systems of classifying rock climbs, usually in numerical order ranging from Class One, the easiest, to Class Six, the most difficult.

Such systems are of dubious value at best. First of all there is tremendous variation in the difficulty of a pitch between a day dry, warm, and tranquil—and a day of rain, cold, and howling gales. Classification can only assume the rare state of optimum conditions. Secondly, climbers are widely different in skill; classification must assume average ability and experience but the intangibility of "averageness" leaves infinite room for interpretation. Finally, there is always the question of who numbered the route. Perhaps it was a young hero seeking to impress the readers of an alpine journal with his derring-do. However, since assigning a high number leaves the hero open to the scorn of competitors, who in a later copy of the journal will demonstrate their superiority by giving a lower rating, some expert practitioners of climbsmanship deliberately undervalue the peak to protect their reputations.

Despite such objections, classification has obvious value in simplifying communication and indicating to a party contemplating a climb the equipment they should carry and the technique they must be prepared to use; the value will greatly increase when all climbers agree on a single system. Perhaps the best approach is not on the basis of climbing difficulty but the degree of protection necessary—always assuming optimum rock conditions and climbers of "average" skill and experience. Also, rather than attempting to give a single number to an entire route it would seem more useful to give a quantitative breakdown, describing a climb as "about 1000 feet of mixed Class One and Two, 600 feet of Class Three, several Class Four pitches, with one Class Five." The following classification, distantly derived from European systems and resembling its immediate parent, that of the Sierra Club, will be used throughout this book, though probably nowhere else.

1. Walking; shoes helpful.
2. Scrambling, using hands; boots desirable.
3. Easy climbing, somewhat exposed; rope should be worn.
4. Moderate climbing, very exposed; belaying essential.
5. Difficult climbing, very exposed; pitons or other anchors used to protect the leader.
6. Extremely difficult climbing; pitons or other equipment used for direct aid.
7. Impossible climbing; supernatural aid required.

It must first of all be noted that the foregoing system has no wide acceptance but neither does any other: until such time as universal agreement is reached a climber must, when told the number of a peak, ask the system. Secondly, one must always remember that even if the numerical value is valid for an average party in dry weather the route's number goes up if the party is weaker than average or the weather is less than ideal.

INTRODUCTION TO TECHNIQUES OF ROPED CLIMBING

In the present definition of Class Three rock, the rope is worn so that if any member of the team slips he will not take a long fall; the slope is so moderate in overall angle, or so thoroughly scattered with trees or rock ledges or projections, that other members of the team can hold him merely by bracing their bodies. In such terrain the possible fall consists mostly of sliding or bouncing and thus does not develop great forces. There is no belaying involved; the positions of the other members are sufficiently secure so that the friction of the rope running over the slope and around projections enables them to make the stop merely by bracing their feet and clutching at holds.

Since the party is traveling in unison, the rope can be very annoying if several rules of courtesy are not scrupulously followed. Climbers cannot move at their individual paces but must mutually accept the complex and irregular pace of the team. For instance, after a person completes a stiff scramble he might wish to dash ahead on easier ground; he must remember that his companions behind are still struggling and go along slowly to avoid jerking them. To eliminate snagging and dragging on rocks, during interludes of Class Two and One terrain the excess rope is carried by the following climbers in neat hand coils, line being taken in or let out as necessary to compensate for differences in pace; each man is responsible for the rope ahead of him, only the leader having both hands free at all times. On awkward pitches the coils must be dropped—the climber ahead, who has just negotiated the pitch and can foresee the situation, then stops and takes in the slack. Finally, as in all roped climbing, all members should be alert to changes in direction or obstructions that might cause the rope to jam and should flip the line as needed to keep it running free.

Class Four climbing—again by the present definition—means the holds are so small or insecure and the possible fall so long that only one climber moves at a time, protected by a companion in a previously-established position; the following chapter, which exhaustively discusses belays, might well be called "Class Four Climbing."

When the leader becomes dubious of his ability to stick to the available holds and concerned about the length of his possible fall, he may drive a piton or bolt into the rock or loop some extra rope over a boulder and run the climbing rope through a carabiner clipped to the piton, bolt, or rope loop, thus in effect bringing his belay point closer to his body. This is Class Five climbing. When the mountain provides no holds the equipment and technique of Class Six climbing are employed. These higher orders of difficulty are the subject of Chapter 11.

The reader has not yet done with the climbing rope, which on snow, ice, and glaciers, and in alpine rescue, is used in still further techniques discussed in succeeding chapters. Moreover, some of its subtler implications are explored in the treatment of party leadership and climbing dangers. By creating the team, the rope, even more than boots and ice ax, symbolizes climbing.

10 *

BELAYING

THE BELAY—in nautical definition meaning the securing of a rope with one or more turns around a wooden peg—was very important to sailing ships, whose masts and spars were held together by rope. The belay is of equal importance in mountaineering, the climbing definition being to bring the rope around some object—most commonly the belayer's body—in such a way that if a belayed climber falls the rope can be secured to stop the fall. Belaying is the technique which gives full meaning to the rope, but good belaying is not a substitute for good climbing. Even when held, falls are always dangerous and usually to some degree injurious. Agile climbing and skillful belaying together contribute to that hard-won ideal, good mountaineering.

In belaying even more essentially than in most techniques, the principle holds true that if a thing is worth doing it is worth doing well. A belay must stop motion—in this case the fall of a climber. A secondary benefit is a sense of security that allows more relaxed climbing—only a benefit, obviously, if the sense of security is not false. A belay must be what it means. The belayer must be in a strong position and know his business through careful and complete practice.

It cannot be too much emphasized that safety in climbing depends generally upon good belaying: it is just as important for the beginning climber to learn the right way to belay as it is for him to learn other climbing skills. As in any other learning process, theory is valuable but only practice makes perfect. Eager mountaineers usually begin the season with warmup climbs to refresh and improve their rock-climbing techniques; on such trips those as wise as they are eager practice belaying every bit as thoroughly as they do anything else. A few seconds before a serious fall may occur is no time to make a quick mental rundown of belaying theory. On actual climbs belaying should be a series of smooth, automatic movements—the result of previous frequent and thorough practice.

The primary requisite of adequate belaying is a mental attitude of constant expectancy. Too often the poorly-trained belayer regards sitting and handling the rope as little more than a rest stop, forgetting that his activities, while less strenuous than those of the climber, are nevertheless more vitally responsible for the safety of the team as a whole. The belayer needs grim determination, for he *must* hold any possible fall. Some so-called experienced climbers have gone serenely on for years without belaying properly, and never having known the sudden terror of a fall they have never considered the consequences. In such mental conditioning lies the explanation of many accidents where seasoned and expert rock climbers have made what seem inexplicably foolish blunders, and suffered—together with their companions—disastrous consequences.

Even without having seen a mountain or a rope the problems of belaying can be glimpsed by considering the forces generated by a falling body. Rare is the individual able to hold a 175-pound weight in his arms, but even so strong a person would probably fare rather poorly attempting to catch a 175-pound man after a 4-foot fall. Withstanding much greater forces is routine in mountaineering; on occasion a belayer may be called upon to stop a companion in a free fall of 20 feet or more. Mere strength is not enough, nor even a sincere desire to spare human suffering; special techniques developed by generations of mountaineers are required.

Belay Stance

The pioneers of mountaineering were so occupied in learning how to move amid steep and unfamiliar alpine terrain they had scant time to study devices for protection. The fullest development of team climbing was expressed in the mandate "be ready to wrap the rope around a rock should a companion slip." It is not surprising that even the greatest climbers of that age put trust in so crude a use of the rope, nor that techniques advanced slowly. Those who learned their inadequacy usually did not survive to enlighten their comrades—and contrarily, those who somehow managed to stop falls saw no urgent reason to improve their ways. Falls are fortunately rather uncommon, but unfortunately their very rarity makes climbers all the more poorly equipped to handle them. The development of modern belaying methods came only when climbers began to seek falls deliberately in practice, test and refine various techniques, and train themselves in their use. The contemporary well-trained climber sees and suffers and holds as many falls in his first day of practice as did the pioneers in their entire lifetimes. Under such a regimen the old "belay after a fall" has completely lost recognition as anything more than a desperate emergency measure. The term *belay* is reserved for a position established before a fall, and the rope management which makes use of this position. The established position is called a *belay stance,* and its description can conveniently be separated from the rope management and related motions considered later as *belay dynamics.* When the moment of truth comes to a climber there is no division of belay elements. Stance and rope and strength and will are fused into a single unit, the belay. However, the only way to understand the complex technique developed by thousands of climbers in hundreds of thousands of falls is to take it apart into pieces. These pieces must then be put back together again by the student in practice, over and over again.

The stance can be broken into even smaller components: *location,* or where the belayer makes his stand; *braking surface,* the parts of his body and other equipment he uses to control the rope; *braces,* his means of holding in position; *direction,* the aiming point of the belay; and the *anchor,* his guarantee of not being plucked completely out of his location.

SECURITY OF LOCATION

The most important factor in a good belay is a good stance. With a well-chosen position even a very long fall can be stopped; in a poor position even a skillful belayer may be dislodged by a small force. Obviously selection of a position deserves considerable care and, if necessary, considerable time. Climbers should not only keep their eyes open for good routes but good belay points. Indeed, the two go together—often a delicate lead is a reasonable risk only if a solid belay can be established. Though the temptation of a quick "token" belay might be hard to resist, the time saved may result in a party lost.

A solid position is not the only consideration. The belayer, not having free movement, is particularly vulnerable to falling rock and his stance must give him as much protection as possible. In gullies or other areas of particularly-heavy rockfall every effort should be made to place the belay either around a corner or under an overhang. Some care should be exercised by climbers above the belay in keeping the rope away from loose rubble and rather taut in order to disturb as few rocks as possible.

Comfort may seem a despicable desire on the part of the belayer but unless a position can be maintained over a long period of time it is a poor position however otherwise solid and safe. Contorted stances must be avoided, as well as those that press sharp rocks into the body. Though initially the belayer may not be disturbed by the pain, his efficiency will eventually be impaired and the urgent necessity to change stance may coincide disastrously with the climber's moment of greatest need.

SITTING HIP BELAY

The soundest stance, combining the best braking surface and the best braces, is the sitting hip belay. In ideal form it has these characteristics:

Fig. 43. Sitting hip belay.

1. The belayer sits in a comfortable position with legs spread well apart for stability, knees straight but not locked, and feet braced against projections.

2. The rope (after a fall) runs from the fallen man up between the belayer's feet, over one leg, around his hips, and is held by his *braking hand.*

3. At the time of a fall, the belayer is braced by his hips and two feet plus his free hand (which until then is employed as the *feeling hand,* as described later); the rope is braked around his leg and hips by the wrapping motion of the braking hand.

The strength of this ideal position derives from the fact it provides a *tripod* stance, the stablest means of suspension on uneven ground. The belayer's two feet plus his hips are the three basic points of support.

The necessity for testing braces to be sure they deserve trust is obvious. If good projections cannot be found for the feet their lack of strength can be compensated for by an extraordinarily-strong hip brace, such as a deep hollow in the rock where the belayer sits as if in a well. Indeed, sometimes the belayer may sit on a narrow ledge with legs dangling over the edge. Though there apparently is no tripod in such a stance, the three points are merely compressed closely together into the hips and haunches. The position is often quite strong, for the rope bends sharply over the lip of the ledge and the angle of the force pulls the hips straight down into the rock; even a minor backsloping of the ledge greatly increases stability. However, an anchor is desirable reinforcement.

Fig. 44. Belaying behind tree.

Sometimes no semblance of a tripod can be established and a sitting belay is placed straddling a tree or rock, a fall tending to pull the belayer into his single brace. If sufficiently large, such braces are extremely strong, but when small the belayer can easily be pulled sideways and dislocated. Both in these and in other circumstances the belayer's free hand can often be used effectively as an extra brace, and such use is planned before the need arises.

A tripod is only stable if the force comes inside its three points of support. If the rope to the fallen climber runs between the belayer's legs the force pulls the belayer into his braces, making his position more secure. If the rope runs outside the legs the sideways force quickly tips over the entire stance. The principle can be illustrated by a camera tripod with a cord attached to the juncture of the three legs. A downward pull on the cord presses the legs more firmly into the ground, but even the slightest horizontal pull brings the tripod crashing down.

STANDING HIP BELAY

In the simplest form of the standing hip position the belayer places himself nearly sideways to the direction of the expected fall, with his forward leg stiff and securely braced, and the rope, after a fall, running close inside this leg and around the hips. There is no tripod in this simple form, which accounts for its instability. Though adequate for holding minor falls, and therefore useful for such purposes as bringing a climber up rock not excessively steep, any very considerable force readily buckles the belayer at the knees or tips him over.

Fig. 45. Standing belay behind boulder.

Modifications, however, can often strengthen the standing stance. Having a good brace for the free hand helps immensely, giving some semblance of a tripod. If the belayer can wedge into a crack or stand behind a boulder, or otherwise arrange himself in conjunction with the rock so that the force of a fall will pull him into his braces, a great variety of standing positions can be improvised—ranging in dependability all the way to being perfectly "bombproof." The belayer must always be anchored, of course, when nature is not cooperative.

MISCELLANEOUS BELAYS

Once a mountaineering technique, however inferior, is accepted by any large number of climbers it dies very hard. In early experimentation many uses of the body for bracing and for braking surfaces were devised. One of these is the "guide belay" which consists simply of holding the rope in both hands, hoping to stop a fall by brute strength and awkwardness. The name as used by amateur climbers is derisive and not entirely fair, for professionals frequently must protect their clients on the easiest ground—or even haul them bodily up the mountain. Any amateur climber, however, caught in the act of using a "guide belay" had best be prepared to defend himself against the wrath of his companions.

There are numerous other strange, silly, and dangerous belays which have worked well in someone's experience and possibly are pet techniques in various circles, recommended as "coming in mighty handy once in a while." There are knee belays, elbow bridges, ankle wraps, and heaven knows what else. Such belays can sometimes stop falls, just as in poker it is possible to draw four cards to a royal flush, but few modern climbers place any value on these widely-assorted maneuvers, for all are inferior in strength to the hip belay which can be adapted for nearly any situation.

The stance most recently discredited in climbing history, and thus most frequently still encountered, is the *shoulder belay*. In one variation the rope runs from the climber below, up and across the belayer's back, forward over his shoulder, and down his chest to the braking hand. In a second, the rope comes up the belayer's chest, over his shoulder, and down his back to the braking hand. The body is braced as in the standing hip belay. Though the shoulder stance makes a very pretty photograph any hard fall demonstrates its weakness, which is that with the rope so high on his body the belayer inevitably bends at the waist under stress—and of course is pulled off balance with extreme ease. With the single exception of Class Six climbing where long falls are not possible, it is difficult to understand why anyone would use the shoulder for friction when the much stronger and more durable hips are available.

AIMING THE BELAY

The most frequent and serious fault of the inexperienced or thoughtless belayer is failure to visualize what will happen in case of a fall. Hardly any person moderately alert would aim a rifle due north to shoot an elephant visible due south, but often a belayer will prepare himself to hold a force from one direction when even the most casual inspection would show that if a fall occurs the force must come from quite a different direction. There are several common causes of confused aim. First, a belayer can be tempted into using a comfortable place to sit down and brace himself, whether or not the resulting tripod has any relation to the probable fall. Second, he can aim his stance at the climber, forgetting that if the climber falls the pull may come from a different direction entirely. Third, once his stance is established he can relax and fail to realize that as the climber changes position his potential line of fall may also change. This is the most insidious and prevalent mistake of all, among novices and veterans alike.

The only way a belayer can avoid such errors is to be a perennial pessimist. He should take a gloomy attitude toward the prospects of the climber, assume a terrible plunge into the abyss is imminent at every moment, and torture himself with a mental picture of the fall and all its consequences to the climber, the belayer, and the rope. Though he does not sabotage morale by loose talk, he always looks upon the climber as a person about to become a falling object, and thinks seriously about where he will fall, how the rope will behave, and from what direction the force of the fall will reach the stance.

The Climber Below the Belay

When the climber is below the belayer the direction of a possible fall is generally self-evident. The sources of confusion are usually absent and the belayer ordinarily has the advantage of having just climbed over the pitch himself.

The Climber Above the Belay

A common error is the failure to study in advance the path which would be taken by a falling climber. If the rock is very steep a free fall can be expected, but on broken cliffs of lower angle it is quite possible for the falling climber to bounce or slide to an endpoint far removed from the expected position directly below the belay.

Just as serious is not taking into account traverses over the belay. The leader may start up a pitch to the left of the belayer and the latter therefore brings the rope around his body in such a manner that his right hand would control a fall. However, if the climber traverses across above the stance, the belayer must note the change at once and reverse the rope so that his left hand is the braking hand, else a fall would find him making no belay at all—just holding the rope in one hand.

Finally, it is easy to be so aware of the yawning gulf below and visualize so vividly the climber tumbling into the void that effects of the rope are forgotten. The belayer's aiming point may not be downward at all, but upward. Even if artificial anchors such as pitons have not been placed there may be trees or jutting rocks to catch the rope. In such case the climber may indeed fall below the belayer, but the force will reach the stance from above.

Indirect Belays

Until now the only braking surface considered has been the human body, but rare indeed is the belay that does not gain some of its strength from the friction of the rope over rock or iron. The belayer has excellent reason to welcome such reinforcement, but he must change his battle plan if it is not to prove a hindrance rather than a help. The position of the climber after the fall is really not the issue at all. *Any object—rock, tree, or piton—that will catch and solidly hold the rope becomes the belay's aiming point.* If there are several, the one closest to the belayer is the target. The simplest and most common example of indirection is any belay on a ledge, where the rope bends at an angle from the stance to the fallen man. Obviously the belay aims not at the climber but at the brink of the ledge. Sometimes, to eliminate trouble, a belayer can place a solid piton close to his body and thenceforward be certain the point of aim will remain constant.

Fig. 46. Belaying.
  a. Correct—controlling hand on opposite side of belayer's body from fall.
  b. Incorrect—controlling hand on same side as fall.

When the pull will come from above, either because of a rock, tree, or piton, an inferior variation of the hip stance is used, the *buttocks belay*. The belayer literally sits in the rope, since the force will pull him directly upward. Braces are sought above the stance, but an anchor is inevitably necessary since the weight of the belayer can rarely if ever counterbalance the force of a fall. Often it is better to place a piton below the feet and redirect the belay. When time or terrain does not allow anchoring or piton-redirection, the belayer had best run the rope under his armpits rather than his buttocks; without an anchor the rope will, in a fall, quickly ride up the belayer's body in any event.

Reflecting back to yesteryear, the *rock belay* deserves proper evaluation. With the intense study of body belays made by contemporary students of high-angle climbing, it is sometimes forgotten that in nearly every fall the rope comes into contact with rock and nearly every belay therefore becomes partially a rock belay. Moreover, because of over-emphasis by the pioneers the modern school has reacted overviolently and given too heavy a measure of scorn to a venerable technique. Its

b

faults are legion and will be apparent later in the chapter, but frequently its virtues are great. If the rock is sound and the rope cannot possibly flip off in a fall, there is no sounder belay. Available friction may be so great that a belayer must control the rope with a very delicate touch to ensure a free slide. More commonly a hip stance is assumed, with the braces—which in such case needn't be overly strong—adjusted toward the rock. Those standing hip belays called bombproof are usually in fact really rock belays.

Caution is needed in any indirect belay and suspicious examination should be made of any object expected to redirect the force of the fall.

If a stance is aimed at a nubbin of rock and the rope flips off, or at a piton and the piton pulls out, or at a tree and the tree topples, the belayer faces the impossible requirement of establishing a new position while the climber is in transit downward.

Traversing, Descending, Ridge-Straddling

On any route other than one that proceeds straight up special problems arise. *Climbing down* is often more difficult than climbing up and more pitons may be needed than in ascending the same pitch. The first man down has an upper belay and feels good about the whole situation but he must remember his companions and anticipate the needs of the last man.

Fig. 47. Belay through piton.

In *traversing* all too often the leader drives a piton to protect himself before attempting a delicate passage and, once across the difficulty, proceeds for some distance on easy terrain without any further placement of ironware. He should remember that the last man on the rope derives no protection from the piton at the start of the difficulty—because he cannot use it—and to have equal protection with the leader needs a piton at the end of the difficulty.

If the leader is out horizontally from the stance and falls, the *pendulum swing* he makes in falling might appear likely to cause the pull to come from behind the belayer rather than below, but in fact the greatest force will come near the bottom of the swing and thus the belay should be aimed directly down.

Protection on a *ridge* requires close coordination between climber and belayer. At the beginning of the pitch they must estimate where the route will probably go and therefore down which side of the ridge the climber is most likely to fall. However, this may be hard to judge. On a narrow ridge possibly the only available stances give an aim horizontal along the crest and therefore the belayer should if possible keep the rope looped around a small gendarme—preferably near his stance—so that the belay will be indirect. The climber must keep this fact in mind and announce to his belayer when he intends to switch sides so that the belayer can flip the rope over the gendarme and make other appropriate adjustments.

On a wider ridge or one without useful little towers along its crest, where the belay is by necessity aimed at the side where the fall is expected, the rope must be kept free from the crest and allowed to droop slightly on the fall side.

ANCHORS

In an earlier age of mountaineering belaying techniques were recognized as ineffectual in hard falls and it was an article of faith that the leader must not fall. Though it is still considered bad form for the leader to fall, the categorical imperative of modern climbing is that the belayer must not be pulled from his stance. Even under ideal condi-

Fig. 48. Belay anchored to rock.

tions the braces of a body stance have rather low limits of strength, and conditions are frequently far from ideal. Whenever a considerable force might be expected in a fall the belayer must find some way to attach himself solidly to the mountain by use of an *anchor*—another borrowing from nautical terminology. The anchor may be a natural object such as a tree, bush, or rock or artificial such as a piton or bolt. Sometimes the belayer may be anchored by another climber.

The anchor rope is best rigged from the climbing rope itself if enough slack is available, using the 4 or 5 feet closest to the belayer. If the anchor is artificial a knot (preferably a figure-eight) is tied in the rope and snapped into the carabiner attached to the piton. If the anchor is a tree or rock a bight of the rope may be passed around the projection and secured with half-hitches. When plentiful slack is available the climbing rope may merely be wrapped around the projection a number of times; even without a knot, friction holds the rope firmly to the anchor.

Sometimes a separate rope is used for anchoring and even carried specifically for such purpose, particularly when it is felt that a sizable portion of the climbing rope cannot be spared. The belayer can tie into the anchor rope if he likes but an easier method is to tie the anchor rope to a carabiner snapped into the waistloops.

Anchors must be rigged with full consideration of the consequences of a fall. *First, the rope must be absolutely taut between anchor and belayer* or it will be of no help in strengthening the stance. Ideally the belayer should be as close as possible to the anchor; the "give" of a long anchor rope will in itself often be enough to allow the stance to be broken. Indeed, sometimes it is better to accept an inferior stance close to the anchor rather than a better one more distant. When the anchor must be some distance away, the belayer can obtain proper tension by first tying into the anchor, and then, after assuming his stance, tightening the anchor rope, if necessary by tying another knot into the waistloops with the unwanted slack.

Second, it is imperative that the *anchor be rigged in line with the direction of pull.* The three lines joining anchor with belayer, belayer with fallen climber, and fallen climber with anchor should all lie in the same plane. If the stance is not on that plane the belayer will be violently flipped out of position. An anchor rigged off to one side is better than nothing, since it will at least keep the belayer from being pulled completely off the mountain, but not much better.

Third, *the climbing rope must always be on the opposite side of the anchor rope from the direction of pull.* If the pull will be down, the climbing rope must be above the anchor rope, and if the pull will be up, the climbing rope must be below the anchor rope. Without this precaution a hard fall can easily force the climbing rope to ride completely off the body. Some protective shield, such as extra clothing, must be placed between the two ropes; a climbing rope running swiftly during a fall can sometimes slice through an anchor rope in a matter of seconds.

The technique of anchoring, though simple in theory and easy in practice, is one of the major recent advances in climbing safety. A sound anchor can make a shaky stance bombproof. Indeed, even if the belayer must literally hang from pitons a good anchor can make the belay completely trustworthy. The single objection to anchoring is the amount of time needed; if the belayer fumbles ineptly for half an hour rigging each anchor there may not be time to finish the climb. Therefore climbers must practice anchoring, over and over again, until they can quickly find anchor points and quickly rig the ropes. With proper skill it is possible to strengthen nearly every questionable stance on a climb, adding immeasurably to security, peace of mind, and enjoyment of the outing.

Belay Dynamics

In describing the stance of a belay the motion of the fall has been implied. However, a belay breaks conveniently for purposes of description into the before and the after of a fall, and the behavior of rope and belayer under a great force is so complex as to require careful analysis. Hundreds of belay stances are established for every fall that is held—but this fortunate fact makes it all the more necessary that the theory of belay dynamics be thoroughly understood.

ROPE MANAGEMENT

Once the belayer is in position and has signaled the climber to proceed, his first consideration is maintaining proper tension in the rope. When the climber is *moving toward* the belay, slack should be kept at a bare minimum to limit the length of any possible fall while still allowing the climber freedom of movement. When the climber is *moving away* from the belay, somewhat more slack is desirable so that the climber can if necessary take a long step without being thrown off balance by the rope. Excessive slack, however, droops around the climber, possibly hampering his movement and surely increasing the distance he can fall.

Both belayer and climber must watch the rope to prevent it from snagging on obstructions or jamming in cracks. If either happens, climbing must stop and the teammates cooperate in flipping the rope free. The rope must also be kept clear of loose rocks; poor rope-management is one of the commonest causes of rockfall, which needless to say can damage not only the rope but the climber or belayer. Being quite literally the lifeline, a rope deserves such solicitous care as keeping it away from sharp edges of rock, or alternatively padding it with an extra sweater or mitten.

The Rope and the Body

The rope coming from the climber passes around the belayer's hips, below the belt line if possible. Not only does the low position bring the force of a fall close to the center of gravity, making for greater stability than if high on the waist, but the buttocks are tougher and less sensitive to pain, besides being usually better protected by clothing. If riding higher, a sliding rope can easily pull out the shirt tail and cause serious rope burns. Often it is worthwhile to protect the body by wrapping a parka or sweater around the hips where the rope will run.

The belayer's hand on the side where the rope comes from the climber is called the *feeling hand*. During climbing this hand "feels" the climber by gentle tugs on the rope, informing the belayer how much tension is present. However, at the instant of a fall the feeling hand is immediately removed from the rope and placed on a previously-selected brace—since it can be of little use in holding the rope but often is very helpful in strengthening the stance.

The other hand, holding the rope on the opposite side of the body, is called the *braking hand*, and is of such key importance that it must never for any reason be removed from the rope during a belay. A rough-textured *belaying glove* is essential for protection from rope burns in hard falls. The braking hand should be kept well forward from the waist to avoid its being dragged back around the body when the rope runs. In a fall the braking hand is brought across the front of the body to gain increased braking surface, with hand pressure increased as needed.

The slack rope not extended between climber and belay must be *kept free of kinks and snarls* so that it can pay out freely in a fall. When the climber is moving slowly, neat coiling of rope is easy, but should he move rapidly and the rope appear in danger of tangling, the belayer should ask him to stop a moment in a safe spot while the coils are arranged.

Taking In and Paying Out Rope

When the climber is in motion rope is always either being paid out or taken in. Though procedure is simple, beginners often have initial difficulty achieving smoothness of rhythm, largely because of the rule that the braking hand must never leave the rope; however, even with this necessary handicap a little practice soon gives proper coordination.

Paying out is easiest since the climber provides tension. By pulling rope forward toward the climber with the feeling hand and pulling backward toward the body with the braking hand, the friction of the rope around the waist can be overcome. Both hands then slide along the rope for another pull.

To take in rope, the belayer first *draws rope from the climber toward his body with the feeling hand*, simultaneously *pulling rope away from his body to the coils of slack with his braking hand*. When the feeling hand has come up near the waist and the braking hand is extended at the full reach forward, the feeling hand slides forward along the rope and *grasps both ropes in front of the braking hand.* The braking hand can then slide back along the rope to the waist without ever removing its grasp. The cycle is then ready to repeat.

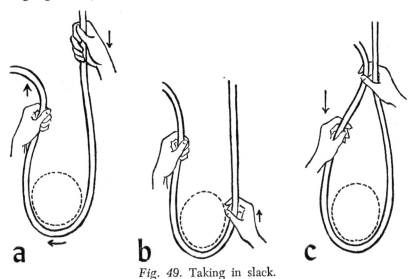

Fig. 49. Taking in slack.

Step a: Braking (*left*) hand pulls rope toward pile of coils while feeling (*right*) hand hauls in slack from climber.

Step b: Braking hand grasps rope; feeling hand slides forward.

Step c: Feeling hand grasps both ropes; braking hand slides back, in position to repeat Step *a.*

The commonest mistake of the beginner is failure to use the full arm extensions, so that in each cycle he may take in only a few inches of slack. However, the *braking hand must not be brought too close to the waist* for the sake of a little extra yardage; a sudden fall at this moment can wrap the arm around the back. Unless both hands are used the friction of the rope about the waist causes it to bind, further slowing the action. Inefficiency at taking in rope is very annoying to the climber, who must adapt his pace to the intake of rope and dares not climb past drooping loops. With practice, slack can be taken in as fast as the climber can move—smoothly and safely, with the braking hand always on the rope and ready to hold a fall.

Climbing Signals

Vocal signals are used for communication between climber and belayer—uttered clear and loud, especially if there is a brisk wind or an intervening obstruction. Whatever signals are selected must be followed rigidly: the certain annoyance and possible danger entailed by calling, for example, "up slack" if "up rope" has been agreed upon is obvious, and increased by the possibility that perhaps only a single word will carry. The following set has been found satisfactory, but is offered merely as illustration.

Belayer (when ready with belay): "Belay on."
Climber: "Climbing."
Climber (when rope is too loose): "Up rope."
      (when more rope is needed): "Slack."
      (for a taut rope to hold his weight): "Tension."
Climber (when safe): "Off belay."
Belayer (responding): "Belay off."
Both (when needed): "ROCK!"
Climber (if it happens): "FALLING!"

If a belayer doubts his position he may wish a test. In this event he calls "test." The climber then answers "testing" and very slowly puts weight on the rope—never by jumping. If the belayer feels insecure or cannot hold the weight he has only to let the rope slide. Belays by a novice should be tested consistently. The knowledge that a pull *will* come aids him in becoming belay-conscious and in evaluating stances. Testing is omitted by experienced climbers except in doubtful positions.

If a climber wants more rope a gentle pull usually conveys the message to the belayer; if not he calls "slack." The belayer must release only sufficient rope for immediate needs.

To tell the belayer to take in rope the climber calls "up rope," or simply "rope." This is short for "take up rope" and is used whether the climber is above, below, or on a level with the belayer.

If a climber is in trouble and wants the belayer to hold him he calls "tension." The belayer then swiftly takes in as much rope as he can and secures it until he hears the signal "slack."

The climber should also give his belayer as much news as possible about his activities—such as clipping into a piton, climbing behind a tree, or being on very touchy holds.

To let an advancing leader know how much rope is available the halfway point may be called out, or silence maintained until the 20-foot mark is reached and that signaled by a sharp "two-oh"; provided that this has been agreed upon, the climber will understand at once without danger of confusion.

Should high wind, generous overhang, or proximity to a waterfall render vocal communication impossible, a brief and simple set of rope signals should be mutually accepted before the lead begins. Some climbers carry whistles for this purpose.

STATIC BELAY

If the belayer secures the rope so firmly around his body or a rock or any other object as to prevent any rope-slide whatever, his belay is called *static*. Early mountaineers knew no other type, and since hard falls can rarely be stopped by such rigid control, sometimes entire parties were pulled off, or the rope broken and the falling man sacrificed. A static belay is obviously proper when the climber is below the belayer, for unless droops have been allowed to accumulate the falling body cannot gain any momentum before the rope comes tight. Under such circumstances it would be pointless and often dangerous to let the rope slide.

Actually no belay is completely static. There is considerable stretch in rope, particularly synthetics, so that never is the falling climber stopped instantaneously. Moreover, the sliding of the rope is largely automatic; when forces become too large for static absorption the rope runs. Indeed, it was realization of this fact that originally led to development of the dynamic belay.

DYNAMIC BELAY

When the second man on the rope belays the leader, the problems of belaying attain their greatest intensity. As the climber moves up and away from the stance his possible fall increases by twice the length of every upward step. After an advance of 5 feet his fall would be 10 feet,

Table 8. Links in the Belaying Chain.

	Pounds
The human body	1750
7/16″ manila rope (over carabiner)	1250
7/16″ nylon rope (over carabiner)	2910
Carabiner	2000
Piton	3000
Piton in rock crack	2200

Source: Adapted from Leonard, Richard M. and Wexler, Arnold, Belaying the Leader, Sierra Club, 1956, p. 23.

and if his weight is 150 pounds he would gain a kinetic energy of 1500 foot-pounds at the end of a free fall, concentrated by the rope on a thin portion of his body; the impact can literally cut him in two. Even if the climber's body can withstand such great forces, perhaps by using some sort of special harness, there is still the breaking point of the rope to be considered, and in Class Five and Six climbing, the danger of pitons or carabiners failing. It is useful to consider the strength of various links in the chain of belaying and the maximum load each can be expected to withstand—remembering that no chain is stronger than its weakest link.

The method that has been developed to hold long falls is called the *dynamic* or *running belay,* the gradual arrest of a fall by letting the rope slide so that kinetic energy is transformed over a period of time into heat by the friction of the rope through the hand, around the body, and over rock and carabiners.

Practice of the Dynamic Belay

The theory of dynamic belaying is easily grasped but not the skill. The only way to attain proficiency is through frequent, intense practice until the technique can be performed without thought as a smooth and automatic conditioned reflex. For anyone planning to climb high-angle rock during a given season one practice session devoted to dynamic belaying is a bare minimum before setting forth on actual ascents.

Rock cliffs seldom are ideally suited for belay practice, and usually present excessive hazard from rockfall and from ironware failure. Also there is often a temptation to have climbers make the falls because other weights are not available; since belaying novices are rarely proficient, the fallers may suffer considerable damage.

Practice is much safer using gymnasiums, stadium bleachers, tall trees, specially-built "belaying towers," or any structure with enough height to provide a sufficient drop, and something like a rafter or a branch from which the weight can be dropped. It is best to simulate the falling climber with a log or a sandbag.

A useful accessory is a pulley to raise the weight for each fall. No great mechanical advantage is needed since there is generally a good supply of manpower. After the pulley rope has raised the weight it is kept taut as a brake while slack is let out on the belay rope. The weight is then released from the pulley rope.

Once the belayer is in position—firmly-anchored, well-padded around the waist and hips, and wearing a belaying glove—he begins by holding several short falls, gradually increasing the length to as much as 15 or 20 feet—or the limit of his ability to hold. A 15-foot fall is generally considered an adequate maximum since in stopping a 150-pound weight the belayer must absorb 2250 foot-pounds of kinetic energy—well beyond the capacity of some links in the belaying chain and close to the capacity of others. Sometimes in holding such extreme forces the belayer may be pulled off his feet, but this is no excuse for letting go of the rope; the belay continues in midair. Generally the beginner first grips the rope too tightly and wraps it around his waist

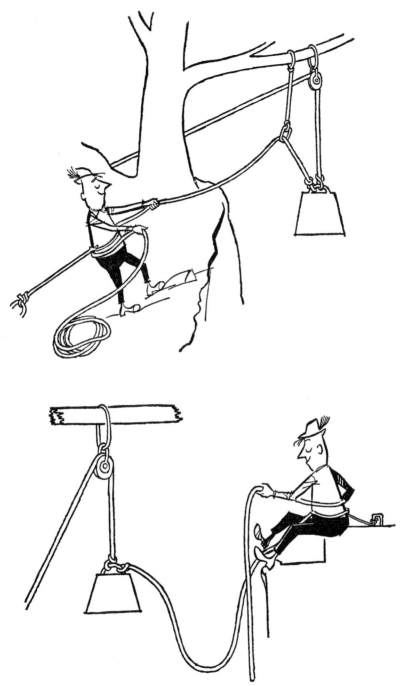

Fig. 50. Dynamic belay practice setups.
Upper: Standing hip or buttocks belay, through simulated piton anchor.
Lower: Sitting hip belay.

too quickly so that either the fall is stopped with a jerk or he is wrenched sharply from position. He then usually overcompensates for his first mistake by being too dynamic the second time so that the weight plunges into the ground. Gradually, however, he gains a feeling for the right amount of rope to let slide, and develops smoothness in braking. It is usually necessary to let rope slide in the amount of about one-third to one-half the distance of the fall. For example, to stop a 15-foot fall the belayer usually must allow from 5 to 8 additional feet of rope to run.

A very common belaying fault since development of the dynamic belay is letting the rope run just for the sake of being dynamic. If the climber hits a ledge while being gradually halted the damage may be much greater than if the belay had been more abrupt. The rope-run is not a virtue, but a necessity.

BELAYING ON THE CLIMB

A climber who has studied the theory of dynamic belaying and has practiced rigorously on the tower until he thoroughly knows what he can and cannot do is prepared to begin belaying on mountains. However, mountains are rarely so conveniently arranged for belaying as practice layouts and a belayer must be mentally active to find the best use of available natural features. Aiming the belay and rearranging the stance to suit constantly-changing circumstances also require an alert intelligence. Pitons or bolts can change the aiming point, an effect often so desirable that the belayer drives a piton close to his stance to make better use of available braces.

The bending of the rope over carabiners adds friction which can be a great advantage but requires special caution. When several pitons are in place the rope is often bent at such tight angles from one piton to another that the leader must actually give a good strong haul to obtain free rope for climbing. In a fall a large amount of friction still exists, and though in such case it would be easy to give the climber a static belay, since the forces that the belayer feels are minor, this would be a grave mistake. If the belayer absorbs too quickly too much of his share of the energy of the fall, the other links of the belaying chain will absorb their shares too quickly also. A long fall held on a static belay will probably kill the climber, snap the rope, or pull out or break pitons and carabiners. When belaying through pitons, therefore, it is necessary to be especially vigilant in letting the rope slide.

The leader must remember that a dynamic belay is not possible if he goes out to the very end of his rope and leaves no remainder in the hands of his belayer. Should he fall, only a static belay would be possible, and would almost certainly fail. When climbing on very steep rock a leader rarely goes more than 10 feet beyond his last anchor point, whether this be the belay stance itself or a piton which in effect brings the belay closer to the climber. Extensive practice has shown that the best-trained belayer with the finest equipment and an ideal stance cannot consistently hold free falls of more than 20 feet.

Even on relatively-gentle slopes the leader should be moderate in the length of each lead, but here the reason is different: though the belayer could perhaps hold a tremendously-long fall of the bouncing, sliding, tumbling variety, the damage to the fallen climber could well be severe. Long leads in climbing, like high speeds in automobiles, are almost certain to bring tragedy if an accident occurs.

After the Fall Is Held

The most rigorous practice never simulates the full effects of a serious fall and consequently little thought is usually given to what must be done after a fall is held. In most cases the climber falls onto or can be lowered to a convenient ledge. Other falls, however, leave him dangling on a steep face or under an overhang.

The belayer's first concern must be to stabilize his own position, since if the belay fails the first fall will be succeeded by a second one including the entire team. Indeed, so fundamental is the maxim that the belayer must not be pulled out that if the stance seems to be collapsing some extra run should be allowed the rope, even risking further injury to the faller. Though stopping the fall, the belayer frequently finds himself in an awkward position, in danger of losing the stance entirely and pinned down by weight of the climber. He must either free himself from the belay by tying the rope to his anchor by means of a pre-prepared prusik sling readily at hand, or preferably summon assistance from another member of the party.

Just as quickly as possible something should be done to assist the fallen climber, for even if uninjured his breathing will be severely restricted if he is hanging from waistloops. If conscious he may be able to assist himself, either gaining lodgment on the rock or taking part of the weight from his waist and chest with a prusik sling attached to the climbing rope and used for a foothold. (When a fall could leave a climber in an inaccessible position, such as under an overhang, he should fix self-rescue slings to the climbing rope before setting out on the pitch, so that he can if necessary employ the prusik technique more usually associated with crevasse rescue.) Recovery of the climber, and evacuation if necessary, are treated in Chapter 19.

Belaying as an Element in Safe Climbing

A climber always has two motives, sometimes in conflict: the desire to attain a challenging objective, and the desire to return home in good health. For most, the second motive invariably takes precedence over the first and such "techniques for safety" as belaying are considered at least as important as "techniques for glory." However, the choices presented by actual, as distinguished from theoretical, mountains are rarely simple. It is conceivable, for example, that under some circumstances the act of stopping to belay might be more dangerous to a party than continuing without belays. In any event belays merely minimize and do not cancel the consequences of a fall. With the most superb belay in the whole wide world it is still better not to fall.

WHEN TO BELAY

The great question is "when to belay?" No rules are unbreakable, no principles apply universally, because each belay is given under unique conditions of weather, climbing difficulty, physical and mental condition of climbers, and time of day. On practice or training climbs a belay is always possible and for sake of experience should be used whether a pitch is difficult or not, and even though there is no exposure. On the way up a peak, if good belays are not possible the ascent may be abandoned. On the descent it is sometimes necessary to balance immediate safety against long-range safety. When the weather looks very threatening it may be better to negotiate easy pitches unbelayed, balancing the slight risk of a fall against the greater risk of being caught by snow or lightning. Similarly time may be a factor, so that one sacrifices belays on easy but exposed pitches to finish a climb before darkness and cold set in. While it is occasionally necessary to avoid loss of time by cutting belaying on exposed pitches, it is never possible to sacrifice belaying when any party member feels insecure. Frequently fatigue is an important factor. What may be a Class Three pitch when climbers are fresh becomes Class Four or Five or Six when finger and arm strength are depleted. Condition of the rock is also of considerable importance; a cliff that offers easy scrambling on a warm, sunny day may require delicate roped climbing in wet weather. A good rule to follow is, "when in doubt, belay!"

XI. North Ridge of Mount McArthur, St. Elias Range. (Franz Mohling)

XII. Mount Index, Cascade Mountains. (Thomas Miller)

11 *

PITONCRAFT AND RAPPELS

Above a certain level of difficulty the rope alone is inadequate protection against falls and anchors must be employed to safeguard the leader, thus distinguishing Class Five climbing from the lower orders described in the two foregoing chapters.

When the rock becomes still steeper or smoother, hands and feet cannot attach the climber securely to the mountain and for further progress the ingenious techniques of Class Six climbing are required. In ordinary terminology both classes are often lumped together under the general name of "high-angle rock," the terrain where pitoncraft and rappels are most frequently used.

The Tools

ROPES

Specialists in high-angle rock usually prefer a 150-foot rather than a 120-foot climbing rope (see Chapter 9) for convenience in longer leads, for additional margin in application of the dynamic belay, and for longer rappels. On extended climbs of sustained difficulty a second 150-foot rope of $\frac{5}{16}$-inch Goldline or 8mm Perlon is sometimes carried to aid in rappels or to reduce the friction of a single climbing rope. Smaller diameters are occasionally adequate but the climber must not be tempted by lighter weight into forgetting the *useful* strength of a rope—meaning the strength when knotted, weathered, frayed, or cut by a falling stone. Synthetic ropes are better than manila because of their greater strength.

Slings, customarily made of ¼-inch rope or various sizes of nylon webbing, are used in a number of ways, such as in prusiking, tying into anchors for belaying or rappelling, making *runners* (slings in single or double loops, used in place of carabiner chains and for anchors over rock nubbins), rappelling, and repairing equipment. Dacron sling rope is preferable to Goldline since it does not have to be under tension to provide a tight anchor. Manila is less strong than synthetics but is cheaper and does not melt under friction. Webbing has the advantage over rope in not unraveling as readily when cut.

Table 9. Strength and Weight of Various Ropes.*

Diameter	Net Weight of 100 Feet (Pounds)		Tensile Strength (Pounds)		
	Manila	Goldline	Manila	Goldline	Perlon
³⁄₁₆-inch	1.47	0.94	450	1100	—
6mm	—	—	—	—	1980
¼-inch	1.96	1.70	600	1750	—
⁵⁄₁₆-inch	2.84	2.60	1000	2850	—
8mm	—	—	—	—	3080
³⁄₈-inch	4.02	3.80	1350	3800	—
9mm	—	—	—	—	3960
10mm	—	—	—	—	4950
11mm	—	—	—	—	5940
⁷⁄₁₆-inch	5.15	5.40	1750	5200	—

For useful or efficient strength, divide by two when knotted; similarly assume lower values when weathered, abraded, or cut.
Manila figures are for three-strand medium.
Goldline figures are for three-strand mountain-climbing lay except for ³⁄₁₆-inch, which is regular lay.
Goldline and Perlon data are not exactly comparable, due to different testing methods by the various manufacturers.
Source: Recreational Equipment Inc., Seattle, 1967 catalogue.
* *For somewhat different data see Table 7 in Chapter 9.*

Stirrups, whose use is discussed later, are fashioned from 1-inch synthetic webbing. When it is known in advance the proposed ascent involves considerable aid climbing, stirrups may be made ahead of time, but generally they are tied on the climb as needed. The stirrups can easily be undone and the webbing used for other purposes.

In order to climb relatively weight-free on difficult rock, the lead man usually climbs without his pack and hauls it up after completing the pitch. For this purpose and also for retrieving the rappel rope and tossing lines over projections, a party often carries a *hauling line,* or *reepschnur.* Dimensions vary widely but 100 feet of ⅛-inch synthetic cord is satisfactory for most uses. For pack-hauling a ¼-inch or larger line is easier on the hands.

To save time on multi-day, high-angle rock ascents, the lead man climbs with an extra climbing rope tied to his waist. After he reaches his high point he fixes the extra rope and then belays his second, who removes the hardware; at the same time the third climber prusiks up the fixed line, hauling the packs a few feet behind him.

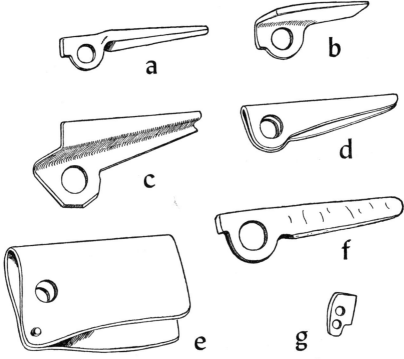

Fig. 51. Representative types of pitons.
    a. Knifeblade with centered eye.   d. Angle.
    b. Knifeblade with offset eye.   e. Bong.
    c. Z-section.   f. Vertical.
                                      g. RURP, or crack-tack.

PITONS

Pitons, or pins, are metal spikes designed for insertion into rock crevices. Sizes vary from the tiny *"crack-tack"* or *"rurp"* (Realization of Ultimate Reality Piton) for very small cracks to giant *"bong-bong"* angle pitons 4 inches or more in width.

The *offset-eye* piton and its variants are perhaps the most used. The *angle* or *Z-section* piton is valuable for its holding power in all kinds of rock. Of the older designs, many *horizontals* continue to have utility but the once-popular *vertical* is now seldom employed. Bong-

bongs up to 6 inches in width can be used in cracks too small for stemming or jamming yet too wide for ordinary pitons.

The number of pitons carried by a party depends entirely on the terrain. Even if it is expected that only one short pitch on the route will be Class Five, a variety of pitons is needed to fit whatever cracks may be available. One angle, one horizontal with a long blade, and one knifeblade might be considered an emergency selection. When a substantial amount of high-angle rock is anticipated, the arsenal required may be 35 or 40 pitons in a number of sizes and shapes, with angles and horizontals predominant.

The recent major advances in pitoncraft come partly from new designs but also from improved metallurgy. The soft iron of decades and generations past has been largely replaced by a chromium molybdenum steel alloy; *"chrome-moly"* pitons are now used almost exclusively by American rock experts, being harder and more durable and having a more reliable spring action than the old-style malleable pins.

CARABINERS AND DESCENDING RINGS

The carabiner, or snaplink, is used to connect the climbing rope to a piton and furnish a smooth running surface for the rope. The most popular is an *aluminum oval* which is light, corrosion-resistant, and has a consistent strength of about 2500 pounds. A *safety* carabiner has a knurled collar which screws over the gate to keep it securely closed; for most purposes screwing and unscrewing the collar is too time-consuming, and therefore the safety design is practical only for rappelling, roping up, or connections where an added margin of safety is desired. Carabiners vary greatly in strength depending on the manufacturer. The stock of any American climbing outfitter can be trusted but it is well to check each individual carabiner before purchase, looking for flaws in the metal and making sure the gate opens easily and closes snugly.

A strip of colored plastic ("mystic tape") may be wrapped just below the gate. The tape serves to readily distinguish gate from hinge, thus expediting snapping into a piton. It also makes clear whether the snaplink has been placed in the proper position, as described below.

Descending rings, circles of iron or aluminum about 1½ inches in diameter, provide a smooth surface for the rope in such instances as setting up a rappel. Being inexpensive they can be abandoned on the mountain without financial pangs, unlike carabiners. Aluminum rings, which cost more than iron but weigh less, have a consistent strength of about 2800 pounds.

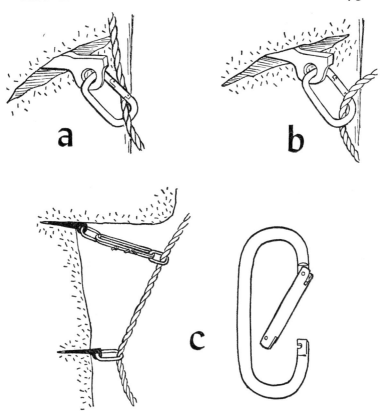

Fig. 52. Carabiners.
    a. Snapping in, wrong.
    b. Snapping in, right.
    c. Carabiner use with runners (loops of
       nylon webbing, tied with water knot).

PITON HAMMERS

Piton hammers with wooden handles or of all-metal construction are available. A fairly-light hammer helps hold down pack weight when only occasional use is planned. If extensive piton- or bolt-driving is expected, a heavier hammer, probably of all-metal chrome-moly steel construction, may be a good choice. To free the hands for climbing, the hammer should have a cord inserted in the handle so that it can be hung from the body. Some climbers tie the cord to their swami belts (see below) while others dangle it from their necks.

A *piton catcher,* a small clip snapped into the piton eye and tied to the body by a string, saves both money and temper.

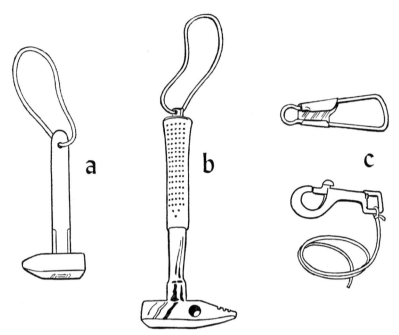

Fig. 53. a. Piton hammer, wooden handle.
           b. Piton hammer, metal handle.
           c. Piton catchers.

BOLTS

A piton can be placed only in a crack. A bolt can be inserted into any reasonably-sound rock, but requires more time and remains permanently in the mountain. Unfortunately, novices who have not mastered the intricacies of pitons have a tendency to "bolt up" and thereby downgrade routes that can be done with pitons or even free by more-skilled climbers. The accepted use for bolts is to provide safe anchors where other types are absolutely unfeasible.

A *bolt kit* includes several drills, one drillholder, one drift (wedge for removing drill from holder), several bolts with hangers (see below), a piece of rubber tubing for blowing dust from the bottom of the hole, and a small carborundum stone for sharpening drills.

The best bolt currently available for hard rock, such as granite, is the *Rawldrive,* whose flanged center section squeezes together when driven into the hole; a ¼-inch bolt, 1½ inches long, is most commonly used. For softer rocks, such as sandstone, the best bolt is the *Star Dryvin,* which resembles a nail and is driven into the sleeve with a hammer; recommended dimensions are a ⅜-inch diameter and a length of up to 3 inches. The *Phillips* bolt drills its own hole as hammered, carrying along a sleeve that later is used to fix the bolt by screwing; tests have indicated ample strength, but in hard rock the bolt tends to lose its cutting edge prematurely.

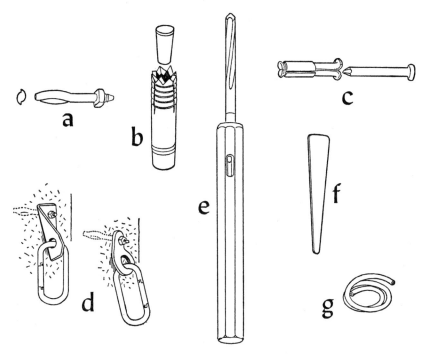

Fig. 54. Bolts.
       a. Stud-type Rawldrive bolt.
       b. Phillips bolt.
       c. Star Dryvin bolt.
       d. Hangers.
       e. Drill and holder.
       f. Drift.
       g. Rubber tubing.

Various designs of *hangers* are available; the offset type applies less leverage on the bolt and thus is by far the most efficient. Bolts remain permanently in the rock and it is therefore good practice to leave hangers in place for the convenience of others following the same route. Many climbers use nutless bolts so the hanger will be sure to remain for those who may not have available the right-size hanger or nut.

SPECIAL GEAR

Improved pitons and methods of placement have radically altered the techniques of high-angle rock climbing. Together with these, other new tools—principally developed in Yosemite Valley—have made multi-day ascents possible with a minimum of gear.

A *swami belt* is a 20- to 30-foot length of 1-inch nylon webbing tied in any number of ways around the waist, thighs, chest, and shoulders to distribute the shock of a fall over a wide area and to facilitate rope-handling in direct aid and rappelling.

A *hero loop*, a length of ½-inch nylon webbing tied in a circle ranging in diameter from 4 to 10 inches or more, is used to reduce the leverage on a single piton or distribute the load on a cluster of pitons that cannot be driven far enough into a crack to be solidly placed. Hero loops are permanently tied into crack-tacks and rurps, whose eyes are too small for carabiners. Most high-angle climbers carry several loops in their pockets, readily at hand for quick use.

Fifi hooks, three-quarter circles of aluminum, are hung on stirrups, which can then be retrieved with a light cord when out of arm reach.

Slings are used in addition to runners, depending on the resource-fulness of the climber, for direct aid on knobs or flakes and to distribute the stress equally on shaky pins.

The customary way to *carry hardware* is on a piece of sling webbing hung over one shoulder and under the opposite armpit. Carabiners are snapped into the sling and pitons hung from the carabiners, preferably with only one or two pitons on each carabiner, but in any event few enough so that the gates can easily be opened. Lightweight wire-type piton catchers, one or two pitons to the catcher, are often used rather than carabiners. Special piton carriers, holding a number of pitons together, are generally less convenient.

HEAD PROTECTION

The *hard hat* or *helmet* (see Chapter 1) is strongly recommended on any lengthy high-angle rock ascent, to protect the head both from falling ice and rock and also from possible injuries when the climber himself falls. The hard hat does not merely act as a barrier between the rock (or ice) and skull, but is also designed to break under a severe impact and thus further cushion the blow. The chinstrap should always remain secured. So numerous are the documented instances of hard hats preventing severe skull or neck injuries that the encumbrance is well worth the trouble.

Anchor Points

On many occasions a climber desires a secure connection between himself and the mountain. Convenient anchors (trees, shrubs, boulders, and rock knobs) may be provided by the mountain. The reliability of such points is often uncertain but common sense fortified by experience generally develops sound judgment. When nature has been niggardly the climber must install artificial anchors—pitons or bolts.

DRIVING AND REMOVING PITONS

The first step in placing a piton is choosing the proper piton for the available crack. In an ideal fit, about half the piton's length can be pushed easily into the crack by hand. The eye should not be driven against the rock surface, since this loosens the piton; the same thing happens if the tip hits the bottom of the crack ("bottoms"). Ideally the pin eye should be just flush with the rock.

Table 10. Holding Strength of Pitons in Hard Volcanic Rock (in Pounds).

	Direction of Line of Pull		
	Perpendicular		*Straight*
Type of Piton	*To Crack*	*Along Crack*	*Out*
Z-section	2450–4250	Not available (NA)	NA
1-inch angle	Over 5000	NA	NA
3-inch bong	Over 4900	NA	NA
Medium-size knifeblade with offset eye	500–4250	NA	NA
Medium-size knifeblade with centered eye	600–4600	2550	950–1150
Vertical	NA	3450–4550	NA

Source: L. J. *Griffin*, The Holding Power of Pitons in Rock, *October 1965.*
Note: The variations in strength of the placed pitons are due to the wide variety of metals in the various pitons (both American and European) and the different configurations of the cracks used.

Perfectly-happy marriages of piton and crack are rare. Moreover, it is not always possible to know in advance of a severe strain exactly how securely the two are joined. Anchor pins should emit a high ring, the best indication of soundness. Figure 55 illustrates various pitons in place, showing relatively good and bad positions. Such information is useful guidance, but developing an ability to predict piton dependability requires years of knocking them in and out. Every piton should be tested by tapping it sideways along the line of the crack. Such tests tell little about how a piton will behave under great stress but at least exclude it from use if very insecure.

However strong the metal of the piton or however firmly inserted into a crack it may be, if the rock is loose or brittle not much protection can be expected. The firmest rock available should be chosen and the

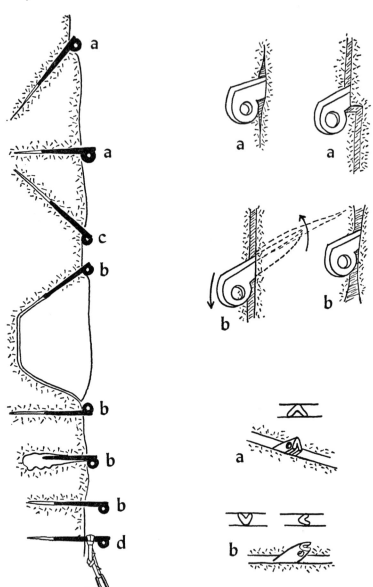

Fig. 55. Pitons in various cracks.
    a. Good.
    b. Bad.
    c. Good only if hard to drive.
    d. Piton tied off with hero loop—used only in Class Six climbing.

walls of the crack observed carefully during driving to see if the piton
is shattering or weakening the rock—or perhaps even wedging off a
huge flake from the cliff. In extreme cases any attempt to clear away
loose surface debris to find a firm crack may result merely in digging a
cave, and about all the climber can do is place a number of pitons and
attempt to distribute the load equally among them. Increasingly-
ingenious methods of piton placement have permitted anchor points
where normal piton placement is not possible. "Backing-up," the
placement of two or more pitons together in unreliable, bottoming
cracks, has developed into an exacting craft. Old-fashioned malleable
pitons are sometimes cut off at varying lengths from the eye for use in
shallow cracks. These are referred to as "trick pins."

Anecdotes abound of climbers who have gained some progress up a
wall on a teetering chain of weakly-placed ironware, fallen, and during
their descent been accompanied by the pong-pong-pong of pitons
flipping into space. It is strongly recommended that the neophyte practice piton placement on some out-of-the-way boulder rather than
trying to learn the craft high on an exposed wall.

In heavily-traveled mountains the climber often finds old pitons in
place. During an earlier era, these were clear evidence that a group of
wealthy men had passed through, and friends of the unspoiled wilderness considered it a point of honor to remove not only their own pitons
but also those left by rich, thoughtless predecessors; in the process they
became quite unpopular in ranges where the high-traffic tours were so
thoroughly catalogued that each particle of iron was listed in the books
or memorized by the guides. With all due respect to the clean-
mountain men of years past, the new rule is that local ironware
customs must always be learned and respected. Very large and/or
cemented-in pitons placed by guides should not be tampered with.
Also, permanent pitons are becoming standard features on many
strictly-amateur routes in some ranges, and if every climber were to
hammer them about and reset them the cracks would soon be destroyed. However, any anchors found in place—pitons or bolts—must
be distrusted, for they may have been loosened by surface rusting or
frostwedging; in any event iron loses its ductility with time and under
stress in a crack can become very brittle. Certainly any such anchor
must be tested with a tug of the rope and a tap of the hammer before
being given even limited confidence.

A piton is removed by hammering it back and forth as far as possible
along the axis of the crack, sometimes employing a larger piton as a
wedge or punch. Frequently a stubborn pin, especially an angle, yields
if the hammering is accompanied by an outward pull. The responsibility of removing pitons lies with the last man, who follows up the route

and "cleans the pitch" quickly and efficiently, an art sometimes as exacting as that of placing the pins. The experienced leader is careful neither to overdrive a piton, making it unduly difficult for his second to remove, nor to place a piton in a corner where its removal becomes next to impossible.

PLACING BOLTS

Pitons of modern metal alloys and of improved designs, and the methods developed for using them, have enormously reduced the need for expansion bolts. Nevertheless, since there are times when a bolt may alleviate a critical situation, the high-angle climber should know the techniques for their rapid and safe placement. However, bolts should always be used with great discretion.

A hole is made by slipping a drill into the drillholder, which is very slowly rotated with one hand while hammered with rapid, moderate blows. Speed in drilling depends on the hardness of the rock, weight of the hammer, and ambition of the driller. When finished the hole must be deep enough so that the bolt will *not* reach all the way to the end, in which case its inward progress will be stopped before it has a chance to tighten against the walls of the hole, or the hole itself may become dangerously enlarged by the rebound of the bolt hitting the bottom.

Class Five Climbing

By definition, Class Five climbing means the rock is so difficult or exposed that the leader on a pitch needs more protection than afforded by a belay some distance below. It is useful to think in terms of *points of protection,* places where the rope connects the climber to the mountain. The chief point of protection, in Class Five as in Class Four climbing, is the belay. However, by attaching his rope to anchors as he proceeds upward the leader provides additional points of protection which in effect bring the belay closer to his body. Thus the leader need no longer judge the danger of a fall by his distance from the belayer, but by his distance from the last anchor.

Changes in technique are made necessary in moving upward to Class Five climbing. Routefinding is so modified by availability of anchor points that the leader may choose a course with good piton cracks even though holds are scarcer than elsewhere. The belayer aims his stance upward, ties his belay anchor below him rather than above, and, because of the tremendous increase in rope friction when passing through several carabiners, must be prepared to give a dynamic belay.

Often the leader can find a good point of protection merely by running the climbing rope above a tree or a rock nubbin; rock flakes should be avoided since the rope may jam during a fall, causing a completely-static belay. When it is necessary to reduce rope friction, the leader ties a runner around a tree or rock, attaching the rope to the runner with a carabiner.

PITONS FOR SAFETY

As the climber soon discovers, it is one thing to experiment with pitons on a practice boulder and quite another to use them effectively in Class Five climbing high on a precipice. Charlie Chaplin and the Keystone Cops together are less comical than a team of novices tangled up in pitons, carabiners, ropes, and steep rock. With practice, however, use of hardware becomes smooth and efficient and vastly extends the frontier of safe climbing.

One of the major problems is that of maintaining balance while driving a piton—which is being driven specifically because balance is difficult to maintain. The wise climber places the piton before it is absolutely needed, while he is still in good balance. Even if his last solid stand is some distance from the ticklish pitch, it is well to have a piton there to give protection while placing another closer to the point of actual need.

After the piton is placed and tested the carabiner is snapped in and *flipped over* so that the catch *is down and away from the rock*, to prevent the gate from being opened by pressure against the rock. Insertion of the rope into the carabiner is the most confusing aspect of the whole business. The aim is to provide the rope with the *straightest possible path between the belayer and the leader* in his advance beyond the carabiner. Overhangs or other obstructions may require the leader to use more than one carabiner, or a runner, to bring the climbing rope away from the rock into a smooth, friction-free path.

If there is a middleman on the rope and the route is straight up, he leaves the pitons and carabiners in place as he climbs by, usually merely unsnapping the climbing rope from them. However, if the leader has made a traverse and at his stopping point is off to one side of the middleman, the third man on the rope may be in a better position to belay the middleman, who thus unsnaps the rope in front of him from the carabiner and snaps in again with the rope that connects him to the third man. If balance is very delicate at this point, he may first snap in the rope leading to the third man, and then unsnap the rope in front.

The last man usually removes the hardware as he climbs. Conversations between the piton-placer and the piton-remover are frequently interesting and instructive. The leader is amused at the grunts and curses of his companion sweating to knock out the iron pounded in with such passionate energy—but somewhat disquieted by the chuckles of his friend who has drawn out with his fingers a piton the leader had suffered agonies to place and trusted with all his heart.

Class Six Climbing: Direct Aid

By definition, Class Six climbing means the mountain has not provided sufficient holds and blank sections of the route must be filled in by artificial devices of one kind or another. Some of these *direct aid* techniques are as old as mountaineering; others are inventions of the recent decades which have seen "rock engineering" advanced by its practitioners to the status of an independent sport which may be enjoyed wherever there is steep rock, and when translated to the mountains has made incredible ascents possible.

BODY HOLDS

An easy introduction to "aid climbing" is the ancient and honorable boost from a companion. Perhaps the leader needs only the pressure of his second's hand against boot to make a slippery foothold solid. Possibly the second can be even more creative by offering as a foothold his cupped hands or his thigh.

Fig. 56. Shoulder stand.

The *shoulder stand* frequently gives a quick lift over a flawless bit of cliff, the leader first stepping into the cupped hands of his second, then onto his shoulder and finally onto the rock. The technique causes the second great pain, regretted by both parties; it also forms an unstable human tower that often must be anchored by tying the second to the rock. Even more complex uses of human holds are described in the literature, including pyramids of climbers with three men at the bottom, tapering to the leader at the top. Circus acrobats could doubtless suggest still further possibilities.

TENSION

The most elementary use of hardware for direct aid is driving a piton to supply a hold, perhaps clipping in a carabiner if the hold is for the hand. On rock of low angle where the climber is able to stand in balance, such artificial holds often are a quick way over a difficulty.

When natural holds are almost totally absent or the rock is so steep balance cannot be maintained, hardware can be employed—but rarely is anymore—for tension technique. In the simplest case the leader drives a piton or bolt, snaps in his climbing rope, and calls for tension on the rope by his belayer. He then leans back into space, bracing his feet against the cliff. Being held securely, his hands are free to reach for good holds above or to drive a higher piton. The transfer from one piton to another is a delicate process, the climber tightly grasping his climbing rope on both sides of the lower piton, then calling for slack, snapping his rope into the higher piton, calling for tension, unsnapping from the lower piton, and stemming up to his new position. Such unadorned tension climbing is extremely strenuous and nowadays is virtually never used by experts and only then for very short passages on a route that otherwise is Class Five or lower.

STIRRUPS

Long Class Six leads are rendered much more convenient by stirrups, the short webbing or rope ladders described earlier. Since both stirrup and climbing rope are attached to the same anchor, it is desirable to avoid rope tangling by using three carabiners: one snapped into the stirrup, a second into a climbing rope, and both of these into the third which is snapped to the anchor.

Stirrups can be used in combination with tension. Held to the anchor by the climbing rope under tension from the belay, the leader climbs the rungs of his stirrup—which serve as holds for both hands and feet. From his stance in the topmost rung he places a higher anchor, another stirrup, and again transfers his climbing rope upward. To ease the strain on the belayer, the leader often ties into his top anchor with a carabiner or runner while working on the next piton.

TWO-ROPE TECHNIQUE

Two-rope technique was at one time considered the most efficient way to eliminate rope friction on a long lead of overhanging or high-

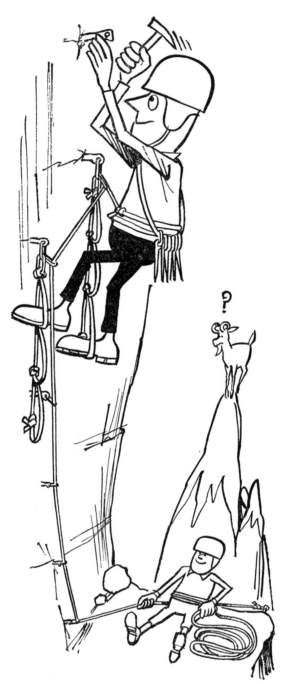

Fig. 57. Direct aid using stirrups.

angle rock, but advances in piton placement and the use of runners have eliminated the need for a second rope. The main use currently is as a training device to familiarize the student with rope management and high-angle technical work.

The principle is very simple: the leader is tied into two ropes and builds two independent lines of connection to the mountain, protected by one line while transferring to the other. The leader drives a piton for his left line as high as he can reach, and to this anchor snaps in both a stirrup and his left-hand climbing rope. Calling for tension on this rope, he climbs the stirrup and places an anchor on the right, and thus continues upward.

A modified use of two-rope technique remains common. The leader climbs the first part of a lead using only one of the ropes. He then snaps the freehanging rope into his highest anchor, divests himself of the first rope by tying it to an anchor, and continues the lead with the second rope, which has not accumulated carabiner friction.

TENSION TRAVERSES

A *pendulum traverse* can be used to make horizontal progress over a holdless portion of rock, but only if several conditions are met. First, it must be possible to climb above the holdless portion and place an anchor from which the leader can pendulum. Second, the distance to be traversed must be reasonable in relation to the height of the anchor pin. Third, on the far side there must be a landing platform or holds easily grasped. If the traverse is over a somewhat-broken slab of moderate angle, the climber employs a sort of stemming technique, pushing with his feet and leaning back against the rope, his belayer letting out slack through the anchor. On very smooth or steep rock a true pendulum swing may work better, the leader first climbing to a point somewhat higher than his landing place, then casting off into space, perhaps kicking at the wall to gain additional momentum. When the traverse is under an overhang and the climber hangs free in space, it may be necessary to swing back and forth several times, gradually building up momentum. A pendulum traverse of any distance is seldom used in climbing, but sometimes is necessary in rescues to evacuate an injured person.

The *Tyrolean traverse* is a means of crossing a deep chasm on a rope anchored at both ends. Though a venerable mountaineering tradition, the technique is seldom practical. One use is in climbing an isolated pinnacle whose summit level can be closely approached on a nearby peak. If the far base of the pinnacle can be reached, a line is thrown over the top and anchored at both ends. Otherwise the summit of the pinnacle must be lassoed, an amusing way to spend a summer day.

Other theoretical applications are in crossing a river, a gorge, crevasse, or a deep notch in a ridge, where it is possible to climb down to the gap and up the far wall but so difficult it is faster for all but the first member of the party to cross on a rope.

Fig. 58. Pendulum traverse.

There are several ways to accomplish the horizontal traverse. In the one illustrated the climber hangs below the rope suspended by his hands and hooked knees, protected by a carabiner snapped into both

Fig. 59. Tyrolean traverse.

the rope and his waistloop. In another—and by some thought much better—the climber lies prone atop the rope, one leg dangling below to provide stability, the other hooked over the rope, his arms extended forward. In both, progress is made by pulling with the arms and kicking with the legs. In a third technique the climber sits comfortably in a "cable car" made of sling rope and tied to a carabiner which slides on the traverse rope.

The Tyrolean traverse creates tremendous stresses in the horizontally-suspended rope and for this reason synthetic is preferred despite the disadvantage of its elasticity. To reduce strain the rope should never be stretched perfectly taut, nor should it ever be tightened to take up slack that develops in use. Again, the most frequent use of this technique is in rescue work.

PRUSIK ASCENTS

The use of prusik or similar knots to climb an anchored line, described in Chapter 19 as a technique for crevasse rescue, has numerous applications on Class Six rock. One is where a leader has climbed an aid pitch and lowers a rope for his companions to climb with prusik knots. Often a better alternative to tension traversing is rappelling to the bottom of the chasm and prusiking up the opposite wall. Finally, sometimes a summit block is so steep and flawless that its ascent by bolts would be interminable. Lassoing may be attempted but it is preferable, if possible, to toss a light line weighted with pitons or rocks over the summit, using it to pull into position a stouter rope which is then anchored.

Several rope-ascending methods are possible. The prusik knot is described and illustrated in Chapter 9. Reliable mechanical devices, such as the commercially-available Jumar, are great time-savers where long rope ascents are involved.

SIEGE CLIMBING

Some of the most notable ascents of recent years have been made on Class Five and Six precipices too long to be climbed in a single day, requiring a party literally to besiege the peak. Traditionally it is customary to bivouac on the route, at or near the highest point attained by a day's efforts, often hanging from hardware or perched on minute ledges. Such bivouacs are not practical during certain months of the year or in areas particularly vulnerable to storms, so parties often retreat each day, leaving fixed lines. The previous high point is regained by prusiking up the fixed rappel lines. On long face climbs the daily descents and re-ascents require so much time that eventually the fixed lines are given up and a final assault is made, usually requiring one or more bivouacs until the summit is gained. Whenever it is practical to do so, experienced climbers always climb straight through rather than leaving fixed ropes; in some areas, indeed, the leaving of fixed ropes for a subsequent continuation of the ascent is considered unethical.

Descending High-Angle Rock: Rappelling

The human body is better designed for climbing up than down, and thus a pitch that is Class Four or Five on the ascent may become Class Six on the descent. Simplest and fastest of all Class Six descending techniques is rappelling (French), abseiling (German), or roping down (English).

Those whose knowledge of mountaineering is gained solely from popular magazines almost invariably believe that climbers spend most of their alpine vacations flinging themselves downward through space. Climbers' photograph albums do not disenchant the lay public, for rappelling is a photogenic technique. Though superficially spectacular, rappelling is childishly simple, consisting merely of sliding down a doubled fixed rope which is then retrieved by pulling on one end.

The novice goes out of his way to rappel, both to avoid climbing down and to be photographically immortalized in poses that will astound his non-mountaineering friends. The experienced climber takes another view. Having learned the pleasures of climbing down he considers rappelling a dull routine that deprives him of stimulating technical problems, or even as a refusal to accept challenges. Moreover, he knows that those who rappel to excess never learn to climb down, leaving a dangerous gap in their training; on traversing descents or over loose rock, rappels are impossible, and sometimes the time required to engineer a dependable anchor may be much greater than that needed simply to climb down Finally he is aware that an alarming proportion of climbing accidents occur during rappelling, which though simple and safe in principle is ordinarily employed on steep and exposed terrain that imparts both the sensational aspect and the latent danger.

Despite such mental reservations, even the enthusiast who takes overweening pride in his down-climbing repeatedly finds it necessary to rappel when the party becomes weary or the weather deteriorates, and rock once Class Three has risen three grades in formidability. Certainly if the ascent was Class Six he has no ethical qualms in adopting what is usually the speediest and easiest method of Class Six descent —rappelling.

RIGGING A RAPPEL

Anchors expected to hold a leader's fall should have a strength, after all deductions for weakening by bends in knots and over carabiners, in the neighborhood of 2000 pounds. Rappel anchors can be considered reasonably safe with a capacity of only 600 pounds, but with so narrow a margin the party must be extremely catlike in descent, since even one sharp jerk may produce an impact-force on the anchor in excess of this strength.

The ideal anchor is a sturdy tree or a rock projection around which the rope can be looped, and with such smooth rounded surfaces that

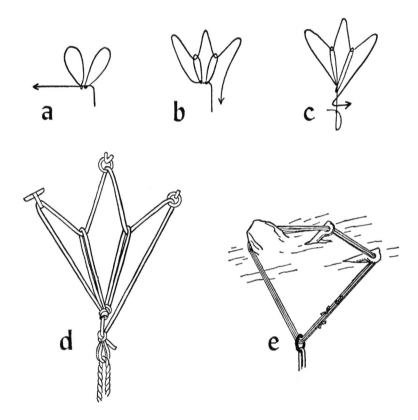

Fig. 60. a, b, c, and d. Steps in rigging a three-piton rappel anchor with sling rope interconnected.

e. Rappel anchor with three separate slings each tied off separately.

the rope will run easily and can be retrieved from below simply by pulling on one end. Usually, however, there are various obstructions, and slings must be used to suspend the rope from the anchor and provide it with a free run. The slings must have cumulatively an efficient strength of at least 600 pounds. The turns of sling rope around an anchor are best joined by a sheet bend, which due to its structure does not come apart so long as one of the turns of rope remains intact. If other knots are used each loop must be separately tied, with care taken that all the individual loops are of the same circumference. One should never be stingy with sling rope.

The 180-degree bend at the anchor produces tremendous friction. To facilitate pulling down the rope it is advisable to thread the slings through a descending ring, through which the rappel rope is in turn threaded, gaining a much smoother running surface. Descending rings are especially useful when two ropes of differing diameters and considerable differences in elasticity are used. In this case the thicker rope will carry more of the weight while the thinner rope is stretching,

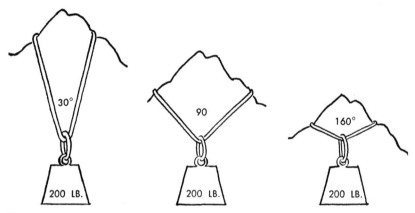

Fig. 61. Importance of slack sling rope, for a 200-pound weight on the sling. If the angle between the ropes is 30° the rope must hold only 103 pounds.   If the angle between the ropes is 90° the rope must hold 141 pounds.   If the angle between the ropes is 160° the rope must hold 575 pounds.

causing the line to slide through the anchor sling. Considerable heat may be produced, enough to sever the sling, if it is not protected by a descending ring.

In the absence of trees or rock projections, the rappel must be from artificial anchors. The questionable dependability of pitons usually leads climbers to place a minimum of two good ones, or at least three dubious ones. Sometimes combinations of natural and artificial anchors can be used, such as a rock knob and a piton, to give doubled protection.

Proper placement of slings around a number of anchors requires careful judgment of their individual value and their values as a group. In the method illustrated in Figure 60-b the three anchors are so tied together that if any one fails the sling system still depends securely on those remaining. It is extremely important to use enough rope to ensure a loosely-hanging sling, something often overlooked by thrifty mountaineers who begrudge every inch of irretrievable rope.

After the anchor has been found or placed, slings and descending ring attached if necessary, the next step is hanging the rappel rope so that it will not snag or fray on sharp edges of rock, and will hang so free from the anchor arrangement that it can be easily retrieved. Once one line of the rappel rope has been passed through the anchor the lines should be thrown down separately to avoid snarling. Each is first coiled, then tossed horizontally into space so the coils have time to straighten out before contacting the rock. It is also important at this time to determine the nature of the rappel route and whether there is a landing point. Rappelling is essentially a straight-line technique,

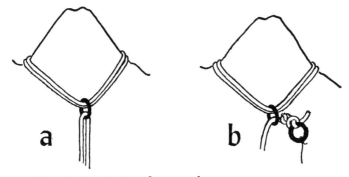

Fig. 62. Retrieving the rappel rope.
a. By pulling on one end of the rappel rope.
b. With reepschnur.

and if there is no stopping point directly below, the party must either find another line of rappel, accept the need for a technique midway between pendulum and rappel, or climb down. If it is impossible to see a landing point, prusik slings must be ready in the event a re-ascent of the rope becomes necessary.

The length of the rappel determines the length of the rope needed. The 150-foot climbing rope can be used for a descent of little more than 60 feet, after deductions for rope wrapped around the body. A party on high-angle rock ordinarily has two such ropes which can be joined to provide a rappel twice as long. If a rope is carried specifically for rappelling, it may be as small as $\frac{5}{16}$-inch in diameter—depending entirely upon the party's calculations of probable requirements. It is well to study Tables 7 and 9.

The rope available which is strong enough to hold a climber in rappel can always be supplemented by carrying a lightweight *reep-*

schnur or *retrieving line*. The rappel rope is first passed through a descending ring dangling from the anchor, then tied to another descending ring, to which the reepschnur is also tied. The climber's weight is held by the full strength of the rappel rope, which is easily retrieved by a pull on the reepschnur.

Retrieving is often troublesome, and all climbers now and then are faced with the nervewracking job of climbing back up to free a snagged line. Proper care in placement of slings and descending rings can reduce the frequency of such problems. Also, to prevent the two halves of the rope from twisting together, each rappeller should keep one finger between the lines while descending or snap a carabiner onto one line and onto a chest loop. The first man down always tests the rope to see if it will pull; the next-to-the-last man repeats the test. Hauling down the rope requires a certain nicety of technique. Usually a slow and steady pull is best to prevent the up-traveling end from flipping around and jamming into cracks. Sometimes, however, it is observed that this loose end is about to settle into a crack and a closely-coordinated jerk must be made to flip it free.

METHODS OF RAPPELLING

A rope can be passed around the human body in innumerable ways to gain friction surface for controlling the rate of descent. As with some other climbing techniques, there are undoubtedly an infinite number of acceptable alternatives, but most climbers use the methods described below, which among them have the versatility to cover any situation.

Dulfersitz

The dulfersitz is the basic method of rappelling, requiring the least special equipment, permitting good control, and being reasonably foolproof. The downhill hand holds the rope on the body, regulating the amount of friction and thus the speed of descent. The uphill hand holds the rope merely to keep the body in balance, and must not clutch tightly or rope burns and fatigue will result—a discovery quickly made by beginners.

The first few feet of any rappel are the most ticklish, since until the rappeller's body is below the anchor his stance is rather unstable. It is best to wrap the rope around the body, then climb down several feet below the anchor. Since rope stretches under load, a rappeller must be especially careful that he does not lean back too far while getting into the rappel; he may suddenly find himself falling out of the wrap due to the unexpected stretching of the line. Once in the rappel the climber braces his feet against the rock and leans out into space so that in effect he is stemming between the rope and the rock wall. Many climbers—particularly when the anchor is dubious—prefer to remain nearly vertical and use such footholds as are available, stemming against the rope only when necessary. However, often the cliff is so smooth the climber must lean well back into space and keep his feet well apart to stay in balance while descending. The leg under which the rope runs should be kept lower than the other to prevent the rope from working up under the knee. Indeed, some climbers use quite an

Fig. 63. Dulfersitz rappel with belay.

exaggerated sideways position for the sake of a better view of the terrain below, and appear almost to be facing downhill.

Slackening the downhill hand's grasp on the rope allows gravity to overcome friction, and as the climber slides he walks down the rock. With a wet rope or clothing, friction may be so great it is necessary to pull upward with the downhill hand to let the rope slide around the body.

Photographs often show "jump rappels," the climber bounding far out into space, sliding many feet down the rope, coming back into the

cliff with sprung knees and bounding out once more. Such rappels are
not only spectacular to watch but frequently spectacular in their consequences. The jerky descent places tremendous strains on the anchor,
which in failure may make the last bound a very long one. Rope burns
are more frequent, and finally the rappeller who in one of his bounds
passes an overhang often gets rather badly battered around the head
and chest when he comes back to the cliff.

Swiss Seat

Friction is needed to control a rappel but in excess can make descent
absolutely impossible. In soaking weather, or on a long or free rappel
with a great weight of rope hanging below the body, the dulfersitz is
frequently difficult and tiring to use, what with the necessity to
laboriously haul the rope upward. In the sling-and-carabiner technique—the Swiss Seat—the rope, instead of wrapping around the leg
as in the dulfersitz, passes through a carabiner snapped to a seat-sling
which is either a simple figure-8 or any of its many variations.

A possible objection to a sling rappel is that there are more things
that can go wrong than with the dulfersitz—more pieces of equipment
that might fail, more possible mistakes in application. The seat sling,
whether made of rope or of more comfortable nylon webbing, must be
at least as strong as the rappel line. For maximum safety either a
carabiner with a safety gate should be used or two regular carabiners
with gates faced in opposite directions.

The greatest danger in a carabiner rappel is that loose ends of the
sling or pieces of clothing may be drawn into the carabiner and foul
the rig. The sling must fit snugly, with knots tied at the side of the
body; parka and shirts must be tucked into the pants. The correct
arrangement of the carabiners and rappel rope is very important. The
carabiners snapped into the seat sling must have the gates *facing up*
and *opening away* from the body.

Carabiner Brakes

The carabiner-wrap and carabiner-brake rappels almost entirely
eliminate body friction. The rappel rope is snapped through the
carabiners and then the *anchor end* of the rope is given two wraps
through the carabiner. If the free-hanging end is looped, the rope will
work its way over and out of the aluminum gates—a very good reason
for using a safety carabiner with a locking gate. The complexities of a
carabiner wrap may be avoided by using a commercially-produced
brake bar across the carabiner; the rope merely slides over the bar with
a minimum of bends.

Being utterly painless, these techniques are considered by some
climbers the only enjoyable ways to rappel. However, the pleasure is
gained at the expense of complexity. Again, there are more pieces of

equipment to fail, and the sharp bends required of the climbing rope greatly reduce its strength, and may weaken it permanently. All in all, when the temperature is low and the wind is high, the snow is driving

Fig. 64. Various rappels.
    a. Arm rappel.
    b. Brake bar, with safety sling attached to rappel rope by prusik knot (moved downward by upper hand).
    c. Carabiner wrap (should also be used with safety sling).

and the rope is frozen, and the intellect is clouded by weariness, the dulfersitz has in its simplicity a great advantage.

An important role of carabiner rappels is in rescue. (See Chapter 19.) Any rappel using the body as its braking surface is limited in control by the amount of heat from friction a person can endure. A climber descending with a heavy load, such as an injured companion, simply cannot stand the heat generated in a dulfersitz and must use techniques that transfer the load to carabiners.

Geneva

The Geneva is a simplified dulfersitz. The rope passes over the hip, but then over the forearm rather than the shoulder, and is controlled in the crook of the arm. There is much less friction than in the dulfersitz and safe use is therefore confined to moderate slopes, such as slippery slabs where a fall would not be dangerous but climbing down would be slow and awkward.

Arm Rappel

Similarly limited to moderate slopes, but providing much more control than the Geneva, is the arm rappel. The climber throws both arms back over the rope, wrapping them once around as illustrated. To lessen friction he unwinds his uphill arm. To increase friction, and thus stop, he brings the lower arm across his chest. The technique is tricky to learn since the natural tendency at first is to fall down backwards, but practice quickly gives the knack.

SAFEGUARDING THE RAPPEL

Rope burns, loose rock, and doubtful anchors, as well as failure in technique, are dangers always present in rappelling. Burns can be prevented by turning up the shirt collar, rolling down the sleeves, padding the portions of the body over which the rope runs, and by stopping from time to time in descent to let heat dissipate. Rockfall danger can be minimized if the first man down carefully cleans the route as he goes and if everyone in the party keeps the rope in the same, cleaned area by avoiding excessive whipping-around of the rappel lines. Anchors can be given greater trust if chosen with careful attention to every detail, and by descending slowly and smoothly, putting the feet on holds when available.

In recent years there have been so many rappelling accidents that the supposed theoretical safety of the technique has been called into serious question. First, there are numerous points of possible failure, any one of which can cause a fall. Second, since rappeling is ordinarily done over great exposure a fall is frequently fatal. Judging the technique both theoretically and statistically, experienced climbers feel that the rappeller must be belayed in every possible case. It is quite true that the belay rope lessens the fabled freedom and pleasure of flying down a cliff like a bird—but all too many mountaineers have started a rappel like a bird and concluded like a stone.

A normal precaution on a high-angle or overhanging rappel is to secure oneself to the rope with a prusik sling chest loop as shown in Figure 64-b. The prusik knot is slipped downward in progress with the upper hand, but should the knot be released it holds the climber fixed to the rope. To prevent an accidental rappel off the end of the rope, a knot should be tied close to the end of each line.

PART THREE

Snow and Ice Climbing

XIII. Mount Logan, St. Elias Range. (Thomas Miller)

XIV. Mount Olympus from Queets Basin, Olympic Mountains. (Charles Allyn)

12 *

SNOW

Iт is not possible to become a snow mountaineer in one season, no matter how intensive the climbing schedule. One quickly learns that the snow of April is but a distant cousin to the snow of August, that the grim flutings of a northern precipice bear not the vaguest resemblance to the slushy crystals on the southern benches, that the same snowfield may be transformed from a fine frozen highway at dawn to a bottomless bog in the afternoon and to a sheet of ice moments after sunset. In one season a climber can learn much, and be conditioned to learn more, but he cannot learn all; the repertoire of snow is too large for all its tricks to be encountered in one year—or in ten.

The substance with the chemical symbol H_2O and the various forms of water, snow, ice, and clouds is too fickle for easy, systematic study. Fundamental to understanding of snow is Chapter 21 with its laboratory outlook; another way to consider snow is from the rough empirical standpoint of climbing technique. For ease of presentation the term *snow* is reserved in the present context for slopes that are neither very hard nor very steep. *Ice,* treated in Chapter 13, encompasses slopes that are hard and/or steep and thus demand a more complex approach. *Glaciers,* the subject of Chapter 14, are almost entirely composed of snow and ice but have some peculiar characteristics, most notably crevasses. Finally—and again for the sake of expedience—throughout these three chapters it will be assumed that the climber never falls; *arrests and belays* are separately considered in Chapter 15.

Selecting the Route

The wise mountaineer begins routefinding long before approaching the peak—starting indeed with observations made during winter. If snowfall has been exceptionally heavy he will postpone a normal "June" climb to July. If the winter has been very mild he will do a "May" climb in April. Sometimes even more specific predictions can be made. For instance, a prolonged thaw in late winter followed by a cold snowy spring spells caution; weeks or months later the thaw's thick crust may hold a heavy load of spring snow poised to avalanche. Finally and quite obviously, the weather and temperature during the ascent and on the days immediately preceding are of the highest importance.

Routefinding on snow is doubly complicated. On the one hand there is the quest for easy walking; on the other the desire to avoid avalanches and collapsing cornices. Choice is particularly excruciating when ease and security are mutually exclusive.

GOOD WALKING

Spring

Snow is considered excellent if the climber can stand on or near the surface, only fair if he sinks to his calves; when immersion is kneedeep or greater it is good only for building character. The *crusts* discussed in Chapter 21 have a major influence on route selection in winter and spring. *Differential consolidation* is equally important. South and west slopes, bearing the full heat of afternoon sun, consolidate earlier in the season and quicker after storms, offering hard surfaces when east and north slopes are still soft and unstable. Similarly, dirty snow absorbs more heat than clean; slopes darkened by rocks, dust, or uprooted vegetation usually provide relatively-solid footing.

The principles that apply in large apply also to *micro-exposures*. The walking on one side of a ridge or gully, or even on one side of a clump of trees or a large boulder, is often more solid than on the other. When the going is very bad it is well to detour toward any surface with a different appearance and possibly better support. Sometimes unstable and stable crust may be only a foot or two apart, and deep slush only a step from hard ice.

Location of the best and easiest route varies from day to day and hour to hour. In cloudy weather snow conditions are unlikely to change significantly around the clock, but a clear cold night after a hot day suggests an early start to take full advantage of the strong crusts on open slopes. As the sun rises higher the search shifts for shadows where remnants of crust linger, or alternatively for dirty snow. Late on a hot afternoon all crusts have deteriorated and the deep shade of trees and steep cliffs gives the best slopes of a bad lot.

Early-season snowcover is scattered with pitfalls; particular caution is needed in the zone between clear ground and deep snow. As soon as snows fall on a hillside it begins a slow, protracted settling called *creep*, moving away from trees and rocks, forming a fissure below each. New snow may fill the holes, called *moats*—or may merely camouflage them. Later in the season the moat below a large rock or cliff may be as wide and deep and difficult as a crevasse. *Differential melting* both emphasizes and initiates fissures; snow adjacent to objects such as logs, brush, or rocks is likely to be hollow. Since the temperature of the ground is always at or above freezing, extensive melting often occurs at the ground-snow interface. Snow surrounding trees and rocks is suspect. The route should follow either solid snow or solid ground, avoiding the margins; when they must be crossed, light, catlike steps prevent wrenched ankles and broken legs.

Summer

As the months progress into summer, walking conditions become so nearly uniform that the major difference is between the hard surfaces of early morning and the morasses of hot afternoons. In the Cascades, June, in an average year, presents summer snow conditions. By August—again on the average—consolidation is so complete that time of day has little effect. However, new vexations develop. *Suncups* may grow into *névé penitentes* through which travel is a relentless, exhausting grind. Moreover, consolidation is not an unmixed blessing, for on the hard slopes of autumn every foot of the route may require crampons or chopping, and the climber remembers fondly the yielding surfaces of spring in which mere swings of the boot made such superb steps.

AVALANCHE HAZARD

Signs and Tests

For obvious reasons instability is suspected during and after snowfall or prolonged heating by sun or wind, especially on steep slopes.

Little *sunballs* roll spontaneously down a slope during the warming of loose snow and frequently indicate deep instability. A slope actively sunballing, or streaked with tracks, may be dangerous, but on the other hand may be perfectly solid beneath the upper few inches. *Spontaneous surface slides* also can occur on fundamentally-sound slopes, the degree of danger depending on the depth of snow involved. *Surface slides which start from the climber's tracks* cause alarm unnecessarily unless they tend to deepen, involving lower snow layers. If any of these symptoms of instability are encountered and the route leads onto slopes that have had even greater exposure to the sun or are steeper than those being negotiated, the need for increased caution is apparent.

Throwing rocks onto a slope is too localized a test to be sensitive, but allows at least some rough conjectures; if a rock can start even a small avalanche a man can do much better. Indeed, short of mortar bombardment the *best test is the climber himself*. A well-belayed person can find out a good deal by deliberate attempts to avalanche a suspected slope; the belay must obviously be so placed that it cannot be involved if the attempt is successful. It must also be kept in mind that danger can vary within the slope. Only a few feet away from a point proven safe, increased steepness or greater sun exposure or some unknown local condition may be just enough to trigger a slide.

Avoiding Hazard

According to the classic law of avalanches there is least danger on ridges, more on the valley floor, and most on inclined slopes. Even when the entire alpine world is shuddering from the roar of sliding snow the ridges may be safe, though perhaps presenting serrate profiles or cornices that cancel their usefulness. A valley floor is the catchment basin for avalanches. In narrow-floored canyons the danger is obvious, but often equally great on a broad plain surrounded by mountains; there are recorded instances of avalanches sweeping over the flat for more than a mile.

Slides rarely start in dense forest or closely-spaced rock projections on slopes, but such obstructions are little protection when a large avalanche starts from above—witness borne by the shattered trees in avalanche fans and the wide swaths cut through old timber. Downslanting brush and small trees tell plainly their slope is so frequently swept that timber has no chance to grow.

Avalanches usually follow existing channels. Gullies are many times more dangerous than adjacent open slopes, their existence proclaiming them as natural chutes. Furthermore, a slide on any one slope within a gully's drainage system can sweep the entire main channel. By undercutting every tributary on its descent the slide may either pick up bigger loads or leave the tributaries poised and ready to discharge their volleys at the slightest disturbance.

The climber should glance upward frequently along the way. He will thus avoid routes exposed to cornices, snow perched precariously on rock ledges, or masses of icicles. Their collapse could cause a fall which even if it does not immediately overwhelm the party might disturb an otherwise-stable slope.

Passage through Danger

A passage through dangerous terrain is sometimes necessary. Although avalanches have been considered thus far as a menace sweeping down on the climber from above, relatively few victims are claimed by such slides. Most avalanches that involve a climber are triggered by the climber himself, posing the twofold problem of attempting not to disturb a slope, and if unsuccessful in this, of minimizing the consequences.

Whenever possible, the party should *keep above the avalanche danger.* If a ridge route is not feasible and sidehills must be crossed, a doubtful traverse is taken high, at the very top of the slope, leaving most of the dangerous snow below the party. It should be remembered that snow is tautly stretched over protuberances and firmly compressed in hollows—convex slopes are thus more prone to avalanche than concave hollows. For instance, the outer lip of a hillside bench may be perfectly sound while the steep slopes below it are weak with tension.

When the route lies up a questionable slope, general stepkicking practice is modified from the switchbacking described later in the chapter, which undercuts snow, to a path *straight up the fall line.*

The party should be so spaced that *no more than one person can be caught* if the slope avalanches. This depends on the width of the danger area: on a long horizontal traverse the minimum separation might be 100 yards; crossing a narrow gully only one person at a time should be in the exposed channel. The value of the rope on difficult terrain must be balanced against its dangers in case of an avalanche. As discussed in Chapter 19, ropes, packs, skis, and axes drag the climber under the surface and interfere with proper "swimming" motion. The choice between the risks of avalanche and an unprotected fall is not always easy.

Avalanches are not to be trifled with. Any safe alternate route, however much longer, more tiring, and difficult, is preferable to one in doubt. When no safe route of ascent can be found the only sensible procedure is to turn back. If, on the return, descent is cut off by imminent avalanching, the party should sit down and wait for afternoon or evening cold to stabilize the slopes. After shadows cover the snow, time must be allowed for it to freeze and consolidate, since freezing itself sometimes starts a slide. During periods of general danger all travel should be in the morning or evening—or even at night.

Two fallacies are worth noting. One is the belief that established tracks are safe; conditions change quickly and climbers have been killed in footsteps made the day before. The other is the common practice of clearing loose snow before the descent; though safe and practicable on small slopes where the descending party will spend but a very few minutes, further slides can result from undercutting.

There is no expert in the world who can precisely calculate avalanche risk. Any climber who repeatedly approaches the limits of safety is certain to make occasional trespasses into danger zones. The way to become an old experienced climber (except prematurely) is to limit oneself to conservative estimates and to allow a comfortable margin for error.

CORNICE HAZARD

The shape of the ridge crest determines the extent of cornice-building. Generally speaking, a ridge that slopes gently on one side and breaks into an abrupt cliff on the other develops gigantic cornices, whereas a knife-edge ridge or one gentle on both sides has only a tiny one, if any at all. When the physical features are right for cornice-building, wind direction decides their exact location, and since storm winds have definite patterns in any given mountain range, most cornices in the same area face in the same direction. In the mountains of Washington State, for example, most storms blow from the southwest and the majority of cornices therefore overhang on the north and east. Since these same exposures were steepened by past glaciation the ridges are ideally shaped for the purpose. It must be remembered that temporary or local wind deflection can contradict the general pattern. In rare instances cornices are even built one atop the other, facing in opposite directions, the lower one partially destroyed and hidden by later formations.

Approach from Windward

From windward a cornice gives little indication of its presence, appearing as a smooth slope that runs out to meet the sky. Observation of surrounding ridges tells a great deal about the probable frequency, location, and size of cornices in the immediate area, not only on the high divides but on subsidiary ridges, knolls, and boulders. Fracture lines from partial collapse are sometimes visible, either as deep cracks or as slight indentations.

Not every snowy ridge conceals a cornice, but great care must be exercised in finding out whether any particular one does or not. If at all possible a safe vantage point should be found—a rock promontory or tree jutting through the crest—from which the lee side of the ridge is clearly visible. Otherwise the belayed leader approaches the ridge at right angles, probing with his ax and testing his weight. Only when the extent of the overhang has been clearly established should other members of the party join him.

To insure a sufficient margin of safety the party must follow a course along a corniced crest well behind the probable fracture line— sometimes difficult to determine since the line of fracture may extend 30 feet or more back from the lip of the cornice. Moreover, though rocks or trees projecting from the snow suggest safety, if they are the tops of buttresses the ridge joining them may curve far back into bays supporting wide cornices. Many a party has looked back along a ridge and quaked at the sight of its tracks poised over a chasm.

The invitingly-flat highway of the cornice is sometimes followed when the windward slopes of the ridge are fluted with ice or gravely unstable. A cornice may, especially in cold weather, be strong enough to support the party if the climbers step lightly and avoid the edge; after all, the enormous weight of snow suspended in the structure is measured in tons and an additional few hundred pounds can release the cornice only if it is extremely weak. However, cornices are temporary and for a good part of their life *are* weak; expeditionary climbers may be able to justify the risk but certainly a party out for a holiday weekend cannot.

Approach from Leeward

From leeward a cornice is readily apparent, resembling a wave frozen in the act of breaking. At close range the overhang is an awesome spectacle but if the weather is cold enough the climber may forge ahead without fear, trusting the cornice to be a strongly-engineered structure. It is even possible, and often necessary, to force a direct passage while crossing a pass or seeking a summit route on the far side of the ridge. A late-season cornice that is almost completely broken down need cause little concern but earlier in the year the route of approach should be chosen with care, keeping as much as possible among trees or along crests of spurs, away from the line of fall. It is easiest to penetrate an overhang where a rock spur leads toward the summit or where a partial collapse has occurred.

Cutting through a healthy cornice is a task only to be undertaken if the structure is judged strong and solid. The point of least overhang is attacked, with a belayer positioned beyond danger. The leader cuts straight uphill, undermining as little of the mass as possible, preferably standing to one side of the path he is cutting. Once he has surmounted the crest his immediate task is to install a sound belay behind the fracture zone before attempting to bring up his companions.

Climbing

CONSERVATION OF ENERGY

In ordinary walking on sidewalks and paths the foot falls first on the heel, rolls forward, and propels the body ahead with a thrust of the toe. This method wastes valuable energy in snow. In hard snow most of the momentum is expended in slipping and skidding; in soft snow a pit is dug at each step.

On flat or low-angle snow slopes the climber uses the *tramp walk*, leaning forward and falling into each step, the sole coming down flat on the surface and rising flat from the surface, the body tottering from side to side. The flatfooted gain distributes the weight evenly over the snow surface, thereby minimizing the force applied to relatively-weak material but giving maximum friction. The stride is necessarily short and means a slower pace, but here as in the fable the tortoise will get there first.

The principles of wide distribution and gradual transfer of weight become even more important in soft, deep snow. To avoid punching deep wells at every step, the climber (who for any reason happens to be on foot rather than snowshoes or skis) leans forward against the snow, supporting some of his weight with knee, hip, ice ax shaft, arms, or even chest and shoulders. On occasion it may be easier to travel entirely on the knees or by squirming snakelike on the stomach; under such conditions no lengthy ascent can be accomplished. When snow is waist-deep or greater, forward motion can only be gained by a bulldozer approach, smashing a trench with feet, knees, arms, and ice ax. In semi-arctic ranges shovels carried primarily for digging camps out from blizzards help make a way through deep new snow.

On *breakable crust* a shuffling sort of tramp walk may keep the climber consistently on the surface, but if not it is best to deliberately smash through the crust to gain a rhythmic pace.

Wet snow has a tendency to stick to boots, packing under the heel and forming a hard, slick mound. Striking the heel with the spike of the ax usually knocks the *snowball* off. If the condition persists the striking of the boot with the ax may be synchronized with each step.

REST STEP

Tramp walk and rest step are two names for the same thing: a uni-adopt a "dash-and-gasp" pace, trying to rush the objective. This inevitably fails, requiring frequent halts to recuperate. The only sure way to gain the summit is to find a suitable pace that can be maintained, and stay with it.

The rest step, described fully in Chapter 4, is the most important form effort patiently expended over a long period of time. The depressing sensation that no progress is being made often tempts beginners to technique of a snow climber and its relaxed machinelike regularity must be practiced to perfection. It is important to remember that the rest step is a coordination of legs, lungs, and state of mind. The upward step, the rest, the breath—these follow a regular sequence, at a tempo that can be maintained without tiring the legs or causing shortness of breath, in a rhythm that ideally could be paced by a metronome. Meanwhile, and often equally important, the climber foils the despair born of monotony and weariness by such spiritual resources as he may possess.

STEPKICKING

In soft snow, pits must be stamped for solid footing. On hard snow the surface is solid enough, but slippery, and level platforms must be kicked. In both cases the step is made by swinging the entire leg—not by pushing the foot alone. In hard snow when one or two blows do not suffice crampons should be put on. (See the following chapter.)

Steps *spaced evenly and rather close together* are easiest to make and easiest to follow in good balance. Often the spacing must be closer than the leader needs for himself, since those following may have shorter legs.

Climbing parties travel in *single file*, letting one man at a time do the work. The physical exertion of the leader is greater than that of any other member of the party, and he is meanwhile constantly on the alert to safeguard those behind him and to choose the best route. The lead should therefore be changed frequently so that no one climber remains in front until exhausted.

The rest of the party members use the same leg-swing as the leader, improving the steps as they climb. The cardinal rule is that the *foot must be kicked into* the step; simply walking on the existing platform does not set the boot securely in position. In compact snow the kick should be somewhat low, skimming off the floor and thus enlarging the step by deepening it. In soft snow it is usually easier to bring the boot down from above, shearing off a layer of snow which strengthens the step.

Etiquette

Climbing is always tiring and sometimes dangerous. A thoughtless climber adds to the weariness, to the exasperation that accompanies weariness, and to the danger. Even when unroped each member of a party is dependent on the consideration of all the other members, and everyone should observe certain simple rules of courtesy.

The leader who has exceptionally long legs or strong ankles and kicks steps useful only for himself is not carrying a fair share of party labor, since the second man must kick new steps. The fellow who breaks out an excessive number of steps should mend his technique—if not to conserve his energy then at least to placate wrathful friends. When a step is broken repairs are, for sake of party rhythm, left to the next man. The stepbreaker should, however, take care to use proper foot-sequence in re-entering the line; those behind do not relish following a person with two left feet. It is unwise to walk in close-order drill. Not only does the man ahead have the unpleasant sensation of hot pursuit but he lacks room to control slips. *Another climber's fall line should always be avoided.* If it is necessary to pass it is done *below* the man ahead. Passing on the uphill side may endanger others in case of a fall and usually fills the steps with snow. Unless each climber maintains a regular pace he breaks the party rhythm. The erratic walker is a nuisance, alternately breathing down the neck of the man ahead and blocking the man behind.

Switchbacking Uphill

Ascending by traverses, which allows body weight to be supported by the entire foot rather than merely the toe, gives the most altitude for the least effort. Therefore when the goal is directly above the climber it is customary to make a zigzag or switchbacking path. There is the additional advantage of alternating strain on feet, ankles, legs, and arms—all of which tire easily on long traverses.

The critical phase of switchbacking is at the point of *changing direction*. If the slope is steep and good balance essential the *pivot is made on the outside foot*. When a climber with the upper slope on his right decides to switchback, he puts his weight on his right (inside) foot and kicks the left (outside) foot directly into the slope. Weight is then transferred entirely onto this toes-in turning step, and the first step is kicked in the opposite direction. The upper slope is now on the left and the right foot has the outside position. The *turning step*, particularly critical since the pivot puts the body temporarily out of balance, is made deeper and wider than others.

Sidehill Gouging

The human body is so constructed as to make stepkicking easier when gaining altitude, but quite often it is necessary to make a long sidehill traverse without any rise in elevation. In this case a different kicking procedure is in order, with the heels rather than the toes taking the lead. During the stride the climber twists his leading leg so that the boot heel strikes the slope first, carrying most of the weight, the toe pointing up and out. As in the plunge step described later in the chapter, the heel makes the platform secure by compacting the snow— which it can do much more efficiently than the toe.

Cutting Steps

Stepcutting is most commonly a technique for ice and is fully discussed in the following chapter, but snow too hard for kicking may also require a modified type of stepcutting if crampons are not being used. If the slope is merely crusted a smashing blow of the ax suffices. Hard, consolidated snow will not smash, and must be cut. Since the pick merely punctures the surface and buries itself, the adze is used with a scraping motion. Should the snow offer too much resistance, a blow that carries the adze into and out of the surface in one shallow arc is the next alternative; a sudden twist on the shaft just before the end of the swing usually breaks out a chunk of snow.

BALANCE: USE OF THE ICE AX

Though all the elements of balance climbing (see Chapter 7) are as important on snow as on rock, vertical stance is particularly so since snow can be made solid only by compression. The temptation to lean

Fig. 65. Three figures on gradually steepening slope.

into the slope is almost irresistible at high angles, yet results only in tearing out steps and pushing the feet off their holds. Methods of holding the ax vary with the terrain. Along trails or gentle slopes it makes a splendid walking stick (see Chapter 4). On steep slopes the ax aids balance and is held ready to check slips and for instant arrest (see Chapter 15).

Balance with the Ax

In ordinary snow climbing only three suspension points are convenient: the two feet and the ax. For vertical position and smooth motion the ax is used either as a cane or in the cross-body position, depending largely on individual preference (experienced climbers disagree, sometimes violently, on which method gives the best balance and greatest security). In a slip the fastest way to stop is to lean on the ax and press the spike into the slope, at the same time shifting body weight to the heels. On steep, soft snow the ax is the best possible anchor since the shaft can penetrate deeper than the feet. If the shaft can be rammed in up to the hilt more support is obtained by grasping the axhead with both hands; if it is only half-buried, one hand grasps the axhead and the other holds onto the shaft next to the surface.

Hanging Onto the Ax

In some mountaineering circles the wrist loop is regarded with derision as an accessory for tourists who have not learned the first commandment of snow climbing: *hang onto the ax*. Other climbers by no means quarrel with the commandment but recognize certain legitimate uses of the loop. All schools of thought agree most emphatically that a climber must learn to hang onto the ax, and not depend on the loop to insure that the ax will hang onto him. Even in a short fall an ax dangling uncontrolled from the wrist can seriously injure the climber. Those who have taken a long ride down a snow slope attached by a short length of strap to a flailing ax are not inclined to repeat the experience, even if they are able.

The loop has several important functions. It frees the hands when needed, as on a *brief rock pitch* amidst a snow climb. On terrain where a dropped ax might be lost and when such loss would be disastrous, as on *long steep slopes* and *among crevasses,* the loop is excellent insurance. *It should never be used except under these circumstances.*

Descending

The route down is sometimes quite different from the route up. By afternoon the upward path may be so subject to avalanching that a steep or circuitous way down on rock is best. Terrain suitable for uphill climbing is often poor for descending, such as icy surfaces that make for good cramponing but poor glissading. Route variations may range from going down a different side of the mountain, which may be hazardous if the terrain is unfamiliar, to moving a few feet from icy shadow onto sun-softened slopes. Snow in good condition is almost the ideal medium for losing altitude rapidly, yielding comfortably under the foot without the jolting shocks that the body must absorb on rock.

Far from increasing the risk, within reasonable limits speed and élan make the footing more secure. Because of these factors and the probability of glissades, snow descents are highly favored.

CLIMBING DOWN STEP BY STEP

When the snow is very steep, speed is the last thing a climber wants. On near-vertical walls it is necessary to face into the slope, cautiously lowering a foot to kick a step with the toes, meanwhile trusting the ax to prevent a slide during the delicate moment when the new step is first entrusted with the climber's full weight. On slopes more moderate, but still too steep or exposed for sliding techniques, the superior facing-out position is adopted, giving better visibility and allowing step-kicking to be done by the heels. The ax, with shaft thrust into the snow at one side and firmly held by both hands, still is the key to security should both feet slip at once.

PLUNGE STEP

As long as a climber keeps his footing the quickest way to check a slip is a reflexive shift of weight onto the heels, or, once a slide has started, by making several short, stiff-legged stomps with the heels. This method is not intended to supersede the ice ax arrest, which must be mastered before a climber can be anything but a liability to himself and the party. However, a flip onto the stomach is not always the best reaction to a slip—the heels can be quicker.

Fig. 66. Plunge step.

The most common use of the heels is in the plunge step, also called "heeling down," a fundamental technique applicable not only on snow but on any similar terrain, such as scree. The ideal plunging surface is a fall-line descent in fairly-soft snow at a moderate angle. From the upper step the climber rolls onto the toe, swinging well forward out into space, and extends a stiff lower leg. The heel of the descending foot strikes the slope with most of the climber's weight behind it, driving as much as several feet through the soft surface, and eventually, by compacting the snow into a hard step, effects a skidding stop. Immediately the body leans to the other side and the opposite leg stiffens for action. The sequence is so rapid that the climber may appear to be running and diving down. The ax held in cross-body position supplies a third balance point when needed. When performed properly the plunge step is a comfortable, rapid means of descent whatever the condition of the snow, and certainly faster and pleasanter than jolting down on hard platforms step by step.

Lunging outward and landing on the heel are essential features of plunge-stepping. Cringing from the outward lunge and leaning back into the slope cause the heel to become, instead of an instrument of compaction, one of destruction. Striking the slope at an acute angle it slices through the surface and out into space, placing the climber in an unpremeditated sitting glissade. On a traversing descent the leg is twisted in midstride—again so that the heel leads.

The angle at which the heel should enter the slope varies with the hardness of the snow: on very soft slopes almost any angle suffices, although if the climber leans too far forward he risks having his leg lodged in a deep well and may sustain a fracture in the next plunge. On hard snow, exactly where the average climber tends to become more conservative, greater abandon is desirable, for the heel will not penetrate the surface unless it has sufficient weight behind it. A timid step causes the boot to skate, again upsetting the climber.

The plunge step must be used with discretion under certain conditions. On hard, steep snow the climber should be familiar with the entire slope and confident he can arrest a fall should it occur. Plunging carelessly in thawing spring snow or among crevasses may well result in compound fractures and difficult rescues. Plunging when roped requires keeping track of companions' progress; progress of the team must necessarily be limited to the speed of the slowest member.

GLISSADE

Face-in Glissade

In descending short slopes too steep for plunge-stepping the face-in or "belly-flop" glissade is faster than kicking or cutting steps. The climber lies prone in arrest position (see Chapter 15), gradually withdrawing the pick from the snow to increase speed, driving it back in to slow down. Once rate of descent is fully controlled he can turn on his side for comfort and greater downhill visibility.

The climber who slips from a step while kicking or cutting down gains momentum before he can contact the slope to make arrest; the face-in glissader is always in arrest position, a very great advantage. Another is speed. Climbing down a bottleneck on the route one by one in a line of steps is agonizingly slow, whereas a controlled slide can bring the entire party down in minutes, perhaps providing the margin between spending the night in a cozy camp or a chill bivouac. Nevertheless the face-in glissade should be used only by experienced climbers with proven skill in the arrest, and even then only on comparatively-short slopes; the technique is tiring to the arms and shoulders and allows quantities of snow to be forced inside the clothing.

The rope complicates this and every other manner of rapid descent. If the condition of the slope is unknown the party must first experiment, sending one man down with an upper belay. If he finds control

Fig. 67. Glissading.
a. Standing—running.
b. Standing—stopping.
c. Sitting.

easy the others can follow, keeping the rope vertically extended at all times. Once all members of the team are underway each watches the others so that all can go into instant arrest if one member seems out of control. Sometimes it is safer to spread the team horizontally across the slope, one man sliding at a time: the two end men go down in sequence, then the middle man, alternation continuing.

Standing Glissade

One of the more graceful methods of alpine travel is the standing glissade. The basic position, similar to that of olden-days skiing, is a semicrouch, leaning back with the knees bent as if sitting in a chair. The legs are spread somewhat for lateral stability and one foot is advanced to anticipate bumps and ruts. For additional stability the spike of the ax can be skimmed along the slope, the shaft held alongside the knee in the arrest grasp, the pick pointing down or to the outside.

Stability is increased by widening the spread of the legs, deepening the crouch, and putting more weight on the spike. Unfortunately all of these decrease speed and increase muscular strain so that the technique becomes awkward, ugly, and tiring—though safe.

Speed is increased by bringing the feet close together, leaning forward until the boot soles are running flat along the surface like short skis, and removing weight from the spike; if gravity gives insufficient impetus a long *skating* stride helps. Unfortunately all of these enable a tiny chunk of ice or rock to cause a spectacular headlong tumble.

To stop, the climber may dig in his heels while throwing most of his weight back on the spike, or as is more commonly done, swing sideways and edge both boots while riding hard on the spike. On steep slopes just barely within the safe limits of the standing glissade this "stop" position, or *sideslipping*, is preferred for the entire descent since the climber is always only a split-second from an arrest.

Another way to check speed is by making a series of linked turns, keeping the boots parallel and shifting weight smoothly from side to side as direction varies. Balance is easy on the traverse where the climber is moving along in "stop" position, but difficult and delicate on the opposite tack, since either the spike has to be brought entirely out of the slope or contact maintained by an awkward stretch of the arms.

Sitting Glissade

When snow is not hard or steep enough to allow sliding on the feet the sitting glissade is the easiest and often the most pleasant way down. There is about as much technique involved as riding a rollercoaster. The climber simply sits in the snow and slides, holding the ax in arrest grasp.

Speed is increased by lying on the back and lifting heels in the air, usually bending the knees. Speed is decreased by dragging the spike and rising into a sitting position. After momentum has been checked by the spike the heels are dug in for the final halt—but not while going along at a good rate unless willing to somersault. Emergency stops at high speed are made by arrest.

Turns are almost impossible in a sitting glissade. The spike, dragged as a rudder and assisted by body contortions, can effect a change in direction of several degrees at most. Obstructions in the slope are best avoided with a right-angled pattern of straight-down slides and straight-across traverses. On fast snow an experienced glissader can do the job with more craftmanship, rising while moving into a standing glissade for the turn, then reverting to a sitting position.

The body's tendency to pivot head-downward is thwarted by rudder action of the spike. On snow that is hard, littered with rocks, or pitted with icy ruts, damage to softer portions of the anatomy is minimized by stiffening the knees and keeping boot heels against the slope to run interference. Generally, however, the heels are kept clear of the snow, since they scrape up a blinding curtain of spray.

Glissade Precautions

A glissade should be made only when there is a safe *runout—* remembering that a runout is not in itself a sound guarantee if the slope is so long and steep that a climber could be abraded and fractured beyond repair during the slide. Unless a *view of the entire run* can be obtained beforehand the first man down must exercise extreme caution and stop frequently to study what lies ahead.

Equipment is adjusted before beginning the descent. Crampons and other lethal hardware are stowed within the rucksack. *Never attempt to glissade while wearing crampons;* it just doesn't work, and the attempt can be bloody. Mittens are donned, snow being so cold and abrasive it can freeze and flay the hands till they lose control of the ax. Finally and most important, if by any chance the ice ax wrist loop is attached it must be removed: glissades should never be attempted in terrain where the wrist loop is needed; the hazards of the wrist loop should never be risked during a glissade.

Avalanche-cushions must be used with caution, the climber being always ready to roll clear. Rather considerable avalanches can be ridden in perfect safety and incomparable comfort but the novice must keep in mind that even a small freshet can be enough to crush him against a rock or hurtle him over a cliff.

13 *

ICE

A NUMBER of substances requiring similar climbing techniques are ordinarily grouped under the family name of ice. Most common is *névé* or *firn,* which on warm days loosens into a coarse-grained snow but in shadows and cold weather freezes hard. Firn that lasts out a summer and is compressed under succeeding winter snowfalls ultimately becomes *glacier ice,* varying from *white ice* with considerable entrapped air to *blue ice* with little (both of these splinter freely and easily) to tough *pressure ice* from which all the air has been squeezed by overburden. Impregnation of pressure ice by sand and gravel results in *black ice,* as resistant to chopping as concrete.

Verglas is any ice thinly sheathing rock. Water, as vapor, mist, or rain that freezes onto the surface, is one source; another is snow melting and refreezing. Whatever its origin, verglas is frequently brittle and often laminated by cyclic repetition of atmospheric processes over a period of days. Thickness varies from a fraction of an inch to a foot or more. Verglas on a severe route forces the party either to retire or to "iron up" the peak; on a moderate route it is usually best to chop the rock clean; on simple staircase routes the rock is forgotten and a delicate climb made on the fragile shell.

The name of ice is also frequently extended to the icy snow in avalanche channels, cornices, moats, and strong crusts. Definition, then, is based not so much on physical structure as on techniques used; in the present context any surface demanding methods more complex than kicking steps is considered ice.

As climbing terrain, ice is intermediate in nature between snow and rock. Snow techniques are used to their limits, then supplemented by others that increasingly resemble those of rock. Indeed, the elements of balance on rock presented in Chapter 7 are even more essential on ice with its low friction and complex, unreliable structure. The route is partly found and is partly manufactured from routeless raw material. When steps can no longer be kicked, crampons give a good bite; when the slope steepens, holds are cut with the ax. Higher in the scale of difficulty the climber drives ice screws and sculptures bollards, employs various specialized tools and techniques—and also uses such rock tactics as counterforce.

The most important attributes of an ice climber are decisive confidence in putting his feet down, good balance, and plenty of experience. All should be gained during practice sessions on easy glaciers (with overhead belays where needed), followed by short ascents at low altitude and moderate ascents at higher altitude, before attempting severe routes. On these latter, time is usually the limiting factor. The weather is often bad (that is why the ice is there) and frequently the pitches are long. A slow and inexperienced party can find itself trapped halfway to nowhere, cold and exhausted, with a storm blowing in, and no safe retreat.

Experts often do difficult climbs with only rope, ax, crampons, and a few ice screws for safety belays. Novices, on the other hand, have a tendency to bring complex gear into play before they can so much as properly stamp across a patch of hard snow. Equipment should be limited to that required for a reasonable margin of safety; unnecessary items delay the climb and thereby decrease rather than increase the margin. In any event, the tools must be thoroughly mastered under relatively-safe low-altitude practice conditions.

Rope and Ax

The most commonly used rope for ice is ⅜-inch synthetic, 120 feet long. Other lengths and diameters may be better in special situations, such as mixed climbs over ice and high-angle rock. (See Chapter 11.)

The standard ice ax described in Chapter 1 is the optimum tool for all climbers most of the time, and most climbers all of the time. However, for genuine ice (as distinguished from steep or hard snow) and for use as a chopping and clawing tool (rather than simply as a cane or arresting tool) the recommended ax has the highest-strength shaft available, a slender spike (drives well into ice), curved adze (less likely than a flat one to stick in hard snow while chopping), and a pointed, slightly-curved pick (the point permits higher pressure and better penetration, the curve allows the pick to slant downward into the ice when the ax is used as a handhold with the shaft resting against the slope). Teeth on the pick are of little value, but may help prevent it from sliding out of hard ice during handhold use. Pick and spike are kept *sharp;* stopping a fall on steep ice with self-arrest technique is virtually impossible, and the best chance lies in preventing a fall by jabbing pick or spike into the slope at the moment of slip.

The *short ax,* with a shaft about 2 feet long or less and an adze somewhat shorter than usual, is designed for stepcutting in cramped positions on steep faces. On the similar *ice hatchet* the adze is replaced by a hammerhead useful for driving pitons. On severe climbs requiring much chopping on steep walls, or extensive clawing (see below), the short ax or hatchet is preferable to the long ax. Also, the short shaft makes for easier stowing in the rucksack, and thus is better for carrying on climbs predominantly over rock but interrupted with patches of ice. Stepcutting below the feet is difficult with a short ax, often requiring other means of descent.

On ordinary ascents all climbers normally carry the long ax, though one short ax may be included in the party gear for occasional leads. The situation is reversed on extremely difficult and extended routes, where all climbers may carry the short ax with perhaps one long ax for special situations.

Crampons

Crampons, or "climbing irons," are used to avoid stepcutting on slopes up to around 35 degrees, depending on the exposure, and in conjunction with steps or aid techniques on steeper terrain.

Numerous designs have been used in the past and many remain on the market, but those most generally accepted nowadays are *10-point crampons with vertical or forward-slanting toe points* and *12-point crampons with horizontal toe points.* The number of points actually has limited significance.

Horizontal toe points, or "horns," are better for clawing (see below) and for stopping slips on hard snow. *Vertical toe points* are easier to place in steps on fairly-steep ice where horns may be an obstruction. *Forward-slanting toe points,* a compromise between the two, are judged by many climbers to be the optimum, nearly as good as horns in most situations and avoiding most of their leg-goring propensity.

Crampons come in various weights. The *heavyweights* may have longer, heavier points, and thus be better in frozen snow and snow-covered ice. The *lightweights* generally are more expensive but because of better craftsmanship usually are equally durable.

The *adjustable* crampon, available in several designs, can be fitted to boots and overboots of various sizes, a great advantage on expeditions. For ordinary climbing, though, it is more to be warned against than

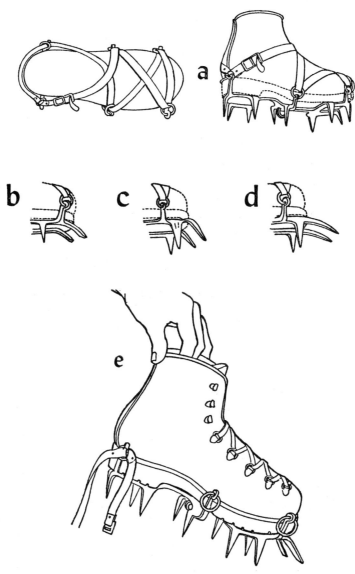

Fig. 68. Crampons.
    a. 10-point with vertical front points.
    b. 10-point with slant front points.
    c. 12-point with slant front points.
    d. 12-point with horizontal front points.
    e. Proper fit.

recommended. The adjustment mechanism must be carefully tested before use, since its breaking or loosening can have serious consequences; it always remains one more thing that can go wrong. Adjustables should not be chosen without advice from those with field experience.

The method of *crampon attachment* is fully as important as crampon style. Best of all is a *buckle-and-rivet harness of oiled, chrome-tanned leather;* non-slip harness buckles with holes in the straps are recommended. The leather does not freeze and therefore permits rapid putting-on and taking-off during cold climbs with much alternation of ice and rock. *Nylon cord* is inexpensive, easily removed, and easily replaced in an emergency. Special care must be taken to lace tightly and to run the lace through each attachment prong or ring, and to tie off the ends with a double knot. *Web strapping* is the least desirable, since it readily picks up snow and frequently freezes at the buckles, sometimes making it necessary to cut straps to remove crampons. The slip-type buckles commonly used with strapping have been known to break.

Proper fit is essential. When purchasing crampons, the climber should carry his boots to the shop. Attachment prongs should contact the boot snugly without significant "bending to fit"; when the boot is lifted from the floor, the prongs should hold the crampon to the boot without assistance from the straps. The front sole points should be close to the toe and all others (except for those in the instep) should be close to the side of the sole.

Before *attaching the harness,* the right and left crampons must be identified (many climbers are unaware that crampons *have* a right and a left). Buckles should be positioned to cinch on the outboard side of the boots. If the crampons do not have heel loops, ankle straps should be long enough to be crossed behind the boot before being secured, in order to prevent boots from sliding backward out of crampons; many crampons have been lost and some exciting situations have developed because this precaution was omitted. If crampons are to be used both with and without overboots, they should fit as snugly as possible on the overboots so they will fit reasonably well on the climbing boots; the length of the harness strap and the location of the buckle holes must be selected for use with both.

Crampon maintenance demands close attention. For maximum effectiveness *points must be kept reasonably sharp,* despite the increased hazard of slicing legs; dull spikes give a false illusion of security and demand greater effort to drive into the slope. *Exact parallel alignment* is important to minimize leg-slashing by splayed points. Many ice routes are interrupted by short passages over rock; crampons are expected to take such punishment without falling apart, but over a period of time the points are inevitably dulled or splayed. Sharpening should be done with a file and never with a grinding wheel, which might overheat the metal and thus destroy the temper so necessary for hardness and rigidity. It is also ill-advised to straighten bent points or frames by hammering; if the weakened metal does not break in the straightening process it may do so under some future climbing stress.

Crampons are dangerous. When they are being worn every step must be taken with care to avoid snagging trousers and gashing legs. When being carried some way of disarming the daggerlike spikes is mandatory; sad experience has plentifully proven the extreme hazard of loose, sharp iron dancing about during a fall. A good method is strapping the crampons point down against a board or piece of metal (though the extra weight is a disadvantage) and then *tightly lashing* the entire package on the *outside* of the rucksack with the points *toward the body*—since there is small chance the points could ever go clear through the entire rucksack. Other possibilities are corks pressed over the points or bits of rubber tubing at least half again as long as the spikes; far better than either of these (since corks and bits of rubber are hard to keep track of) is using a rubber-spider crampon-point-pacifier and carrying the crampons inside the pack.

CRAMPONING

Crampons are used chiefly to eliminate kicking or cutting steps but also to increase security when standing in steps. Whenever footing is slippery they save time and help prevent falls. They should always be carried if there is a chance they may be required, remembering that a wet snow climb may become an ice climb after the sun goes down. Need should be anticipated, and bindings checked periodically to make sure straps are not loose or cut; tying on—or retying—irons while teetering on a wall is peculiarly unpleasant.

On smooth surfaces of moderate angle, the essence of good cramponing is *stamping all points firmly into the slope*—not just those on one side of the boot; these, being overweighted, can easily tear out. The necessary flat contact of points and slope requires the painful position known as "cramponer's ankle." Frequent switchbacking provides a welcome relief to strained muscles and joints, as does a route selected to take advantage of suncups and other irregularities. Short steps are most comfortable; long strides are extremely tiring and require extra attention to balance.

On ice as on rock, the legs should carry most of the weight; entrusting the position to ax or dagger (see below) alone is undesirable, since often they cannot properly puncture hard surfaces. *The crampon must be decisively placed;* the smooth transfer of weight recommended for climbing rock is *not* desirable with crampons, which must be smoothly but positively set into the ice. On hard slopes, most of the body weight should be squarely over one crampon at a time to provide maximum pressure on the points.

The ax is used to give a minimum two-point support, the spike (on moderate slopes) or pick (on steep slopes) being driven into the

Fig. 69. Climbing with crampons and **ax.**
a. Ascent, correct.
b. Ascent, incorrect.
c. Descent.

surface, the crampons moved in sequence, and the ax then redriven. Care must be taken to keep the weight over the crampons, resisting the tendency to lean heavily on the ax and into the slope and thus removing the body weight that forces the points into the ice.

In descending it is more important than ever that all points have a good bite. The knee is therefore bent so points can be stamped flat into the slope. If by accident the heel points dig in first, the weight must be quickly rolled forward to implant the forward points; otherwise the rear ones might flake out ice and cause a spill. Just as in plunge-stepping, the ax is used as a third point of support.

Rock climbing with crampons is poor fun, but when pitches of ice and rock alternate frequently and rapidly it is a lesser evil than repeatedly putting on and taking off irons in awkward stances. Crampons are employed sometimes to gain purchase on ice-covered rock, a use justified only when the ice is firmly frozen to the rock surface and tough enough to hold weight without flaking off.

Stepcutting

When the slope reaches a steepness no longer secure for crampons alone, an angle that varies widely with experience and ice conditions, the climber either claws (see below) or cuts steps. The pick is the usual tool, though in hard snow or névé steps can be scraped or scooped with the adze, as mentioned in Chapter 12. The design of the step and its reliability differ considerably with the type of ice. Laminated ice has an annoying habit of flaking off in layers; the pick must be used with dainty pecking strokes, and even then the danger remains of crampons splitting out the step. Glacier ice compressed into an homogeneous mass is much more reliable, ordinarily requiring only a few well-placed blows. Black ice takes hard and persistent chopping, or rather chipping, but gives indestructible steps.

The most important thing to be said about stepcutting is that it must be *rhythmic*. The second most important point is that the best way to learn is by watching an experienced iceman at work, and then practicing.

For the most comfortable chopping stance the climber stands sideways to the slope with body erect, feet well apart, one holding most of the weight and the other steadying balance. Sometimes the outside foot should be to the rear and below, holding the weight, and sometimes the inside foot. Only experimentation can determine which is most secure on any given pitch. On steep slopes the leader should be protected by ice screws (see below) or other anchors that allow him to do his best work without worry. Though one-handed cutting is necessary on very steep slopes, whenever possible the ax is held with both hands close together next to the spike. The swinging ax ordinarily has enough inertia to split the ice and it is unnecessarily tiring to bring the shoulders and torso into the blow, woodchopper style; most of the thrust should come from arm motion, particularly at the end of each stroke when the pick is given a slight snap to aid in flaking out ice. In all cutting the wristloop should be attached.

Size and shape of the step depend on the type of ice, steepness of slope, and skill of the chopper; frequently a single hard two-handed

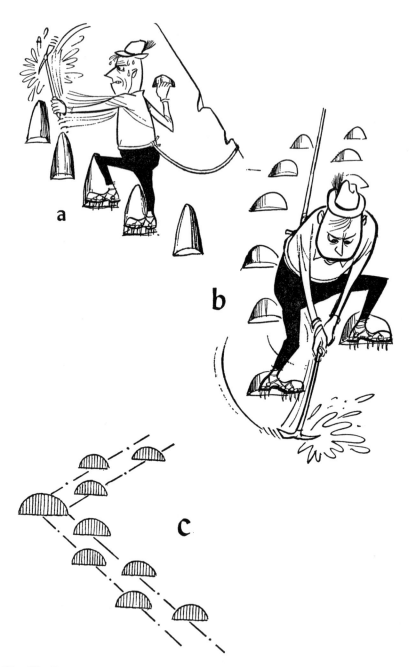

Fig. 70. Stepcutting.

      a. Single step line, climber cutting one-handed, using handhold.
          Can cut two-handed if handhold is not needed.
      b. Double step line, descending.
      c. Switchbacking.

stroke is adequate. The first blow or two are usually horizontal into the base of the step, the next two or three nearly vertical, the job completed with a few cleanup strokes. The platform should be ample to accommodate crampons and boot, but if too large one simply wastes energy. In order to stand upright on very steep slopes room must be cut for the calf and knee.

The ideal step pattern is a zigzag. On moderate slopes a single straight line of steps is sufficient, but on steeper terrain two parallel lines are cut, one for the lower or outside foot, another for the upper or inside foot. The climber cuts two or three steps ahead of his stance to gain the full swing that utilizes momentum of the axhead.

At the precarious turn from a zig to a zag an oversize step is cut; on a very steep slope, this step must be large enough for both feet. The *pivot should invariably be made on the outside foot* of the zig, the first step on the zag being made by the inside foot of the zig which during the pivot becomes the outside foot for the zag. When possible the first pair or two of steps beyond the turn are cut beforehand, the changed relationship of the feet being kept clearly in mind.

Chopping is so tiring a way to gain elevation that conservation of energy is supremely important. The leader selects a route to take advantage of humps and cracks that provide natural steps, times his blows to approximate the energy output of the rest step, and cuts platforms just large enough for his own needs, leaving additional excavation to those following—who generally have plenty of time to elaborate on his outline, especially on steep ice. The optimum interval between steps varies with the slope and the individuals, but each step should make the greatest possible safe gain in distance and altitude.

Changing the lead at regular intervals is desirable in principle to share the labor. However, the change-over is time-consuming even on moderate slopes, and of doubtful value unless several skilled axmen are available. On steep terrain, particularly where fixed ropes, ice screws, and other contributors to confusion are present, it is best to change choppers only when clearly necessary.

On rock the climber, having two hands and two feet, aims always to be supported by three of these. On ice he often has only three points available—feet plus ax—and must move with two-point support. Fortunately the ax generally is a good anchor. On moderate slopes it maintains balance. On steeper slopes it provides two varieties of handholds. The *two-handed pick hold* is actually the arrest grasp described in Chapter 15, the axhead held firmly by one hand with the pick rammed into the slope, the other hand holding the shaft; the *one-handed pick hold* dispenses with the latter hand. Pick holds are strong in névé but in glacier ice may be inferior to *cling holds* chopped deep and solid about shoulder level, the pick first chipping a niche, the adze then scooping out a curved groove for the fingers to grip. On steep ice, pick and cling holds are often used in combination to gain three-point support—supplemented by dagger holds.

Cutting steps downhill is clumsy business. The best stance is usually sideways with the upper, or inside, foot bearing most of the weight and placed slightly ahead of the lower or outside foot. The leader is always firmly belayed from above, or on extreme pitches perhaps is lowered to the bottom meal-sack fashion to cut steps back up for the benefit of his companions, though in such cases rappelling may be much simpler. Descending in steps is much like climbing down on rock; it is preferable to face outward or sideways but on steep slopes often it is necessary to face in, using cling holds or pick and dagger.

In several special conditions ice does not lend itself to an ideal cutting position or step pattern. In narrow gullies or on slim towers the route must go straight up, with steps made to accommodate toe-in boots. When chopping overhead it is essential to work well ahead to allow the arms a full swing. The undercut is an awkward affair and excessive zeal in the downward strokes can split out several steps in one fell blow. Atop the crest of a knife-edge ridge steps can be made with a single blow, but balance is so precarious that often it is better to cut steplines on both sides, using the crest for a handhold. In the traverse of an extremely-steep wall, stepping from platform to platform may be entirely too touchy and a ledge must be chopped. In passing overhanging bergschrunds and cornices sometimes a trench must be dug.

Screws

The first ice pitons were extra-long, blade-type, rock-type pins embellished with holes, notches, or bulges to give a better grip on the ice. After World War II climbers experimented with new designs, T- or X-shaped or tubular in cross-section, with a greater shaft area to decrease the load-per-square-inch on the ice and with holes to help the shaft freeze into the slope. In the early 1960s the screw-type piton, or "screw," appeared, with a large thread surface that grips the ice and tenaciously resists pulling out.

In the opinion of enthusiasts, screws have revolutionized ice climbing, bringing security to slopes where previously the only rule was "the leader must not fall, and nobody else, either," and permitting direct-aid ascents of long and extremely steep, even overhanging pitches. The annals of recent expeditions are full of screws, and so too are the current seminars of icemen discussing experiments with new techniques on local seracs and walls; the revolution has only just begun. Critics, however, feel screws are not all that superior to older tools, which continue to have a place; they point to serious accidents resulting from screw failure and suggest that much must be done to improve current designs and raise current standards of quality control.

The *lag-bolt* screw, with a long shank and a ring, or eye, about ½- to ⅝-inch diameter, is driven about two-thirds of its length into the ice

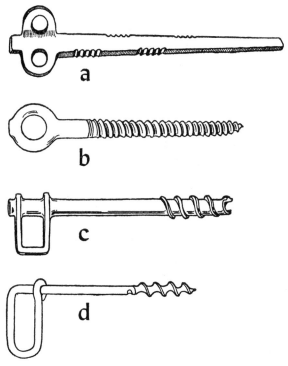

Fig. 71. Ice pitons and screws.
        a. T-shaped ice piton.
        b. Lag-bolt screw.
        c. Tubular screw.
        d. Coathanger screw.

with a piton hammer, then screwed in with ice ax pick or other instrument until only the ring is exposed. The lag bolt is used in soft ice where its large cross-section resists sideways cutting—particularly important on Class Six pitches at low and possible-warm altitudes. Lacking an offset eye, it can sometimes be accidentally unscrewed by direct outward tension.

The *tube* screw (smaller shank and less weight than the lag bolt; offset eye) is similar to the coathanger screw (see below) except that the shaft is larger and tubular and the thread flukes are smaller. A hammer is usually necessary to start the driving, which can be slow work in hard ice. The tube is most notable for its resistance to sustained side-loading. Before re-using, ice should be removed from inside the shaft.

Most popular of all, both at high and low altitudes, is the *coathanger,* which has a small shank with large threads, an offset eye integral with the shank, and is about half the weight of the lag bolt. A hammer is not required; the screw is inserted into a starter hole made by a stroke of the ice ax pick and then screwed up to the eye by hand or with another screw. In most cases a coathanger can be installed *with one hand* in less than 30 seconds. Several lengths are available. In one test where a short coathanger was placed in the soft white ice of a low-altitude glacier snout on a hot day, four strong men were unable to dislodge or appreciably affect the placement by sustained pulling and jerking from any and all directions, including straight out. However, the small shaft of the coathanger makes it less resistant than the other types to sustained side-loads in soft ice. It also may break when inserted through soft ice into hard ice which begins (after final placement) at the top of the threads, and this situation should be avoided by chopping if necessary.

All screws should—in general—be inserted at an angle of about 10 degrees above a perpendicular to the line of pull; this angle, however, is not critical. Placement in direct sunlight should be avoided; when it cannot, the screw should be set in an ax-cut depression and covered with snow to prevent melting out.

USING SCREWS

Though first associated (as was true of rock pitons) with difficult climbing, ice screws have a potentially-major role, not yet fully exploited, in providing protection on easy but hazardous pitches. For example, a party may need a reliable belay to cross a crevasse, by bridge or leap (see Chapter 15); screws may be the only feasible answer. Rock climbers have long carried an emergency selection of pitons even on quite-simple routes; ice climbers now are similarly well-advised to include several screws in the party gear.

Screwcraft is in most essentials identical or similar to pitoncraft. To apply Class Five and Six rock technology to ice, one should re-read Chapter 11, mentally making proper substitutions.

One major difference between the use of rock pitons and ice screws must be remembered: unlike rock, ice melts or creeps under heat or pressure. Screws should therefore not be subjected to sustained tension or straight-out pulls, particularly in warm temperatures.

Any loaded screw should be reinforced by an anchor screw, *with the anchor line (from one screw to the other) left slightly slack.* Movement in the loaded screw can be detected by noting any lessening of slack, thus providing a warning of failure; otherwise, with a tight anchor line, a sustained pull might dislodge both screws simultaneously, resulting in sudden and complete failure. When used as belay anchors, screws should not be under strain—except during a fall.

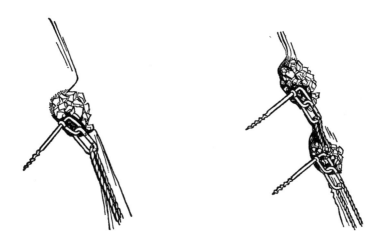

Fig. 72. Using screws. *Left,* well-placed screw. *Right,* anchored screw.

Bollards and Pickets

A *bollard* is a tear-shaped or round pillar fashioned from snow or ice by boot-stamping or chopping, then slightly undercut at the back and sides to prevent the rope from slipping off. In soft snow the horizontal width must often be as much as 6 to 10 feet and the trench as deep as boots can stamp. In hard ice a width of 1 to 3 feet and a depth of 3 to 6 inches may be ample. However, variations in the strength of snow and ice are so great that no standard dimensions can be given; extensive personal experimentation in bollard-making is essential before trusting one on an actual climb. Homogeneous ice is not only most dependable but requires the smallest dimensions and least effort. Laminated ice may split rather easily if the applied force is parallel to the planes of cleavage. Snow might seem utterly worthless, but stubbornly resists decapitation if two or more strands of sling rope are inserted into the undercut and snow stamped in on top. Bearing surfaces of rock, wood, spare clothing, or whatever material is available and dispensable are also helpful in hindering slicing action.

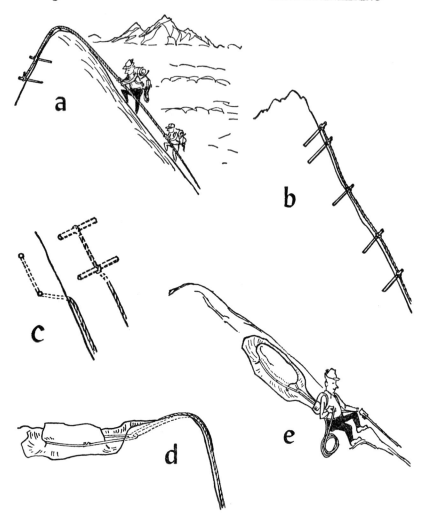

Fig. 73. Pickets and bollards.
  a. Pickets placed on opposite side of ridge.
  b. Pickets anchoring a fixed rope.
  c. Pickets buried in snow horizontal to line of pull.
  d. Bollard for rappel anchor.
  e. Bollard for belay anchor.

Bollards may fail either by the rope slipping off the top (the major danger on ice, where the undercut is particularly important) or shearing away the top (most common in snow). Terrain conditions can be evaluated by making a small-scale bollard, then testing it to failure. One must always keep in mind that the bollard may be melting while in use, thus steadily deteriorating in dependability.

XV. Puyallup Glacier in the Sunset Amphitheater, Mount Rainier. (Bob and Ira Spring)

XVI. Mount Robson, Canadian Rockies. (Thomas Miller)

A bollard has the immense advantage of being a "piton" always at hand on snow and ice, and requiring no special equipment. For this reason the technique should be familiar to all ice climbers, if only for emergencies. Use as anchors for leader protection is too time-consuming to be more than rarely practical, but on the descent a single bollard may enable a party to negotiate considerable difficulties, either on a fixed rope or a rappel. During the evacuation of an injured climber bollards can be quite literally lifesaving.

The most common *picket,* or "snow piton," is a tube or angle of aluminum about 3–4 feet long, 1 inch in diameter or width, that can be driven into snow or soft ice. As belay anchors pickets are used in pairs, one anchoring the other; as anchors for fixed ropes, they are sometimes placed singly. Pickets are especially reliable when located on one side of a ridge with a pull coming from the other side, or when wedged between rocks.

Fixed Ropes

Though the human body is poorly designed for any sort of climbing (by comparison with a spider, for instance), it works even worse going down than up. Consequently, ice that extends the leader to his limit on the ascent often requires a fixed rope to provide a safe descent. Also, steps put in on the way up may not be available on the way down, having melted or been filled with snow during the interim. Since stepcutting below the feet is time-consuming and tiring, a fixed rope may save long minutes or hours, and perhaps a bivouac or worse.

Because of these factors, the fixed rope has become the mainstay of climbers attempting difficult ice, particularly on peaks of expeditionary caliber. On a long route the key to success—and safety—is keeping open the line of fast retreat—fast and safe in storm or darkness or both, when stepcutting is completely infeasible.

The most common purpose of the fixed rope is to provide the climber with a steadying handhold or to stop a slip before it develops into a fall. In this case rope is not selected for strength, since expected loads are small, but for good friction with mittened hands. The usual diameter is ¼- or ⁵⁄₁₆-inch polyethylene or manila: polyethylene because it is light, strong, and can be obtained in easily-visible black; manila because it is cheap and rough-textured. Strength becomes important—and polyethylene, polypropylene, or other synthetics thus preferable—when fixed ropes are used with Jumar or similar metal ascending devices to move climbers and equipment up very steep and long pitches.

Rope intended for fixing along the route should be cut into lengths of about 200–300 feet and neatly coiled so it can be easily uncoiled on steep slopes; it should be possible to tie one end to an anchor, toss the other down, and have it hang free without snarling.

The lead climber, or climbers, carry as much extra rope and other gear as they can handle. Otherwise time is lost transferring ropes, screws, and pickets from the rear of the party to the front.

Special Techniques

ICE DAGGER

Among items of special equipment, one of the most interesting is the dagger, which is stabbed into ice to provide a balancing handhold or to permit clawing (see below), and thus may be described as an ice ax pick without the rest of the ax. Having long recognized that the best handhold on steep ice is frequently the ax pick, climbers have sometimes carried both a long ax and a short ax to have good holds for both hands; with the second ax not available, an ice hatchet or a long piton, such as an angle, has been employed. The dagger has evolved in the search for an improvement over earlier expedients.

CLAWING

By saving stepcutting and therefore time and energy, clawing has made possible safe and fast ascents of routes previously slow and thus dangerous. Several different though related techniques are covered by the term.

On steep slopes firm in texture yet easily punctured by crampon points and ice ax pick—frozen névé is the perfect condition—the climber holds the ax in arrest grasp and thrusts the pick up to the hilt before moving his spiked feet. This *crampon-crawling* often saves a great deal of cutting without any sacrifice of safety, though like any counterforce technique it is tiring. Alternation is the general rule: when ankles begin to quiver, the lead is changed or steps are chopped; when arms grow heavy, crawling is resumed.

Many a novice has discovered during crampon practice that he can run up short pitches too steep for him to walk up. This seeming anomaly derives first from the quick transfer of weight from one foot to the other, and second from the increased impact of the boot and the consequent firmer contact with the slope. From the discovery was developed a technique which might be called the fast crawl, or *clawing*. Though a climber can do some elementary clawing equipped with nothing more elaborate than vertical-point crampons plus ice ax, the ideal outfit is horizontal toe-point crampons, ice ax (long or short), and dagger. With sharp spikes for each foot and hand, the climber moves fast—but not very far in any single rush, since the technique is too strenuous for leads much longer than 10–20 feet. Before setting out, the climber must either have in sight a ledge, niche, or other secure resting point offered by the terrain, or must be prepared to place a screw or chop a quick step.

Fig. 74. Clawing. *Left,* with ax. *Right,* with short ax and dagger.

From the original short-dash application, clawing has been extended to much-longer slopes. Rather than cutting steps every foot of the way, the leader claws 20 feet or so, chops a step, places a screw or picket, snaps in, and then repeats the sequence. On slopes of medium steepness, both members of a two-man rope team may move together; on extreme slopes the second man may have to belay. When there are more than two teams in the party, the second man may scratch rudimentary steps as he climbs, and on arriving at a screw or picket attach a fixed rope for the benefit of following teams. These may improve the steps if desired—as would be the case in an expedition where following climbers are carrying heavy loads—and in doing so have the protection of a rope from above. Through this method the effort of chopping is distributed among all members of the party without the nuisance and danger of changing rope positions.

Clawing with pitons and piton hammer is not a technique anyone ever plans to use, but in emergencies has proven extremely helpful to rock climbers encountering unexpected snow or ice on their route.

DIRECT AID

Until quite recently the technology of ice was so primitive compared to rock that the two had little in common. However, the new tools and techniques described in this chapter have made possible application on ice of the Class Five and in some cases Class Six methods discussed in Chapter 11.

Doubtless each season will rapidly advance skills in direct-aid ice climbing; the best advice possible here is to consult the current journals. Four generalizations can be made: Class Six techniques should be mastered on rock to attain the necessary speed and proficiency before attempting them on ice; these techniques are most suitable for hard cold ice and thus the climb should be timed to avoid sunlight and warmth on the critical pitches; since Class Six climbing is slow at best, routes should be selected that are relatively free from avalanches and falling rock and ice; and finally, ice is a medium that provides great scope for imagination and ingenuity.

Routefinding

PERCHED ICE

Ice in the indentations of a precipice is variously called perched ice, hanging ice, ice patches, ice fields, ice aprons, plaques. Such slopes commonly are preferred to the surrounding rock, since on steep cliffs ice may occupy all the shelves and ledges, leaving clear only very steep rock. When rock must be used for connecting links, crampons may come on and off repeatedly and ice axes and hammers continually shuttle in and out of rucksacks. On these combination climbs sometimes each two-man team has a rock leader and an ice leader, the former wearing rock shoes, carrying rock hardware and a short ice ax or dagger; the latter wearing boots, carrying ice screws, and—for clawing—horned crampons, ice ax, and dagger.

COULOIRS

Deeply-shaded couloirs, or gullies, are more often floored with ice than snow. Even in springtime when all open inclines are deep slush the couloirs may be hard ice—from frost or from avalanche-scouring.

Whether on a glacier or snaking upward into a rock precipice, ice gullies are often the key to passage, having a lesser angle from bottom to top than the cliffs they breach. However, the inviting aspect of a couloir in morning, contrasted with the forbidding menace of its enclosing cliffs, frequently proves in afternoon to have been a crocodile smile. Gullies are the garbage chutes of mountains, and however quiet during night begin with the sun to transport toward sealevel such rubbish as avalanching snow, rocks loosened by frost-wedging, ice blocks weakened by melting. The climber strives to be out of the couloir before the sun comes in, which means an early start to accomplish a round trip, an alternate route for descent, or a bivouac. Most, but not all, the debris comes down the center; even keeping to the sides it is well to cock a sharp ear for suspicious sounds above and have one member of the team watching for quiet slides and silent bounders.

In a steep couloir avalanches often erode a system of deeply-incised *guts* that usually are either avoided or crossed with all possible haste. However, early in the year gut floors offer the soundest snow available and in cold weather may be quite safe enough—particularly in fast descent.

Couloirs can become increasingly nasty the higher they are ascended, presenting such nuisances as extreme steepness, verglas, moats, rubble strewn loosely over smooth rock slabs, and cornices. Many lead into traps, or *cul-de-sacs,* the gentle angle at the bottom compensated for by culmination in a frosty chimney. The rule is by no means invariable; when the couloir heads at a col it can well afford to offer a lower average angle than the face.

Despite negative aspects many ice routes follow gullies. Generally the techniques are simple cramponing and cutting, but crevasses and moats and suncups, or blocks of fallen rock and ice, make rock-climbing techniques useful. Some irregularities are welcome for the sake of their belay potential.

When the bed of the gully is uncompromisingly steep, *moat-crawling* along the side of the gully is often delightfully secure. During the morning ascent cramponing or cutting may be faster; in afternoon a nervewracking descent on steep ice is hardly tempting compared to stemming down a moat with its lessened exposure and increased protection from rockfall.

RIDGES

Routes along or near the crests of ridges are characterized by freedom from falling debris and avalanches, but are exposed to wind and weather. Also, ridges are frequently topped with dangerous cornices (see Chapters 12 and 21) and may be composed of partly-rotten ice in the vicinity of rock outcrops. However, in regions of heavy snowfall they may prove the only wise choice when the ascent is at all lengthy. Routefinding is generally less critical than on other portions of a mountain and a safe retreat is usually open if proper equipment has been installed on the ascent. Ridge routes are less sensitive than others to the time factor, ordinarily not being threatened by avalanches and falling debris resulting from sunlight and warming conditions occuring late in the day, but they are subject to hazardous cornices; if these are suspected, the safest line of progress lies below the crest on the side away from the cornice. Any sharp ridge that appears flattened when approached from windward must be considered suspicious.

ICEFALLS

The advisability of an icefall route depends on the stability of the icefall in question; fresh debris, or the lack of it, may indicate what can be expected. Icefalls are often protected from avalanches by the broken nature of the terrain, but it is most important to be aware of any snow or ice masses poised above. Routefinding can be tricky, with progress suddenly and abruptly halted by an enormous crevasse or a blank wall. Once in the icefall, the view may be restricted to the array of seracs and crevasses in the immediate vicinity. For this reason one should gain a distant look before entering the icefall, and where practical select in advance each portion of the route and each avenue of escape, taking special pains to memorize salient landmarks, particularly those adjacent to unstable areas that must be climbed as rapidly as possible and at the optimum time of day. Appearance or disappearance of the sun can cause thawing or freezing, and in both cases avalanches. Exits or refuges, such as cleavers, should be noted for use in case of need.

14 *

GLACIERS

IF it were not for crevasses a separate consideration of glacier travel would be superfluous, since nearly all the techniques are treated in preceding and following chapters, particularly 5, 9, 12, 13, 15, 19, 20, and 21. On the other hand, with very slight adjustments this entire book could as well be called "Glacier Travel"; to many climbers it is, indeed, an article of faith, "no glacier, no mountain."

Route on Glaciers

Too much emphasis cannot be placed on the oft-stressed *distant view*, taking into account all the many features of a glacier discussed in Chapter 20. Approaching a glacier the long angle from the valley frequently tells more about the surface than the foreshortened perspective from the surface itself. A downward or cross-valley view is even more valuable. From a distance the route may be perfectly obvious, while once amid icefalls and crevasse fields finding passage may be a matter of blind luck. Often it is worthwhile to make a quick pencil sketch of signpost features: a distinctive block of ice may mark a gully that penetrates an icefall, or a bump on a moraine a narrow lane through a crevasse field. The distant view is no panacea, for closer inspection reveals much new information, but at the very least the main outlines of the route can be blocked out.

On large glaciers *routemarking* is essential to a safe return. It is easy to become confused in the bewildering monotony of the great white world of ice even in bright sunshine, not to mention fog, and footprints are far too perishable to be trusted. The traditional marker is the *wil-*

low wand cut from thickets near the glacier, but parties nowadays ordinarily carry willow wands that are neither willow nor merely wands.
Most commonly used are bamboo garden stakes about the diameter of
a pencil and about 3 feet long, the ends notched and cloth flags inserted, bound with rubber bands. Fluorescent orange cloth is most
visible at a distance and in all conditions of light. Square flags are
better than long rectangular streamers, which tangle together while
being carried in a bundle and shred in the wind once placed. Wands
are placed on the ascent whenever the descent might be confusing,
very much like blazes in a forest: several hundred feet apart when the
route is a straight line, a rope length apart for a twisting path, in pairs
to mark turns or crevasses.

Travel Among Crevasses

The crevasse is the special problem of glacier travel, its distinction
being that the more harmless the outward appearance the greater the
danger. The most casual observer is scared into taking protective
measures by huge gaping chasms; the hazardous holes are those that
show on the surface as mere narrow cracks or are completely invisible.
It is easy to move from a snowfield onto a snow-covered glacier without recognizing the need for added protection. Also, even after much
experience a climber who has traveled under a lucky star may imagine
himself able to negotiate glaciers without special precaution, confidently depending on his wisdom to predict when and where he will
come upon a crevasse; an alarming percentage of such gifted seers,
however, eventually lose either their second sight or their luck.

PROTECTION: THE ROPE

The first law of traveling snow-covered glaciers is to *rope up.*
Whether stepping onto a known glacier or onto a snowfield of unknown status, whether or not crevasses are visible, whether or not
crevasses have ever been reported as existing in the past, the law
without exception is: *rope up.* Even though a fortunate climber makes
hundreds of climbs during a score of seasons and never once steps into
a crevasse, if he is as wise as he is lucky he has kept up the premiums
on his climbing insurance by wearing a rope during all of these climbs,
realizing that too frequently a climber's first unroped fall into a
crevasse is his last.

More is involved than merely roping, which can in fact be the visible
declaration of a suicide pact; it is well for each member to ponder for
a moment the reasons why the rope is used and to visualize in detail
the consequences of a fall. If this is done no one will need urging to
keep the rope extended at full length between members to minimize

falls. Climbers who march in friendly proximity through crevasse fields, whether dragging long loops of slack or carrying neat coils, are liable to continue their close association as a rope team all the way to the bottom of a crevasse.

The *preferred number on a team for glacier travel is three* climbers to a rope 120 to 150 feet long. With but two on a rope a crevasse fall must be arrested by a single ax; more than three on a rope necessitates such short intervals between climbers that if one man drops in a hole often another is dragged down before he has time to take any action. Due to the difficulty of crevasse-rescue procedures (see Chapter 19) *two rope teams are the recommended minimum for glacier travel.* A single rope may be insufficient to effect rescue and in any event extra equipment and manpower expedite matters, many times having proven the margin between failure and success.

Before stepping onto the glacier other measures of protection are taken. *Prusik slings* are attached to the rope. Ordinarily each climber affixes one sling (the middleman two, one on the rope in front and one on the rope in back) for use in modified bilgeri, but in a small party each climber should place three slings for prusik technique. (Both rescue methods are described in Chapter 19.) The iciness of crevasse interiors must be remembered and *warm wool clothing* worn or carried; a climber can die of cold within easy speaking distance of companions who are sweltering in the sunshine. All *equipment is secured* —pockets buttoned, loose gear safely stowed, rucksack straps tightened. The *ice ax wristloop is kept on the wrist at all times.* The *ax is held always in arrest grasp.* (For the reasons behind both these rules, see Chapter 15.) Finally, *competence in the rescue methods* detailed in Chapter 19 is an absolute prerequisite to glacier travel.

Rope team order on glaciers is sometimes slightly different from that described in Chapter 9. Usually the first man should be the one most experienced in crevasse detection and avoidance, but when crevasses are thoroughly masked the best policy is for the lightest member of the party to lead, followed by the climber most skillful at belays and arrests.

The great wish of glacier travelers is to avoid falling into crevasses. It is even more fundamental, however, that the members of a team must never fall into the same crevasse. Consequently, whenever possible the team *crosses the visible or suspected crevasses at right angles.* When the route forbids such a course *echelon* formation is used, somewhat awkward but good insurance that if one climber plunges into a chasm his companions will not immediately join him; at the worst they will topple into neighboring chasms, a sufficiently-unhappy situation but better than everyone landing in the same hole.

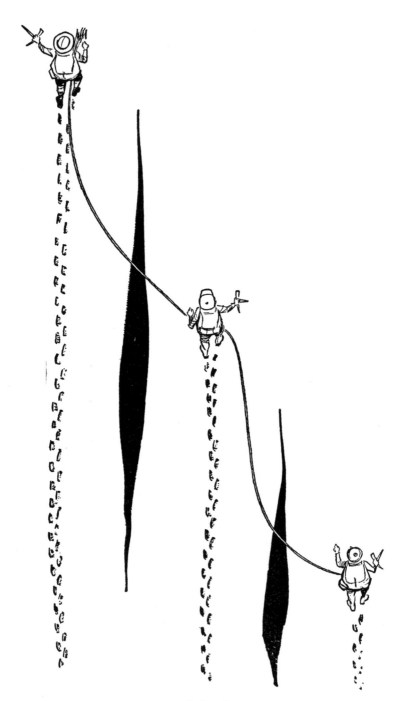

Fig. 75. Echelon formation.

An alarmingly-common blunder is for a party to cluster closely together at rest stops. A number of alpine tragedies have resulted from this convivial instinct when a chosen rendezvous proved to be the bridge over an unseen crevasse, strong enough to support one or two climbers at most. If areas of indisputable safety cannot be found the rope must be kept extended during rests just as during travel. A party establishing a camp on snow-covered glacier similarly remains roped for a long period, stomping and probing the surface thoroughly before according any trust to their névé home.

During extended periods of glacier living, skis and snowshoes are often of inestimable value. The climber equipped with such footgear distributes his weight more widely than when clumping along on boots and by placing less strain on bridges falls into fewer crevasses. Neither skis nor snowshoes can be considered substitutes for the rope, but in semi-arctic ranges or winter mountaineering they may be needed for easy travel and if available give considerable bonus protection.

AVOIDING CREVASSES

Except when photography is the object of the trip the best route is one that completely avoids all crevasses. Simple and self-evident as such strategy seems, the distant view may be misleading. Scale is difficult to estimate from far away and often a crevasse judged to be the merest crack turns out to be many feet wide. Moreover, if one crevasse can be seen from several miles away, odds are that on close approach it will prove to be merely the largest of a cluster. Finally, even if the climbers have a near view of the terrain to be traveled and can see every tiny break in the surface, hidden crevasses must always be suspected.

Familiarity with the mechanics of glacier motion, described in Chapter 20, is essential to wise routefinding. An understanding of where crevasses are most likely to form may allow a party to proceed rapidly and safely even in the extreme case of a glacier surface entirely free from visible breaks but honeycombed with chasms beneath the snowcover.

DETECTING HIDDEN CREVASSES

The climber should continually search the route ahead with a roving eye for suggestions of hidden holes. Suspicion increases in areas likely to be crevassed, such as the sides of the glacier, around nunataks and icefalls, at any sharp bends or drops. Memory is useful, for on many glaciers crevasse patterns change little from year to year. A thin snowcover which masks crevasses without bridging them is particularly hazardous, and extreme caution is mandatory in late spring, after

snowfalls, and near exposed ice. Once one crevasse is discovered the
climber does well to keep in mind that crevasses usually form in
parallel belts, and usually have hidden extensions.

When a crevasse is suspected the climber seeks visual clues, and all
of these stem from the natural inclination of snow arching over
emptiness to *sag* under the pull of gravity, creating a shallow trough
with a linear form that distinguishes it from suncups, which tend to be
circular. A sag smoothed over by a continuing succession of storms

Fig. 76. Crossing a bridged crevasse.

gives no surface indication of its existence, but any interval of good
weather allows gravity to do its work; the sag may then give itself
away by a slight difference in sheen, texture, or color. Snow in the
trough may have a flat white look and a fine texture from being newer
than the old névé, or be dirtier from collecting windblown particles of
dust, or have the chalky appearance typical of a windslab, since the
trough presents the wind with a lee slope. (See Chapter 21.) Proper
light helps in spotting sags. In the dull illumination of fog and in the

blinding glare of noon details are blurred. With moderate light from a low angle, such as in early morning or late afternoon, differences in snow texture are distinctly revealed and shadows outline the characteristic linear form of the sag.

Very commonly there is not the slightest clue to the location, size, and direction of crevasses, and the party must *probe* the surface. *Probing with the body* might seem the very negation of technique, but when a very large area must be crossed which probably is riddled with hidden fissures it is the only economical procedure. The entire team must remain constantly alert during such travel, with the lead man ready to leap back from a crumbling bridge, or lean forward to span the gap, or if worse comes to worst, to extend his arms and ax hoping to find support within his reach. It is essential for each member to hold the ax firmly in arrest grasp whatever happens; everyone is watchful for a breakthrough and ready to drop instantaneously into arrest.

Probing with the ice ax is nowhere near so positive a way to find crevasses but much more comfortable. Continuous probing is scarcely practical through a large suspected area but is advisable at points of maximum probability; that is, on the lips and at the ends of open crevasses, across all sags and dubious bridges.

The axhead is held firmly in the arrest grasp and attached to the climber by the wristloop. The shaft is thrust into the surface well *in advance of the climber's weight*, with a *smooth sensitive motion*, the angle as *nearly vertical* as convenient, since otherwise the climber is merely skimming the surface rather than penetrating the underlayers. If resistance to the thrust is uniform it has been established that the snow is solid at least to the depth of the shaft. If resistance abruptly lessens, probably a hole has been found, and further thrusts are made to establish its extent. The value of probing depends largely on the climber's sensitivity to changes in resistance and his skill in interpreting the meaning of such changes. The shaft may seem suddenly to plunge into space when actually it has merely broken through a buried crust into a softer stratum. In the structure of the ax (see Chapter 1) a smooth line from spike to shaft is essential for accuracy; a blunt-pointed spike or a jutting ferrule may give a false reading. The length of the shaft remains a limiting factor, since obviously all one can find out is whether a bridge is as thick as the shaft is long.

Passing a Crevasse

END RUN

If a crevasse pinches out anywhere within reasonable distance the end run is much preferred over any tactical maneuver; even though it should involve traveling half a mile to gain a dozen feet of forward progress the time taken to walk around is generally much less than in forcing a direct crossing. The great fact to remember in an end run is the almost invariable hidden extension of a visible crevasse. A frequent error is aiming at the visible end; unless the true, or subsurface, end has been clearly seen during approach it is wise to make a very wide

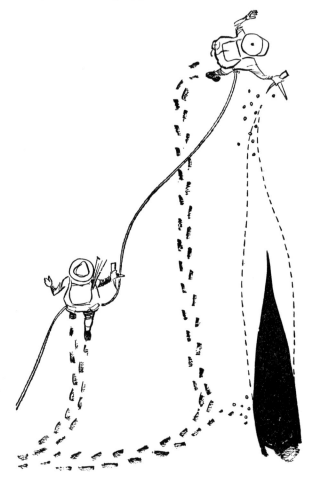

Fig. 77. Skirting a crevasse.

swing around the corner. In late summer the visible end is often the true end of a crevasse, but early in the season even the tiniest surface crack may be a chink in the roof of an immense cold mansion.

BRIDGES

When end runs are impractical because of the distance involved or because the ends of the crevasse are adjacent to other crevasses, the party looks for bridges. One variety consists of remnant snowcover sagging over an inner vacuity. Another kind is less of a bridge than an isthmus between two crevasses with a foundation that extends downward into the body of the glacier.

Ideally any bridge should be closely and completely examined before use. A side view may give a stamp of such unqualified approval that the party can stride across in perfect confidence. If overhanging snow obscures dimensions the leader must explore at closer range, probing the depth and smashing at the sides, walking delicately all the while and equally ready for an arrest or a deep tumble. The second man gives a belay, anchored by the third man, who is also prepared to start rescue if the leader falls.

A bridge excessively narrow for walking or apparently quite weak may be crossed by straddling, or even slithering on the stomach, both of which methods lower the center of gravity and distribute weight over a broader area. When the bridge is extremely dubious but still the only feasible route, the smallest climber in the party should be the first across, the followers walking with light feet and taking care to step exactly in the established tracks without the slightest deviation.

Bridges vary in strength with changes in temperature. In the cold of winter or early morning the thinnest and airiest of arches can have incredible structural strength; when crystals melt in the afternoon sun even the grandest bridge may suddenly collapse of its own weight. Each must be tested with care, neither being abandoned nor trusted until its worth is determined. Moreover, dependability in the morning does not mean that testing can be omitted in the afternoon.

JUMPING

Narrow cracks can be stepped across, but increased width requires jumping, often faster than an end run and sometimes the only possible passage. Crevasse-jumping, however, is one of the alpine techniques dramatized far beyond its importance, although distinction must be made between the routine hops of fact and the long desperate leaps customary in novels.

Care must be taken to find the precise edge of the crevasse, which usually overhangs. The jumper holds his ax in the arrest grasp in case he falls short and must claw for lodgment on the far side. Any jump must be belayed—*dynamically* to minimize bounce-back damage in event of failure. The belayer leaves slack in the rope exceeding the width of the crevasse; on occasion a jumper has made a splendid effort but while still in forward flight has suddenly been snapped backward by a taut rope.

A running jump can carry somewhat farther than a standing one, but not so far as usually expected. With full glacier gear including crampons it is difficult to get up much momentum, particularly since the dashing climber is likely to plunge deep into the snow, or perhaps even through the overhanging lip of the crevasse—an inglorious conclusion to a thrilling beginning. If the jump is so long a run is required the approach is first carefully packed. Before takeoff the lead man leaves his rucksack and other encumbrances with companions, rolls down shirt sleeves and puts on mittens, checks his waist knot and prusik slings. In point of fact, running jumps are not often practical; most are made from a standing start or with but two or three lead-up steps. Unlike the heroes of fiction the ordinary real-life mountaineer does not try much more than 5- or 6-foot leaps on a flat surface; if he falters in midflight he at least has a fighting chance to claw over the lip with ax

Fig. 78. Jumping a crevasse.

and boots. A jump is obviously much less dangerous once one climber is across, for then the belay is on the landing side and if the second man falls short he has assistance from the rope in scrambling out of the hole.

Downhill jumping, such as from the overhanging wall of a bergschrund, is a different matter entirely. With momentum from a descending run a climber may perhaps clear prodigious horizontal distances. Such leaps, however, are made only in desperation. Danger can be minimized by a proper landing position, with the feet slightly apart for balance, knees relaxed to absorb shock, ax held ready for arrest, and the belayer alert. Still, the landing platform is an unknown quantity that may be so weak the climber plunges through into the crevasse, or so hard that he breaks both legs. Moreover, the choice between jumping and slower methods of passage usually is made late in the day when weary climbers are apt to forget the brittleness of bones, the forces generated by a falling body, and the world record for the broad jump.

Fig. 79. Crossing a sunken bridge.

COMPLEX METHODS

Expeditions with facilities for heavy transport often employ ladders or poles as artificial bridges. Rope traverses of the sort described in Chapter 11 have been theorized, if never actually used. More than one anecdote tells of a lead climber being hurled by his companions over a crevasse. Somewhat less rare is descent by rappel into a crevasse and ascent of the far wall, or a traverse along the crevasse bottom until a weakness is found in the defenses of the upper wall. This is more properly the realm of ice climbing.

15 *

ARRESTS AND BELAYS

To repeat a point which scarcely needs emphasis, it is better for a climber never to fall, but when he does he should stop without delay. On snow and ice there are three divisions of the technique of stopping: the *self-arrest* by an individual; the *team arrest* of a roped party; the *belays* with which a moving climber is protected by a stationary companion.

Self-Arrest

On any slope where a slip could lead to a fast, rough slide the climber travels in constant readiness to make arrest. An *eye for consequences,* continual awareness of what lies around him wherever he walks, is as characteristic of the experienced mountaineer as an eye for the weather. Always in his mind are the chances of a slip and the dangers of a fall—the length and steepness of the slope, the rocks or cliffs or crevasses below.

Physically the climber rigs for arrest by rolling down shirtsleeves, putting on mittens, securing loose gear, and most important of all by making certain the ax is held correctly. Mentally he prepares by recognizing the importance of *instantaneous application.* A sloppy but quick arrest often has a better chance of success than a stylish but leisurely one.

POSITION

1. One hand on head of ax with thumb under adze and fingers over pick; the other hand on the shaft next to the spike; both hands with firm grip.

2. Pick pressed into slope just above shoulder of the hand holding the axhead so that the adze approaches top of shoulder; shaft crosses chest diagonally; spike lies close outside opposite hip or thigh.

3. Chest and shoulder pressed strongly on shaft; spine arched slightly to distribute weight chiefly at shoulders and toes.

4. Legs stiff and spread apart, toes digging in.

5. *Hang onto the ax!*

The firm grip on the head of the ax holds the pick close to the shoulder. The other hand must be *at the very end* of the shaft lest it act as a pivot around which the spike can swing into the thigh, inflicting a nasty wound.

The pick must be close to shoulder and spike close to hip to employ all the body weight. If the pick rides uphill away from the climber it cannot be forced into the slope and thus has negligible braking effect. If the spike moves laterally out from the hip the shaft approaches a right angle to the line of fall and the pick cannot be driven in.

The pick and the toes are the most effective brakes. A slight arch of the spine concentrates body weight on the toes and on the chest-and-shoulder region which presses on the shaft, driving the pick in. With a limp backbone much of the abdominal mass lies wasted on the snow. However, the slight arch must not be confused with the ineffective and unstable very-high arch of novices unwilling to get chest and face down into the rough, cold snow.

Particularly in soft snow the stiff, outspread legs with digging toes give the pick important help and also add stability. However, when arresting on hard snow or ice while wearing crampons, the knees must do the job described above for the feet. Under these conditions the feet must be held away from the slope until speed is reduced, so that crampons do not catch and flip the climber backwards.

The prime law of snow is that it takes an ax to turn a hiker into a climber. When the ax is lost in a fall there is no longer a climber but only a hiker attempting with fingernails and teeth the pick's proper job. In other words, *hang onto the ax.*

ARREST IN WILD FLIGHT

Most arrests are applied to check a slip resulting from a stumble or a simple breaking-out of a step. Even a halfhearted arrest can usually stop such low-speed slides, if indeed hopskipping of the feet is not enough to restore balance. The smaller proportion of arrests is also the more critical—those applied while the climber is flying blindly and wildly, half in the air and half in the snow, whirling, spinning, and bouncing until he quite literally cannot distinguish up from down. Such falls quickly separate the good arrests from the bad.

The first step in making arrest is gaining the ideal position—sliding on the stomach with feet downhill. The climber *sliding on his back rolls onto his stomach toward the head of the ax.* If his axhead is on his right shoulder he rolls to his right. Rolling left might jam the spike into the slope before the pick, wrenching the ax from the climber's grasp.

Fig. 80. Self-arrest.

      a. Correct—rolling toward head of ax.

      b. Incorrect—rolling toward spike.

To *pivot into an arrest from an on-back head-downhill* position the climber can use either of two methods, both of which should be practiced until mastered so that in a fall one reflexively chooses the best method for the situation.

In the *roll pivot* the climber first rolls from back to stomach—toward the head of the ax—then starts his arrest while still with head downhill.

The drag of the pick allows the lower limbs and torso to move with greater relative speed and thus swing around the pick into the lead. The pivot takes place faster if the body is cocked at the hips to help the legs make the swing. In soft snow it is also necessary to scramble with the feet, since the pick has insufficient drag.

In the *tuck pivot*, the falling climber, while still head downhill on his back, jams the pick into the slope beside his hip, with the ax shaft held across his body. If the axhead happens to be in the left hand, the pick

Fig. 81. Self-arrest from headfirst fall on back, using the roll pivot. (To arrest from headfirst fall on stomach, follow steps 4, 5, and 6.)

is driven into the slope by the left hip; in the right hand, by the right hip. With the pick as a pivot, the body flips from back onto hips and side and then onto stomach while feet swing around into the lead. In the flip, which can be expedited by a downhill kick of the legs, the body falls onto the ax in correct arrest position.

ARREST VARIATIONS

In loose snow of winter and early spring the pick cannot reach compact strata and the usual self-arrest is useless. The falling climber being nearly submerged, his most effective braking instruments are feet, knees, and elbows, all widely spread and deeply pressed. The greatest drag potential of the ax lies not in the pick but in the shaft—thrust vertically into the slope, exactly as the alpenstock **was** used by an earlier mountaineering generation. Pivots are usually

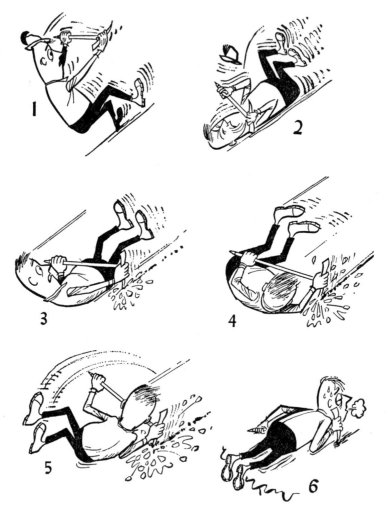

Fig. 82. Self-arrest from headfirst fall on back, using the tuck pivot.

unnecessary, the fall often being stopped while the climber is still head down.

Under any snow conditions, the speed with which the arrest position is attained is the key to success. In soft snow the reflexive speed of ramming in pick and toes brings the quick stop. On hard slopes the arrest must still be instantaneous but in addition *dynamic*—applied immediately but gently, with pressure increased rapidly but carefully, slackened at the least tendency of the pick to ride uphill from the shoulder, resumed when the ax is again under control. The startled climber who slips on hard snow and rolls into the reflexes of a panic-stop, jamming his pick deep, finds himself sliding down the hill all alone with his ax awaiting his return precisely where he jammed it. Moreover, in hard snow the feet should be kept out of the slope in the early stages of the fall; a sudden thrust of the toes may cause a calamitous backflip, especially if crampons are being worn. When the rate of fall has been stabilized at a fairly-slow speed by the pick, the auxiliary brakes are brought into action—the spread legs and digging toes and arched back; even in hard snow these are usually necessary to complete the stop.

On hard snow a quick stab at the slope with the pick or spike—or even boot heels—may stop a fall before it gets started. On the other hand acceleration is so terrific that the first instant of fall is often the whole story—*dynamic does not mean belated.* Once underway on hard snow the climber commonly rockets into the air and crashes back to the unyielding surface with stunning impact, suffering dreadful pains of laceration and concussion, completely losing uphill-downhill orientation.

The arrest on ice is very difficult to impossible, but should always be applied whether or not a belay is also available. Occasionally in the first instant of fall the pick lodges in a crevice or behind a hump and effects a stop even on a very steep slope. If not, the lower hand must raise the shaft off the slope, changing the angle at which the pick meets the slope until it can begin to dig in. As mentioned above, crampons must be managed with extreme care during a fall. Presumably a party on steep ice will belay unless the slope is short with a snow runout below, in which case if the arrest is begun on ice it can more easily be completed on the snow.

LIMITS OF THE ARREST

The arrest stops a fall by friction of ax and body against the snow. When the slope is too steep or slippery—too "fast"—not even the most skillful technique can reduce acceleration. Moreover, even successful arrests require at least a little time, during which the climber slides some distance. Therefore the value of the self-arrest is *limited by speed and length of a slope.* Obviously the arrest is ineffectual if the slope is too fast. Also, though a climber may be confident that under a particular set of conditions he can stop within 100 feet of slide, his faith in the arrest is misplaced if the slope is only 75 feet long with a cliff below.

Even when friction potentially available from the slope-climber contact is plentiful, still the arrest is *limited by strength and skill.* The athlete with perfect timing and bulging muscles may be able to arrest a bounding fall down a cliff of ice while the tourist slides helplessly to disaster on a gentle snowfield. However, the learned skill is more significant than native ability. Arrest with ax is not instinctive. Instinct tells the novice to do foolish things, such as throw away his ax and claw with his fingers. Only thorough practice can provide him with reflexes stronger than his instincts.

A climber must *at all times be aware of his arrest limits.* If the slope seems too fast or too short, or if he is not sure of his strength and skill, the self-arrest should be supplemented by other protective techniques.

Team Arrest

The team arrest is intermediate between self-arrest and belays. When there is doubt that an individual could arrest his own fall—such as on crevassed glaciers and steep snowfields—and yet conditions are not so extreme as to render belaying necessary, the party ropes up and travels in unison. Should any member fall he is *arrested by two or three axes,* not one.

If it is to be a safety device rather than a hazard, the *rope between the climbers must be fully extended* except for one or two coils carried by the second and third men. These not only allow easy compensation for pace variations but if one person falls give the others time to hit the slope before being yanked into the air by the rope. However, slack is kept at a minimum to bring the second and third axes into action at the earliest possible moment.

When a roped climber falls he *immediately screams "FALLING!"* It is not advisable to delay the alarm to see how the self-arrest will come out; the partners may then hear the signal only after they have already begun their trajectories. When a roped climber *hears the cry "FALL-ING!" he reflexively drops into arrest.* Turning in slow amazement to watch the catastrophe wastes seconds that may prove precious.

Hip Belays

At this point the reader would do well to refer back to Chapter 10, for the principles of belaying are everywhere the same. Though on snow and ice belays using the ice ax (described below) are also available, the preferred stances are identical with the body belays used on rock. Snow requires even closer attention to dynamic application, since the rope is most commonly wet and thus has more friction than when dry, and since frequently the stances are weak. It is some consolation that usually there is assistance from the falling climber's self-arrest.

HOLE STANCES

Glaciers and snowfields offer a variety of surface openings which can be utilized for belay stances. There are the true crevasses, small and large, of glaciers; the crevasse-like holes found in snowfields; the moats between snow and rock; the oversized suncups around fallen rocks or dirt.

Small holes (crevasses or moats or other) which pinch out or have a solid bottom at a depth of 3 to 10 feet, and are wide enough to admit the belayer's body as a sort of human piton, provide splendid bomb-proof stances. Not only is the belayer's body securely lodged but the friction of the rope bending over and trenching into the lip of snow

Fig. 83. Belay in moat.   *Fig. 84.* Belay in small crevasse.

gives a great deal of additional purchase—so much that if dynamic application will be desirable the belayer should interpose his ax between rope and snow.

Wide, deep crevasses or other holes should for obvious reasons be utilized only with caution. Frequently a sunken bridge offers a secure stance, but if visual inspection leaves any doubt the belayer must be belayed while making closer investigation.

Shallow and narrow "finger" crevasses which will not admit the body, and also large suncups, can be used in a different way, the belayer sitting above the hole or in the suncup, bracing his feet on the lower edge. A bit of work with the ax can improve such stances immensely.

PROJECTION STANCES

Particularly on ice but also frequently on snow various features project above the slope and are sufficiently large to provide the belayer with a good stance, either bracing his feet against the uphill side or less desirably straddling it. In various terrains the following may be encountered: trees, notably useful in early-season low-altitude climbing; seracs and ice blocks; fallen rocks firmly frozen into the slope; rock outcrops thrusting through the surface. Some of these afford very strong positions, but often a projection is more effectively employed as an anchor, as described later.

STANCES KICKED OR CHOPPED

In soft snow a stance can be established by stomping the feet and wallowing the hips. If the possible fall is moderate, ease of construction makes such a belay worth consideration, but since a hard fall might pull the feet through the braces the alternative ice ax belay should be compared in value. Whenever such a body belay is placed in snow the ice ax should be adjacent to the bracing hand; in a fall the belayer grips the axhead so that if pulled out of stance he can go into arrest.

Fig. 85. Sitting belay in snow.

In hard snow or ice an absolutely bombproof stance may be possible by chopping. On steep slopes the amount of time required is usually too great, but on gentler slopes a few quick strokes may create a superb position.

ANCHORS

As emphasized in Chapter 10, often an anchor is the difference between a shaky and a sound body belay. Details of anchoring on snow and ice are the same as on rock; once again the only distinction is in the anchor points characteristically available.

The most common anchor is a back-up belay by another climber, especially recommended because stances on snow and ice are typically less strong than on rock. Generally such an anchor would be desirable if not essential for the belays shown in Figures 85 and 87.

Projections, as noted previously, are often better anchors than braces. For example, a serac with a 3-foot diameter is too narrow for a good tripod stance but as an anchor may warrant full trust even if the position below is not strong. The natural tendency is to feel more secure with the feet braced against a solid point, however narrow and shaky the base of support; a full analysis usually shows that a "hanging belay," anchored by the solid point, is far stronger.

Fig. 86. Standing belay anchored to ice screw or picket.

When steep snow slopes are adjoined by rock walls or interrupted with outcrops or blocks of rock, as they frequently are, the rock-type ironware discussed in Chapter 11 can provide anchors. Ice screws and pickets and bollards, described in Chapter 13, have obvious use.

The ice ax, if well-placed, can also serve as an anchor. However, if the belay and anchor are unsound a wild ride may result with a flailing ax tied on behind—an experience few are inclined to repeat, even if they can. Furthermore, the belayer has no chance to attempt a self-arrest if he is pulled from his stance.

Ice Ax Belays

On many slopes of snowfield or glacier there are no holes or projections adaptable to hip belaying, and chopping a stance is too long a job to be practical. In these circumstances ice ax belays can be employed. Though inferior as a class to body belays, they often are quite strong enough and usually are installed rapidly if they can be installed at all. A fast adequate ax belay is preferred to a slow bombproof body belay.

The two factors determining the potential of an ax belay are (1) strength of the snow; (2) depth of shaft penetration. The ideal condition is snow which offers resistance but after a battle allows the shaft to be buried up to the hilt; in such case an excellent boot-ax belay can be placed. When the shaft enters too easily and has considerable lateral play, strength is less than ideal, though stamping a compact platform around the shaft helps. When only a small fraction of the shaft can be inserted strength is also less than ideal. Under this condition it is necessary to brace the upper end, as in the hip-ax belay. If only a few inches can be buried, other types of belays must be used.

BOOT-AX BELAY

The simplest, strongest, and fastest utilization of the ice ax for belaying is in combination with the boot, the ax providing an anchor to the slope, the boot bracing the ax, and both together giving friction surface over which the run of the rope is controlled.

Before proceeding, clarification of the terminology to be used is in order. The belay position applies both on the flat—as in protecting a crevasse passage—and on an incline. In all circumstances the belay must always be *oriented toward the endpoint of the potential fall,* the final location of the fallen climber, and thus the direction from which the force reaches the belayer. For the sake of descriptive convenience the commonest case of a fall will be assumed; the term "downhill" will be used rather than the cumbersome "endpoint of fall," and "below" rather than "final position of the fallen climber." The reader must, however, keep in mind that in some cases the force may reach the belayer horizontally or even from uphill.

Boot-Ax Position

1. Shaft is jammed in snow as deep as possible, tilted slightly uphill to resist pulling out.
2. Pick is parallel to fall line, pointing uphill, thus applying the strongest dimension of shaft against force; also the length of pick prevents rope from running up the shaft and over the top.
3. Belayer stands below ax: facing at approximately a right angle to line of fall; facing *toward* the side on which the climber's route lies.
4. Uphill boot is stamped into slope against the downhill side of shaft at a right angle to the fall line, thus anchoring shaft against downhill pull.
5. Downhill boot is in a firmly-kicked step below the uphill boot, bracing the belayer against the expected force.
6. Uphill hand is on the axhead in arrest grasp, bracing the shaft against downhill and lateral stress.

7. Rope from below crosses toe of boot, which prevents the rope from trenching into slope.

8. Rope bends around the uphill side of shaft, then down across the instep of the bracing boot. It is controlled by the downhill hand and brought back uphill around the heel, forming the "S bend" to apply braking. A less-strong method uses the "C bend," with the rope wrapped around the shaft and the heel of the bracing boot in a single bend. In either method the downhill hand is the braking hand and, as in any belay, must never leave the rope. The uphill hand must guard the ice ax, help manipulate the rope, and scratch the nose as required.

The switchbacking nature of snow climbing demands that every climber be equally adept at installing the boot-ax belay with either foot uphill, since above all it is essential that the belayer face his climber's fall line; *if the climber falls behind the belay obviously there is no belay.*

Fig. 87. Boot-ax belay.
a. "S bend."
b. "C bend."

Taking in slack when the climber is approaching the stance is difficult in any ax belay. Ideally the controlling hand should never leave the head of the ax, but friction is usually so great there is nothing for it but to use both hands to reef in slack. Fortunately a fall on snow takes a few seconds to develop momentum so that in most cases the belayer has enough time to return his uphill hand to the axhead. However, if the shaft can be driven only partway into the snow, a constant force in the uphill direction must be applied to the upper shaft to maintain the strength of the belay position. This force is provided by the knee and/or the uphill hand.

Dynamic application is as essential to the success of this belay as of any other, both to reduce initial impact and to allow a gradual stop during which the strength limits of the stance are never exceeded. However, excessive run of the rope is dangerous. Braking begins immediately. Additional friction as needed is gained chiefly by bringing the rope farther around the bend of the boot heel and secondarily by tightening hand pressure on the rope. If the belay seems about to fail because of the shaft pulling out, pressure is momentarily slackened until control is regained. If the stance fails the belayer goes into arrest.

For most conditions the boot-ax position is superior to any other ax belay. The opposing forces—downhill pull of the fall, uphill push of the belayer—meet in a small area, namely the bend of the rope around toe, shaft, instep, and heel. Moreover, this focus of opposing forces is close against the slope, an important stabilizing factor. The sharp angle of bend provides a great deal of friction yet can be easily varied by slight motion of the controlling hand. Running the rope over the toe prevents it from trenching so deeply into the slope that the belay becomes abruptly static.

Not only is the boot-ax stance theoretically strong but it is easy to learn and apply, thus insuring maximum realization of the belay potential even by inexperienced or physically-weak climbers. In speed it is unsurpassed. A well-practiced climber with one sweep catches the rope with the shaft and jams the shaft into the snow, then stamps in his boots and places his hands—the whole process complete in seconds. On very steep slopes, however, placing the uphill boot next to the shaft and the downhill boot in a comfortable step may require near-impossible contortions.

HIP-AX BELAY

Though more complex and in general less stable, the hip-ax stance is adaptable to the steep slopes where the boot-ax position becomes difficult.

Hip-Ax Position
1. Shaft is jammed in snow as deep as possible.
2. Pick is parallel to fall line, pointing uphill.
3. Belayer stands below the ax facing uphill, turned slightly so that the fall line is in front of him.
4. Downhill leg is straight and firmly footed.
5. Uphill leg is bent with the knee braced against the shaft where it emerges from the slope, the foot firmly placed. Usually the bent leg is approximately horizontal from knee to hip.

6. Uphill shoulder and chest are pressed against the axhead.
7. Uphill hand is on axhead in arrest grasp.
8. Rope from climber below runs along downhill leg, bends around
   the shaft, back downhill around the hips or buttocks, and is controlled by downhill hand.

Additional friction is gained as needed by bringing the downhill
hand more sharply around the body until finally it may be bent across
the waist. The shaft is braced against lateral stress and vertical pullout
by the hand on axhead. The shaft is braced against downhill stress by
the knee and thigh, reinforced by shoulder and chest pressed against
the axhead. Force of the fall presses the shaft downhill against the
knee, which in turn is pressed uphill by the rope on hips.

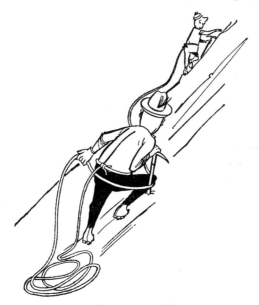

Fig. 88. Hip-ax belay.

The hip-ax stance is very much less stable than the boot-ax. Stresses
are extended over longer distances in four dimensions: along the fall
line between hip and shaft; across the fall line over the width of the
hips; vertically normal to the fall line between slope and hip; in time
by the interval between first impact of the running rope on downhill
leg and final impact on downhill hand. The force diagram is so
complex, with so many points of possible error, any one of which
upsets the entire stance, that realizing the belay's theoretical strength is
very difficult.

The usual point of failure is the uphill hand. When braking is too
rapid the shaft slides down along the uphill leg. The proper corrective

measure is to momentarily slack off on braking with the downhill hand while pushing the shaft back to upright position with the uphill hand. If braking is not slackened quickly enough, however, the ax pulls out shockingly fast; the human arm is ill-designed to resist violent side-motions. Despite its limitations the hip-ax stance is sometimes the only one possible; it should not be used if anything better is available, and never without a clear realization of its weaknesses.

An exception must be noted—a special application of the hip-ax belay which is very strong indeed. When the shaft can be placed behind a firm boulder of rock or ice or in a tiny crevasse, the stance has exceptional strength and can be very rapidly installed. Frequently a *hip-ax belay with natural reinforcement for the shaft* (often called a "K-2 belay," recalling its use on that peak to save an entire party) makes better and faster use of a small boulder or crevasse than as brace or anchor for a body belay. However, if the belay is too static the overload comes directly on the shaft and since it cannot pull out it breaks instead.

OTHER BELAYS

In the literature innumerable snow and ice belays are presented. Some have apparently been theorized without testing. Others are inferior variations of the boot-ax and hip-ax stances recommended here. A few of these miscellaneous belays are useful in special circumstances.

Though not constituting a stance, *multiple turns of rope around the shaft* have status as a variation of every shaft belay. Every loop of rope around the shaft adds friction that is very undesirable where a sudden load and rapid run of the rope is expected; many a pulled-out ax and many a broken ax is directly attributable to superfluous rope around the shaft. The friction is welcome in a static belay since the tension of holding weight is transferred from the climber to the shaft. Multiple turns are standard practice for an anchoring belay, when the third man on a team is holding a tight rope on the belayer who is giving a running belay to the leader. The extra turns are also desirable when there is no conceivable necessity for dynamic application, such as in crevasse rescue. Even in a dynamic belay, once the fall has been held the belayer may be able to throw extra loops around the shaft to stabilize the situation and allow relaxation.

On hard snow or ice when the shaft cannot attain useful penetration, and the belayer is above the climber, the *pick belay* gives a little support. The pick is rammed into the slope above the belayer and held there by his hand in arrest grasp, the rope from below is passed over the head of the ax between the holding hand and the slope, controlled by the other hand.

The Swiss Guide Association once conducted tests to find the most effective belay—short of excavation—for steep ice. They abandoned all ax belays, especially those using the pick, in favor of the *belay around a crampon*. The crampon must be stamped firmly into the slope and carry the entire weight to be effective. If crampons are being worn this stance is probably at least as effective as that using the pick, but both are primarily "guide belays."

The entire emphasis here has been on "in-place" belays assumed by parties moving one man at a time. Climbing manuals of the past speak about an entirely-different technique, the *ice-ax-loop belay* applied after a fall. Each climber ties a small loop in the rope connecting him to his fellows, using an overhand knot. The loop is at such a distance from the climber that it reaches his feet when dropped free. The ax shaft is inserted into the loop and kept there during travel. Should any member of the team slip his companions jam their shafts into the slope. On cursory inspection the technique seems to have immense virtues and for many years was widely used—and did, indeed, stop many falls. However, in the long years vices became apparent. First, if the snow is hard the shaft cannot be rammed into the slope and even a small force pulls it out. Second, if the shaft can be deeply imbedded and the fall develops any momentum whatsoever the force comes upon the shaft abruptly and all at once—a classic example of a completely-static belay—and the shaft breaks. For every minor success to the credit of the technique a dozen catastrophes are recorded where parties rode the slope all the way to the bottom accompanied by splintered axes. Though the ax-loop belay has occasional uses, such as on steep slopes between crevasses where there is no space for arrests yet fixed belays are not deemed necessary, in general it is downright dangerous. If the team arrest cannot control the potential fall, in-place belays must be prepared; the "belay after a fall" is a snare and a delusion.

Technique of Practice

Committing this entire chapter to memory would flatter the authors but would not stop any falls. Yet a good many climbers venture above snowline with even less preparation, having no idea at all how slides on snow are controlled beyond a vague impression that the ice ax is somehow supposed to do the job. Arrests and belays are difficult enough at best, involving as they do close coordination of many muscles and tools. Without thorough practice to imbed the proper reactions deep in the reflexes, successful stops under extreme conditions are a rare and random chance.

Practice of the arrest begins by lying against the slope and point by point checking correctness of each detail of grip and posture, then by "hitting the deck" from a standing position—checking to see if after flopping down the details are still correct. Downhill motion is then introduced, the climber sliding in sitting glissades, rolling toward the head of the ax into arrest. The pivot follows, practiced first by sliding head-first on the stomach and finally by toppling backward out into space, hitting on the back with head down, pivoting and arresting.

The next phase of self-arrest practice can best be combined with team arrest. When any one person calls "Falling" all members of the team flop on their axes. Then one slides without arresting, leaving the job entirely to his companions. Finally two or more slide, testing the ability of one climber to hold the entire team.

Belay practice begins with manual hauling on the rope from the belayer, to test the stance, then progresses into use of glissades for a testing force. The "faller" makes short glissades, then increasingly-longer ones, and if the belayer can hold one person in the longest slide the rope will allow, another faller ties in, and another, until the belayer is pulled out.

The cardinal rule in practice of arrests and belays, as of any other technique, is that *the limits must be found.* Success is only half the practice; the point of failure must also be discovered, since otherwise it is impossible for a climber ever to intelligently set his margin of safety. It goes without saying that a practice slope must have a clear runout so that discovery of the limits does not endanger the student. Moreover, progression of practice into more intense stages must be gradual, and once a student has found his limits he should not be asked to exceed them; forced practice is as pointless as it is dangerous.

Practice of arrests and belays can start before the climbing season with sessions on convenient slopes of lowland sand and gravel. The first trial on snow should be under fairly-soft conditions or at least quite-gentle slopes. However, a day on soft snow gives no opportunity to learn the dynamic arrest of hard snow. Two or three days of intense work, under as many radically-different snow conditions, can in one season make a competent journeyman of the greenest apprentice. To become a master, though, practice must continue. An easy way to learn the tricks of many slopes and to gain the constant repetition necessary for reflexive efficiency is to mix a little practice with any climb. For instance, while climbing a frozen slope in early morning, taking a moment during a rest stop to try out the speed of the snow; while glissading home in the afternoon, occasionally rolling into an arrest.

Just for the fun of it, too, a climber should try an arrest sometime while carrying a full overnight pack.

Research

The methods described here represent hundreds of thousands of man-days of strenuous practice. Limits have been sought relentlessly, axes and ribs cracked in wholesale lots, belayers flipped like rockets from their stances—and numerous hallowed techniques forthwith abandoned and condemned. The boundary of safe climbing on snow and ice has been greatly extended, but many standard routes remain marginal, and many noble and unattempted ones beyond reason.

New concepts have been stated, tested, and proven in the past few years. More concepts are in order, and also many more systematic testing programs employing strain-gauges to measure forces developed in falls—and simultaneously, to make the data meaningful—inclinometers to record slope angles, thermometers to record air temperatures, and other instruments to find the water content and particle size of the test slopes. It would be fascinating to know the foot-pounds required to break various belays under identical conditions, how fast a fall a self-arrest can ever, in the most ideal circumstances, be expected to control, and exactly how strong are bollards, pickets, screws—and axes.

For a single basic example, the arrest has reached its apparent limits (though these are not precisely measured) with the present ax, which is first and foremost a tool for cutting steps. Since a more frequent use of the ax is for arrest, conceivably the day might come when a party carries "arresting tools" individually and one "stepcutting tool" per team. Here, and in every other technique and tool, there is ample room for ingenuity and patient investigation.

PART FOUR

Safe Climbing

16 *

THE CLIMBING PARTY
AND ITS LEADERSHIP

The Group

In most areas of life man works in groups to achieve his goals more completely, whether the goals are social or individual. In mountaineering he climbs in groups because he has found that with the help of others he can climb more safely, more successfully, more enjoyably.

The climbing party is more than the sum of its members. The individual members feel more confident—more aggressive in ascent and more enduring under stress—when they know they are part of a group. Mountaineers have discovered this; shipwreck survivors and explorers confirm it. Perhaps it is for this reason that the mind in ordeal situations offers the delusion of the "extra man" as a fortification. Whether he knows it or not, the man who needs no group has not yet been born.

On the other hand the group is nothing apart from its members. The group is created and sustained by their will; the members have a group only as long as they continually will to be together, to work together and to sustain each other. There is also a place for individuality in mountaineering: brilliant individuals can make brilliant contributions, both to particular climbs and to alpine lore. But the individual makes these contributions *to the group* and *within the framework of* the group. To be in a group is to abide by the group's decision. To be in a group is to help translate the group's decision into group action. Not to abide by this, to do it differently, is the way of the saboteur, the rebel, ultimately the way of the suicide. The individual earns the support of the group only as far as he continually reaffirms the existence of the group, in mountaineering as in the rest of life.

Leadership

The group must not only have unity it must also have direction. But direction involves two things: steering and propelling. The group must steer in one direction and be propelled in that direction. This is the aim of leadership.

Any mountaineering trip involves a rich spectrum of choices and makes continual demands on the will. A route must be found, equipment selected, dangers evaluated; the tired body must be inspired with the will to move. Without leadership even a strong party will wander aimlessly, or sit paralyzed with indecision, or lie abed while only the sun climbs. With good leadership even a weak party will come near finding what it seeks behind even the subtlest ranges.

Leadership may be present in parties that appear to have no leader. Some mountaineers have argued that the climber's training should include some solo climbing. Indeed, Frank Smythe writes that when the climber is alone he is more cautious and more alert, and can learn more, than with a group. Implicit in this description of an ideal is the assumption that a climber is directed by a leading principle of intelligence and alertness. The solo climber is not necessarily schizoid; he is—or should be—of one mind, one cautious mind.

In a democratic culture many mountaineering parties are composed of friends and have no explicit, official leader. Some parties of this sort will explain: "No member of our team is obviously outstanding and fitted to be the leader," or "We all cooperate so well we don't need a leader," or even "Leadership is a European institution that has no place in a democratic culture." Whatever the explanation, whatever the boast, the party will attain its aim only if someone is always implicitly leading. Someone must alert the others, someone must say, "Let us discuss and vote," someone must say, "Our decision seems to be so and so," someone must say, "Let us do it now." It need not always be done by the same person, but when it needs to be done someone must do it, and that person is the leader.

Much successful mountaineering has been done by so-called leaderless parties. And perhaps the most enjoyable weekend trips are those taken by small groups of friends with no explicit leader. But a safe rule is: the larger the party and the larger the mountain, the more definite and explicit the leadership must be.

When there is no leader or the leadership is weak it is all too easy for little things to become big. Trivialities become magnified, irritations become aggravated. Friends forget to vote, or ignore the vote; friends fall out. What should be challenging novelty becomes destructive chaos. Happy are the parties that know none of this; many are the parties that have tasted, and still taste, the bitterness of it. After a lifetime of climbing and exploration Gordon Brown wrote: "If you would stay friends, climb not as friends but as leader and led." The question, really, is not "Shall we have a leader?" but rather "What sort of leadership shall we have?"

In small parties group leadership is often best. Most climbers enjoy (and learn from) participating in the decision-making. An individual is always fallible in some respects; when several individuals make decisions together they balance each other, compensate for each other's fallibilities. Experience and wisdom can be pooled. Often a particular decision can be assigned to one member of the group; the routefinding, for example, is best done by the person who has been on the peak before, or by the person with the best eyesight or with a special flair demonstrated in past experience. Or, with a rope team that is climbing "leapfrog," the decisions will be made by whoever is leading at the moment. In parties where everyone shares in the decisions, everyone is that much more alert. Everyone is ready to contribute toward a decision or to make the decision himself. This makes for great flexibility in the party and it makes each climber more self-reliant. If some disaster occurs the individual is ready to operate on his own if necessary. Finally, where everyone has helped make the decisions everyone will thereby share more deeply the party's success.

On the other hand there are many occasions when it is necessary for one person to be explicitly acknowledged as leader. Inexperienced climbers need guidance, both for their own safety and to train their judgment. Many climbers would rather follow than lead, so that in some parties perhaps only one person has the imagination and initiative necessary for leadership. In large groups where it is impractical to assemble, discuss, and vote on every issue, the leadership should be vested in one person.

The great difference between group and individual leadership is one of efficiency. Whether one or the other is chosen for a particular climb depends largely on the purpose of the trip. If a small group of friends wants merely a good time in the mountains, the formal appointment of one person as leader is usually unnecessary; and for some climbers the naming of a companion as leader definitely inhibits enjoyment. On the other hand a group which has one firm objective, such as the climb of a particularly-difficult peak with other motives secondary, will do well to designate one strong person as leader and to abide by his decisions. Both the ancient and the modern democracies have found that in time of crisis it is necessary to appoint a strong leader who is given extraordinary powers. The same is true in mountaineering.

Organizing the Party

In any mountaineering venture an early decision of great importance is the choice of party personnel. If a definite climbing objective has already been designated, a party must be chosen which will be adequate to the climb. A party is adequate not by its size alone, but also according to the strength and experience and morale of its members. If the trip involves glacier travel the party should include men who have practiced crevasse rescue. If the climb involves difficult rock the party should include a man skilled in pitoncraft. And of course any long trip requires a person willing and able to plan food.

If the party is found to be weaker or stronger than the organizers anticipated, the objective can be changed, although often the objective is not chosen until after the organizers have evaluated the strength and desires of the party.

Organizers cannot be too careful in selecting party members. The more exacting the trip the more care is needed in selection not only for climbing prowess and knowledge, but also for the various traits that make up character and personality. These are subtle and intangible factors—until they become most horribly tangible, as when the fellow is caught stealing from the food supply, or becomes hysterical in a thunderstorm. One should know his companions and know them in advance. Here even gossip may help. Mountaineers gossip a great deal, talking about each other's exploits, eccentricities, weak points, and humors. In climbing, the justification of gossip is that it may function as an exchange of information. Some of this is merely malicious backbiting, but some of it may become of life-or-death importance and prove valuable in selecting the party.

The leader of the group can be chosen in any of several ways. According to the casual method the person who organizes the party is tacitly assumed to be the leader. Sometimes the leadership changes during the climb; one person starts as leader but after awhile it becomes obvious that another is better fitted to lead, either because he is able or more willing to take the responsibility. Two men may work well together and prefer to be joint leaders; sometimes a triumvirate is appropriate.

Not everyone can lead; some climbers are incapable of doing so. On the other hand there are those who are incapable of following. The best mountaineers, however, can both lead and follow, and are perfectly willing to do either. Every climber should, if possible, lead occasionally, even if only on easy trips, for the sake of developing confidence. On some mountains it is possible to appoint as leader a relatively-inexperienced person; he makes the decisions but can consult the more-experienced members of the group when he wishes, thus in a manner of speaking serving out his apprenticeship.

In special cases a leader may be imported into the party. A group of young climbers planning a trip overseas, for example, can organize their group and define their objectives, and finally invite a more-experienced outsider to join the group as leader.

Leading

THE LEADER AND HIS LEADING

The leader is responsible for the success of the trip and the safety of the party. To lead, and to choose a person to lead, are difficult.

Personality is crucial. Character, intelligence, and alertness must be combined in certain ways, and people with the right combinations are the natural leaders. Although experience is important it is not the only requirement. The members of a party will look instinctively to the person who inspires the most confidence. This may not be the man with 20 years' climbing experience, if those years were spent in compulsive climbing motivated by greed, egotism, or thrill-seeking. Rather it might be the man with only 2 years of climbing experience if he also has a lifetime accumulation of common sense and good judgment. Physical agility and strength are desirable but not necessary, since the leader need not lead a single pitch of the climb; he may even be the rearguard. What matters is that the party looks to him for judgment and decision.

Experience must be coupled with self-confidence if the leader is to be accepted as such by his party. The man without confidence in himself is hardly one to inspire confidence in other people. The man with the most dynamic personality, the best-liked and most aggressive, is likely to be chosen leader, although another man may have more knowledge to back his judgments. It is in any case a mistake to follow a man who is incapable of making or expressing decisions; that way lies chaos.

The leader must be inspiring, as inspiring as the occasion demands. If the rising hour is 2 a.m., the leader rises then; he may not want to, but he does. If the summit is near and the time is short, he does not merely decide to continue or retreat; he gets everyone to decide the same way. In crisis he is firm; in ordeal he is the example of fortitude; in disaster he controls himself, and leads his companions to control of the situation. He must combat lassitude and despondency; he must curb greed and anger; he must avoid panic and despair. He may be the strong, silent type or the "talk it up, gang!" type; whoever he is, he must inspire and control himself before he can inspire and control others.

THE LEADER AND THE PARTY

In a small group of good friends the friendship is usually enough to insure party harmony. Where the party is larger, problems of leadership are more complex. The leader cannot do everything himself, nor should he try. Rather he should delegate duties to others whenever possible, not only to insure that these jobs will be done, but also to build party morale by giving more of the members positions of responsibility. For a very large party the leader may designate someone to plan food, another to plan transportation, another to arrange for a pack train, and so on. He will appoint an experienced and patient member as rearguard, and may send several fast climbers ahead to pick a campsite or scout a route or cut steps. When he divides the group into rope teams and appoints a leader for each he also delegates important duties. It is also the better part of foresight to appoint a deputy, a second-in-command who will assume command if anything happens to the leader.

The good leader has a variety of techniques for getting others to follow him. In most cases he needs only to say what he thinks is best and the group will act accordingly, out of friendship or respect. Often the leader will consult some of the others before making up his mind, or even ask everyone's opinion. In these instances the members will tend to follow the leader because they know they helped make the decision. Some leaders make a habit of oozing confidence and enthusiasm, but most leaders find it more useful (and prudent) to make cautious and tentative statements so that the others in the group will feel free to express their own views—which may, in the final analysis, prove to be better than the leader's. Whenever possible the good leader is subtle. He persuades gently and indirectly; he persuades the stubborn few by enlisting the support of the majority. He makes guesses and suggestions; he says "Wouldn't you like . . ." He is not an autocrat so much as a stabilizing influence. Occasionally he must be decisive, be firm, give orders, and then he leaves no doubt as to what is to be done. There are times when the leader cannot consult with his companions, and times when the minority is implacably stubborn, and times when the leader is himself in the minority. Perhaps the majority is weak, or apathetic, or paralyzed with fear, or epileptic with panic—or calm, sincere, but adamant. In these cases, if the issue is merely one of making the summit or not, the leader's resourcefulness reveals itself: he coaxes, argues, wheedles, cajoles, challenges, inspires. But in emergencies where the issue is life or death the leader can call heaven as his witness and hell as his servant: there is nothing he may not or must not do then for the safety of his party.

In a crisis the leader must call forth in himself and his companions all the strength and resources they have, their individual and collective resources. But in the routine of the normal trip also the good leader will challenge the resources of his party. He will try to find outlets for the energy and talent of the members of his team. Let the engineers rig the Tyrolean traverse; let the untiring young pick a route on the nearby peak. The leader is here an artist, using his human material to the party's best advantage.

While inspiring the best in his party the leader is also extending the party's best. He is training its members to do better. The beginners are taught how to climb and climbers are taught how to lead. Training others to lead is the acme of leadership. It takes patience, intelligence, and generosity. Nor does the leader neglect to train himself. On a particular trip he is always thinking ahead, anticipating the problems that will arise and planning their solution. In camp he is thinking of the climb; on the ascent he is thinking of the descent; in success he plans retreat. His eye is on the horizon, on that little cloud no bigger than a man's hand. He knows how tired his companions have become and therefore what strength he can count on in a crisis. If the party is ascending a face he studies the ridges on either side. If the party is ascending a ridge he studies the faces on either side. He plans for bivouacs or alternate routes of descent. He observes and plans, and calls the attention of his companions to these things, for any of them might suddenly become leader. Everywhere on the trip the leader is crossing bridges before he comes to them. He does more: he borrows trouble. What would I do if we lost the rucksack here? What would I do if my belayer were hit with a rock? By keeping these things in mind, by being alert and thinking ahead, the leader to that extent is master of what happens on this particular climb, and he will to that extent increase his ability to lead in the future, anywhere.

SOME HIGHER VALUES

The leader leads on the climb by leading before the climb. He sets the tone of the party's ambition; he can curb the overconfident and inspire the timid. He determines the standard of conscientiousness, the degree of alertness and care in planning. More important, however, is the leadership he displays after the climb. Here too he sets the tone of the party's attitude, whether it is one of brag, sourness, or good-natured modesty. On the peak and afterward the conscientious leader follows the example of those leaders of great spirit—like Frank Smythe, pausing to let his Sherpa be the first on the summit, or Charles Evans, whose account of the ascent of Kanchenjunga closes with a farewell to "our untrodden peak . . . a symbol of what is always beyond."

Following

A party needs good followers as much as a good leader. There is an art to following well, and in some situations it is harder to follow than to lead, for the follower must not only climb well and climb as he is directed; he must also be alert, ready to become leader himself at any time. He disciplines himself to summon the patience, courage, and strength that the moment requires. Often it is harder to belay than to lead the pitch—harder to belay smoothly and calmly while knowing only that the leader is somewhere high above, on doubtful rock.

The follower has to be alert and sensitive to the leader's suggestions; if he is by nature neither alert nor sensitive, he must at least be able to understand and obey a direct, explicit order, even if the suggestion may appear unnecessary, or the order may appear too demanding. If one is tired or afraid it is easier to ignore the suggestion and shirk on the order.

The good follower will discipline himself for the sake of the party discipline. He must remember also that if he shirks on this trip he will not be asked by these companions to join them on future trips. The pride he takes in the beauty of a perfectly-functioning team will make self-discipline easier. This is the sort of team that he hopes to lead in the future himself; he earns the right to lead such a team, he earns the right to expect smooth functioning, only as far as he understands what self-discipline, and the discipline of a good follower, is.

The Party and Its Strength

Several things make a party strong or weak in relation to its goals. One is the mountaineering proficiency of the members, another is the size of the group, and another is the party's morale. Morale is difficult to analyze; in general a party has good morale when it has good leadership and good followship.

Mountaineering proficiency involves many things: chiefly, climbing ability, experience, and physical condition. A strong party would consist of several or more experienced, well-equipped mountaineers in good physical condition, each agile on rock and each able to handle rope and ice ax with ingrained reflexes. What constitutes a weak party is not so easy to define. In some cases a party is strong enough if it has only two strong climbers in addition to many weak climbers. In other situations a group of ten strong climbers and one weak climber is too weak a party. The weak man might merely be clumsy or slow or stupid, and yet his weakness might jeopardize the entire party. A party with no experienced members is a weak party in any situation.

The size of the group is a matter of simple numbers, but good judgment about the best size for a group is not easy. The minimum size for a party is the number of people who could adequately handle an accident situation. Traditionally the party of three has been standard: if one climber is hurt the second can stay with him while the third goes for help. Variations from the basic unit of three depend on the particular situation. On difficult climbs where it would be dangerous for one man to go for help alone, four is the safe minimum. On the other hand if there is a support party nearby, a rope of two can safely climb by itself. On a glacier climb four to six people are needed where a speedy crevasse rescue may be necessary. A climb to a remote area where there is no support for hundreds of miles must plan for complete self-sufficiency and therefore becomes an expedition of relatively-large numbers. A party gains in strength if there is a group of supporting climbers waiting nearby, or if there is another climbing party in the area. The latter case often proves to be merely a parody of safe mountaineering, because the other party might itself be exhausted or need rescue. To be useful the support party must be willing and able to do rescue work, and ready, moreover, to initiate rescue automatically at a prearranged time. In cases where there would ordinarily be no support in the area the climbing party should arrange in advance to have it available somehow, as near to the area as possible, leaving its plans and time schedule with a responsible person who will dispatch help if the climbers do not return when due.

A mistake to be avoided is the belief that a larger party is always a safer party. A larger party can start bigger avalanches and kick down more loose rock. It can retard itself in many ways, both in camping and climbing. No matter how well-organized and led, the largeness of the group tends to breed overconfidence and carelessness, even among good climbers. And, of course, there are some mountain circumstances under which no party—and no climbing—is really safe.

In mountaineering time is vital for safety and for success. The party will be safe and successful according to how it uses its time. The factors cited above (proficiency, size, morale) contribute to the party's strength in many ways, but the most important of these is the way they enable the party to use its time efficiently. The trip planners allow a reasonable amount of time for making the trip safely, and when they leave the trip schedule with a support-dispatcher they also allow some extra time for minor mishaps, harmless bivouacs, and the like. The extra margin of time gives an extra margin of confidence, for the party can climb more cautiously and slowly than it had planned to. Nevertheless, no matter how generous it is the time allowance fixes a definite limit to the group's activity, just as the hours of daylight or the months of summer impose limits; and the party is strong according to how well it can use its limited time.

The climbing ability and physical stamina of the party affect its time-use directly. If the climb is on steep rock all members of the party must be agile and strong. If the climb is a predawn-to-afterdark tour, the members must have stamina to maintain a good pace for the whole time—and reserves of strength for coping with the unforeseen.

The experience of the party affects its time-use directly. An experienced routefinder can choose a route with little waste of time, and the route he chooses will be the fast one. Likewise the experienced leader can evaluate situations and make good decisions faster than the less-experienced person. Experience adequate on easy trips may be inadequate on harder trips, but in general an experienced leader has not only an accumulated store of knowledge to draw on, but also the very habit of decision-making, so that his lack of experience with the details is compensated for by his confidence and shrewdness in on-the-scene decision-making. The more experienced the leader the less he will be slowed and awed by unfamiliar situations.

The size of a party affects its time-use directly. A rope of two can move faster on rock or ice than a rope of three. A rope of two leaders can move faster than a rope of one leader and one follower. A rope of three can move faster on a glacier than a rope of two, because it can effect crevasse rescues more quickly and hence can also travel more confidently and quickly.

The morale of the party affects its time-use directly and in many indirect ways. If the individual climbers have good morale they will be willing to exert greater effort and follow more challenging decisions. If the group has good morale as a group, if it is cohesive and harmonious, its decisions will be agreed on faster and carried out more effectively.

For high morale there must first be good communication among members of the group. Each must know his companions and their habits of speech: that John always exaggerates and Joe always uses "interesting" to mean "impossible." Knowledge of this sort becomes doubly important on a large mountain or in a foreign country. In situations of cold, fatigue, or danger, as at high altitudes, communication tends to congeal into a series of croaks and grunts, and the possibility of misunderstanding increases. And of course, where the party includes native porters, the climbers should know as much as possible about this other people: their temperament, desires, and communication habits. In general, the larger the party, the more time is required to build an effective network among the members. Once it is built the more time-saving the actions of the party will be.

Secondly, harmony is based on agreement in values. If there are personality differences between members the party organizers must decide whether these differences are harmless or whether they will flare up seriously in a climbing situation. Some climbers are intensely ambitious and this may in itself be a source of friction; the peakbagger and the hillwalker are often good friends in town, but may become as oil and water when on the mountain. In a smooth-working party there is agreement not only on the objective and the time schedule, but also on the overall mountaineering values of the party. There must be agreement on the casualness or intensity of the climb; nothing is more frustrating than to be middleman between two climbers pulling in opposite directions, one toward the summit and the other toward the meadow.

Strengthening the Party, and Oneself

It often happens that one member of the party has done much less climbing than the others. For easier climbs a little practice in fundamentals may suffice to bring his proficiency to a level where he can climb safely with the group. A simple review of knot-tying and belaying, or a little practice in arrests, might make all the difference. It may happen, however, that a short practice is not sufficient. In this case the inexperienced climber cannot be depended upon and the climb must be made with greater caution. Better still, the person should be left in camp or sent on an easier trip with another party.

Sometimes, in a remote or unfamiliar area, a whole party may feel inadequate to handle a mountaineering situation. Even a local and familiar peak can be so difficult that it awes good climbers. In such cases the party must be especially alert and cautious.

As has been reiterated throughout this book, mountaineering experience can be gained only by climbing. On the one hand it is important for beginning climbers to adopt a conservative attitude toward climbing; they will thus avoid getting into frightening situations which destroy self-confidence. On the other hand, in order to widen his experience the climber must attempt peaks of increasing difficulty. An inexperienced climber can learn both from climbing with more experienced mountaineers and from being with friends of his own ability. By climbing with more experienced companions the beginner can learn new techniques and develop good standards of judgment. Climbing with other beginners will develop his ability to make decisions. As the climber's experience grows he will find that the more he is able to depend on himself the more personal challenge he will find in mountaineering.

The Trip

PLANNING

Once the party is organized and the objective chosen, a time schedule must be drawn up. Good scheduling requires thorough consideration of many factors but usually swings the balance from failure to success.

Some groups like to make "adventure" their objective, and strike out into the wilderness deliberately ignoring available "cookbook" information, thus enjoying even on the most heavily-traveled peaks the challenge of a pioneer ascent. Most parties, however, aim at a more definite objective, and to attain it they first gather all the information they can concerning the best approaches, the best campsites, the location of the various climbing routes and their difficulty. For many climbs it is possible to consult both friends and the proper guidebook. For most climbing areas there are maps, so that the party can orient itself to the terrain in advance. Even if the trip is for exploration, some knowledge, however basic, will be available. One can perhaps study the geology to learn the nature of its rock and the glaciation. One can study the local meteorology to become familiar with the prevailing weather. Not only the prevailing but the imminent weather must be ascertained. If the weather is in a state of change one must determine from the signs whether it will be good or bad. Both safety and enjoyment may be involved.

In planning a time schedule one should allow for emergencies, though even the most-experienced leader cannot foresee everything that will happen on a trip. On the typical weekend climbing trip a starting time must be set which will allow ample leeway for driving and hiking to the basecamp. Drawing up a climb schedule is often left till the night before the departure, but it is better to do this further in advance for the simple reason that if a rising time has been scheduled beforehand there is little likelihood of disagreement the night before. In allowing time for the ascent one first of all considers the traveling speed of the party, then the condition of the peak, the time to be spent on the summit, and the desirable hour of return.

Consider, for example, a party camped at 5000 feet, below an 8000-foot summit. Ascending to 7000 feet will be straightforward and will take 2 hours. The next 500 feet is steep ice and may take 1½ hours. The final 200 feet of rock and 300 feet of scrambling will take 3 hours. The ascent will therefore total 6½ hours from camp to summit. Descending the rock by rappel will take 1 hour; descending the ice will take as long as ascending, 1½ hours. The long glissade down the bottom slope should require only ½ hour. Hence the total descent will require 3 hours, and the total climb 9½ hours. On this particular day darkness comes at, say, 8:30. The hypothetical party happens to want an hour on the summit and 2 hours of daylight left after the return to camp. Two hours must be allowed as a margin of safety. Thus, the starting time from camp in the morning is—no questions asked—6 o'clock. A similar projection of estimated times along highways, trails, and through the brush will fix the necessary departure time from home in order to reach high camp at a decent hour.

It is always necessary to consider the time of year. The amount of available daylight is a function of the season. Some climbs are most feasible early in the summer, when brush is covered with snow; other climbs can be executed only in late summer, when snow melts away from rock. Perhaps a particular season is best because of prevailing weather conditions; in some parts of British Columbia the best season for climbing is late August, while in Mexico it is winter.

Plans have to be made for food, equipment, and transportation. Food is chosen to please the tastes of all concerned. Similarly for equipment: John may suffer claustrophobia in the only tent that Joe finds comfortable. There is the trip itself to plan for, the probable delays, and the possible emergencies. The best rule: take somewhat more food and equipment than anyone anticipates using. The plan should also include which members are to provide what items, who is to carry how much weight, and finally (in detail) who is to carry what.

THE APPROACH

Most long climbs involve camping for one or more nights. There are obvious advantages to placing the final camp as high as possible. A high camp usually provides a better view of the peaks, especially in the early or late hours of the day. Also, the higher the camp the later the start can be made the next morning. A disadvantage is that it is often colder at higher altitudes because of reduced protection from the wind. And, although the fledgling climber may not realize it, every scenic camp high on a ridge is attained only at the cost of a long, pack-laden trudge up from the valley bottom.

Most high climbs necessarily involve early starts. The leader must decide on the rising time in advance and then resolutely ignore the moan of the indolent and the cry of the dissenter. The leader remains adamant.

On the trail or on the peak many problems can be avoided if the leader sets a good pace. "Fast" and "slow" are relative terms; what is fast for one party might be slow for another, and what is fast for one terrain might be slow for another. Chapter 4 has already discussed other aspects of pace which the leader must keep in mind.

If the party is large the leader keeps the group moving at a steady pace, with only short halts, because a large group tends to waste time straying, for in a large group a stray may not be missed till the end of and move slowly. Its members must also be kept together to prevent the day. Such mass travel is unwieldy and often obnoxious. If possible it should be avoided. Frequently a better plan which is also pleasanter may be substituted—that of traveling in small teams, though in this event the leader must visit horrible punishment on any team whose members arrive separately in camp or at designated checkpoints.

ROPING UP

One of the first things a climber learns about the rope is that it is primarily a safety device, and that its use is not a sign of weakness. A good rule to follow is to use the rope whenever a possible unchecked fall would result in a serious accident. The time to put on the rope is before the climbing becomes difficult and while there is still a spacious and protected stopping point available.

The leader assigns the climbers to rope teams according to their experience, speed, and personality. If there is more than one rope team in the party, it is desirable for the best climbers and belayers to be on the first rope—though not at the expense of leaving another rope without an adequate leader. The best climber then leads, putting in pitons or chopping steps, while the best belayer secures him. If both climbers on a rope are good enough they can "leapfrog," both thus having alternately the pleasures of leading and resting. This method also alerts two people to the problems of routefinding, instead of only one. Other aspects of the rope team are discussed in Chapters 9 and 15.

TURNING BACK

As his experience widens the climber begins to understand the frequent necessity of turning back before the objective is reached. A party may turn back for any one of several reasons, such as bad weather, approaching darkness, difficult or dangerous terrain.

Very often it is almost impossible to recognize signs of bad weather far enough in advance, for example when a storm approaches from the other side of the mountain. And it doesn't take much in the way of a storm to transform a pleasant peak into a miserable one. New snow makes rock slippery; all climbing is brought to a halt by freezing rain. Fog on a glacier makes it difficult to find a route through the usual maze of crevasses. The greatest discomfort—and perhaps the greatest peril—are the climber's wet, cold hands that refuse to obey the mind's orders. The sensible and safe place to be in a storm is in a warm tent.

The time to turn back because of oncoming darkness may be as early as noon if the descent is likely to take as long as the ascent. Generally the descent requires half as much time as the ascent, but there are climbs where the descent takes even longer than the ascent. This would be the case, for example, where long delicate descending traverses must be made. It is always wise to decide in advance what the latest time for turning back will be, summit or no summit.

There are other reasons why a party will turn back on a climb. Terrain too difficult is easy to recognize; terrain too dangerous is more subtle. An avalanche slope, or a traverse beneath an icefall, are examples. A party may turn back when it discovers that one member is sick, or simply because someone forgot his goggles. On the other hand inadequacy of climbing ability should turn the party back automatically.

Common sense usually dictates a retreat when it is necessary. There are times when the weather is miserable, yet still safe enough for the climb to continue. An avalanche slope dangerous in the afternoon might be crossed safely early in the day. The more experienced the climber the better his judgment about turning back.

BIVOUACS

Sometimes the decision to turn back is made too late or the descent takes longer than was expected. In such cases the climbing party is forced to spend the night away from an established camp. On some trips the climbers plan in advance to bivouac, because the objective is worth a long climb and a night in the open. But an unexpected bivouac is usually the result of a late start, poor routefinding, bad weather, or accident. If the party is caught by darkness it should continue climbing only if the route is well-defined, or if ropes are unnecessary. At the end of a long day the climber is cold and rather groggy. Because of fatigue he may not comprehend dangers of trying to go on in the dark when he is colder and more tired than he thinks.

Usually the climber has some forewarning of a bivouac. If he is still ascending he can begin looking for bivouac sites. If he is descending he can choose whether to keep going as far down as possible, or to stop at a site which has water or firewood. In any case it is wise to stop an hour before dark; even in this short time much can be done to make the night a comfortable one.

The leader has an especially-important role in the bivouac situation. Tired climbers may sag stupidly to earth without first trying to prepare an adequate bivouac, trusting in their fortitude and the inevitable return of morning. The attitude is heroic but foolish; such a night often drains away an important share of party strength. The leader, then, sets an example. He encourages everyone to keep busy at least until darkness is complete; there are wind walls to be built or firewood gathered. Everything possible must be done to keep the body warm; it is not enough to keep the teeth gritted. The grit will be necessary anyway; no matter how adequate the preparation there will be opportunity for fortitude and humor.

The Margin of Safety

In all his planning and all his decisions the leader must think in terms of a *margin of safety*. Even with the most detailed planning and the greatest alertness there is always the unexpected. The margin of safety is the ability a party retains for meeting extra trouble. Several precautions can be taken to insure this margin.

The party must be stronger than the mountain, with surplus food, clothing for colder weather than is anticipated, more rappel slings and pitons than needed, an abundance of extra flashlight batteries and bulbs. To emphasize a point already discussed, in setting the starting time the leader plans for a reasonable margin of daylight. The leader also takes the precaution of roping his party before it is absolutely necessary, rather than waiting till the very fine line between Class Two and Three climbing has been crossed. In making decisions regarding turning back or bivouacing, or failing to make them, if the leader does not make ample allowance for turning back the bivouac is sure to follow. If the party is caught by darkness, however, the leader insists that they bivouac while still on easy ground rather than climb until hung up. Obviously it is better to bivouac while still fresh than climb till exhausted.

The more experienced a climber, the more he realizes that the margin of safety is a good half of the enjoyment. The student need not be experienced, however, to realize at this point that the more efficient the leadership the more smoothly the climbing party functions as a group.

CLIMBING DANGERS

A Basic Consideration: Sense of Proportion

MOUNTAINEERING is a very complex sport, encompassing every-thing the climber does from the time he leaves home until he returns from his expedition. He must be fed, clothed, and sheltered. He must be intimately familiar with specialized techniques and equipment which enable him to move with safety over rock, snow, and ice. He must be deeply concerned with the forces of nature perpetually ar-rayed against him. Moreover, he should learn something of the flora, the fauna, the clouds, and the geology if he is to fully appreciate the scenes of his travels.

In the exercise of his mountaincraft the climber finds rewards on different levels. On the physical level he enjoys all the sensations of an outdoor life and the skilled use of his body. Intellectually he encoun-ters problems of route, equipment, organization, and safety. Finally, he derives significant rewards on an emotional level—the pleasures of comradeship, the confidence instilled by increasing self-knowledge, and the satisfaction of dealing successfully with intricate and stimulat-ing adventures.

If mountaineering is the most rewarding of sports it can also be the most demanding. The dangers, like the rewards, are found on both physical and psychological levels; disregard or ignorance of any of these hazards may cause the loss not only of the pleasurable benefits, but even of life. This book would be incomplete if it did not outline the elements of danger in the mountains; understanding the demands and responsibilities of the sport is essential for a true appreciation of its rewards.

From the very outset every climber should realize that the burden of accident prevention rests with him. He has the ability, through skill, knowledge, suspicion, and caution, to reduce his probability of accident almost to nil. At no point in his climbing career should he fail to weigh the expected rewards of his endeavor against the possible penalties. He should never forget that all other considerations are secondary to his ultimate goal of returning safely from the mountain. In short, as Geoffrey Winthrop Young wrote many years ago: ". . . in mountaineering our aim is to make sure of the highest form of adventure consistent with our sense of proportion."

A Standard of Judgment: A Climbing Code

A climbing party of three is the minimum, unless adequate prearranged support is available. On crevassed glaciers, two rope teams are recommended.

Carry at all times the clothing, food, and equipment necessary.

Rope up on all exposed places and for all glacier travel.

Keep the party together, and obey the leader or majority rule.

Never climb beyond your ability and knowledge.

Never let judgment be swayed by desire when choosing the route or turning back.

Leave the trip schedule with a responsible person.

Follow the precepts of sound mountaineering as set forth in textbooks of recognized merit.

Behave at all times in a manner that will not reflect unfavorably upon . . . mountaineering.

The more one climbs the broader becomes his positive knowledge, and yet there always remain factors just beyond his experience, new situations he has been unable to predict, things he does not understand, and all around him phenomena he does not even detect. In this uncertainty lies much of the charm of mountaineering: the infinite variety of experiences confronting the climber, the elusive perfection always sought but never quite attained. In this uncertainty also lies the major cause of the many tragedies which have claimed the lives of the unsuspecting throughout the history of mountaineering. With the best intentions in the world it is often difficult for a climber to maintain a sense of proportion in the face of unanticipated circumstances.

There do exist, however, certain fundamental rules which no climber can afford to ignore. One set of such rules is the Climbing Code of The Mountaineers, reproduced above nearly in its entirety. The code is based on the incontestable principle that sensible climbers want control over the outcome of risky or doubtful situations. They want strong chances of success; they want safeguards in case they have misjudged those chances; and they want the ability to retreat when it becomes evident that the chosen path leads to grave danger. These are the controls which assure a reasonable proportion between risk and reward. The Code is a means to implement these controls and help the climber maintain his sense of proportion when faced with the unforeseen. Similar codes have been developed in other areas by other climbers, based on careful observation of the habits of skilled climbers and upon thoughtful analysis of tragic accidents in their own experience.

By no means a step-by-step formula for conquering summits, the Climbing Code is rather the key to safe and sane mountaineering, an expression of the boundaries which the veteran mountaineer knows from experience he must not exceed, and which the newer climber, with less experience, must learn to accept as his guide lest he overstep the bounds of safety into the unknown. The layback he can learn in one lesson, but judgment he cannot acquire without years of mountain travel. Therefore, he *must* adhere rigidly to a sound climbing code, particularly in his first two or three seasons; follow it blindly if necessary even though he may not understand it at first; with the growth of wisdom, judgment, and responsibility he will make it his own, and never will stray from it as long as he climbs.

Each year the value of the Climbing Code—and similar expressions —is re-emphasized in the minds of those who work for the safety of beginning climbers as each year adds to the list of alpine tragedies. Investigation of each tragedy invariably reveals one or more departures, either thoughtless or deliberate, from the safe framework of rules stated by experienced mountaineers.

Elements of Danger: The Statistical Picture

Sooner or later in his career the climber encounters situations of potential accident, and it is well for him to be forewarned of the most common factors which contribute to mountain accidents, and to reflect upon the basic sources of mountaineering hazards.

Since 1947 the American Alpine Club (from 1961 in conjunction with the Alpine Club of Canada) has published annual descriptions and analyses of climbing accidents in North America. These are available in booklet form (see Appendix 3) and demand close study by every mountaineer. During the first 8 years, 198 accidents were recorded in the United States, 81 of which were fatal. In the 6 years between 1959 and 1964, 355 accidents were listed from the United States and Canada, killing 120 people. Only true climbing accidents are included in these totals, as distinguished from those which merely occur in mountain regions. Moreover, the tally shows only those accidents voluntarily reported. Numerous others, even fatalities, occur each year which are never publicized beyond the immediate vicinity. Furthermore, these recorded tragedies are but a fraction of the total world loss; in Europe and in Japan, where large numbers of people regularly engage in mountaineering, the toll is many times greater than in North America.

The statistics published in these annual reports roughly indicate the elements of danger in the sport of climbing, and they show basic patterns which recur again and again. Although every accident is a little different from every other, many of the contributing factors are surprisingly common; and most of the varied causes involve human frailties. Failure of ropes, slings, knots, and pitons due to improper use is frequent. Injuries from failure of half-learned techniques in exposed situations are common. Mistakes in judgment are as varied as the personalities of the people who make them. Hundreds of accidents could be used to illustrate these points but detailed analysis of statistics is not the purpose here.

The purpose, rather, is to illustrate one of the methods by which the climber comes to understand the hazards of climbing, and develops techniques and attitudes to minimize those hazards. Study of statistics enables the mountaineer to make use of the unfortunate experience of others to evaluate his own actions. As the climber absorbs the experience of others he begins to realize that the maxims of the Climbing Code are not arbitrary but have been forged from actual misfortune. He begins to study the inherent qualities of mountains and the men who climb them, and evaluate the qualities which lead to danger. Finally, from his thought and experience, he develops a philosophy which expresses his relation to the sport. He develops a sound judgment and an attitude which limits danger to a sane proportion of the endeavor. He understands the demands and accepts the responsibilities and thus he becomes a mountaineer.

The Physical Hazard: The Mountain

The hazards of mountaineering fall into two basic divisions, and an understanding of the dual nature of the problem is essential to the development of a safe attitude. Perhaps the most easily recognized is the physical hazard inherent in the very structure of mountains. No less important, but far harder to evaluate, is the psychological hazard which arises from the complexity of the all-too-human climber.

The physical hazard is objective, including all the natural processes which operate inevitably whether or not man is involved. Darkness, storms, lightning, cold, precipitation, altitude, surface disintegration— all such impersonal factors fall into this category.

Mountains are turbulent places, full of swift violence, where humans are dwarfed by comparison. In the natural process of building and destruction, the entire mountain range is forever being reduced to sealevel. Heat and bitter cold crack huge blocks from the solid rock. Lightning blasts the summits. Tons of rock and snow avalanche down into the valley. Rains and meltwater continually wash away supports so that gravity can go to work pulling away debris. Little insidious constant forces and tremendous crashing ones all work toward just one end, the leveling of the entire region. Through an eternity the forces keep chipping away. Time has no meaning here; neither has man, except as he may trigger a process prematurely.

This is the ground the climber seeks for his sport, an arena of the elements where destruction of a human is too minor an accomplishment to be worthy of note in the annals of nature. Through the labyrinth of these physical factors the mountaineer must thread his way. The climber who cultivates the dynamic view of the mountain will be amazed at the persistence of the continuous destructive forces but never surprised by the rapidity with which conditions can change. The snow that loosens all day and slides in late afternoon, the little lunchtime cloud that unleashes lightning at 3 o'clock—these are things the mountaineer cannot control and therefore must learn to recognize and avoid. He is awed by the part they play—and wisely arranges to be elsewhere while the game is on.

To avoid destruction by these invincible forces the climber depends on two things. First, he observes that there are places on a mountain where the devastation proceeds more slowly, with long time intervals between events. Second, he develops the keenness of his observation and the astuteness of his judgment to choose the right route by way of such places, at the right time to avoid being caught by what he calls accidents.

Finally, a factor of the physical hazard is the weakness of the human body. Against the background of mountains man is a vulnerable creature. A falling pebble or a slight stumble can kill him, and yet in pursuit of his sport he must climb where entire mountainsides sometimes move and must cling to cliffs with exposures measured in hundreds of feet. His tolerance for cold is extremely limited, yet he travels where temperatures can drop from intense heat to zero cold in a few hours, where wind and rain can drain his energy even at temperatures far above freezing. He cannot live off the land and must carry with him all the food his body needs for strength and warmth until he can return to habitable regions. These are some of the physical limitations which govern the climber.

The Psychological Hazard: The Climber

Man cannot control the physical nature of mountains, nor can he do much about his own physical limitations. He can and must, however, bear all these in mind, and a failure in awareness is the other basic element in mountain tragedies. Looking back upon an accident one always finds both physical and psychological causes—neither alone is sufficient. The destructive processes daily at work on the mountain are inconsequential unless a human being is in their way at the crucial time. The subjective controllable factors seldom in themselves cause death; but they do provide the steering which sets the climber on a collision course with one of the objective hazards. It is the combination which is dangerous. A slope may be ripening to an avalanche tomorrow—a climber, ignorant of snow structure, may trigger it today. A rock, slowly weakening by natural processes, may be preparing to fall next week—the weight of a careless climber may pull it loose today. This subjective psychological factor, which brings a particular climber to a given danger point at just the perilous time, is not amenable to statistical summary but is nearly always at the root of a climbing accident.

A climber seeking to control the mountain danger will ask himself what the factors of the psychological hazard are that he *can* control. There are subjective elements in every phase of a climb: the party management, the choice of route, companions, equipment, and techniques, the effort spent in acquiring skill and knowledge, even to a great extent a basic philosophy of approach to mountaineering. If all these elements are under thoughtful control the potential physical danger may never strike.

Of all the psychological hazards the most deadly is ignorance; and second is its partner, overconfidence. The perils of ignorance can be avoided very simply by study and experience; the background of mountaineering knowledge which a climber should have is the scope of this book. However, even the educated and experienced climber can be guilty of overconfidence. One of the most subtle forms arises from familiarity with a given climb. People have been killed because a strong experienced leader thought he could repeat with novices a climb he had made before with experts. Any climber should recognize a danger signal in his thinking when he finds himself imagining that he knows *all* about a given climbing problem.

Another aspect of this danger is the generally-recognized fact that an individual's ability does, through elusive psychological factors, vary from time to time. Every experienced mountaineer can remember days when his climbing lacked the usual "feel" and he has had difficulty with pitches well below his normal standard. If a false pride prods him into persisting on a difficult climb during one of his off days, danger can develop. The safe climber accepts his temporarily-lowered ability and chooses an easier objective with no loss of enjoyment.

Other forms of overconfidence are involved in many a mountain accident. There are thrill-seekers who in any activity insist on teetering at the brink of disaster; yielding to this urge on a climb they sometimes get the fatal nudge. The person with show-off tendencies may be driven by ego to climbing beyond his abilities with no margin of safety for the unexpected. An example is the talented young climber who continually overdrives his limits in order, so he thinks, the sooner to win acceptance among his more-experienced fellows. Although they will probably regard the youngster with amusement or shock—never the longed-for respect—he persists, and unfortunately he can induce others to follow him, people who would rather climb sensibly but who are shamed into stretching their luck to match him.

Another prominent factor in accidents is the attitude common to nearly every individual: namely, the feeling that *he* dwells under an umbrella provided by his own special providence, while accidents happen only to the other fellow. This narrow misconception results from confidence in the certainty of one's own knowledge and in the information provided by the senses, without a suspicion that these may be far from complete.

Group overconfidence—the fallacious belief that there is safety in numbers—is an insidious danger, which it is the task of leadership to control. The demoralizing effects of fatigue, illness, cold, wind, and bad weather also contribute to the psychological as well as the physical hazard. It is a basic duty of the leader to understand such influences on his party as well as on himself.

Psychological danger is present on every climb. Its control lies in awareness of all the varied factors which influence decision-making in the mountains. A climber who gains perspective by learning to back off from himself in order to judge his actions from an objective point of view develops a sense of responsibility for his conduct, and is never content to fumble or gamble his way up or down a mountain.

The Accident Situation: Fundamental Causes

To this point, the endeavor has been to analyze the dual nature of climbing danger and to emphasize some of the knowledge fundamental to a safe attitude on the part of the climber, an attitude which permits no more than a reasonable proportion of danger on any climb. Evaluating the experience of others contributes greatly to this knowledge. Nearly every mountaineer sooner or later is involved in a rescue operation, and such close contact with an accident is an educational, if a sobering, experience. Any climber who has participated in a rescue knows the risks encountered and the miseries endured by all, and he redoubles his resolve never to let *his* mountaineering provide the reason for such effort by self-sacrificing strangers and friends.

On another level, firsthand acquaintance with a rescue demonstrates the nature of the accident situation and illustrates the process by which such misfortunes come about. The important characteristic is seen to be that there is never a single cause or contributing factor. In every case one can trace back through a series of linked events. A slight alteration at any point in this chain could usually have prevented the accident.

In a typical glacier fatality, for example, the rescuer can detect a long list of such factors. Three or four friends get together for a climb in late spring. They all have about the same degree of experience, 2 or 3 years at most; none has more mountaineering knowledge than the others. They are all good friends and anticipate no disagreement, so no definite leader is appointed. Each person carries the same equipment, none better prepared for emergency than the rest, and none familiar with crevasse rescue technique.

They choose a route that skirts obvious fissures on the glacier and appears to lead safely over a smooth snowfield. However, they have failed to take into account the exceptionally-heavy snowfalls that spring which have concealed many deep crevasses; they proceed on their way unaware they are crossing one thin snowbridge after another. There is no leader to say, "We will rope up, because we always rope on glaciers"—and the party does not rope. The weather turns warm, the snow softens, the bridges weaken. Everything seems to be going well, the climbing is easy, the party is entirely confident of success. Suddenly a life is snuffed out deep in a hidden crevasse.

Throughout this chain of events appear weak links where even one slight change could alter the entire outcome. Another rope team for strength, well-defined leadership, an item of emergency equipment, a thought as to past weather, a little more planning—or even lacking all these, plain and simple adherence to the rule "rope up on glaciers" —any could be enough to save a life. Through the entire sequence, as the stage is slowly set for disaster, each member of the party has had a chance to detect each weakness, and failed.

The rescuer, reviewing such an accident situation, is impressed by the necessity for objective evaluation of both the mountain and the party at every stage of an ascent. From such close encounters with accidents the climber-rescuer becomes alert to the simple elements which lead to the complex accident situation, and he continually reevaluates his own climbing in a search for fundamental causes of accidents.

The Safe Attitude: A Basis for Control

The development of a safe mountaineering attitude proceeds along three lines:

First, each climber must be instilled from the very beginning with a respectful attitude toward mountains, a realization of the basic relationship between their steady destruction and his limitations.

Second, each person must develop the climbing skill and knowledge of specialized techniques and equipment which supplement his natural abilities.

Third, each must encounter—preferably vicariously—the actual situations which teach him the distinction between safety and danger and enable him to evaluate his margin of safety at all times.

The development on all three lines is parallel; with increasing knowledge and practice of technique comes experience in practical mountaineering situations as well as an intellectual investigation of the fundamentals of the sport. Progress is made when the climber comprehends the reasons for a climbing code and resolves to follow its rules without exception. Further study and experience bring understanding of the danger inherent in both the mountain and the climber himself. Using this knowledge the mountaineer can evaluate any climbing situation and is equipped to recognize the fundamental causes—the seeds —from which an accident can grow.

By the time he has understood this much about climbing danger, the mountaineer will have some definite ideas on the kind of climbing he wants to do and how he wants to do it. These ideas make up his attitude toward the sport, in which a paramount element is his consideration of safety.

Of first importance is an attitude of continual suspicion. There is always something in the complex situation that he could have overlooked. Ever alert, he thinks his way up a mountain, analyzing and evaluating, basing decisions on sound reasoning, continually probing for hidden peril and planning ahead to meet it, above all forever suspecting that there is something undetected just beyond the limits of his awareness.

As a corollary to his suspicion, every climber must be thoroughly familiar with both the preventive and the corrective safety technique. The safe climber is ready to deal with danger should it develop. High on a glacier far above timberline he asks himself, "Could I live here if something unforeseen should happen, if we were unable to descend on schedule and were forced to remain all night?" Study of first aid and rescue technique, plus adequate equipment for emergency, enable him to answer "Yes" invariably, on every climb.

One element of the safe attitude is a generality which applies to every hazard ever encountered in the mountains, and that is always to minimize the time of exposure to danger. Often a calculated risk cannot be avoided, such as when retreating from the peak in a sudden storm. Whatever the reason for taking the risk, it is no more than common sense to better the odds of survival by moving through the danger area as quickly as is consistent with safe travel.

"Margin of safety" is a concept often discussed by climbers, and the individual's evaluation of this margin most fully embodies his attitude toward climbing danger. No one can predict infallibly the boundary of safety, the exact demarcation between routine travel and catastrophe, and the wise mountaineer allows for this uncertainty by keeping the margin of safety as a cushion between himself and peril. The margin is not an absolute thing; it changes character continually to meet changing conditions, but ideally it affords a constant degree of protection for the climber.

Since safety rests upon a number of factors, whenever a weakness appears in one respect the margin must be maintained by adding strength somewhere else. For example, ignorance of the precise breaking strength of rock, or the exact friction between boots and wet vegetation, leads the climber to add the rope. When the moving team might be unable to catch a fall, he adds a belay. If the security of the belayer is in doubt, he adds an anchor for the belayer and pitons for the climber. In doubtful weather he carries extra clothing, food, even bivouac gear, and marks the route carefully. Knowing that rappels sometimes fail, he uses the technique with caution and belays the rappeller. If a member of the team is weak or inexperienced, a balance of strength is maintained by the addition of another strong companion— or by choosing a less-difficult objective. The list can be elaborated endlessly, but the principle is always the same: the weakness of one safety factor is neutralized by the strengthening of others.

Such are some of the elements of mountain safety. Only the innocent ignorants are content to set forth blindly on a haphazard struggling journey. The well-trained climbing party proceeds safely into the mountains skillfully directed by responsible leadership that has planned carefully for every eventuality. At the same time, each member of the team is prepared to cooperate, if need be subordinating his own will; the group responsibility found among mountain climbers is seldom matched in any other human endeavor.

Setting a proper margin of safety and controlling climbing danger—the supreme test of a climber's attitude—depends upon his knowledge and his sense of proportion. His sense of proportion determines how he uses his knowledge to remain always within the boundaries established by his never-forgotten climbing code. Out of his understanding of the dangers and responsibilities grows a deeper appreciation of the rewards of mountaineering.

18 *

FIRST AID

WHEN accidents occur in the mountains a doctor's services are seldom available, and it is therefore every climber's responsibility to possess a working knowledge of how to examine and properly care for disabled persons until professional services can be obtained. To this end it is desirable for all climbers to take, in addition to the Red Cross first aid courses, the specific mountaineering first aid training offered by many outdoor clubs.

The treatment here has been deliberately focused on aid that should be given in the absence of medical help; only the most common situations the climber is likely to encounter are covered. For discussion of infrequently-occuring problems and for specialized information, the student is referred to *Medicine for Mountaineering*. (See Appendix 3.)

Turbulent emotions after an accident frequently cloud the mind. There is an optimum sequence of actions in first aid and it is well to memorize this sequence, and in addition to carry a procedure checklist in the first aid kit. (This chapter is published separately as a miniaturized booklet suitable for carrying in the kit—see Appendix 3.) Then when an accident occurs a dependable formula is available. For ease in assimilation and reference the following discussion is presented largely in outline form.

General Procedure

1. Keep cool. Well-intentioned haste may be fatal.
2. Keep the patient lying down and warm. Do not move him until extent of his injuries has been ascertained.

3. Examine gently and observe for:
    a. Hemorrhage
    b. Cessation of breathing
    c. Shock
    d. Lacerations
    e. Head, neck, and spine injuries
    f. Fractures
    g. Dislocations
4. Treat severe bleeding and cessation of breathing immediately, as time is of utmost importance in avoiding certain death.
5. Keep the patient as comfortable as possible. Reassure him.
6. Preferably the most-experienced person should direct first aid. While he makes a careful examination of the patient an assistant gathers first aid kits and assembles supplies. After the immediate treatment:
    a. Decide if the patient can be evacuated under his own power. If there is any doubt, assume that he cannot.
    b. Decide if the party has sufficient manpower for evacuation or if it should summon further aid. Procedure in this event is discussed in Chapter 19.
7. If unable to evacuate the patient, make preparations for bivouacing in the area. If possible transport the patient to timberline; a fire is a valuable morale-builder, besides helping to keep the injured person warm.

The Personal First Aid Kit

Mountaineering first aid begins with the first aid kit, an essential which must be carried by every person on every trip. The kit should be small, compact, sturdy, and waterproof; a polyethylene box with a tight lid makes a good container.

Each person should have the items listed below in his personal first aid kit, plus any medications he needs because of individual medical problems, such as allergies. Parties going on long trips or to regions remote from medical aid may wish additions to their group first aid kit. The majority of these require a doctor's prescription and special instruction by him in their use and their hazardous side-effects. For details, consult *Medicine for Mountaineering*.

Tape, not waterproof	2 in. roll	For sprains, securing dressings, etc.
Bandaids	6, 1 in.	For small lacerations.
Butterfly bandaids	6	For closing small lacerations.

Steri-pad gauze flats	4, 3 in. × 3 in.	For larger wounds.
Razor blade, single-edge	1	For shaving hairy spots before taping.
Needle	1 medium size	To remove splinters, etc.
Moleskin	½ pkg.	For blisters.
Elastic bandage	1, 3 in.	For sprains, applying pressure, etc.
Phisohex	1 oz.	Mild antiseptic for abrasions, cuts.
Salt tablets	12	To prevent exhaustion and cramps due to heavy perspiring.
Aspirin	12, 5 grains	1 to 2 every 4 hours for pain.
Antacid (Tums, Rollaids, etc.)	6	For nausea, upset stomach.
Darvon compound (requires doctor's prescription)	6, 65 mgm.	1 every 3 hours for more severe pain than can be controlled with aspirin.
Burn ointment (Nupercain-al, etc.)	½ oz.	To relieve minor burns.

Hemorrhage

Hemorrhages are of two kinds, arterial and venous. *Arterial bleeding* occurs in pulses or spurts and the blood is usually bright red. Since a large amount of blood may be lost in a very short time, quick action is vital. *Venous bleeding* is usually dark and flows smoothly, without spurting.

The following steps are taken to control any hemorrhage:

1. Place a sterile gauze pad over bleeding area and apply pressure. If feasible, elevate bleeding area. This stops the vast majority of hemorrhages.
2. If Step One fails, inspect the wound and place the finger on top of a sterile gauze pad directly over the bleeding point. Maintain pressure for 5–10 minutes.
3. If Steps One and Two fail, and the wound is on a limb, and *only if the hemorrhage is severe and life-threatening*, apply a tourniquet, as follows:
   a. Use only if there is no other way to control a severe, life-threatening hemorrhage. Realize that sacrifice of the limb may result.
   b. Apply one handbreadth (about 4 inches) below the crotch for leg wounds, and about halfway between the elbow and shoulder

for arm wounds; the least pressure is required at these points to
shut off the blood supply.

c. The material used should be cloth at least 2 inches wide.

d. Tighten by twisting the loose ends with a stick or piton. The
tourniquet must be applied tightly enough to *completely shut off
the hemorrhage;* otherwise the bleeding may actually be aggravated by blocking the venous blood return without shutting
off the arterial flow.

e. In 30 minutes release tourniquet and simultaneously apply
pressure over the wound with sterile gauze pad. Hold for 5
minutes. Then gradually release pressure and see if severe bleeding has stopped.

f. If severe bleeding continues, replace tourniquet. Repeat Step e
at 30-minute intervals.

g. Always label the patient as having a tourniquet in place so that
all concerned with the evacuation and later treatment will know
of it.

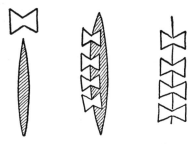

Fig. 89. Use of adhesive butterfly in closing wound.

Wounds are classified as incisions (clean cuts), lacerations, puncture
wounds, or abrasions. Clean *cuts and lacerations* are closed in the
absence of suture material with butterfly bandaids or 1½-inch strips of
adhesive tape. *Puncture wounds* are not pulled together but are left
open and covered with sterile pads. *Abrasions* are simply washed with
soap and water and covered with a sterile dressing.

Shock

Shock is a profound depression of all body processes caused by circulatory failure. It may follow *any* injury, even a relatively-minor one,
but hemorrhage, pain, cold, and rough handling are intensifying
factors. The patient feels weak and listless and may faint in the upright
or sitting position. The skin is cold and clammy, the pulse weak and

rapid. Shock actually can be more serious than the initial injury and must be assumed to exist in every casualty.

The following measures are used both to prevent and to control shock:

1. Place the patient in a supine position, flat on his back with head lower than his feet to make the blood which is circulating available to the brain, heart, lungs, and kidneys. If there are no complicating head or chest injuries, the patient is kept preferably flat or with head and chest elevated above feet.
2. Keep the patient warm with all available clothing. If he is badly chilled from exposure to cold, apply external heat, but not above body temperature; otherwise, merely prevent heat loss.
3. Eliminate contributing factors:
    a. Control hemorrhage.
    b. Relieve pain.
    c. Avoid rough handling which causes further injury and pain.

Head and Spine Injuries

Injuries to the head, neck, and spine give the alpine first-aider his worst moments. These portions of the anatomy are so delicate that the slightest mistake may cause further injury, yet often symptoms are so confusing it is difficult to choose a course of action. Usually indecision

Fig. 90. Compression of scalp wound.

revolves around the question of whether or not the victim can safely be moved, or whether medical treatment on the spot is essential. Many climbers, particularly those who have once undergone the agonies of having to make this life-or-death decision, carry the following detailed checklist of symptoms in their first aid kit. The sequence of examination and treatment is important, and must be accurate.

HEAD INJURIES

The head may be injured in any number of ways—by rockfall, wall collisions, or falls. Fracture or severe concussion make stretcher evacuation mandatory. Minor concussion and surface injuries do not. Treatment, diagnosis, and decision as to method of evacuation are thoroughly intermixed. The following is the proper sequence of action and thought.

1. Control obvious bleeding from the scalp by finger pressure—one finger on either side of the incision. This will compress scalp arteries and stop bleeding usually in about 10 minutes.
2. Loss of consciousness means probable concussion—a bruising of brain tissue by swelling or hemorrhage which create unusual pressures within the skull. There may or may not be a skull fracture.
3. Look for bleeding from ears, nose, or mouth, the symptoms of basal skull fracture. If observed, elevate the head to lower blood pressure within the skull and thus lessen bleeding. Scalp wounds may cause a puddle of blood in the ear which confuses diagnosis: wipe the ear clean with a handkerchief; if blood collects again there may be a basal skull fracture.
4. Examine the pupils. Are they equal or unequal? When there is brain damage the pupil on the side of the injury is usually larger and does not react to light. To test for light reaction shade the eye with the hand, then suddenly remove the hand, exposing the eye to bright sun (or to a flashlight if it is a dark day). A normal pupil will contract.
5. If the pulse is very slow or respiration fluctuates noticeably there is probably hemorrhage within the brain and increased pressure inside the skull.
6. If the patient is conscious, ask him if he has a headache. If generalized over the entire head it may be caused by interior bleeding. If merely local at the injury site it may, in absence of any other symptoms, safely be assumed due strictly to surface wounds.
7. Determine if the patient is oriented as to time and place. ("Where are you? Who are you? What day is it?")
8. Test for loss of muscular power or sensation. In the absence of other injuries any weakness or loss of sensation on one side is indicative of damage to central nervous system.
9. If the patient has none of the above symptoms, have him stand with eyes closed. Swaying or falling may indicate damage to the brain or to the labyrinth (balancing organ).

10. If the patient has none of the above-listed symptoms of concussion or fracture he may be evacuated by walking; if any of the symptoms are found the patient must be carried out—even though he may be able and may desire to walk.

11. When evacuation by walking has commenced the patient must be watched during the next 6 hours for evidence of drowsiness, nausea, vomiting, or increased headache. These may occur in injuries where there is an extradural hemorrhage between the skull and the membrane lining the skull.

SPINE INJURIES—CERVICAL (NECK)

Fractures of the neck are most frequently caused by a blow on the head during a fall or when struck by falling rock. Examination for neck injury should always be conducted simultaneously with examination for head injury.

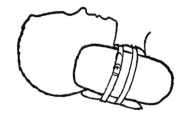

Fig. 91. Splinting for cervical fracture.

1. Determine if the patient's neck hurts. If pain is severe, but there are no local bruises, suspect a neck fracture or hemorrhage in the membranes covering the spinal cord.

2. A patient with a broken neck is apt to have a great deal of muscular spasm and will not want to move his neck.

3. If other injuries permit, test for:
    a. Loss of muscular power in the arms or legs by asking the patient to move them.
    b. Loss of sensation. Stroke various parts of patient's body with a finger, asking if sensation is felt. Always check both right and left sides. If doubt remains concerning presence of a cervical fracture treat the patient as though he had one.

4. Treatment: Turn the patient on his back, being sure that his body and head are at all times held in perfect alignment. One man holds the head and exerts slight traction; he rotates it in line with the body as others carefully roll the trunk and legs. For evacuation one pad should be placed under the neck to prevent compression of the spinal cord, and others on both sides of the neck to prevent

rotation. A belt or piece of clothing tied around the three pads adds stability. Patients with such injuries must be evacuated by a rigid stretcher.

SPINE INJURIES—THORACIC OR LUMBAR (BACK)

Crushing of the vertebrae often results when a climber falls some distance and lands on his feet or buttocks. Vertebral fractures most commonly occur in the lumbar region (small of the back) or the last two thoracic vertebrae, from which the 11th and 12th ribs originate. The first and second lumbar vertebrae are particularly susceptible.

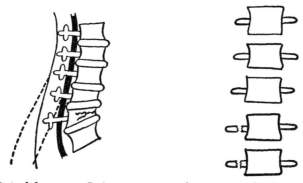

Fig. 92. Spinal fractures. *Left,* compression fractures; *right,* fractured transverse process.

1. Check for loss of motor power and sensation by asking the injured to move his legs, feet, and toes, and by testing his sensitivity to touch.
2. Treatment: slowly and gently turn the patient onto his back with one man keeping patient's legs constantly in line with his body. Put a small pad under the back to hyperextend it, as there is less likelihood of injury to the spinal cord if the back is arched backwards. If there is any doubt regarding the extent of injuries evacuate by rigid stretcher.

Fractures

SYMPTOMS

Fractures are classified in two general categories: *closed* (simple), with no break in the skin; *open* (compound), having a skin wound communicating with the fracture. One or more of the following signs or symptoms are usually present:

1. Pain and tenderness at fracture site.
2. Deformity (may or may not be present).
3. Patient is unable to move or bear weight on the affected part without pain.
4. A grating sensation may be felt or even heard during motion of the affected part.

TREATMENT

Following are the general principles of treatment:
1. Whenever in doubt, treat an injury as a fracture.
2. Splint both the joint above and the joint below the fracture.
3. The extremity may usually be splinted in a position of some deformity. If it is apparent the fracture might produce penetration of the skin (for example, in the case of some ankle fractures), a gentle attempt at reducing this pressure may be made by applying traction and then straightening the deformity.
4. Carefully pad splints.
5. Check splint ties frequently to be sure they do not interfere with circulation.
6. In open fractures, cover the wound with a sterile dressing prior to splinting.
7. Above timberline, splint materials are scarce and a good deal of ingenuity is required to immobilize the fracture. Ice axes or uninjured portions of the patient's own body may be the only splints available. Inflatable plastic splints are now on the market which effectively immobilize an arm or leg; inclusion of one of these in the group first aid kit should be considered.

Fractures of the jaw, rather uncommon, are held rigid with adhesive tape. It is well to place steri-pads or bits of clothing between the teeth before taping, to allow later ease in drinking. *Fractures of the collar bone* are held rigid by adhesive tape and by immobilizing the affected arm over the chest. *Forearm and wrist fractures* are best treated by taping to a splint applied on the inner side of the arm, and then supporting the limb with a sling. In *fractures of the upper arm or humerus,* the weight of the patient's arm helps to overcome the pull of the muscles, which are in spasm following the fracture. The patient's ribs are used as a splint, and the forearm supported in a sling. For *fractures of the hand or fingers,* the hand is folded around a rock or a rolled bit of clothing or bandage, and fastened with adhesive tape. *Fractures and dislocations of the elbow* are best splinted and supported with a sling in the position of maximum comfort; a position acutely bending the elbow should be avoided, since circulation to the

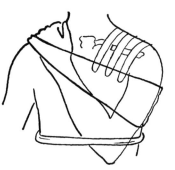
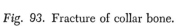

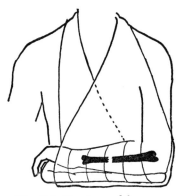

Fig. 93. Fracture of collar bone.   *Fig.* 94. Fracture of forearm.

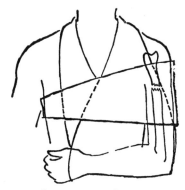

Fig. 95. Fracture of upper arm. (Position same for elbow.)

Fig. 96. Fractures of hand.

forearm might be cut off. *Fractured ribs*, if on one side only, are best treated by four to six overlapping strips of 2-inch tape extending from slightly beyond the midline in back to slightly beyond the midline in front, starting at the top and working down. If fractures occur on both sides, one band of 2-inch tape around the lower ribs will frequently immobilize the chest enough to control the pain and motion.

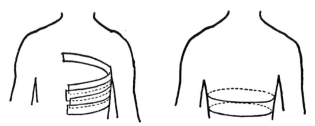

Fig. 97. Taping of fractured ribs. *Left*, fracture on one side; *right*, fracture on both sides.

Injuries to the pelvis are most frequently of a crushing sort. There is agonizing pain and possibly swelling or bruising at the fracture site. Fractures most frequently occur in the front and the greatest hazard is rupture of the bladder; for this reason any attempt to urinate must be discouraged. In such case it is essential to limit fluids to less than 1 pint per day. Pelvic fractures are immobilized by tying the legs together at the knees and ankles with a thick pad of clothing between the thighs.

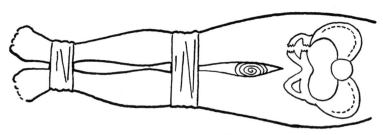

Fig. 98. Fracture of pelvis.

A *fracture of the thigh* is difficult to treat because of the powerful thigh muscles. The broken ends tend to be displaced inward and frequently slip over one another causing great pain. A splint may be improvised, as illustrated, extending from the foot to the rib cage on the outside of the leg and from the foot to the groin on the inside. The splint must be well-padded and held in place by strips of cloth or other material. *Fractures of the lower leg or ankle* may be treated by splints improvised from ice axes, alpine trees, or by taping to the opposite leg, making sure to loosen the boot lest the swelling impair circulation.

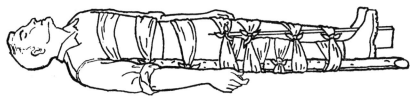

Fig. 99. Fracture of thigh.

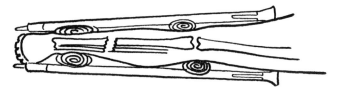

Fig. 100. Fracture of lower leg.

Dislocations, Sprains, and Strains

DISLOCATION

A dislocation is a tearing of the ligaments around a joint, followed by displacement of the bone from its socket. Most common in mountaineering is dislocation of the shoulder. The shoulder appears more angular, the arm cannot be moved, the muscles are in spasm, and there is considerable pain. A depression can be seen or felt below the tip of the injured shoulder, as compared with the normal side. *Reduction of a dislocated shoulder should be attempted only by trained personnel, since permanent damage can be caused by improper procedure.* If reduction is absolutely necessary it is best carried out by the Hippocratic or "dirty sock" method. Mountaineers venturing to remote areas would do well to learn the method under a doctor's supervision, for the ability to reduce a dislocated shoulder may mean that the patient can walk out rather than be carried on a stretcher. If reduction appears unwise the arm should be supported in a loose sling, the pain controlled by aspirin or other drugs.

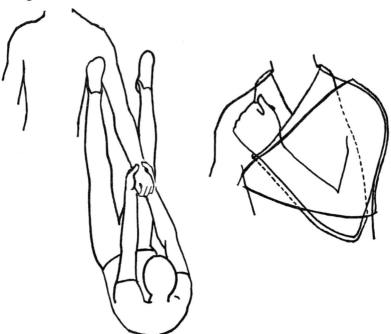

Fig. 101. Dislocated shoulder. *Left,* reducing dislocation, dirty sock method; *right,* immobilization.

SPRAIN

A sprain is a stretching or tearing of ligaments in the region of a joint, followed by hemorrhage, swelling, and tenderness. The most common and distressing type from the standpoint of mountain evacuation is a sprained ankle. If there is pain in the region of the ankle bones or in the region of swelling, then there is probably a fracture. It is often impossible to tell without an x-ray if the ankle bones are broken. All severe "sprains" should therefore be treated as possible fractures until proven otherwise. A person with only a sprained ankle can usually be walked out after adequate support with adhesive tape, but it is unwise to walk a person with an ankle fracture. If a sprain has just occurred, the ankle should be elevated and a cold pack applied for 30 minutes to control internal bleeding. The ankle is then taped. The first strip of tape is brought from a handbreadth above the ankle down under the foot and back to the same level on the opposite side, with the sole of the foot at right angles to the leg and turned slightly toward the side of the sprain. Next, three or four overlapping strips of tape are applied longitudinally (up and down) and numerous strips horizontally, taking care with the latter not to encircle the leg with any one strip, thus restricting circulation. The strapping should include the arch of the foot. Pain is alleviated with aspirin.

STRAIN

A strain is a rupture of the lining covering a muscle, or a tear in the muscular fibers. It is differentiated from a sprain by its occurrence over a muscle belly rather than in the region of a joint. Localized tenderness is present. Treatment is by cold applications, plus taping in a position which removes some of the strain from the muscle.

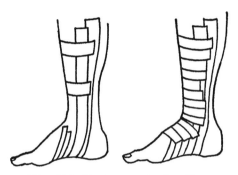

Fig. 102. Taping sprained ankle.

Other Mountain Emergencies

Other disabilities occur in the mountains, not necessarily caused by climbing accidents, but such as to prevent a person from being evacuated under his own power, and sufficiently serious to make correct treatment mandatory.

CESSATION OF RESPIRATION

In mountaineering the stoppage of breathing from causes other than death results most frequently from *crushing chest injuries, electrocution* by lightning, or *drowning* in streams or lakes.

Resuscitation is best carried out by the mouth-to-mouth method. The victim is placed on his back with head tilted and *jaw pulled upward into a jutting-out position, where it is held throughout resuscitation.* The operator takes a deep breath, opens his mouth wide and places it tightly over the victim's mouth, at the same time pressing his cheek against the victim's nose to pinch or press it closed. The operator blows air vigorously into the victim's mouth (any obstruction is readily apparent at this time), then removes his mouth and listens for the rush of exhaled air. Usually the elastic recoil of the lung furnishes adequate expiration, but in some cases it is necessary to apply downward pressure on the chest with the free hand. The process is repeated about 12 times per minute for adults and 20 times per minute, with shallower breaths, for children.

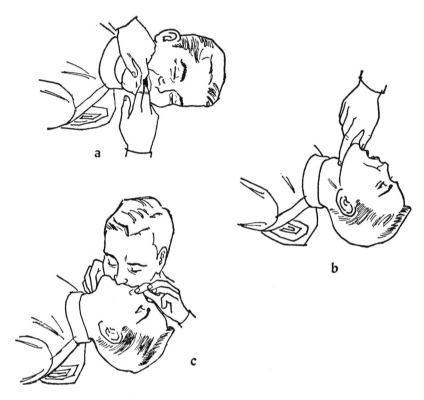

Fig. 103. Artificial respiration, mouth-to-mouth method.

EXPOSURE

Exposure results from loss of body heat by prolonged cooling. In the first stage heat production is increased by shivering, which increases oxygen consumption and metabolism four to six times. Available carbohydrate reserves determine how long this phase can be extended; in exhaustion, followed by accident, the shivering phase is very short. Below the critical body temperature of 92°F the victim cannot produce enough body heat to recover. In this second stage he has a masklike face, glassy stare, mumbling voice, and mental confusion. Blood pressure and heart rate are reduced. A diffuse, foamy, pulmonary edema may occur. The victim slips rapidly into the third stage, with slow irregular heart beat, leading to death.

Treatment is aimed at supplying heat to a victim unable to generate his own. Some useful sources are: prewarmed garments, sleeping bags, warm tent interior, hot, wrapped rocks. Perhaps a fire can be built on each side of the patient, or two climbers lie beside him, all three wrapped in tarps. Warm fluids with sugar may help.

FROSTBITE

Frostbite, or freezing of the tissues, most commonly affects the toes, fingers, and face. There are several degrees of severity. In *first degree* frostbite the affected part is cold, white, and numb; after warming the area is reddened and resembles a first degree burn. In the *second degree* a blister forms after warming. In *third degree* the skin becomes dark, dusky, and very painful; there is gangrene and loss of some skin and subcutaneous tissues. In *fourth degree* there is never any warming; the skin remains cold, dark, and lifeless, and the affected part usually is lost.

Frostbite occurs when an extremity loses heat faster than it can be replaced by the circulating blood. It may result from direct exposure to extreme cold or high wind, as happens with the nose, ears, and hands. Damp feet may freeze because moisture conducts heat rapidly away from the skin and destroys the insulating value of socks and boots. With continued cold or inactivity blood circulation to the extremities is steadily reduced, speeding the freezing process.

Prevention

With adequate equipment frostbite does not occur. The feet, for instance, can be protected by proper boots and socks. The insulated boots described in Chapter 1 are mandatory for cold climbs, particularly at high altitude where blood circulation is slowed. Whenever the feet and toes feel cold they should be vigorously exercised, and for this reason the boots must not be too snug nor too tightly stuffed with socks. Insoles and socks are effective insulation only when dry: wet socks increase the heat loss; obviously a change to dry socks is immensely helpful.

Hands and face are protected from frost by adequate clothing, but of equal importance is conservation of heat in the trunk of the body so that blood circulation to the extremities is not reduced.

Treatment

Frostbitten areas are warmed by being placed against warm skin: feet, against a companion's abdomen or in his armpits; fingers, in a person's own armpits.

Most emphatically the temperature of the frostbitten area should not be raised much above body temperature, such as by warming near a fire. Such misguided efforts to give speedy relief invariably increase the injury. Furthermore, the injured part *must never be rubbed*, especially with snow. The additional cooling and the abrasive action of the snow can only add further damage to already devitalized tissues.

The treatment of serious freezing is fairly complex, and is discussed at length in *Medicine for Mountaineering*.

Mountain Miseries

Climbers suffer from numerous afflictions in the mountains. In their least-severe forms such miseries only lessen enjoyment of the outing, but any can in extreme cases be disabling.

HEAT EXHAUSTION

In hot weather, particularly during intense exertion, a climber may sweat so much that his body becomes excessively dehydrated and salt-depleted. All or some of the following symptoms may be present: nausea, cold and clammy skin, faintness, weakness, and perhaps a rapid pulse. Treatment consists of rest, with plenty of liquid and salt tablets—perhaps combined in a salty soup.

SUNSTROKE

When exposed to excessive sun the body may become so overheated that it is provided too much blood through the cooling effort of the circulatory system. Symptoms are a flushed, hot face; rapid, full pulse; pain in the head; weakness; dizziness. Sunstroke is relatively rare among climbers since proper headgear is usually effective prevention. Treatment is rest in a shaded area, cooling of the head and body by snow or water, and administration of cold liquid.

MUSCULAR CRAMPS

Leg cramps caused by an accumulation of lactic acid in the muscles and loss of salt through perspiration sometimes make it impossible for a climber to continue. Such cramps appear suddenly, usually after strenuous exertion for several hours, and the pain is excruciating. During ordinary activity the blood removes lactic acid as it is formed, but in long-continued exercise a surplus may build up. Resting, to allow the blood to carry away the lactic acid, is the first step in the treatment. Deep breathing, and stretching of the cramped muscle as quickly and completely as possible—painful as this may be—gives further relief. Salt tablets should be administered immediately to remove the other cause; indeed, many climbers, after finding their cramps quickly dispelled by salt intake, wisely prevent them by using salt tablets at periodic intervals on any climb where they perspire heavily.

SNOWBLINDNESS

Snowblindness is caused by failure to use adequate dark glasses during brilliant sunshine on snow or light-colored rock. The eyes ache and are bloodshot. The treatment is application of cool, wet compresses to the eyes, and then having the patient wear two pairs of dark glasses. Holocain hydrochloride eye ointment relieves the burning and pain but does not improve vision; it should not be used any oftener or any longer than absolutely necessary because of risk of damage to the cornea. Aspirin controls the pain. Occasionally it may be necessary to cover the eyes and lead the casualty out by the hand. Recovery may take 2 or 3 days.

BLISTERS

Blisters result from rubbing of the skin against the socks, either because the boots are too large or laced insufficiently tight, or because

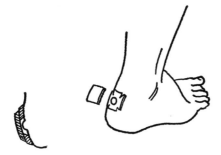

Fig. 104. Blister protection, using moleskin.

the socks are lumpy or wrinkled. To prevent blisters, shoe and sock should be removed at the first sensation of pain and the foot examined for reddened skin areas which indicate undue friction. A wide band of adhesive tape, applied smoothly over—and well beyond—the margins of the "hot spot," relieves discomfort and prevents blistering. Application of tincture of benzoin prior to taping makes the tape adhere more firmly. A hole may be cut in a piece of moleskin, which is then placed over the blister to protect the area from further direct contact. The moleskin is secured with tape.

Because of the risk of infection blisters should not be opened unless absolutely necessary. If it must be done the area is washed with soap and water and a needle sterilized with a match is inserted under the skin just beyond the blister's edge. Fluid is gently pressed out and a sterile bandage applied. If the blister has already broken it should be washed and bandaged in the same manner and carefully watched for subsequent infection.

SUNBURN

Protection from the burning rays of the sun is discussed in Chapter 1. At high altitude and on snow nothing but coverage by clothing is completely effective, and a degree of burning is inevitable. Lips are particularly vulnerable and some climbers develop severe lip sores unless they exercise special caution. Reflection from snow causes burns in areas not ordinarily affected, such as under the chin, around the eyes, inside the nostrils and ears, and on the roof of the mouth. Lack of a hat when hair is short, thin, or absent may result in scalp burns.

First degree burns with skin-reddening are common, as are second and third degree burns with blisters, the climber often miscalculating intensity of the sun or being too weary to take preventive action. As with any burn—from sun or fire—if the affected area is large, toxic substances absorbed by the body can cause generalized illness.

Sunburn usually is treated on first notice by further applications of sunburn preventive. In severe cases burn ointment should be applied, plus cold compresses if there is much swelling, aspirin for pain, and (at a cold camp) warm liquids to reduce the violent shakes that may occur.

HEADACHE

Headache in the mountains usually results from inadequate sunglasses, tension in neck muscles, constipation, or some pre-existing physical condition. An occasional cause is "water intoxication," with actual swelling of the brain tissue, when over a period of several days a climber has sweated excessively and drunk great quantities of water without taking salt tablets. In any case of headache the source of the trouble should be sought; better protection of head or eyes, stretching and relaxing neck muscles, salt tablets, or a laxative may eliminate the cause. Aspirin alleviates the immediate pain.

MOUNTAIN SICKNESS

Whenever a person ascends rapidly to an altitude greater than that to which he is accustomed his system adjusts to new conditions. Breathing becomes more rapid to extract the necessary oxygen from the thinner air. The blood also must adjust by increasing its proportion of oxygen-carrying red corpuscles. In the extreme case, such as when an airplane pilot climbs thousands of feet in minutes, unconsciousness results. The mountaineer, moving upward foot by foot, suffers less-drastic but very uncomfortable symptoms. First comes general malaise and loss of appetite, followed by increasing weakness and lessening of desire. If forced by social pressure or inner resolution to continue the climb, the sick person eventually becomes apathetic, nauseated, dizzy, and sleepy. Bleeding at the nose and hallucinations are rare.

Symptoms of mountain sickness can occur even at relatively-low altitude. Tourists driving in automobiles to 8000 feet sometimes feel lazy or dizzy, or experience palpitations. Climbers generally have more time to acclimatize, and except for shortness of breath usually feel only minor effects until elevations of 12,000 feet or more are reached. However, in regions such as the Pacific Northwest where climbers live at sealevel yet ascend to over 14,000 feet on a weekend, mountain sickness of greater or lesser severity is the rule rather than the exception.

Proper use of the rest step is the first remedy. Next come rest stops, with forced deep breathing ("overbreathing") to hyperventilate the lungs. Nourishment in the form of the simple sugars in candy, oranges, or fruit juice should be taken. In an extreme case, if a person has been able to climb a mountain but is too sick to get down, dexedrine is helpful.

Above 12,000 feet *high-altitude pulmonary edema*, a rare but dangerous condition, may occur. The victim is restless, coughs, and eventually brings up frothy, blood-tinged sputum. The only treatment is immediate descent and a continuous supply of oxygen, if available. See *Medicine for Mountaineering*.

Snakes and Insects

SNAKES

Venomous snakes are unknown in alpine terrain. Their danger to the climber is limited to low-altitude practice rocks and approach marches. Even in infested country reasonable alertness is usually sufficient to avoid close encounters. Rattlesnakes live on the sunny eastern slope of the Cascades but rarely venture above 3000 feet. In the Rockies and Sierra they range more widely and to higher altitudes. In Arizona and New Mexico lives—fortunately not in conjunction with mountains—the dangerous multi-colored coral snake, a cousin of the cobra.

Treatment of snake bite is touchy business; see *Medicine for Mountaineering*.

INSECTS

Chapters 1 and 2 discuss avoidance of insects. In some persons numerous bites cause allergic reactions, with general sickness and considerable pain. Antihistamines may control the allergic reaction, and aspirin the pain.

Potentially the insect most dangerous to climbers is the tick. In some areas of the West ticks carry germs of *Rocky Mountain spotted fever,* characterized by high fever and a large hemorrhagic spotted rash. Before the advent of antibiotics the mortality rate was 50 per cent, but with timely treatment by chloromycetin or the tetracyclines the figure is close to zero. The disease may be entirely prevented by immunization before entering an area known to contain infected ticks. Another tick-transmitted disease, *tick fever,* is difficult to recognize since the symptoms are approximately those of a bad cold. Danger from tick-derived illnesses can be minimized by following precautions suggested in Chapter 2.

19 *

ALPINE RESCUE

ANYONE who climbs very often for very long must expect sooner or later to be involved in misfortune, if not his own then someone else's. The very nature of the sport rules out much chance of help from casual passers-by; climbers usually must be rescued by other climbers, often at great risk and sacrifice. So high a degree of mutual responsibility requires every mountaineer to be familiar with emergency procedures.

One of the first decisions that must be made after an accident is whether to call in outside help or to proceed with available personnel. Sending for help means delay, and also means imposing considerable inconvenience upon volunteer rescuers. The party should attempt to remain self-sufficient; many times a handful of climbers can do a difficult rescue job speedily and efficiently using only such labor-saving and safety devices as they can improvise from ordinary climbing tools. This chapter approaches the rescue problem from the viewpoint of a small team. (For a more comprehensive discussion, read *Mountain Rescue Techniques;* see Appendix 3.)

When something goes wrong swift action may be less important than correct action; a spontaneous, shortsighted effort has less chance of success than one more deliberate but more carefully considered. In mountain travel once any person is beyond voice range of his companions the party has lost control over his subsequent actions. Therefore, there must be no hasty separation; everything must be thought through to the very end, everything prearranged, including what each member is to do under all conceivable conditions until he has completely played out his part in the rescue drama.

If there has been no recognized leader on the climb then one must be elected for the emergency. Once he accepts the task companions abide by his decisions without argument, although he still should remain flexible enough to consider suggestions. Strong intelligent leadership and strict discipline are requisites of success in alpine rescue.

The leader and his group sit down to plan. Every aspect of the situation needs cool analysis: seriousness of the victim's injury, time of day, weather, distance to the road, terrain; the number of people on hand, their mental and physical condition, their experience, their equipment, food, and first aid supplies. Then, and only then, should a course of action be selected. If possible the leader organizes his people, delegates jobs, and begins the rescue at once. If he feels the party is too weak in numbers or strength, or if medical aid or special equipment are needed, then messengers are sent for help, those on the scene doing what they can to make the victim and themselves comfortable during the wait.

Search

WHEN TO SEARCH

Search is ordinarily not begun until reasonably certain the missing person is delayed for no normal reason. After straying from the route he may recognize his mistake, retrace his steps, and rejoin the party within a few hours. If he is healthy, experienced, and well-equipped, and has been traveling where injury is unlikely, search can even be deferred overnight.

Under some conditions there should be no hesitation. Immediate search is mandatory if the lost person might have wandered onto steep rock or a crevassed glacier, or if a physical disability such as diabetes is known to be present, or if he is very fatigued, inexperienced, or poorly equipped. Similarly, if an entire rope team is missing on difficult terrain or after a lightning storm or in avalanche conditions, there should be not the slightest delay.

SEARCH PROCEDURES

There are three basic search methods. A small party may be able to make no more than a hasty search along a limited track. With a half-dozen people available there probably can be a perimeter search. A large group, if it finds these ineffectual, can then proceed to comb thoroughly over a considerable area.

Regardless of the method adopted, before beginning the search each person must know the full plan. If the party is to divide, then each division must know the location of the others. Audible signals such as yodels, yells, and whistles, or visible signs with smoke, mirrors, or lights should be prearranged. All members must know the rendezvous point and the time at which they are to meet there regardless of whether or not their search has been successful.

Hasty Search

For safety, searchers should travel in pairs, or at least remain always within earshot of one another. This means that a party of two or three people can cover only a narrow strip of ground and their best chance is outguessing the lost person, putting themselves in his place and visualizing the logical errors, the blunder into the wrong one of two gullies similar in appearance, or onto the wrong ridge. The most likely places, such as the exits of wrong gullies and ridges, are checked first; failing there, the party retraces its original trail while casting about for tracks showing where the lost person wandered off. Once such a point is found the searchers proceed swiftly along the most likely path, watching for footprints in snow, mud, sand, or on footlogs. When such track-showing ground is intermittent the party fans out to broad intervals, calling to each other regularly, and also pausing frequently to listen for calls from the lost person. If after several hours no clues at all have turned up then probably it is time to seek additional help.

Perimeter Search

The method of a perimeter search is to intercept the lost person's trail by cutting perpendicular to his expected direction. The leader sends several teams traveling on different contours of the mountain; if any team crosses a track which seems to be the one sought, the teams above are signaled to discontinue. It helps to know the footwear of the missing person, not only for identification but because this may influence his choice of route.

Once a promising track is found it must be carefully preserved— marked clearly with wands, stone cairns, or anything else suitable, then followed a few feet to one side, not by walking directly over it. With a large party it may be best to hold the main group in reserve while a small team pursues the trail. If the track fades out it often can be rediscovered merely by choosing the most logical route, or by casting about among several possible ones, either dividing the team or calling in others from the reserves.

Area Search

When no tracks are found, or in heavily-traveled country where there are too many, an area search usually becomes necessary, requiring a large party and very exact organization. The leader first establishes the search area and divides it into sections. He forms teams of two or three members and allots each an area of reasonable size, defined by natural boundaries or by grid lines drawn on a map. Each team then conducts a perimeter search of its assigned area, and this failing, proceeds to a foot-by-foot combing. Sometimes the area of initial search must be greatly broadened, hundreds of people recruited, radios, airplanes, and helicopters employed.

When an Accident Happens

When a climber is injured the first response of his companions often invites further accidents. The victim must of course be reached quickly, but not at the expense of additional casualties. Under rockfall or avalanche hazard those not needed immediately take cover. On diffi-cult terrain only one or two men should be dispatched to reach the victim. If he is out of sight or hearing—as in a crevasse—then all signals and actions must be predetermined before a rescuer is lowered to the spot. Remaining calm is important. Belays and anchors are not to be ignored in the confusion. Excitement only contributes to further accidents; self-sacrifice is spirtually commendable but in the mountains can have the effect of sacrificing everyone.

First aid should be rendered at the first possible moment—bleeding stopped, breathing restarted, shock relieved, and fractures treated. Impending danger may force the party to move the victim at once to a more sheltered spot; if so, methods must be used which do not compound injuries, though sometimes there is a very difficult choice to make between the dangers of the accident site and of moving the victim.

If for any reason an injured person must be left unguarded, even for a few moments, he must be tied to the mountain. All too often a hurt person left alone has in his confusion fallen or wandered to his death—sometimes even untying himself to do so. Companions must anticipate that he may become irrational and tie him so securely he cannot possibly work free.

Transport on Technical Terrain

On terrain so difficult as to require technical climbing even a minor handicap can render a person completely incapable of descent without help. Because of reserve strength and plentiful equipment, a large group may be able to choose almost any route for the evacuation, devising elaborate traversing and lifting devices, sending scouts ahead to prepare these in advance of the main party.

The small party has less choice. Though short lifts and traverses can be made, generally the lack of party strength makes it necessary to evacuate in the fall line, which uses the least energy and equipment. Frequently the party must descend by a different (and unknown) route, with hidden dangers. The prime object—moving the injured person—

is naturally uppermost in all minds, yet the safety of each individual must never be forgotten. A rescue inherently is more dangerous than a normal climb over the same ground because attention is focused upon the victim instead of upon the surroundings and one's own movements. Therefore belays may be required—and solid ones—both for the casualty and those aiding him, even where superfluous under ordinary climbing conditions. If ropes are in short supply rescuers can be served by a fixed line to which they attach themselves with prusik slings. Since in a small party the normal equipment may be insufficient for rescue purposes, many climbers carry in their rucksack—depending on the climb—such emergency items as extra sling rope, extra carabiners, pulley, brake bar, folding saw, snow shovel, ice screws, and plastic tarp—as well as all the basic essentials described in Chapter 1.

LOWERING

With slight injuries a person can climb down under tension from a tight belay, assisted by a companion who helps him place his hands and feet. On snow or ice large platform steps can be prepared. If the victim has no head injury or symptom of shock he can sometimes be allowed to rappel—always of course with a safety belay.

Fig. 105. Lowering injured climber.

Rope Seat

If neither down-climbing nor rappelling is possible but the victim still has use of his legs, he can be lowered in a rope seat. As a companion pays out the belay line through a braking device, he guides himself down with his feet. He can also descend on the back of a helper, using the double rope seat illustrated.

Both the single and double seats are constructed similarly. For the single seat a bowline on a bight is tied at the end of the climbing rope, each loop just large enough for one of the victim's legs. To prevent overturning he uses a chest sling, the simplest version of which is just a loop high under the armpits, attached to the main rope at about face height with a prusik knot.

The double seat for two people uses two climbing ropes. A seat is tied in the end of each and they then are joined by a square knot about 2 feet above the bowline of one seat and about 3 feet above that of the other. Chest loops are provided on both ropes. The helper sits in the lower seat, with the victim on his back in the upper seat, and backs down the slope in a rappel stance, lowered by helpers above with braking devices. Both people should be belayed separately by additional safety ropes. The double seat can be improvised on one climbing rope if necessary. The helper's seat is tied as before; then about 3 feet above its bowline a small middleman's loop is tied. The seat for the victim is made from doubled sling rope and tied to this loop or snapped in with a carabiner.

Fig. 106. Basket for lowering injured climber.
(*Note:* For simplicity in illustration, only half the actual number of loops are shown.)

Rope Basket Stretcher

When a badly-injured person cannot sit in a rope seat, he can be immobilized and lowered in a rope basket stretcher. To construct this device a small loop is tied on each side of the middle of a climbing rope. Stretched out, the loops measure 20 inches from tip to tip. Then working toward both ends, more small loops are tied with tip-to-tip distances measured down the rope from the middle loops as follows: three at 20 inches, three at 32 inches, and three at 36 inches. The rope now contains ten small loops on each side of the center, with loose ends of at least 5 feet remaining. Laying the two halves parallel on the ground, and starting at the rope center, the loops are crisscrossed to form the stretcher.

The victim lies on the stretcher with his head toward the loose rope ends; either these ends or sling rope can be used for gathering and tying the loops together. A cloth band around his head and a sling to support his feet complete the stretcher, with extra slings and carabiners to adjust the various points of support for the most comfortable posture. The illustration shows the finished product in use; for simplicity only half the actual number of small loops are pictured. After a fatal accident the task of guiding the stretcher is less grim with the victim's head in his rucksack and the body bound in a tarp or extra clothing.

The basket stretcher is tied to the end of a climbing rope, a seat and chest sling for the helper prepared at the end of a second rope, and the two ropes joined with a square knot. The stretcher should hang horizontally across the helper's chest so that he can hold it away from the wall with his legs. If there is a rope shortage, the helper's seat can be made of sling material and suspended from a small loop in the main rope above the stretcher. As always, separate belay ropes should be used for each person if at all possible.

Rigid Stretcher

When a badly-injured person must be completely immobilized before being moved, a rigid stretcher may be more-or-less satisfactorily improvised with poles and rope, but usually a metal stretcher such as a Stokes must be brought from outside. Sling ropes from at least six points around the rim attach the stretcher to carabiners on the end of the main lowering rope. These slings are tied individually so that failure of one will not overturn the load, and the victim is securely lashed in as an added precaution.

Friction Brakes

Ropes are weakened quickly by braking around rocks or trees and therefore a special brake made of carabiners and sling commonly is used to control the descent. This *carabiner brake* is very versatile; it can be doubled for very heavy loads, it can be operated from either an upper or a lower station, and it can be used for descents of more than one rope length. If available, a *brake bar* does the same job more simply.

Several slings are fastened to a solid anchor. A carabiner is laid atop the climbing rope and a loop of rope pushed up through it. Another carabiner is snapped into this loop, rotated so that the rope hangs from its solid side, then flipped over the upper end of the first carabiner so that its gate hangs underneath. When snapped to the anchor, the brake is ready—after examination to make certain there is no pressure from the rope or the ground tending to open either of the carabiner gates. Braking comes from pinching and bending the rope in the device. Swinging the free end of the rope upward releases the brake, while swinging it down parallel to the loaded end adds friction. By substituting a strong stick, or a piton hammer handle, a brake can be rigged using only one carabiner.

The brake usually is placed near the top anchor, but occasionally it can more conveniently be situated below or at one side. In such case the rope runs from the load through an upper carabiner or pulley and down to the braking station.

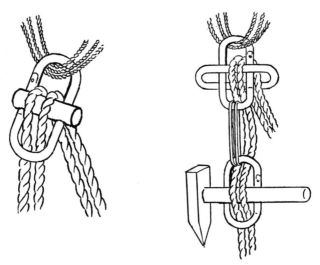

Fig. 107. Left, brake bar. *Right,* carabiner brakes.

On a long pitch it is sometimes desirable to tie in additional ropes while the load hangs in midair to allow an uninterrupted descent of several rope lengths. The problem is to bypass the joining knot around the carabiners without dropping the load. Two men can accomplish this without difficulty. When only about 2 feet of rope remain, they halt the descent. One man belays the rope while the other attaches a prusik sling to it just below the brake, then wraps this sling several times around an auxiliary carabiner anchored above. He holds this sling—it must not be tied—while his partner eases the load onto it, removes the brake, and ties on a new rope. This he inserts in the brake with the knot already past the carabiners; now as the wrapped sling is allowed to slide the load returns to the climbing rope and the descent continues.

RAISING

To assist a person up a steep face rescuers have a choice of three common methods. Two depend upon the climber's own efforts, while the third can be used to lift even an inert weight. All three are usually associated with crevasse rescue, but they work equally well on steep rock and snow. The following discussion will cover only bare fundamentals; the refinements, special applications, and limitations peculiar to crevasse rescue are dealt with later.

Prusik

With three slings a person can climb the length of a fixed rope, the slings attached with prusik or similar knots that grip tightly when loaded yet slide when the load is removed. Prusiking is strenuous and requires the use of both hands and both feet, hence it is no system for a badly-injured person.

Fig. 108. Prusiking.

Manila is recommended for slings because of its high friction and lack of stretch. Although for pictorial simplicity the slings are illustrated as single strands, they actually are double, consisting of a simple loop of sling rope. The foot slings should extend to about shoulder level with loops just big enough for the foot, while the chest sling is just long enough to keep the climber from toppling backwards. In all techniques where foot slings are used they *always pass down inside the waistloop and spiral around the legs as shown,* reducing the tendency to lean backwards and also keeping the feet from slipping out of their loops.

Standing upright with all his weight bearing on the foot slings, the climber slides the prusik knot of his chest sling upward. He then lifts one foot and raises its unweighted knot. Now, stepping up into this sling, he repeats with the other foot. The climb is less tiring if the foot slings are of different lengths so that he can take equal steps with both feet. Some difficulty can be expected in sliding the knots when the rope is wet; spinning also can be troublesome under overhangs where the wall cannot be touched to maintain stability.

Bilgeri

Bilgeri is more commonly used than prusik, being faster and less strenuous. It still requires both hands and both feet, however, and therefore is also limited to cases of relatively-minor injury. A simple application of the method showing a crevasse rescue is illustrated. The principles are the same on rock. (*Note:* With a synthetic climbing rope, the stretch of the fiber makes bilgeri useless when the victim is more than 30 feet down.)

Fig. 109. Bilgeri.

Two ropes are held by belayers at an upper station, the ropes bearing on a smooth object to reduce friction and abrasion. The climber stands in loops at the ends of these two ropes—loops formed either by bowlines tied in the ends, or by attaching prusik slings. He unweights his right foot, calls "Right!" and as soon as the slack has been drawn upward by his helper above, steps up into this sling. Now unweighting the left foot, he calls "Left!", waits for this rope to be tightened, and takes another step upward. Done properly, bilgeri is little more fatiguing than climbing a ladder.

Up above, when the signal "Right!" is heard, a helper pulls the slack from that rope, reapplies his belay and then calls "Right!" to indicate that he has complied. At the signal "Left!" the other helper does the same. The obvious advantage of the bilgeri method is that the helpers never lift the climber's weight; they only pull alternately on slack ropes.

Body belays have the advantage of speed and simplicity. However, occasionally one man may have to do the job alone. Then each rope is anchored at the top with a prusik sling. At each signal the helper pulls the slack from the proper rope and slides the prusik knot down for a new grip.

Pulleys

Neither of the previous methods can be used when the victim is incapacitated. Even so he can be lifted easily—and an accompanying helper if necessary—by rigging a pulley system that more than doubles the lifting capacity of the rescuers.

Any pulley system gains its mechanical advantage by multiplying the number of ropes lifting the load. If two ropes can be employed, then each carries half the weight but the rescuer has to haul in 2 feet of rope to gain 1 foot of elevation; three ropes reduce the pulling force to one-third, while the rescuer hauls in three times as much rope as the distance lifted. With several frictionless pulleys very large weights can be hoisted by small forces—lightweight rescue pulleys, however, are not frictionless and this fact imposes a definite limitation on the force multiplication of such improvised systems. The one illustrated can theoretically lift a weight three times the pulling force, but friction reduces the best measured value to about 2.5. For simplicity the illustration shows typical loads in the ropes in the absence of friction. (Carabiners can be substituted for pulleys if the latter are not available, but add much friction.)

The drawing shows pulleys in use for crevasse rescue, but there is little difference on rock except in the anchors and edge protection.

In the simplest and commonest system the main anchor is placed as far from the edge as possible, and an anchor sling attached. The climbing rope is laid out in a "Z" pattern, one apex of which is snapped into a pulley on the anchor sling. A short sling, fastened with a prusik knot to the climbing rope near the cliff's edge, is snapped with a pulley to the other apex. As the rope is hauled in, the pulley of the short sling moves upward toward the anchor pulley. Now the rope is anchored with the long prusik sling while the pullers slide their short sling down

for a new grip. Too long a pull at one setting must not be attempted—
if the two pulleys touch, the "Z" will snap out of the rope and the
mechanical advantage will suddenly be lost, with a corresponding
jump in pulling force.

Fig. 110. Raising injured climber with pulley system.

Sometimes the terrain is cramped and a pull in the opposite direction
may be necessary, toward the cliff's edge. Then the same mechanical
advantage with reversed pull can be obtained, with a system similar to
the one illustrated, by rigging another pulley from the anchor.

For a long lift when two ropes are tied end to end there is a method of bypassing the joining knot around the pulleys. When the knot reaches the pulley, the prusik knots pass easily over it but the joining knot balks at the first pulley. Now the long sling holds the load while the main anchor sling is lowered slightly and its pulley relocated below the knot. The pull continues until the knot reaches the second pulley; again the long sling holds while this pulley is changed to the other side of the knot. Finally the system is free to operate for another rope length.

TRAVERSING

If the descent route must deviate far from the fall line, transport becomes very difficult. A *pendulum* is useful on terrain where rescuers can traverse overhead. Suspended from an anchored rope, the victim is pulled sideways by a second rope also anchored from above. As tension is gradually released from the first rope he pendulums to a position underneath the second anchor. The first rope is re-anchored farther along for the next swing.

For a *suspension traverse* along a taut climbing rope, most commonly employed in crossing a gully or notch, the victim hangs in a seat or stretcher from a pulley sliding along the anchored rope. He is pulled, or braked, by control ropes running from this pulley to both ends of the traverse. Two control ropes are essential because the suspension rope sags under the load and near the end of the traverse an uphill pull is required. A rigid stretcher should always be suspended at each end from pulleys joined by a short sling, otherwise the ride will be rough and erratic.

The pull exerted on the anchors by the taut rope is often much greater than the weight of the suspended person. To illustrate—at the halfway point of a level traverse, if the rope sags 5 degrees below the horizontal the anchors are subjected to almost six times the victim's weight. Ten degrees of sag alleviates this load by half, but too much sag makes pulling difficult. The need for stout anchors is obvious.

While the suspension traverse is ordinarily done in midair, it can just as well be used elsewhere. On a rope stretched across the face of a cliff a victim—or his helper—can fend away from the wall with his legs while being drawn across by a control rope. On steep snow the load can be slid along the surface.

Rescue on Steep Rock

Falling stones are responsible for a large proportion of the injuries incurred on rock, and the danger is many times magnified during rescue. Loose rock is then a particularly-serious hazard because of the many dragging ropes, and because the attention of rescuers is diverted, and because the operation may continue into night. Anyone working above the victim or rescuers must be doubly careful. Those below, with small chance for dodging, should wear hard hats and pad vital spots with extra clothing. If possible, sentries should be posted to warn of barrages. The first man down attempts to scour the route of loose stones; if the danger persists, it may be wise to lower an extra man just above the victim—a man with quick reflexes who holds in his hands a well-padded rucksack to field flying rocks.

Rescue on Steep Snow

Stonefall, avalanches, the ice ax, flailing tumbles or falls onto the rocks below are the common causes of injury during snow climbing. On snow there is particularly-urgent need for protecting the victim from exposure while administering first aid and planning evacuation. He should be wrapped in extra clothing and insulated from the snow by packs, ropes, or the body of a companion. If he cannot be moved quickly a trench or low wall will shield him from the wind. For overnight stays a snow cave can be dug.

Rockfall from cliffs above often makes this first phase of snow rescue deadly for all concerned. On more than one occasion lives have been saved by quick-thinking lion-hearted "shortstops"—companions who have grabbed rucksacks and lined up across the slope above the victim to smother a barrage.

As rapidly as possible the casualty should be removed to a sheltered spot or down to timberline where a fire can be built. The quickest method is by *human toboggan.* An uninjured person dons all available clothing, including a parka with the tail outside of his trousers. He lies in the snow with his head in the direction of travel and the victim is laid on top of him, head uphill or down as the injuries require; on a steep slope the two should be tied together. Belayed by the ankles, the "toboggan" is towed by his arms—for hard pulls a tow rope can be added, with the load distributed over his body by a harness. If angle of slope permits, the head-first pull is preferred because the toboggan slides more easily and comfortably. Under proper snow conditions the toboggan allows an evacuation pace little if any slower than that of an ordinary climbing party in a hurry to get home. Usually it is necessary to change toboggans every mile or so—more frequently on rough snow.

Other methods also depend upon sliding rather than carrying the victim. Sometimes the victim can be lowered in a *sitting glissade* position, well-wrapped in extra clothing, perhaps riding in back of a companion who smooths the track—the two tied together and carefully belayed. If injuries are relatively minor and the slope not excessively steep he can be roped in with two or three companions who slide slowly as a team, constantly under control. In addition, any of the general methods of transportation already described are applicable on snow.

The ice ax belay usually is not strong enough for rescue purposes unless two or more are used. Hip belays are preferable, particularly in very hard or very soft snow. Moats often provide superb lowering positions; in narrow chutes belay ropes can run to both sides. Rock islands in the snow are often solid, and sometimes can be created artificially by piling boulders in an excavation. The bollard is always worth consideration. A pole buried in a snow trench at right angles to the pull can be very strong.

Crevasse Rescue

To an unroped climber a fall into a crevasse is almost certainly fatal, for even if he survives the tumble, death from exposure is only a matter of hours. Traveling roped, but with improper technique, the result can be the same. On a slack rope a person can plunge freely to the bottom, the rope being no more than a retrieving line; companions unskilled in the self-arrest can be dragged in with him. Many people, although stopped by the rope, have died in midair because companions did not know how to extricate them. The history of glacier climbing is punctuated with frustrating examples.

Today such fatalities are largely needless. Modern climbing and rope-handling techniques can virtually eliminate injuries in crevasse falls, and rescue methods have been devised which are successful under almost any circumstances. This knowledge is available, yet all too often climbers venture onto glaciers before learning these skills. In time of trouble they must then rely on primitive techniques which are as untrustworthy today as they were a hundred years ago.

PREPARATION FOR ACCIDENTS

The success or failure of crevasse rescue depends very largely on advance preparations. Most glacier accidents occur while the whole team is moving, a plunge without warning into a hidden crevasse being much more common than a fall protected by a belay at an obviously-dangerous spot. Since a falling climber can easily drag in a single companion, it is best to travel roped in threes. Furthermore, to provide needed strength and equipment there should be at least two teams; a single team sometimes is pinned down in arrest position, unable to make the motions necessary to begin rescue.

A small party may have to depend upon the ability of each member to prusik from a crevasse; hence in such cases each climber must travel with *two slings and chest carabiner* (to snap into climbing rope) or *three* slings already attached to the rope and put down inside the waistloop, the loose ends tucked away where they can easily be reached.

In a party of two or more teams, to expedite the bilgeri or pulley systems each *end climber travels with one foot sling* attached to the rope; the *middleman needs a sling ahead of him and one behind,* since in a fall he might be caught by either rope; all climbers wear a chest carabiner. The sling allows a fallen climber to relieve the strain on his waist while waiting for rescue. It should already have been passed through the waistloop; after a fall the climber spirals it around his leg and inserts his foot. With bent knee he slides the prusik knot upward a few inches, places his weight on the sling, and stands in comparative comfort. Regardless of the rescue method he expects to use, this is his first move—without the sling he must dangle by the waist until help comes. His next move is to snap the chest carabiner over the climbing rope to hold himself upright.

Besides slings the party carries cumulatively a sufficient supply of spare rope, plus pulleys or carabiners, so the pulley method can be used if needed.

Knowing he might be trapped for a long time in ice, each climber must remain dressed for survival; clad in shorts and a thin shirt for a hot day he will not survive long in the depths of the glacier.

WHEN A CLIMBER FALLS

Assuming a three-man team, the instant a fall occurs team members drop into arrest, and as soon as the fall is checked, use their emergency slings to escape from their prone arresting positions: with an end man in the crevasse, either of the two partners may be able to hold the load alone while the other attaches a prusik sling to the rope near the crevasse and loops it over his anchored ice ax; if the middleman has fallen and is held from both sides, one partner holds as much of the load as possible while the other rises and anchors his rope. The first man now relaxes and seeks some safe way to reach the other side of the crevasse so that rescue can begin. If one of a two-man team falls, assistance from another rope team is usually essential to rescue.

ORGANIZING THE RESCUE

Hidden crevasses always are assumed in the work area, which if possible is probed thoroughly and safe boundaries marked before anyone moves about unroped. Without fail, those who must work in dangerous spots are belayed.

The lip above the fallen climber is reconnoitered. If overhanging or thinly bridged, a new access hole is cut at least 10 feet to one side. *The hole directly above the victim must not be enlarged*—he can be smothered or injured by snow and ice dropped in the process. All communications and rescue activity are conducted through the access hole.

Often a little ingenuity makes the rescue easier. The victim may be hanging near the bottom or above a ledge to which he can be lowered to wait in comfort. With a narrow place in the crevasse nearby he probably can traverse and climb out, or someone can stem down to him (stemming with crampons in a narrow crevasse is just as easy as stemming in a rock chimney). If it appears that surmounting the lip will be difficult, the victim might be swung along the crevasse to a better spot by means of the suspension traverse described earlier. If the rescuers are working on a steep slope above the crevasse, they should if feasible transfer operations to the lower edge to save time and reduce risk.

If someone must descend to render first aid he can rappel through the access hole and prusik out again. However, the party must make certain before he enters the crevasse that he can get out again and will not merely double the problem.

A line with a carabiner can be lowered to bring up the victim's ice ax and pack, and warm clothing sent down in the same way. Once the ax has been retrieved it is placed crosswise at the edge of the crevasse to *prevent the rope from trenching into the snow*. A canteen, rucksack, or other gear can be substituted if the ax cannot be spared, or has been lost in the fall.

IN THE CREVASSE

Down below the victim first steps into his emergency sling, dons warm clothing, and when a line is lowered sends up his pack and ice ax. If prepared to prusik he adjusts his three slings and sets out immediately for the surface.

For the modified bilgeri (described above) an end man stands in the sling until his companions lower the other end of the rope (or another rope entirely) with a foot loop; having run it through his waist-loop and around his leg he steps into it and begins to climb as already described. The technique for the middleman varies only in that he stands in both his slings immediately and is ready to climb as soon as his companions anchor both ends of the rope.

The bilgeri as originally invented makes no use of an emergency sling, and the victim hangs by the waist until a rope with loop is lowered. Once he can stand in this foot loop the climbing rope is slackened so that in it he can tie the second loop about 3 feet above his waist knot, pull it down, and begin his climb. The middleman must dangle while each end in turn is slackened enough for him to prepare his loops.

An unconscious or badly-injured person must be raised by pulley. If possible he is immediately swung to a place where he can rest comfortably. A companion descends quickly to render first aid, add warm clothing, remove pack and ice ax, and rig a seat sling or rope stretcher. Sometimes these duties must be performed under extreme difficulties, even hanging in midair. Once completed the helper may return to the surface, or he may guide the victim up if enough lifting power is available to raise their combined weight.

ON THE SURFACE

While the fallen climber is ascending via the prusik method his companions have little to do except guard the anchors and prepare to lift him over the edge.

For the bilgeri method, they lower the second foot loop tied in the end of a climbing rope; both ropes run on an ice ax shaft or other gear. The illustration shows two rescuers, using hip belays; often boot-ax belays are preferred. By substituting ice ax and/or bollard anchors and a prusik sling on each rope, one man can with skill and luck do the job alone.

The pulley system is set up as illustrated, though bollards also can be used. A trough must be dug beneath the rope so that the pulleys and prusik knots slide easily. For greatest efficiency the anchor should be well back from the crevasse, and all ropes should pull as nearly parallel as possible to the loaded rope. A long lift with each setting of the prusik knots speeds the operation.

CREVASSE LIP PROBLEMS

With all three rescue methods great difficulty can be encountered bringing the victim the final few feet to the surface. The climbing rope tends to slice into the crevasse edge in stopping the fall; unless buffered with an ice ax it saws deeper still during the rescue and may utterly vanish into a deep groove, freezing there so that no amount of effort will budge it. A person thus stalled can be in serious trouble.

One solution is to tunnel down along the rope, taking care not to drop debris on the victim. Failing that, rescuers can drop a spare rope to which the victim shifts his weight while cutting the other free. Sometimes it suffices to drop a rope from the other side of the crevasse, with a carabiner which the victim snaps to his climbing rope above his head. This rope is then pulled until the carabiner is over the middle of the crevasse, relieving pressure on the crevasse lip.

If spare line is not available the stuck rope must be salvaged. In the prusik method a person usually, by the time he reaches the buried section of the rope, is trailing enough slack to reach his rescuers. He unties his waist knot and on a retrieving line sends up the end. With this anchored he can retie his foot slings on the free rope and resume ascent. There is always in prusiking a last few feet, when the knots bear against the wall, that must be surmounted by a scramble or a hard upper haul. In a pulley or bilgeri rescue the last bit may similarly require brute strength, though usually by the time the imbedded portion of the rope is reached enough slack has been hauled in for free ends to be lowered.

A final method has thus far been used only in fatal accidents to roll the corpse up an overhang like a barrel. It might be extended in an emergency to raise a living person. With the victim rigid in a horizontal position a few feet down the wall, a loop of rope is slung under his feet and one under his upper body. Anchoring the ends which bear against the snow, the outside ends are pulled simultaneously and the body rolls up the wall, even out from under a sharp overhang. The pull required on each rope is only one-fourth of the victim's weight.

SPINNING

If the climber cannot touch the crevasse wall, spinning may defeat both the prusik and the bilgeri methods. In prusik a loaded rope, because of its twisted construction, tends to unwind. In bilgeri the two ropes sometimes cross and wind up, the resulting friction stopping all progress. The cure for spinning in bilgeri is simple. Rescuers can stop it by increasing the distance between the two anchors. The victim often can stop it by grasping both anchored ropes and pushing them sideways.

Avalanche Rescue

CROSSING AVALANCHE SLOPES

Chapters 21 and 12 discuss respectively the stability of snow and the techniques of choosing the safest route in avalanche conditions. There remains to be considered how the hazards can be minimized for a party forced to cross a questionable slope.

Only one person crosses at a time, the others watching from safe places, ready to warn him if a slide starts or to rescue him if he is caught. If the slope is very narrow a firmly-anchored belayer can safeguard each climber, but if there is more than one rope length to go the rope is not used. A belayer should not tie himself to the rope, for once a climber has been engulfed in a wet, heavy avalanche his belayer might as well try to snub an express train, and risks being snatched into the slide himself.

Before venturing onto a suspected slope each person should put on warm clothing and mittens so that he can survive if buried. All equipment should be loose and free to be thrown away, not only so that it will not drag him down, but also because loose articles provide clues to the location of a buried person. The rucksack may be carried in the hands, ready to throw away or to clutch in front of the face to gain breathing space. During winter mountaineering where many of the slopes traveled are of dubious stability each person should trail from his waist about 100 feet of bright-colored avalanche cord.

The crossing is made gingerly on foot, with long smooth strides, taking care not to cut a trench across the slope—such as is efficiently done by skis. Persons following the leader step carefully in the same footprints. The party is silent, the better to hear the start of an avalanche and sound the alarm.

WHEN AN AVALANCHE STARTS

Trying to outrun an avalanche is futile; the climber should dash for the side of the slope or at least for a rock or tree to which he can cling. As a last resort, he should throw aside all equipment, jam his ax deeply into the underlying snow, and hang on. If carried away he should fight to keep on the surface, swimming on his back with head uphill, flailing his arms and legs. If buried he must, before the snow stops, inhale deeply to expand his ribs and raise his arms or hands over his face to make a breathing space.

Dry, powdery snow poses slight danger of quick suffocation, containing trapped air and being loose enough to allow respiration. In heavy, wet snow immediate suffocation is probable, even if a person's face is above the surface. A cubic foot of wet snow weighs as much as 55 pounds; packed solidly after the slide stops, it holds the climber as in a vise, compressing his ribs and preventing respiration. Thus he must obtain breathing room while in motion. Rescue must come quickly, for wet snow contains little air and his breath will soon glaze and seal the surface around his face. Once the avalanche stops and struggling appears futile, he must conserve his energy and oxygen by waiting quietly for help, listening for the sound of rescuers, shouting only when there is some chance of being heard.

HASTY SEARCH

When a companion is swept away, the rest of the party must first of all remember the *point on the slope where he was caught,* and second the *point where he disappeared,* noting these with respect to fixed objects nearby—trees or rocks. At the same time the party watches— until it stops—the *point on the moving surface of the avalanche where he disappeared.* If successful in observation they have three points on his path and know he is somewhere on or near the line between the lower two, probably closer to the lowest point.

While lookouts watch for further slides, the upper two points are quickly marked. The group hurries down the victim's line of fall toward the lowest point, searching carefully as they go for items of his gear, or for his avalanche cord. They look especially hard at trees or outcroppings which might have stopped him, and scan beneath any blocks of snow that lie on the surface. They shout at intervals, then maintain absolute silence while listening for a muffled answer.

It is important to keep in mind that sliding snow flows like water, faster on the surface and in the center than on the bottom and at the sides. When an avalanche follows a twisting channel the snow and the victim conform to the turns. Both these facts have obvious influence on search.

If any loose equipment is found on or near the surface the buried victim probably lies not far uphill, and rescuers immediately begin to probe and dig in the vicinity. If no equipment is found, the party should mark the observed stopping point of that portion of the avalanche surface where the victim disappeared, and quickly search and scratch the area just above, where he is most likely to lie. If nothing is found they begin to probe, using blunted willow wands, taped ice axes, or reversed ski poles. Sharp probes must never be used because at this time it is assumed the victim is still alive.

SYSTEMATIC SEARCH

If the hasty search proves futile a systematic probing is required. This is best done as a team, not by individuals, and hence may be beyond the capability of the small party except on a very limited basis.

While a sentry watches for further avalanches, searchers line up across the bottom of the search area. They stand no more than 3 feet apart, facing uphill. All movements are coordinated by signals of the leader; at the count each person probes as deeply as he can push his probe, first directly in front, then 1 foot to his right and 1 to his left. Thus a line has been probed at 1-foot intervals all across the track. By signals the group proceeds uphill with short steps.

All the while the group keeps quiet, listening for the victim's voice. At this stage he may still be alive, although his chances diminish rapidly with time. People have lived for a week in dry snow, and in the

Cascades a youth once survived some 9 hours in a wet avalanche, his life saved by an airspace between big blocks of snow. The party should not give up as long as it can continue the search with any hope of success. Even a small group usually had better exhaust its strength trying to save the victim's life, rather than sending for distant help which may arrive too late. Only in ski areas where large rescue parties can be organized quickly might it be best to send for help.

Probing should continue as high as the second point on the victim's track, the marked point where he disappeared beneath the surface. It also should extend well on either side of the estimated fall line, since he may have been sidetracked into an eddy. If probing is completed without success the victim is deeply buried and can be found only by digging. It is unlikely he will be found alive.

TRENCHING

As a final effort the avalanche is trenched, an operation which requires many men with shovels and probing poles. The first trench is dug horizontally across the bottom of the avalanche, the full depth of the slide. Then at 1-foot intervals both walls of the trench are probed to the full length of the pole. If the first trench reveals nothing a parallel one is dug exactly two pole-lengths away. The procedure is repeated until if necessary every foot of the avalanche is probed. Several days may be required to complete the job, working from a basecamp established nearby. Continuing avalanche danger obviously makes such a prolonged effort in an exposed location unwise.

TREATMENT OF VICTIM

Once the person is found first aid begins at once unless rigor mortis is positively diagnosed. As soon as the face is uncovered artificial respiration is started by the mouth-to-mouth method. Treatment for freezing, shock, and physical injuries can be conducted simultaneously, but it is above all important to concentrate on restarting breathing. Here rescuers must not be discouraged too soon. There are cases on record of revival by artificial respiration several hours after all hope was seemingly lost.

Transport on Nontechnical Terrain

In many rescues the hardest job begins when the steep terrain is past and ropes are put away. No longer aided by gravity, the party must carry its burden, very fatiguing work on rough ground. Under some conditions, however, a few simple techniques extend the capacity of the small team so that it need not call for help.

ONE- AND TWO-MAN CARRIES

A strong climber can carry a person on his back for long distances, provided the weight is distributed properly. For the *rucksack carry* a large rucksack is slit on the sides near the bottom so that the victim can step into it like a pair of shorts, the drawstring tied snugly around his waist. He rides piggyback, wrists tied over the carrier's chest if need be. For the *coiled rope carry* rope is coiled in a circle about 4½ feet long and twisted once to form a figure-8. The victim inserts his legs into the loops and the carrier inserts his arms as though putting on a pack.

The *four-hand seat* is useful for short distances. Two carriers stand side by side, and each grasps his right wrist with his left hand—or vice versa—with palms down. Then each carrier grasps the wrist of the other with his free hand to form a four-hand seat. For longer distances the *ice ax carry* is better, rucksack-wearing carriers standing side by side with the shaft resting between them in their pack straps. The victim sits on the padded shaft with an arm over the shoulder of each helper.

DRAGS

For a *travois* two small trees are cut and laid parallel about 18 inches apart. The branches are stripped from the upper side, those underneath left to cushion the ride and add braking, though on level ground they too are best removed. Two crossbraces are lashed atop the trunks about 6 feet apart. A rope is used for diagonal bracing and then laced in zigzag fashion from side to side to form a bed. A single rescuer slips both butt ends in his pack straps or two men grasp one each. Under ideal conditions the travois allows one or two rescuers to move the casualty. The major disadvantage is the rarity of usable trees at high altitude. Alpine conifers tend to be thick and heavy at the base; slide alder and other deciduous species tend to be excessively limber.

Ski mountaineers can from skis and poles improvise a travois, or alternatively a *toboggan*.

STRETCHERS

When injuries demand rigid evacuation a stretcher of lashed poles is best. Here again alpine species are deficient, being either too heavy or too limber. At lower elevations vegetation is more cooperative.

A simple semi-rigid structure can be made by inserting poles through the loops of the previously-described rope basket stretcher, adding strength with crossmembers, then bracing diagonally with sling rope.

For a more durable rope stretcher two small loops are tied about 18 inches apart near the middle of a climbing rope. Then, proceeding toward both ends, three or four more loops are tied at the same interval over a finished length of about 7 feet, at which point the ropes are joined with a square knot. This knotted section of the rope is laid in a rectangle on the ground, the hand loops along the sides; the remaining ends are laced diagonally back and forth from side to center—twisting once over each other at the center and returning to their original sides. Lacing continues until all the rope has been used in making a bed, supplemented by sling if necessary. Six or eight men can now carry the victim by the hand loops, inserting poles or ice axes for additional rigidity.

Obtaining Outside Aid

There are occasions when a party cannot cope with its own emergency. Then help must be requested—from climbers on nearby peaks, from people living or working in the region, or from a regional mountain rescue group. At all times a party should know what help it can expect if its own efforts fail, where and how to get it, and how to cooperate.

GOING FOR HELP

The group must have a clear grasp of the problem and of its own capacities and needs before deciding how much and what form of aid to request; once a runner has been dispatched there is no way to control what he does or says. An excited messenger hurrying to the road with little idea of his party's needs only causes confusion.

Ideally two climbers should travel out together—partly for safety and partly because two people do a better job of obtaining help. Written instructions should be carried so that nothing is forgotten. Messengers carry a minimum of equipment and travel swiftly, marking on the way a plain trail to facilitate the return.

Once in contact with civilization the messengers call the local authorities in charge of the region—perhaps Forest or Park Service personnel, a law enforcement agency, a logging or mining company, or the military. These are asked either to immediately relay a message to the local rescue group or to provide the needed help themselves.

The messengers' job is not ended here. They must make certain messages are sent at once, accurately, and that they reach the destination. Often the organization of a rescue depends upon a chain of communication, message relayed from person to person via telephone and radio until finally a rescue leader is reached. Along the way vital information may be lost by non-mountaineers who do not understand the words they are asked to convey. For this reason a messenger is always much happier when he can talk directly to some trusted fellow climber. The messenger must not allow the chain to break. If he cannot personally contact the leader he must be insistent with intermediaries to the point of being obnoxious. Messages garbled along the way—or simply not forwarded—have directly caused a tragic number of rescue failures.

The leader will want to know:

1. Where, when, and how the accident occurred.
2. The number of casualties, the nature and seriousness of injuries.
3. Distance from the road and the type of terrain and thus the probable difficulty of evacuation.
4. How many people are still at the scene, and their strength.
5. If the climbing party will wait at the spot or must move to safer ground.
6. What method of evacuation will be necessary—carrying by rigid stretcher, sliding on snow, lowering down steep cliffs.
7. Where the messengers are, and where he can meet them. Enough information must reach the leader so that he can decide:
   a. If a doctor is needed.
   b. How many men are necessary in various stages of the rescue and what skills they need.
   c. How long the job will take.
   d. What equipment and supplies must be supplied.
   e. What support to provide, such as aircraft, radio, or basecamp facilities.

Once the messengers are assured the rescue is in good hands they should personally inform relatives of people in the climbing party of the situation. In a large group this requires making a written list of names and telephone numbers before leaving the accident scene. It is cruel to place family members in anxiety for hours or days.

A last and important function of the messengers is to meet the rescue party at an agreed rendezvous and be rested and ready to lead the way to the accident scene. If incapacitated by fatigue or injury it is all the more important that they have marked the trail on the way out.

SPECIALIZED RESCUE EQUIPMENT

Rescue organizations often bring equipment specially designed to make their task easier. The average climber may not be familiar with these items, but he should know what they are and what they can do. Most important is a rigid metal stretcher such as the Stokes which has a framework of metal tubing and a wire-mesh basket that closely fits the body outlines, even to separate troughs for the legs. Such a stretcher is mandatory for spinal injuries or severe fractures. Some designs are demountable for carrying in sections and have provision for attaching either a bicycle wheel or a ski. For snow rescues there are several types of toboggans designed for use by rescuers on skis or snowshoes.

The aerial tramway—consisting of long lengths of steel wire with pulleys, fittings, and a wooden drum for a friction brake—has been spectacularly successful in the Alps. On the taut cable a casualty can be traversed high across a chasm or sent from the top of a cliff to a point many hundreds of feet down the mountain without relocating anchors.

Numerous smaller items occasionally are used, such as body harnesses of webbing, and the "Dolfer hook," a complexly-bent steel rod used for braking by a person sliding down a fixed rope. There are special pack frames with seats for injured persons. For avalanche rescues there are aluminum shovels and sectional probing poles. For transport of corpses, zippered, airtight body bags are useful and in evacuation by horse essential.

RADIO COMMUNICATIONS

Two-way radio communication, when the gear is both light and efficient, immensely facilitates mountain rescue. The main problem is obtaining reliable transmission and reception despite heavy timber, intervening ridges, long distances, and bad weather. Transmitters operating by amplitude modulation (AM) on frequencies between 2000 and 5000 kilocycles are most dependable in timber, valleys, and over long distances but need considerable power, which means considerable battery weight. Frequency modulation (FM) radio uses less power and thus the units are smaller and lighter. However, FM is limited virtually to line-of-sight and is worthless in timber, from one valley to the next, or over great distances.

Many organizations serving both public and private interests have excellent radio facilities. However, in most cases they operate on incompatible fixed frequencies. For a satisfactory rescue radio network the following are needed:

1. Portable sets for each group in a ground party, all on the same frequency.
2. A powerful mobile station at the road, capable of relaying messages to distant centers.
3. Portable sets that can be carried to intermediate vantage points for links between the mobile station and the ground party.
4. Airplanes equipped to relay messages back and forth over intervening ridges where (3) is impractical.
5. Fixed stations in the population centers from which rescuers and equipment must be drawn.

Ideally a rescue organization should own items 1 and 3, but usually they must be borrowed from public agencies. Items 2 and 4 may be provided by police, Civil Air Patrol, or the military. Item 5 includes facilities of these same people, plus those of radio "hams." Without a great deal of preparation beforehand to ensure that this assorted equipment works on compatible frequencies there is no reliable link between the rescue team and the outside world—or even between the ground rescue party and the aircraft a few feet above.

AIR RESCUE

Light Airplanes

Fixed-wing aircraft have limited utility in rescue. In rare instances float or ski planes have landed at high altitude on level glaciers, but ordinarily the light airplane is most useful for communications, being sometimes invaluable for relaying radio messages, or with a loud-speaker for shouting instructions to ground rescuers or a lost person. Dropping supplies is another occasional role.

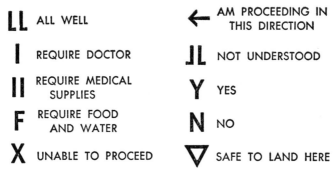

LL ALL WELL

I REQUIRE DOCTOR

II REQUIRE MEDICAL SUPPLIES

F REQUIRE FOOD AND WATER

X UNABLE TO PROCEED

← AM PROCEEDING IN THIS DIRECTION

JL NOT UNDERSTOOD

Y YES

N NO

V SAFE TO LAND HERE

Fig. 111. Ground-to-air signals.

The international symbols illustrated are familiar to the majority of pilots and it is well worth a climber's time to jot them down on a slip of paper to be carried in the first aid kit.

Helicopter

The helicopter has revolutionized mountain rescue. It has plucked persons from cliffs and glaciers and rushed them to hospitals in hours rather than the days required by ground transport—over and over again meaning the difference between life and death. However, large ground parties are not a thing of the past: there still are times and places where helicopters cannot operate; weather is often the determining factor, as well as the availability of qualified mountain pilots.

Helicopters, now usually supplied by the Air Force, have made innumerable rescues in Northwest America. Rescuers have been deposited and casualties picked up at elevations as high as 12,000 feet. Landings for other purposes have been made at altitudes well above 14,000 feet. As machines with higher performance become available they will play an increasing role, and therefore the climber should know the principles of helicopter operation, and also the limitations.

A helicopter can take on a load either by landing, or when this is not feasible, by hovering and lowering a sling on a cable attached to a power winch. The most important factors governing its ability to evacuate are visibility, wind velocity and turbulence, and air density.

In mountain flight continual visual contact with the ground is essential, and thus in poor weather the helicopter cannot operate. It can maneuver safely in winds up to about 35 miles per hour, a wind of about 10 miles per hour being indeed better than still air. The turbulence which usually accompanies high winds is dangerous, although under some conditions steady breezes are actually helpful. The maximum altitude at which a helicopter can work is determined by air density, which decreases at high altitude and in high temperature, thus reducing the lifting power of the rotor blades.

As a helicopter nears the ground, downwash of the rotors creates a cushion of compressed, dense air on which the craft floats. Only when such a cushion can be built can the helicopter hover or land. When there is no flat surface against which the rotors can push, or when the air is too thin for floating, the helicopter flies in exactly the same manner as a fixed-wing airplane—that is, it must keep moving forward to remain airborne. It can stop forward motion and rest on a cushion only when within "reach" of the ground; the reach of most machines is less than 50 feet at sealevel, and much less at any altitude. Contrary to lingering misunderstanding, a helicopter cannot stop forward progress high in the air and descend vertically hundreds of feet onto a dime.

Because he must make an airplane-like approach, the helicopter pilot must have a clear lane into his proposed landing or hovering area. Windward slopes are desirable for the extra lift provided by steady updrafts; lee slopes with downdrafts are to be avoided. The landing or hovering spot need not be exactly level, but should be reasonably so. The pilot prefers "falling off" the top or side of a ridge crest or the lower edge of a hanging valley rather than rising vertically from a valley bottom. From a flat landing spot he may be able to climb only a few feet before losing his cushion and having to fly forward. Thus the ground party must have selected a spot with a clear exit into the wind. In timbered areas trees may have to be felled both to provide the approach lane and the necessary lateral clearance of at least 100 feet. The ground party should clearly define the touchdown spot with boughs or ropes, remembering that the hurricane blast of the rotors will blow away unweighted objects. On winter snow, where the downdraft stirs up a blizzard that hides the ground, the pilot needs a fixed point of reference; a guide, dressed in a bright-colored parka if possible, stands in a prominent place giving hand signals that let the pilot know when he is approaching touchdown. A smoke column from green plants thrown on a hot fire shows wind conditions. Usually the pilot makes several close passes to test the air. If the cushion feels slippery he may not land but merely rest one wheel on the ground while loading, or perhaps he dares only hover, lowering a line. If even hovering is dubious, the helicopter may lower a line and make a slow pass over the ground—much slower than any airplane could manage, but still with some forward speed to supplement the cushion. *Warning:* one should never approach a helicopter unless signaled to do so by the pilot or a crewman.

RESCUE GROUP ORGANIZATION

In the Alps, with its large corps of professional guides, organized rescue is all part of the business. In North America climbing is done almost entirely by amateurs, and so is rescue. To search out skilled mountaineers, to overcome their native hatred of mass organization, to integrate their efforts, is no small task. Nor is it easy to weed out—as must be done—the sensation-seekers who carry cameras and collect photographs of corpses, the headliners who gravitate to any activity that promises to get their names in the newspapers or their faces on TV, the honest do-gooders with a sense of pity greater than their physical ability.

Of primary importance is a pool of leaders who thoroughly know rescue work and the local mountains and are able from fragments of telephone information to analyze a situation and decide quickly what action to take. With the help of a call committee they round up the necessary manpower and equipment. Since without such a leader the rescue is likely to be ineffective, and since on any given day of the season most of them will be on climbs of their own, a group must have many competent leaders available. Dependence on one or two "indispensable" men sets the stage for tragedy.

The manpower is contributed by volunteers from among the local climbers, ready to answer a call at any time, ready to finance their own way, use their own equipment, and take time from their jobs. The call committee should have the current addresses and telephone numbers of these people, as well as a knowledge of their climbing experience and specific skills. The mere act of volunteering should not be accepted as a sufficient test of capability.

In most areas, responsibility for rescue now rests with law-enforcement agencies, the Forest Service, the National Park Service, or some comparable arm of government, and volunteer rescue groups work closely with such authorities. To put the problem in perspective, it remains true that most rescues are accomplished by one (1) call committee, one (1) leader, and either four dozen (48) stretcher-bearers or one (1) helicopter.

PART FIVE

The Climbing Environment

MOUNTAIN GEOLOGY

WHEN a climber reaches a summit and looks out over ridge after ridge of peaks he may imagine he is on the crest of a gigantic wave heaved up by a turbulent ocean. His fancy is not so very wrong, for even the geologist often likens mountain ranges to stormy seas, though the storm is inside rather than outside the earth's crust. Nor do the waves of rock ever achieve the perfect form of waves in water, for as fast as the mountains rise they are attacked by elements of the very air they have displaced and degraded by the gravity they defy. Sun and frost, water and wind, tear down the peaks grain by grain.

The tempests in the earth's crust have a duration measured in eons rather than hours, and man clambers about among the crests and troughs for too brief a span ever to see—except in imagination—the rise of mountains from plains and their degradation into plains once more. However, just as the master mariner knows the nature of wind and water so that he can navigate even in the hardest blow, so does the master mountaineer know the nature of the more complex storms that toss up the mountains and tear them down. The following brief survey of mountain geology contains information that can make alpine navigation easier, and climbing a much richer experience than any mere athletic exercise; the sincere mountaineer will desire a more complete understanding and is referred to any of the many fine texts available. (See Appendix 3.)

Foundation of Mountains: The Earth

One theory of the earth's formation suggests a catastrophic near-collision of the sun with another star which spattered surrounding space with fiery particles that assumed orbits and became planets. According to another theory the entire solar system, sun and planets, slowly coalesced from diffuse cosmic dust about 4½ billion years ago. Many scientists believe that as the dust coalesced the pressure produced in the center of the growing mass and radioactivity of the interior caused the spinning solid juvenile earth to heat up and melt. With cooling, chemical compounds formed, the heavier ones gravitating inward until ultimately the earth differentiated into at least three concentric spheres. Others feel that this differentiation could not have taken place in the allowable time before the oldest crustal rocks formed at least 3½ billion years ago. It has even been suggested that the outermost layer of the light shell of the earth—the continents with their mountains—began as great splashes of late-arriving meteoric material.

Whatever the origin of the earth, earthquake waves (seismic waves) show it to have a relatively-rigid crust, a layer of rock some 22 miles thick with an average density of about 2.5 (that is, weighing about 2½ times more than water, which has a density of 1). The middle shell has an approximate density of 5, or a good deal heavier than basalt. Virtually nothing is known about the inner core, by far the major mass of the earth. Having a density of between 8 and 12, it could be a nickle-iron alloy, like some meteorites, but many scientists believe that under the extreme pressure and temperature of the earth's center atoms do not have the same characteristics as in the crust, so that the core is a substance utterly unlike any material familiar to man, having the properties of both a highly-compressed gas and a tough metal.

The climber is most interested in the outer shell, the crust that crumples and ruptures to form mountains. Though the highest mountains and the deepest valleys are nothing more to the earth as a whole than the scratches and dust on a billiard ball, man himself is sufficiently small to find the scale impressive.

Building Blocks of Mountains: Minerals and Rocks

THE MINERALS

Mountains are made of rocks and rocks of minerals, compounds not broken apart except by chemical action, so that a climber can begin his study of mountain construction considering minerals as the basic building blocks. Over a thousand are known, but only seven are common, and these—constituting most of the earth's outer shell—are called the *rock-forming minerals*. The element silicon is as ubiquitous in rock as carbon in living things, 90 per cent of the crust being either silicon dioxide (*silica*) or compounds of silica and other elements (*silicates*).

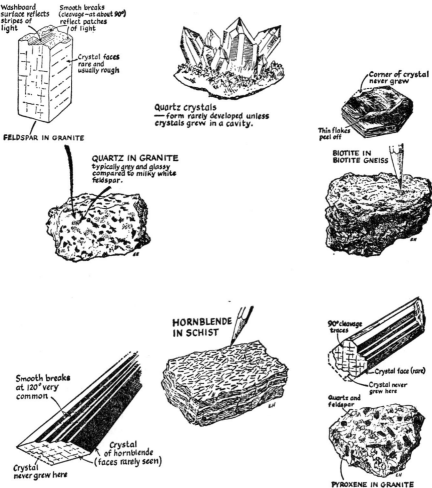

Washboard surface reflects stripes of light

Smooth breaks (cleavage—at about 90°) reflect patches of light

Crystal faces rare and usually rough

FELDSPAR IN GRANITE

Quartz crystals
— form rarely developed unless crystals grew in a cavity.

QUARTZ IN GRANITE
typically grey and glassy compared to milky white feldspar.

Corner of crystal never grew

Thin flakes peel off

BIOTITE IN BIOTITE GNEISS

HORNBLENDE IN SCHIST

Smooth breaks at 120° very common

Crystal of hornblende (faces rarely seen)

Crystal never grew here

90° cleavage traces

Crystal face (rare)

Crystal never grew here

Quartz and feldspar

PYROXENE IN GRANITE

Fig. 112. Some rock-forming minerals.

Among the group of seven, only calcite does not have silicon in its molecule.

IGNEOUS ROCKS

Now and again within the crust, internal friction, heat of radioactive decay, and/or release of pressure creates *magmas,* melts of silicate minerals which on cooling solidify into igneous rocks. If the process is completed deep in the earth, the minerals crystallizing slowly, the rock is called *plutonic.* If in addition the melt moves upward, propelled by its own lesser density, perhaps dissolving and incorporating the overlying masses, or forcing them aside, an *intrusive* rock results. Should the liquid erupt onto the surface and cool rapidly, it becomes *volcanic,* that is, *extrusive* rock.

Table 11. The Rock-Forming Minerals.

Mineral	Common appearance	Occurrence	Chemical composition
Quartz	Many colors, but usually colorless, white, or gray. Irregular glassy masses around other minerals or discrete grains in sedimentary rocks.	Almost all rocks except dark igneous ones.	Silicon dioxide.
Feldspars (A group of minerals)	White, gray, or pink, usually well-formed rectangular crystals.	All types of rock. Especially prominent in granite and gneiss.	Potassium or sodium and calcium aluminum silicates.
Muscovite (White mica)	Colorless to silvery flakes or foliated masses. Usually transparent and flexible.	Light-colored igneous, metamorphic, and sedimentary rocks.	Complex potassium aluminum silicate plus water.
Biotite (Black mica)	Like muscovite but generally brown to black.	Light-colored igneous and metamorphic rocks.	Complex potassium iron magnesium aluminum silicate plus water.
Amphiboles (A group of minerals)	Light green to black. Grains or long crystals. Common variety is *hornblende.*	Igneous and metamorphic rocks.	Complex of calcium magnesium iron aluminum silicates plus water.
Pyroxenes (A group of minerals)	Green to black. Short, stubby crystals. Difficult to distinguish from amphiboles.	Dark-colored igneous rocks and some metamorphic rocks.	Complex of calcium magnesium iron aluminum silicates.
Calcite	Colorless to white, yellow, or gray. Glassy to dull. Often mass of crystals of uniform sugary texture. Scratches with knife.	Limestone, marble, fillings in veins and cracks of all rocks.	Calcium carbonate.

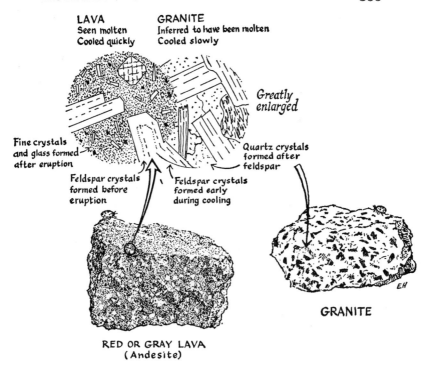

LAVA
Seen molten
Cooled quickly

GRANITE
Inferred to have been molten
Cooled slowly

Greatly enlarged

Fine crystals
and glass formed
after eruption

Quartz crystals
formed after
feldspar

Feldspar crystals
formed before
eruption

Feldspar crystals
formed early
during cooling

GRANITE

RED OR GRAY LAVA
(Andesite)

Fig. 113. Volcanic and plutonic igneous rocks.

As the following table shows, the name of a rock derived from a magma depends on two things: mineral content and rate of cooling. The same molten mass that becomes granite when crystallized slowly becomes rhyolite if erupted at the surface.

Table 12. Extrusive and Intrusive Equivalents.

	Rich in Quartz Light in Color	No Quartz Dark	Very Dark
INTRUSIVE OR PLUTONIC (visible crystals, granular)	Granite	Diorite	Gabbro
EXTRUSIVE OR VOLCANIC (only spots of visible crystals, glassy or sugary)	Rhyolite Dacite (Explosive eruptions)	Andesite (Explosions and flows)	Basalt (Mostly flows)

Plutonic or Intrusive Rocks

Slow crystallization from deeply-buried melts generally means good climbing, since the minerals formed are relatively large and interwoven into a solid mat. Weathering develops protrusions of relatively-resistant minerals which either make for a rough-surfaced rock with excellent friction, or, if the resistant crystals are very much larger than the enclosing mat, one with numerous knobby holds. Many of the rock routes in the Cathedral Peak area of Yosemite afford just such crystal climbing.

Intrusions are variously named according to location and size. Very large masses of plutonic rock are called *batholiths*, being with rare exception in the *granite* family: granite, granodiorite, diorite, and others, all similar in composition and formation, differing only in the relative amounts of minerals contained.

There is a core of such batholiths in every major mountain system in the world. In the Alps, Sierra Nevada, North Cascades, British Columbia Coast Range, and most other ranges this core is at least in part exposed, providing some of the finest and steepest rock climbing.

Small bodies are *sills*, forced between sedimentary strata, and *dikes*, fissures which crosscut the strata. Many small intrusive bodies are quickly cooled, so they may look like extrusive rocks.

Volcanic or Extrusive Rocks

Explosive eruptions, most characteristic of melts with a chemical composition producing rhyolite, eject molten rock so abruptly into the atmosphere that it hardens into loose airy masses of fine crystals and uncrystallized glass. When this ash is bound together, either while still partially molten or after cooling, it is called *tuff*, a weak rock that disintegrates rapidly and erodes easily. Loose ash, or *cinders*, are of no interest whatsoever to the rock climber. Pinnacles National Monument in California, however, has become a bolt-climbing playground, since its rhyolite *breccia*, a solidified aggregate of rhyolite chunks, affords few dependable piton cracks and a wealth of treacherous holds.

Quieter eruptions with the molten rock flowing from large fissures as *lava* are most characteristic of melts producing *basalt*. The plateau of eastern Washington and Oregon is composed of innumerable basalt flows extruded during many eons.

Volcanoes built almost exclusively of basalt flows have broad bases and gentle slopes, such as Mauna Loa in Hawaii, while those explosive in origin are steep cinder cones. Many are complex, their history including eruptions of flows and ash ranging from basalt to rhyolite in composition. Examples are Fujiyama in Japan and the Pacific Coast volcanoes, from Lassen in California to Garibaldi in British Columbia. On these peaks snow and glacier routes are usually preferred; the nightmarish slopes of shifting cinders and ice-carved cliffs of rotten andesite rarely tempt a climber.

Jointing

The importance of joint systems has been discussed in Chapters 6. In plutonic rocks joints or cracks are caused by internal stresses such as from contraction during cooling or expansion when overlying rock is eroded away. Some joints tend to follow a consistent pattern throughout an entire mountain and their existence can often be predicted. For instance, when a ledge abruptly terminates the climber does well to look around the corner, for perhaps the joint—and thus the ledge—resumes.

When molten rock extrudes onto the surface of the earth as a lava flow or even when it intrudes into a cold surrounding mass as a dike or sill, the contraction from rapid cooling commonly causes such a profusion of joints that, in contrast to plutonic rocks, the climbing is most treacherous. However, not too seldom the jointing is so regular as to present the appearance of massed pillars, the classic example being the Devil's Tower in Wyoming, where most routes are strikingly vertical.

SEDIMENTARY ROCKS

Igneous rocks originate deep in the earth, but sedimentary rocks are born high on the mountains, where the erosive forces pluck away debris and pass it along to rivers for transportation to places of deposition in valleys, lakes, or arms of the ocean. As sediments accumulate, the underlayers are solidified by pressure and by mineral cements precipitated from percolating groundwater. Gravel and boulders are transformed into *conglomerates;* sandy beaches into *sandstone;* beds of mud into *mudstone* or *shale;* shell beds and coral reefs into *limestone* or *dolomite.*

Though in general sedimentary rocks are much more friable than those cooled from fiery magmas, pressure and cementing often produce very solid rocks. Indeed, by sealing up cracks cementing can result in a disturbingly-flawless surface, particularly in limestone. Most of the high mountain ranges have some sedimentary peaks. The Canadian Rockies are almost exclusively so, and offer every degree of sturdiness. However, except for scattered regions such as the Italian Dolomites, sedimentary rocks rarely offer high-angle climbing comparable to that on granite.

METAMORPHIC ROCKS

Pioneer geologists quickly became adept at distinguishing between rocks of fiery and aqueous origin, but not so quickly did they recognize that many rocks—though grossly resembling igneous or sedimentary rocks—have been so profoundly changed by heat or pressure that they have become something quite different. These are the *metamorphic* rocks, that is, changed rocks. No rock is fixed in a permanent state; all change in time. Sand does not become sandstone without pressure—and what constitutes a magma if not melted older rocks? Metamorphic rocks bridge the gap between sedimentary and igneous, though on either side the boundaries are ill-defined.

After sediments are solidified they may be subjected to such great pressures and high temperatures, meanwhile being permeated by hot water, that the minerals recrystallize. The bedding may at the same time be distorted by folding and squeezing. Shale is transformed into *slate* or *schist*, sandstone and conglomerate into *quartzite*, limestone into *marble*. The changes may be slight, producing slightly-altered sediments, or so considerable as to produce *gneiss*, only distinguishable from igneous rock by a banded structure that betrays a sedimentary origin. Indeed the end result of continued pressure and heat and circulation of hot water is a rock with all the characteristics of granite even though it has never been melted. By this process of *granitization* have been created many of the granite massifs formerly assigned a magmatic origin.

Most rocks called metamorphic have a recognizable ancestry in sedimentary rocks, but some can be traced back to an igneous origin. *Greenstone* or *amphibolite* may be metamorphosed basalt or andesite. Even gneiss can be derived from rhyolite or a crushed and squeezed granite, and many of the favorite climbs in the North Cascades are just such gneissic granite.

Metamorphic rocks may have not only joints and bedding, but *cleavage*, a series of thinly-spaced cracks imparted to the rock by the pressures of folding. Blackboards were once made from cleaved slabs of slate. Because of this cleavage, the lower grades of metamorphic rocks may be entirely unsuitable for climbing, the mountains quickly wasting away to uninteresting low angles, or if steepened by glaciers, altogether too rotten for pleasure—the inner Olympic Mountains being a prime example. However, the higher degrees of metamorphism or metamorphism of the right rocks provide superb sport. In Boulder Canyon in the Front Range of the Rockies high-grade metamorphic rocks present a variety of high-angle climbs. An example of low-grade metamorphism of the right rocks is the Sir Donald group in the Southern Selkirks, composed of a durable quartzite sound enough to stand solidly at high angles and yet so well-broken by bedding, jointing, and cleavage that rarely is much investigation needed to find the next hold or the next belay.

Mountain Building: The Grand Pattern

Two steps are necessary in the building of a mountain. First a land area must rise above sealevel. Second, erosion must dissect the crustal protuberance. Both are essential, for mere altitude does not make a mountain. The high plateaus of Colorado and Tibet, not yet deeply eroded, are of little interest to the climber. To understand mountain building it is logical first to study events that lead to the elevation of a portion of the earth's crust above sealevel; later will be considered the forces of erosion that sculpture peaks out of the elevated crust.

GEOSYNCLINES AND MOBILE BELTS

The earth's crust seems hard and brittle in man's view of things, but in the geologic measure of time the crust is fairly plastic and subject to all manner of distortion. It sags under great weights, bulges when pushed from beneath, wrinkles when compressed from the sides, and when it cannot relieve pressure by bending, cracks into pieces which slide along each other. None of the many hypotheses presented to explain the origin of these mountain-building stresses satisfies all the evidence, but even if the "why" is unknown the "how" is well understood, for certain invariable similarities make it possible to tell a general story that summarizes the history of any mountain mass.

Compared to rocks elsewhere, folded sediments of mountain chains are extremely thick, commonly 8 to 10 miles before folding. A gigantic downwarp in the earth's crust is necessary to accommodate such a mass, and this great sag, along with the sediment, is called a *geosyncline*. Every major mountain range, past and present, had its beginning in one or more geosynclines. When a geosynclinal downwarp occurs so rapidly that sedimentary processes cannot keep up, oceanic troughs or deeps are formed, examples being those in the western Pacific which have measured depths of over 7 miles. When the downwarp is constantly filled by detritus derived from a nearby continental mass a true geosyncline forms.

All mountains are born in the sea—and all are seeded by more ancient mountains. Today the Pacific Ocean along the west coast of the Americas is a geosyncline. Sediments from the Rockies, the Cascades, the Sierra Nevada, and other ranges are dumped into coastal waters by many rivers. It is more than likely that the Coast Ranges of California and Oregon and the Olympic Mountains are embryonic folds of this geosyncline; West Coast dwellers of the present may be living near the crest of a mountain range which will rise millions of years from now.

Not only are the rocks of the major ranges unduly thick, but they are complexly folded, especially in the cores. These contortions indicate that the crust in the range was subjected to intense deformation, and this complexity can be contrasted to stable continental areas such as

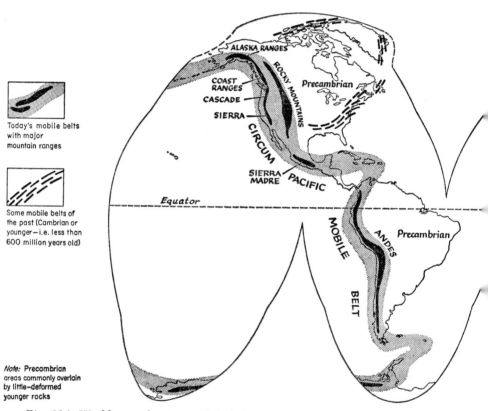

Today's mobile belts with major mountain ranges

Some mobile belts of the past (Cambrian or younger—i.e. less than 600 million years old)

Note: Precambrian areas commonly overlain by little-deformed younger rocks

Fig. 114. World map showing mobile belts, past and present. (Note shape distortion towards poles.)

the midwestern United States where the thinner-bedded rocks are flat-lying or gently undulating for scores of miles. What is more, as has been noted, major ranges have cores of metamorphic and granitic rocks. The ranges were not only squeezed, they were heated, locally to the melting point. The folded sedimentary rocks themselves give evidence of hot crustal activity beneath them even during the geosynclinal stages of the mountain cycle, for the sediments of the mountain cores are interlayered with flow after flow of dark basalt and andesite, much of which erupted on the ocean floor.

Thus it is said that major mountain ranges lie in belts of great mobility. The crust in these belts was folded, faulted, and heated. Modern day *mobile belts* are characterized by such exciting symptoms of crustal instability as active volcanoes and earthquakes. And the mountaineer finds today's two major mobile belts most interesting, for here

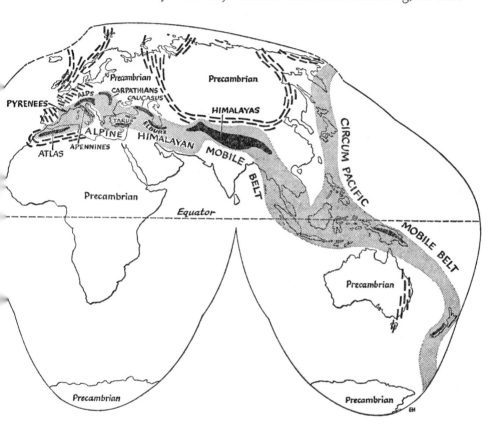

are some of the world's highest and most rugged mountains. The *Circum-Pacific Belt* swings in great arcs around the Pacific Ocean and includes the Andes, Sierra Nevada, Cascades, Canadian and Alaskan Coast Ranges, Aleutian chains, and others, not to mention innumerable volcanoes from Rainier to Fujiyama. The second is the *Alpine-Himalayan Belt*, containing both the birthplace of mountaineering and its ultimate challenge.

ISOSTACY

Some years ago an engineer surveying in the foothills of the Himalaya noticed he was accruing large errors. His plumb bob did not hang straight, pointing at the center of the earth as expected, but seemingly was tugged over toward the great peaks towering to the north. On consideration he was not surprised, since it seemed quite obvious that a huge mountain range would have a certain gravitational attraction. The significant thing is that further careful measurements have shown the displacement is not as great as it should be if the mountain mass had the same average density as the rest of the earth's crust. The only explanation is that a mountain range is lighter than the crust as a whole and floats like an iceberg in a denser material, partly thrust high into the atmosphere, with the more massive "roots"—which essentially consist of the sediments that filled the geosyncline—lying deeply submerged in the crust.

As the geosynclinal depression fills with sediment, more-rigid blocks of crust outside the mobile belt squeeze and crumple the growing pile. Some of the sediments melt to form granites, others are metamorphosed. Some mountains are born as this folding takes place; the pile is thickened and pushed both down into the earth and up above the sea, and this might be called the first step in raising the mountains. Ultimately the downward movement of the crust ceases, and the geosynclinal rocks now pressing deep into the denser substratum of the crust tend to rebound or float upwards, isostatically responding just as a cork pushed under the water bobs up when released. This is the second step in the mountain-building process and has been the most important in elevating today's highest mountains. Once the mountain block emerges above the sea erosion begins stripping off the upper layers, promoting further upward motion—as an iceberg, when its upper surface melts, thrusts more of its submerged portion above water.

The total life history of a mountain range is a complex series of slow-motion events; although uplift can be thought of as occurring in two steps, it is not always easy to determine where one step stops and the other begins, and in fact at times both go on together.

GEOLOGIC TIME AND ANCIENT MOBILE BELTS

Only a century ago there was a very considerable weight of geologic opinion favoring a view of the earth's history aptly called *catastrophic*. Proponents theorized that in the not very distant past there had been awful convulsions of the crust that virtually overnight made the mountains and the valleys. Another school watched the ceaseless small washing of ocean waves against the beach, streams against rock, and having

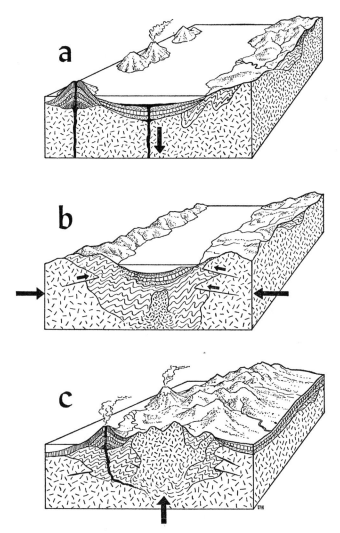

Fig. 115. Geosyncline formation and mountain building. (Vertical scale grossly exaggerated.)

 a. Sediments accumulate in deepening basin. Volcanic islands contribute debris and ocean-bottom lavas incorporated in sediments.

 b. Old rocks in crustal blocks to either side move in and squeeze sediments now depressed into hot region where they become metamorphosed and melted.

 c. Compression stops and geosynclinal mass rises. Erosion exposes granitic core. Volcanos form where tension cracks extend down to hot rock at depth. A new geosyncline begins to fill at left.

Table 13. Geologic Time and Mountain Development.

Era	Period or System	Began (millions of years ago)	Mobile Belts	Some Events of Interest to the Climber
Cenozoic	Recent (Epoch)	1/100		Emergence (?) from Ice Age glaciers; ice caps retreat. Growth of Circum-Pacific volcanoes.
	Quaternary Pleistocene (Epoch)	3		The Great Ice Age; continental glaciation. Chamonix, Yosemite, Mt. Katahdin, N. E. Appalachians, Cascades, etc. steepened by glaciers.
	Tertiary	70	Circum-Pacific Mobile Belt / Alpine-Himalayan Mobile Belt	Much vulcanism along the American Cordillera: Columbia Plateau lavas, Oregon and Washington Cascades, Yellowstone, San Juan Mountains of Colorado. Isostatic uplift of Alps, Himalaya, Andes, Sierra, Cascades. Folding of the Alpine and Himalayan Geosyncline. Deposition and folding of rocks of Olympic Mountains.
Mesozoic	Cretaceous	135		Rocky Mountains rise out of the sea. Emplacement of Sierra and B. C. Coast Range granites such as those of Yosemite and Mt. Waddington. Appalachians rise isostatically.
	Jurassic			Folding and uplift of mountains all along the west side of North Amer-

Table 13 (*cont.*)

Era	Period or System	Began (millions of years ago)	Mobile Belts	Some Events of Interest to the Climber
Mesozoic	Jurassic	180	Circum-Pacific Mobile Belt / Alpine-Himalayan Mobile Belt	ica (Circum-Pacific Mobile Belt). Granites of Sierra and Coast Ranges emplaced in geosynclinal sediments.
Mesozoic	Triassic	225		Deposition of limestone (dolomite) in southern Alpine geosyncline.
Paleozoic	Permian	270		Folding and mountains in the Appalachian and Hercynian mobile belts of eastern U. S. and central Europe-southern England. Chamonix granites and others emplaced.
Paleozoic	Carboniferous	350		
Paleozoic	Devonian	400	Caledonian Mobile Belt / Appalachian and Hercynian Mobile Belts	
Paleozoic	Silurian	440		Deposition of lower Silurian conglomerates which have become the Shawangunks and other prominent Appalachian ridges. Folding and mountains uplifted all along the east coast of U. S., Scotland, Scandinavia.
Paleozoic	Ordovician	500		
Paleozoic	Cambrian	600		
	Pre-Cambrian	3500		Many mobile belts and mountains on all continents (see Fig. 118). The igneous and metamorphic rocks of this era provide fine climbing country the world over, from the Needles of the Black Hills and high peaks of many Rocky Mountain Ranges to the Isle of Skye in Scotland.

with a mighty effort freed themselves from traditional notions that the earth was created one fine week a few thousand years ago, grasped the cumulative effect of apparently-puny forces continuing over immense periods of time. *Uniformitarianism* does not deny that some dramatic changes in the earth's crust, such as volcanic eruptions, occur before the very eyes of man. However, these are small matters compared to the building and destruction of a mountain system.

Study has steadily extended backward the life of the earth: the individual accustomed to thinking in terms of hours and years must strain his comprehension to digest even the spans of historic time; a much greater effort is required to accept geologic time. In analogy, if the height of Mount Everest (29,028 feet) equals the age of the earth before man evolved, then a tall climber on the summit represents the time mankind has existed.

Geologic time is divided into *eras* and the eras into *periods*. Their current names use terms from various older classifications, and thus are rather an assorted lot. Tertiary and Quaternary, for instance, are remnants of an early division of geologic time into four major divisions. Later scientists found a system with additional divisions more useful and during necessary revision of the geologic calendar some of the old eras became periods, some were dropped, and the new system was superimposed on the hodgepodge of names.

Until quite recently ages could only be determined relatively, largely by examination of fossil life, studies of evolution having established a progression of life forms from simple to complex. It could not be said how old a particular rock was, but only that one rock was older than another. Lately the measurement of rates of nuclear disintegration of radioactive elements present in tiny amounts in many minerals has provided a means of establishing absolute age. Much has been done to confirm the relative time scale, and the history of the earth prior to the evolution of life (the Precambrian) is finally being deciphered.

The cycle of mountain building—filling of a geosyncline, folding and heating, isostatic uplift—has occurred many times in many locations in the earth's long past. Geologists once thought these cycles took place at widely-spaced intervals. Such a view is convenient for organizing data but there is much to indicate, especially in the latest chapters of geologic history, that there have never been long periods of quiescence; in fact, it may well be that mountains have been under construction somewhere around the earth at every moment of the past.

There is a pattern, however. Since Precambrian times, 600 million years ago, several mobile belts and their mountain progeny have come and gone, moving like waves more or less parallel to the continental margins. But during the Precambrian, a time almost six times as long, untold mobile belts lived and died. They can be counted up across the now stable continental platforms, side by side like fossilized waves. The mountains are gone and the old belts are overlain by relatively-thin layers of younger undeformed sedimentary rocks; beneath this sod of stability the old rocks are crumpled, contorted, metamorphosed, and intruded, proof of their once-lively mobility. The continents, in part at least, appear to have grown by accretion of these petrified mobile belts.

The youngest mountains, all of which occur in today's mobile belts, are of greatest interest to the climber. Older ranges such as the Appalachians, in a belt whose mobility appears to be waning or gone entirely, may still rise relatively high in response to isostacy, but the surge of youth is gone and erosion rounds them as fast as they rise. Only the most-resistant rocks stand on high as mountains—the granites, gneisses, and schists of the White Mountains of Vermont and New Hampshire, the greenstones and schists of the Blue Ridge of Virginia. The former has been freshened by glaciers, the latter by streams. Even at worst—from a climber's standpoint—the near-truncated roots of bygone ranges, cores of granite or metamorphic rocks, can offer exciting rock climbing if cut by a vigorous river, such as the gorge of the Potomac outside Washington, D. C.

THE THEORY OF MOUNTAIN BUILDING

As mentioned earlier, little is known of the *why* behind the crustal motions which produce mountains. Several theories are in vogue today and probably each has in it part of the story.

The continents are composed of the eroded roots of ancient mountain ranges, long-dead mobile belts packed side by side. They have a lower average density than the crust and must therefore float on a heavier inner stratum. In the *continental drift* theory it is speculated that all continents were once part of a single land mass, gradually separating and being set adrift by some force, perhaps one connected with the rotation of the earth. There is some evidence, for instance, that Africa, South America, and Antarctica were once joined, ultimately splitting apart and floating to their present positions.

The stresses produced in the continental margins as they plow through the denser substratum of the earth or drift against one another could give rise to the mobile belts. There is much evidence to suggest that the Alps, composed of the world's most strongly-squeezed rocks, have been caught between the crustal blocks of central Europe and Africa.

Another theory calls for a density convection current in the middle layer of the earth, a region where the rocks may well be hot and plastic enough to flow very slowly. As an overturning current of rock moves by the rigid crust above, it sucks the latter down, providing the geosynclinal depression. Such currents could even push blocks of crust together to crumple the wedges of sediment in between.

Mountain Building: The Internal Structure

The various horizontal and vertical stresses that act on the rocks of mountains commonly produce complex patterns. However, each kind of stress, if left to itself, would produce a certain ideal *structure;* some ranges can be described in terms of these simple structures.

The first mountain structure to be considered is called with apparent incongruity *plains-plateau,* where sedimentary strata have been lifted upward and dissected without being tilted much from the horizontal. Such ranges may occur adjacent to mobile belts or within them where rigid blocks resist the geosynclinal deformation, like a nut in the porridge. Some sections of the Canadian Rockies on the edge of the mobile belt evidence such a simple history, but perhaps the best example is the mountain range now being sculptured from the Kaibab Plateau, where the Grand Canyon is the first good cut, so to speak. As erosion progresses in future eons there will be steadily more peaks and less flatland.

A simple upward bulge of the crust forms *dome mountains* such as the Ozarks of Arkansas and Missouri, and in a more complicated way, the Olympic Mountains of Washington and the High Uintas of Utah.

Often accompanying upwarp is faulting, or cracking of the crust into large chunks, resulting in *fault block mountains.* A great variety of forms are created by motion of these chunks along the faults. The ranges of the desert country of California, Nevada, and Utah present most striking instances of faulting; the breakage extends to the surface and often during an earthquake—caused by slippage between the blocks—fresh scarps many feet high develop. Sometimes a block is faulted on both sides and rises or falls as a unit, but the Tetons of Wyoming and the Sierra Nevada are faulted on one side only: along the single zone of faults the range heaves up impressive steep scarps, while on the other side the mass bends but does not break, leaving a gentler slope from the base of the range to the crest. Blocks may drop as well as rise. A clear example is Death Valley, which is below sealevel and thus most certainly could not have been carved by erosion. The adjacent upfaulted block bears Telescope Peak, 12,000 feet above the floor of Death Valley. Motion is not always merely up and down—slippage along the notorious San Andreas Fault of California is essentially lateral, and elsewhere are instances of blocks that move both horizontally and vertically.

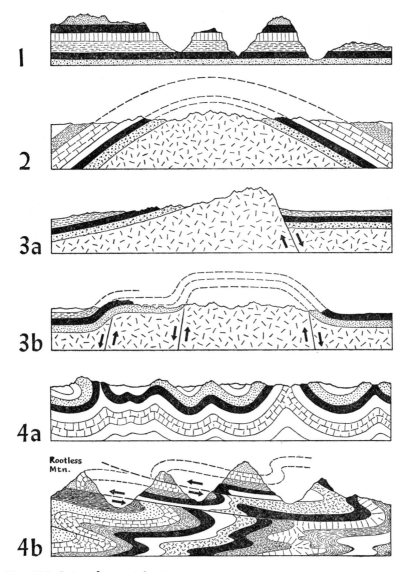

Fig. 116. Internal mountain structures.

1. Plains-plateau mountains: Canadian Rockies.
2. Dome mountains, eroded to expose granite core: Raft River Range, Utah.
3a. Fault block mountains, one side faulted: Sierra Nevada.
3b. Fault block mountains, deep-seated faults: Southern and Middle Rocky Mountains.
4a. Fold mountains, gentle folds, highly eroded: Appalachian Mountains.
4b. Fold mountains, tight folds and overthrust fault: Alps.

More subtle examples of fault block mountains are the ranges of the Central and Southern Rocky Mountains, from Wyoming to New Mexico, elevated by faulting but with the planes of breakage deeply buried under the surface strata, which are bent above the faults but commonly unbroken—a condition not always easily distinguishable from compressive folding. The Rocky Mountains are on the edge of the Cordilleran Mobile Belt and these faults may be flaws in one jaw of the vice which squeezed the geosynclinal pile to the west.

Perhaps the most common architectural style is a rococo of complex folds. When erosion strips down the geosynclinal pile that has risen out of the ocean, the folds and contortions are most evident. The Alps are one example of *fold mountains*. The Appalachians are another, but much older; the only rocky summits are remnants of resistant strata.

When the squeezing of a range is intense, the rocks of the mountain mass first fold but may then break and parts of the rocks be pushed sideways and override others. Eons later when the geologist attempts to decipher the history of the region he may well be puzzled, finding older rocks perched atop younger ones. Isolated blocks of the *overthrust* mass may form when erosion strips away links connecting them with their place of origin. The rocks of the Alps have been shoved to a large extent into foreign locations.

But an overthrust structure may also form in another way. As a large mountain range rises very high, large masses of rock, measured in miles, creep out over the lowlands at the base of the mountain. These may be likened to a landslide, and although their motion may be of a geologic slowness, they may move considerable distances. Rootless Chief Mountain and its progenitor, the Lewis Overthrust of the Montana Rockies, may be the results of this latter type of process. Almost every range of folded mountains in the world exhibits an overthrust of one sort or another.

Volcanic mountains are in a class by themselves, an exception to the rule that both uplift and dissection are needed to produce peaks. The Pacific Mobile Belt also includes the Rim of Fire—from Katmai in the north to Tierra del Fuego in the south, from Rainier and Popocatepetl on the east to Fujiyama and Krakatoa on the west. However, the Pacific has no monopoly on volcanoes; Kilimanjaro in Africa and Etna in Europe are no mean examples.

Mountains can be categorized by ideal structure for convenient description, but most ranges are *complex mountains,* with portions that have been simply moved upward without tilting, with other portions folded, domed, and faulted, frequently with a sprinkling of volcanoes. Moreover, the processes described occur both on a large and a small scale. A single gigantic fold may form an entire mountain peak, but there are also folds measured by a rope length, and tiny folds confined within a handhold. A single fault may build a mountain front, but the climber encounters smaller faults that form ledges and gullies.

Mountain Sculpture: Weathering and Erosion

Having surveyed the processes that elevate portions of the crust, it is time to consider the sculpturing of highlands into peaks and valleys; although the uplift of the mountains has been discussed separately, it is well to remember that the minute a land area rises above the sea, the forces of erosion begin to tear it down. Were it not that uplift gains an edge, the mountaineer would have nothing but broad rolling hills for his pleasure.

Two processes cooperate in carving the mountains. *Weathering*, both mechanical and chemical, breaks the rocks into smaller particles without moving them. *Erosion* encompasses all the activities of gravity, wind, water, and ice which not only break or grind the rocks but transport the degradation products.

WEATHERING

The consequences of weathering to the climber in choosing his route are considerable and have been mentioned in Chapter 6. *Chemical weathering* constantly attacks exposed rocks, since many minerals, which crystallized within the hot earth, are unstable at the cooler surface where they are exposed to air and water. Chemical weathering is not uniformly intense on all rocks in all places. Some minerals, such as quartz, are extremely stable, so that quartzite or quartz sandstone are little affected. Feldspars and other complex silicates, on the other hand, break down readily into clays, while calcite dissolves. Water is the prime factor in chemical weathering; a limestone cliff is very durable in a desert but rapidly crumbles in a humid climate. Carbon dioxide and humus acids in solution immensely increase the solvent power of water, so that weathering is accelerated in the presence of vegetation, attaining its fastest tempo below timberline in a moist climate.

By way of contrast, *mechanical weathering* is particularly severe high on the mountain peaks, especially *frost-cracking* or *wedging* by water that trickles into minute cracks and in freezing exerts a tremendous expansive force. Many high summits consist entirely of shattered rock; some areas are aptly called a rock ocean, or *felsenmeer*. In arctic ranges cracking is so intense that often no unshattered rock is found, merely heaps of loose rubble. In more temperate climates the climber does well to keep in mind that even routes thoroughly "cleaned" by generations of travelers may present new dangers after the freeze and thaw of winter.

Exfoliation does much of the sculpturing in granitic areas. Mechanism of the process is not fully understood, but the results are quite distinctive. By chemical and mechanical action curved flakes of the surface are loosened and break away from bedrock. A combination of exfoliation at the surface and tension jointing deep in the rock produces the spectacular granite domes of Yosemite Valley. On a smaller scale, exfoliation alone makes the characteristic rounded and scaling boulders often seen on high mountains.

GRAVITY AND WIND EROSION

Gravity does its very best to clean up the peaks, and by rockfall indefatigably clears away fragments loosened by weathering and climbers. More terrifying, though rare, are *landslides*. In December 1963 a series of landslides on the north side of Little Tahoma on Mount Rainier delivered some 14 million cubic yards of broken rock to the glacier below, via a climbing route, and sent debris 4 miles down the valley at rates up to 90 miles an hour. Evidence of a recent landslide is an unweathered cliff or slope standing out in sharp contrast to darker and more vegetated surrounding surfaces, or a heap of tangled trees and rocks and earth where a timbered slope has slid from the bedrock. Landslides are usually set in motion when the ground is saturated and thus lubricated with water, such as after heavy rains or when the winter snows are melting, good times to avoid steep and unconsolidated slopes such as those on river terraces and moraines. *Mudflows*, especially wet landslides which act like viscous streams of water, are common on the flanks of volcanoes; climbs of volcanic peaks often begin on gentle ramps of mudflow debris.

All loose soil and rocks steadily *creep* downhill under the pull of gravity. In steep meadows creep produces striking patterns of contoured terraces. These wrinkles in the hillside are usually attributed to animals; actually both game and humans help transform them into "trails," but their origin is quite different.

A special kind of creep promoted by freezing and thawing of ice deep in a pile of coarse rock rubble produces *rock glaciers*. These streams of rock, found in many deglaciated cirques, advance downstream like a glacier and are commonly mistaken for concentric arcs of terminal moraine. Geologists are not agreed as to whether they are actually related to a preceding glaciation or not. Examples abound in the northeasternmost Cascades, the Olympics, and the Colorado Rockies.

Wind is least significant of the erosional agents, though playing an important role in deserts, sandblasting rocks into weird forms and impelling sand dunes in their steady march. Occasionally in geologic history wind has had free play across great plains, blowing dust to rest in deep beds of *loess*. The Yellow River region of China and the Palouse Hills of Washington are loess deposits—the latter thought to be derived from glacial outwash, rich in powdered rock.

STREAM EROSION

In all but the iciest or driest ranges, ultimately every particle of every mountain, however it begins its downward journey, enters a stream of water and is ground boulder against boulder, pebble against pebble, grain against grain, until—given sufficient time—nothing remains but sand and silt. Meanwhile, the stream carries steadily its burden of milling rubble to the sea, moving the mountains piecemeal to the seeding places of a future range.

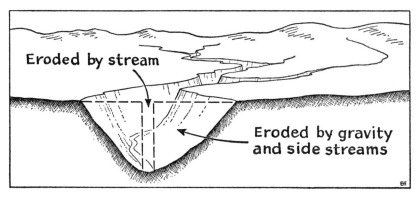

Fig. 117. Erosion by a stream.

Though the highest and most interesting peaks are chiefly carved by glaciers, streams retain an important role. Glaciers rarely if ever originate valleys, rather tending to follow and modify those previously dug by rivers. Actually the digging of the river valley is a complex business. The stream or river saws a notch into the rock, using the rubble it carries for abrasives. As the notch deepens, weathering, gravity, and side streams all work to eliminate the steep walls of the notch, ultimately producing a V-shaped valley. The climber, whether fording a rushing stream or following a river to its alpine headwaters, constantly must cope with erosional effects of streams. In some places, indeed, such as the cliffs along the Great Falls of the Potomac and the impressive Dalles of the Columbia, he finds practice climbs on rocks whose steepness is almost entirely due to sculpturing by the load carried in the stream.

The Life Cycle of a Stream

A river system and its drainage area progress through a cycle from youth to maturity and old age. In a simple case, the cycle begins on a smooth piece of the earth's crust, uneroded and lifted well above sea-level. During *infancy* rainwater rushes in sheets down the slopes, collecting in depressions to form lakes. Quickly the water tends to funnel into channels which are steadily deepened, the lakes meanwhile overflowing and sending streams downward to lower lakes.

In *youth* the main valleys are V-shaped and steep-sided, but a complete system of tributaries has not yet been established, the divides between valleys being flat or rolling, interspersed with numerous lakes, plateaus, and hillsides only slightly indented by gullies. In the Sierra Nevada of California, for example, many of the valleys are youthful, while the high intervening divides retain the gentler relief of infancy.

When the landscape has been so dissected that every portion of the area is thoroughly drained by deeply-incised valleys and gullies, rills running into creeks, and creeks into rivers, the streams and the region are mature. Divides are sharp, the major rivers have flood plains, and relief between summits and valley is at the maximum attained during the cycle. The North Cascades of Washington are in major part mature.

Steadily divides are lowered and rivers move more slowly, expending less energy in downcutting and more in meandering across their valleys, leveling and widening. Wide valley floors of adjacent drainages merge, leaving mere remnants of the original highlands. *Old age* has been reached, with sluggish streams and low rounded hills. Still further erosion eventually creates a *peneplane* of flood plains interspersed with a few *monadnocks* of resistant rock.

As in many things theoretical, nature rarely approaches the ideal case; probably there never has been a simple life cycle of stream erosion. A region may be comfortably established in maturity or old age, and be suddenly uplifted once more, causing a *rejuvenation* of its streams that superimposes elements of youth. Retreat of glaciers causes retrogression to infancy even in a maturely-dissected mountain range, leaving lakes and swamps that are not drained for millenia.

Along a single river every age in the cycle may be seen. The Mississippi has infant headwaters, gloriously-young and gracefully-mature tributaries, and far from the mountain front, it loops and curls in contented senility to the Gulf of Mexico.

The Graded Stream

Unladen water in running downhill gains velocity and thus energy, energy to transport; the swift water seizes hungrily on any loose material until fully *loaded*. If the gradient of the hill lessens, the velocity

Youth

Maturity

Old Age

Terrace

Older
Terrace

Rejuvenation

Fig. 118. Life cycle of a stream and accompanying landscape.

and energy must decrease; the stream is overloaded and drops its load of sand and gravel, building a new and steeper gradient.

The supreme desire of a stream is to make its bed form a smooth curve from its headwaters to its mouth, or *baselevel,* a curve steep at the upper end, flat at the lower. When the ideal curve is achieved, the stream uses all its energy to carry all the debris dumped into it by side streams and gravity, and the stream is said to be at *grade.* Since perfect grade is elusive, a stream is always in flux, rarely satisfied for long. Lakes and waterfalls are particularly abhorrent. To fill the former the stream slows down (it must) and drops its load; to eliminate the latter it speeds up (it must) and picks up more tools to gouge away at the steep face, causing the falls to migrate upvalley, and leaving behind a deep gorge.

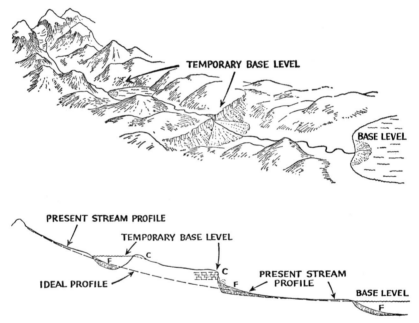

Fig. 119. Graded stream profile and baselevels. Stream is cutting at C, filling at F. Dashed line is ideal profile.

The mountaineer soon learns to avoid the temptation of riverside routes when marching into the hills, realizing that he may arrive at an impasse of cascading water and damp, sheer cliffs. A lake or waterfall acts as a *temporary baselevel,* and the stream above grades itself in relation to it, meanwhile trying to remove the lake or fall from the true grade curve.

A river issuing from the front of a retreating glacier is almost invariably overloaded, since the melted ice is charged with rock debris picked up by the glacier and the gradient in front of the glacier is very low. The river drops part of its burden, thereby obstructing its own course, moves to a new course and in turn fills that up with debris, finally creating a system of *braded* channels and the wide plains of gravel commonly encountered below a glacier terminus.

A river flowing at grade may have built itself a flat flood plain. Rejuvenation—by a new uplift of the land or a change of baselevel, such as the elimination of a lake downstream—causes the water to slice deeply into the sand and gravel it had previously deposited, leaving remnants of its abandoned floodplain perched high above the river. Often the mountain traveler can make good use of these *terraces* or benches, which provide smooth pathways along the valley. However, such benches are not unmixed blessings, for both the main stream and its tributaries gouge into the old fill, making steep and unstable gravel or sand cliffs that are sometimes troublesome.

GLACIER EROSION

Of all erosional agents, glaciers are most significant to the climber. Many mountaineering routes are largely the work of past glaciation; others lie upon the surface of presently-active ice. A knowledge of glacier habits is indispensable. The ultimate beginnings of a glacier are described in the next chapter, which describes the metamorphosis of snow into ice.

The Hierarchy of Glaciers

A *cirque glacier* is one confined to its place of origin, either because it has not yet gathered sufficient mass to venture further, or because it has retreated from a previously-greater extension. As a climbing problem it may be no more severe than a snowfield. If the place of origin is on a steep cliff, a *hanging glacier* results, perhaps consisting entirely of icefalls. When the pressure of increasing snow layers on the underlying ice becomes too great it flows down from the cirque, becoming a *valley glacier*. If ice advances downvalley to the plains beyond the mountain front, a *piedmont glacier* forms. Vast regions of ice lower the average temperature so that more and more snow falls and less melts. The valley glaciers thicken and spill over divides to merge with other ice streams, the piedmont glaciers advance steadily, and ultimately only the highest peaks rise above an *ice cap*.

Features of Glaciers

In the *accumulation zone* of a glacier, annual snowfall exceeds annual melting; in the *ablation zone* melting predominates. The boundary between the two is called the *firn* or *névé* line, though usually it is a wide belt rather than a narrow line. The vitality of a glacier depends on at least as much ice flowing from the upper zone as melts in the lower, and the location of the firn line is a good indication of whether the glacier is advancing or retreating. Many glaciers of the Canadian Rockies, for instance, are chiefly bare ice, *dry glaciers,* with only small patches of snow at their upper limits; these are extremely unhealthy, steadily retreating. If the firn line marches down toward the glacier *front, snout,* or *terminus,* a growth or advance of the glacier may be expected.

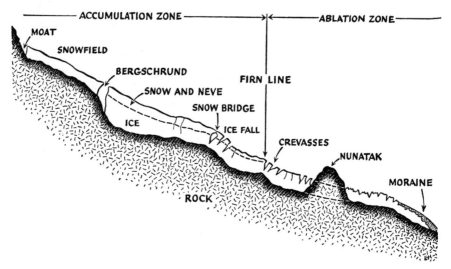

Fig. 120. Cross-section of a valley glacier.

The depths of a glacier are solidly compressed and without cracks but the brittle surface layers fracture under the strains and stresses of motion down steep slopes, around corners, and along rock walls. These *crevasses* are rarely deeper than 200–250 feet but even when much shallower, as is usual, they are the major problems of glacier travel. Specific climbing tactics have already been discussed in Chapter 14, but understanding what controls crevasse formation is immensely helpful in planning a route.

Crecentric crevasses develop wherever the ice increases its rate of flow, commonly where the glacier bed steepens. The change in angle may be so small it is not evident on the surface and is only indicated by belts of crevasses forming long arcs concave downvalley, at right angles to the direction of flow.

If the incline is very steep an *icefall* forms, the surface broken into a

MOUNT ALABASTER
19,536

Fig. 121. Glacier nomenclature and moraines.

Ice features

A. Moat
B. Bergschrund
C. Firn line
D. Crecentric crevasses
E. Nunatak
F. En echelon crevasses
G. Marginal crevasses
H. Terminus or snout
I. Braided outwash stream

Moraine features

1. Lateral moraine
2. Medial moraine
3. Terminal moraine
4. Outwash plain (and ground moraine)
5. Erratic
6. Old terminal moraine
7. Old lateral moraine

profusion of crevasses extending every which way, with large ice towers or *seracs*. Below a sharp declivity crevasses are often absent, since
the glacier is slowing down after its plunge, but sometimes pressure
from the cataract above buckles the surface into *pressure ridges*, with
attendant crevasses. In a steep icefall a considerable portion of the
downward advance is by avalanches, a hazard that influences routes
both through a fall or anywhere underneath one.

Lateral or marginal crevasses are opened by the faster motion of a
glacier's center relative to its sides, where friction along the valley walls
has a restraining effect. Lateral crevasses invariably trend upvalley.
The characteristic of both crecentric and lateral fractures to angle upstream toward the glacier center is frequently useful in guessing the
hidden extension from a single surface hole. Crevassing, however, is
not so simply methodical, for minor surface stresses produce random
fractures which follow no pattern whatsoever. Protuberances of rock
through the ice, *nunataks,* usually have a halo of crevasses and thus are
best avoided, but if the rock does not quite reach the surface, the
crevasse pattern may completely baffle the routefinder. The only general rule applicable to crevasse location is that they can occur anywhere and anyhow on a glacier.

As Chapter 14 emphasized, crevasses are most hazardous to the
climber in the zone of accumulation, where they are frequently
bridged by snow. New snow may completely fill the depths, or with
the assistance of a cornice-building wind, build an arch over inner
emptiness. The entire structure may melt away or collapse of its own
weight during the summer, leaving an obvious pit. Often glacier motion widens the crevasse and by stretching the bridge cracks it open;
the climber who assumes the visible thin fissure represents the entire
width of the chasm can be unpleasantly surprised.

At the glacier's upper limit is a giant crevasse, the *bergschrund,*
formed between the glacier and the rock by the movement of the glacier and melting or both. Sometimes the bergschrund is the final problem of the ascent, with the summit only a short stroll above. If the glacier is diminishing, the surface lowers, leaving a steep arcuate precipice
above, which may be capped by hanging glaciers with still more
menacing crevasses and bergschrunds. Above the highest bergschrund
there is often perched a snowfield separated from the rock face by a
randkluft or *moat,* formed partially by melting and partially by creep,
thus being similar to origin to a bergschrund and frequently every bit
as difficult to cross.

A glacier continually receives debris from its headwall, from its bed
which it scrapes and gouges, and from valley sides; it incorporates and
carries all this burden along. In the ablation zone the glacier thins and

the rubble emerges on the surface; when the ice is entirely melted the debris is dumped in *moraines*.

If the glacier terminus remains in one place for a long time a *terminal moraine* is built, a steep ridge generally concave upvalley in accordance with the usual shape of a glacier front. Deposits along the sides of the glacier, on and off the ice, are *lateral moraines*. When two valley glaciers come together the lateral moraines merge into a *medial moraine*. When a glacier swiftly retreats, debris is widely and thinly scattered, leaving a formless *ground moraine*. The unstable rubble of moraines is usually a nuisance, but sometimes lateral or medial moraines provide easier walking than the surface of the glacier.

Whereas running water sorts sediments so fastidiously that in any one bed particle size may lie within a narrow range, ice carries along particles sized from the *rock flour* produced by milling of rock against rock, all the way to boulders as big as small mountains. Such unsorted deposits are called *till*, the general term for all the material found in moraines. The boulders, when left perched far from their source, are called *erratics*. The flour gives to glacier streams their characteristic opaqueness and when carried in suspension is the *rock milk* which makes fording a blind and chancy job. Within till there are usually inclusions of bedded sand, gravel, and clay, evidence of a vanished river or lake at the margin of the retreating ice.

Land Forms Produced By Glacial Erosion

Few unglaciated mountains have any attraction for the climber. Glaciers deepen the valleys and steepen the slopes, and thus create the sharp relief called "mountainous."

A cirque glacier erodes headward in a complex way. Most of the damage to the rock wall of a bergschrund is done by the freezing and thawing of ice; the loosened blocks fall down into the bergschrund and become incorporated in the glacier. The bottom of the cirque is lowered by the scratching, scraping, and gouging of rocks frozen in the ice: a glacier is a giant rasp. Even in the northern Appalachians and the hills of Britain, where glaciation was never prolonged, whatever cliffs exist have been provided by headward cirque erosion, which produces *biscuit-board* terrain, generally gentle of profile interrupted by occasional cirques.

When glaciation is more prolonged and two cirques work toward each other they lower the divide into a razor-sharp *col*. Three or more cirques plucking backward into a common mass of rock make a *horn*, which in ideal form has three cirque walls, three *aretes* separating them, and culminates in a steep sharp summit. The Matterhorn is the classic example. Forbidden Peak in the North Cascades and Sir Donald in the Selkirks are splendid American horns.

A distinction must be made between a *valley*, which represents erosion under the leadership of a stream of water or ice, and a *channel*, the actual space occupied at any time by that stream of water or ice. Cross-sections of both river and glacier channels are U-shaped. However, ice moves much more slowly than water, and a glacier requires a much larger channel than a river to drain a watershed. For a given amount of precipitation, a river might have a channel 100 feet wide and 5 feet deep; a glacier might need a channel—the U-shaped valley —1 mile wide and 2000 feet deep.

Abandoned glacier channels are very widespread in today's mountains and give the traveler some interesting moments. Typically in the North Cascades, the wide flat floor of the U is a swampy tangle of brush and morainal hillocks, and the walls are steep. In many ranges it is not always easy to distinguish a glacier channel from a water-carved valley, for talus and alluvial fans rapidly obscure the U, smoothing it into a V. Such modifications often provide ramps through the cliffs of the U.

Fig. 122. Stream- and glacier-cut valleys.
      a. V-shaped valley.
      b. U-shaped valley.

Tributary glaciers with their smaller flow cannot keep pace in downcutting with the main valley glacier, and *hanging valleys* are characteristic of ranges once heavily glaciated. Reaching these valleys from below can be as challenging as ascending the peak.

A glacier-cut valley is seldom an evenly-graded highway to the alpine country. Most commonly the history of glaciation includes the birth and death of several generations of glaciers which when born as cirque glaciers did not always form at the same elevation. Thus *multiple cirques* are occasionally encountered. In the North Cascades, the upper cirque may still support a glacier, while the steep cliffs of the lower cirque, plucked by vanished ice, are stoutly defended by waterfalls and cedar trees. Mountaineers tend to devalue these pitches with humor, feeling that the effort demanded to overcome them is considerably less noble than that needed to scale clean rock crests, but in truth the lower cirque is frequently the crux of the climb.

More commonly the valley is broken into cliffs or *steps* due to differences in rock resistance, the glacier more rapidly eroding the weak rocks than the strong ones. Commonly in jointed granite terrain, large blocks of rock are quarried by the ice, leaving a vertical step along the joint plane when the ice is gone. Steps may also form where several tributary glaciers join a main one, the additional ice volume increasing the erosive power. Any rock protuberance overridden by a glacier, especially one on the edge of a step, is plucked and steepened on the downvalley side and streamlined on the upper side, leaving a *roche moutonée*.

Glaciers, being viscous masses with some strength, have the ability to flow uphill and thus erode a sizable depression in their bed—a feat only achieved by water when it gains extra energy by falling off a cliff to dig a plunge pool. *Grinding down at the heel* is quite typical of glacial erosion and has produced such features as the deep fjords of Norway and British Columbia, long lakes in glaciated valleys such as Lake Chelan of Washington and the Finger Lakes of New York, and the round lakes or *tarns* in evacuated cirques.

Glacial Cycles

World climate has fluctuated radically in past ages. A lowering by only several degrees in mean annual temperature of the atmosphere is sufficient to cause a general advance of glaciers; such fluctuations have occurred many times in the geologic past and with them have come ages of ice.

The ultimate reasons for the coming of an ice age are not known exactly, though responsibility has been assigned to a variety of things. Popular for many years have been theories which more or less assign a single cause, such as clouds of dust which shield the earth from the sun, either the passing of the solar system through a cosmic cloud or clouds produced by accelerated vulcanism on earth. Current thought favors more complex relationships which not only involve changes in average summer and winter temperatures due to orbital and rotational eccentricities of the earth, but the configuration of mountain belts and distribution of hot and cold ocean currents.

Whatever the cause, the world is now either in or emerging from a cycle of glaciation, the Pleistocene Ice Age, which is one of the most extensive ever to have occurred. The glaciers were most widespread between 10,000 and 25,000 years ago, at which time a continental ice cap covered all of Canada, most of Alaska, and much of the northern United States. Another reached from Siberia and Scandinavia far south into Europe. The Antarctic cap was thicker and bigger than it is today and extensive systems of valley and piedmont glaciers entwined all mountainous regions of the world.

Subsequent to the time of maximum ice cover, world glaciers have been in general retreat. The so-called "climatic optimum" of 4000 to 6000 years ago, when all but a few ice caps disappeared, provided warmer and drier climates the world over than have been enjoyed since. Following that period the climate has fluctuated several times, sending mountain glaciers charging down their valleys. Records in Europe show considerable advances in the 16th and 17th centuries. In Chamonix, the glaciers of the Mont Blanc chain descended into the main valley and overwhelmed several villages.

In the United States the record is less complete. There appears to have been a rebirth and growth of mountain glaciers in the high cirques of the Northwest about 2500–2000 years ago and several resurgences since then. While Europeans explored and settled the New World the ice revived, reaching a maximum in the 18th century; throughout the Northwest mountaineers commonly encounter moraines from that period. Another lesser advance climaxed around 1900, and since then recession has been general and worldwide with but minor exceptions. However, glacier lovers have been excited recently by the general resurgence of ice in the Cascades and Olympics. It would be premature to herald a new age of ice, for so local a phenomenon could be the effect merely of a temporary shift in storm tracks. It would also be unwise to suppose that the Ice Age is over; only time can tell whether contemporary glaciers will increase their dominion or become extinct.

Certainly the world is not so chill as during the Pleistocene Epoch, but it is much colder than it has been during most of the geologic past. The Antarctic continent is almost completely submerged in an ice cap of some 5 million square miles and locally almost 3 miles thick. The Greenland ice cap, though only an eighth as large, has been estimated to be almost 2 miles thick. Continental North America is blessed with over 30,000 square miles of glacier, mostly in Alaska and Canada, but also sprinkled in generous samples through the Cascades and Olympics of Washington, and in meager bits through the Rockies and Sierra Nevada.

The Mountaineer as Geologist

It is interesting that most early climbing was done by geologists who sought the secrets of mountain origin. The novice climber asks what ancient geologic history has to do with his struggle to reach the register book. The devout mountaineer answers that freedom of the hills comes only with understanding. The next handhold, the next belay, the next twist in the route, all express the interplay over millions of years of the forces that both build and destroy mountains. Whether the climber seeks his sport high on granite spires that are the remnants of a magma once buried deep in the crust, or navigates the icy avenues of a glacier, he can choose his route with more confidence, and gain a more intimate feeling for his mountain, if he knows its history and its present state of flux.

21*

THE CYCLE OF SNOW

WHEN the climber leaves behind the rock crags and cliffs of lesser hills and ventures into the zone of perpetual snow, he passes from terrain of stable, known, and reasonably-predictable character to a region where change is the rule and where, as a consequence, his previous experience is often of little avail. He enters a world where snow and ice invest high mountains with a beauty foreign to lower peaks, mold their form and character, at the same time presenting him with some of his more strenuous difficulties, unpredictable hazards, and most thrilling moments. The almost infinite variety of conditions which snow and ice can assume at different times of day and season, and in different locales, confronts him with an infinite variety of problems. The techniques necessary to deal successfully with these elevate the skill of an adequate climber to the craft of a competent mountaineer.

Complete familiarity with the behavior of snow and ice, if attainable, would require a lifetime spent dwelling above the snowline, for the first rule the climber learns is that mountaineering on snow and ice is indeed a craft, and must be learned by direct participation rather than from books. However, his apprenticeship will be shortened if he departs for the hills equipped with a basic understanding of the way snow behaves, how it becomes ice, and the manner in which meteorological factors affect the entire process. The following sections are intended to provide the background for this understanding. Emphasis is placed on presenting fundamentals which will enable the mountaineer to face intelligently the problems of snow and ice travel wherever he may go, and in whatever season. Once the basic physical laws which govern snow behavior are understood, logical explanations can be drawn for phenomena observed in the field, a method established for their prediction, and a firm foundation set up for the training of an experienced craftsman.

The Hydrologic Cycle

The conditions of geology, climate, and life on this planet are determined by the existence of a temperature range wherein water, the commonest substance on the earth's surface, can exist in all three states of matter—solid, liquid, and gas. It is difficult to conceive what the face of the earth would look like if the cycle of evaporation, condensation, and runoff were eliminated by temperatures high enough to keep all the water in the form of vapor, or low enough to keep it all in the form of ice. Because the temperatures that do prevail permit water to pass readily from one state to another, a complex hydrologic cycle exists. All three states of water are active participants in the hydrologic cycle, but the solid state—snow and ice—represents a temporary storage on the earth's surface of water substance which is not immediately available to the continuous cycle of evaporation, condensation, and liquid runoff. This storage may be of short duration, as in the temporary winter snowcover, or it may be for centuries or millennia when the solid state takes the form of glacier ice. In either case, water owes its perpetuation in the solid state on the earth's surface to the fact that a great deal of energy is required to return it to the liquid state once it has been deposited as a solid. The amount of heat required to melt a given weight of ice, without any change in temperature, is seven times that required to melt the same weight of iron, and thirteen times that for the same weight of lead.

The various forms which water assumes during the solid phase of the hydrologic cycle are displayed in Figure 124, and are discussed in the following sections.

Formation of Snow in the Atmosphere

Snow may occur whenever water vapor is precipitated at temperatures below freezing. Snow crystals are known to form around centers of foreign matter in the air, such as microscopic dust particles. The first step is collection around the nucleus of a small ice crystal, which grows by the deposition of additional ice from water vapor in the atmosphere. (The transfer of water directly from the vapor to the solid state, or vice versa, is known as *sublimation.*) Recent investigations suggest that minute water droplets (i.e., diameter around 1 micron) may also contribute to the growth of snow crystals. These crystals in general assume a hexagonal pattern, but variations in size, shape, and

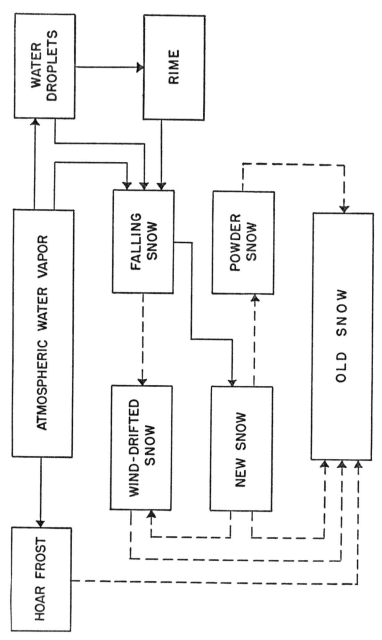

Fig. 123. Solid phase of the hydrologic cycle.

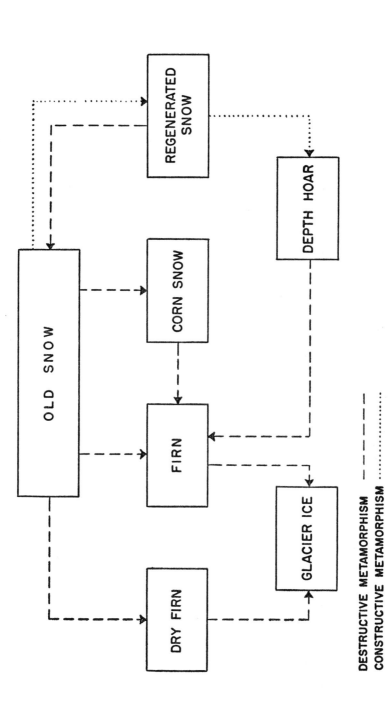

DESTRUCTIVE METAMORPHISM - - - -
CONSTRUCTIVE METAMORPHISM ....

OLD SNOW

REGENERATED SNOW

DEPTH HOAR

CORN SNOW

FIRN

GLACIER ICE

DRY FIRN

Term	Remarks
Plates	also combinations of plates with or without very short connecting columns
Stellar crystals	also parallel stars with very short connecting columns
Columns	and combinations of columns
Needles	and combinations of needles
Spatial dendrites	spatial combinations of feathery crystals
Capped columns	columns with plates on either (or one) side
Irregular particles	irregular compounds of microscopic crystals
Graupel (soft hail)	isometric shape. Central crystal cannot be recognized
Ice pellets (sleet)	ice shell, inside mostly wet
Hail	

Fig. 124. Types of solid precipitation.

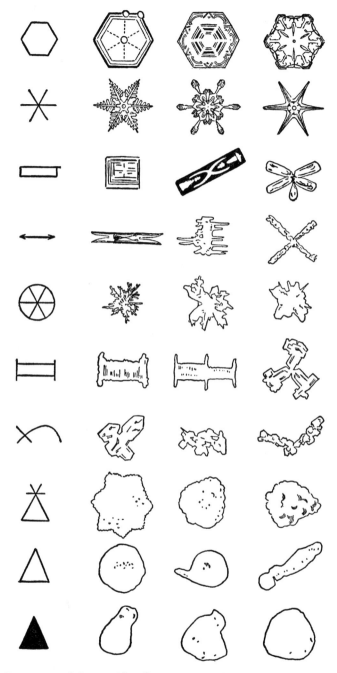

From International Snow Classification.

form are almost limitless. A general classification according to form divides snow crystals into stars, needles, columns, and plates. Combinations of these forms may occur, and irregular crystalline aggregates are found. The particular form developed in the atmosphere depends on the air temperature and the amount of water vapor available. When a snow crystal falls through different air masses with different temperature and water vapor conditions, the more complex or combined types may develop. Crystals formed in, or falling through, air whose temperature is near the freezing point stick together to become aggregates of individual crystals, or *snowflakes*.

When snow crystals fall through air which contains water droplets, these droplets freeze to the crystal as a *rime* deposit. As the amount of rime on a crystal increases, the original shape is obscured and a rounded ball results, giving rise to the type of snow commonly known as pellet, or tapioca. The technical term for these rimed crystals is *graupel.*

The percentage of water in new-fallen snow prior to settlement may range from 1 per cent to 30 per cent or higher. The average for mountain snowfalls is from 7 to 10 per cent, depending on climate. For some extremely maritime climates, this average may be as high as 25 per cent. The lightest snow is deposited under moderately cold and very calm conditions. At extremely low temperatures a fine, granular snow is deposited with somewhat higher densities. The highest new snow densities are associated with graupel or needle crystals falling at temperatures near the freezing point. In general, new snow density increases with air temperature, but density can vary widely in the range of 20° to 32° F. As air temperature falls, density variations become smaller and lower densities predominate. High winds break up falling snow crystals into small fragments which pack together on deposition to form a dense, fine-grained snow structure.

Formation and Character of the Snowcover

Formation of the snowcover is in some ways analogous to the formation of sedimentary rocks. Solid precipitation from the atmosphere (*sedimentation*) builds up the snowcover layer by layer, yielding a stratification that displays the history of weather variations which occurred during its development. With the passage of time, structural and crystalline changes within the snowcover (*metamorphism*) obscure the original stratigraphic differentiation and convert the snow into new forms.

The metamorphic process within the snowcover is a continuous one which begins when the snow is deposited and lasts until it melts. The normal path of metamorphism tends to destroy the original forms of the deposited snow crystals and gradually convert them into rounded grains of ice (*destructive metamorphism*). When the crystals of new snow have been altered by this conversion so their original form is no longer recognizable, it becomes, by definition, *old snow*. The physical process causing these changes is not entirely understood, but transfer of water vapor by sublimation from the points of the crystal branches to the more central portions of the crystal appears to play an important role. The process is strongly influenced by temperature, and proceeds at a rapid rate when the temperature is near freezing. At extremely low temperature metamorphism is very slow, virtually stopping below —40°C. All types of crystals tend to approach the uniform conditions of rounded grains as this process takes place, and the snowcover becomes more homogeneous. The rate of metamorphism is influenced by pres-

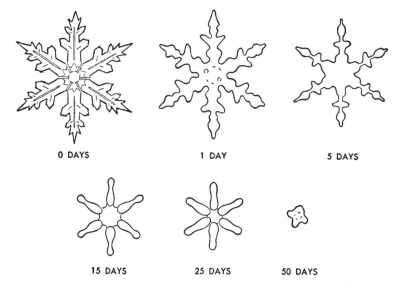

Fig. 125. Destructive metamorphism of a snow crystal.

sure as well as temperature (*pressure metamorphism*), and the weight of additional snowfalls over a given snow layer causes acceleration of the crystalline changes within it.

The destructive metamorphism of the snow crystals results in a reduction of the space a given amount of ice occupies. With this increased density the snowcover shrinks, or settles. *Settlement* is a continuous, visible indication of metamorphism. Rising temperatures cause an increase in the settlement rate.

Constructive metamorphism may also take place in the snowcover. This occurs when water vapor is transferred from one part of the snowcover to another by vertical diffusion and is deposited in the form of ice crystals with different characteristics from those of the original

snow. These crystals often have a scroll or cup shape, appear to be lay-
ered, and may grow to considerable size (several millimeters in diameter). They form a very fragile mechanical structure which loses all
strength when crushed and which becomes very soft when wet. The
snow form produced by this type of metamorphism is known as *depth
hoar* and is sometimes popularly referred to as sugar snow. The necessary conditions for its formation are a large difference in temperature
at different depths in the snow (large, or steep, temperature *gradient*)
and sufficient air spaces in the snow so that water vapor can diffuse
freely. These conditions are most common early in winter when the
snowcover is shallow and unconsolidated.

Because of its plastic nature, whenever snow is situated on a sloping
surface it tends to move slowly downhill under the influence of gravity.
The snow layer deforms internally, the upper layers moving downhill
faster than those next to the ground. This internal deformation, called
creep, proceeds most rapidly at the freezing point and diminishes with
falling snow temperature. The entire snow layer also *glides* on the
ground if the interface between snow and earth is at the freezing point.
If the ground surface is smooth, (grass, for instance), gliding is the
dominant form of snow motion. The slow combined motions of creep
and glide often go unnoticed by the casual observer, but they cause the
snowcover to exert enormous forces on obstacles in its path. These
forces increase with the square of snow depths and may achieve mag-
nitudes of several tons per square yard. Such forces must be taken into
account when designing mountain installations such as avalanche barriers, ski lift towers, and snow sheds. The stresses produced by uneven
creep of snow are an important factor in avalanche formation.

Variations in the strength of snow are among the widest found in nature. The hardness of windpacked old snow or frozen firn may be as
much as 50,000 times that of light, fluffy new snow. Tensile strength
also varies widely. Strength characteristics continually change as a result of metamorphism, and also depend on temperature for a given
snow type. When snow is disturbed mechanically and then allowed to
set, it undergoes a process known as *age-hardening*. This results in a
gradual hardening of the snow for several hours after it has been disturbed. The greatest source of mechanical disturbance in nature is the
wind, and an increase in hardness is always associated with wind-
drifted snow.

Thermal Properties of the Snowcover

Properties of snow that have been mentioned are all functions of
temperature. Indeed, the thermal properties of snow are the key to its
whole behavior and its stability.

There are three basic characteristics of snow which strongly influence its thermal properties. First is the high heat of fusion of ice already mentioned. For each gram of ice at the freezing point, approximately 80 calories are required just to convert it to liquid water without any change in temperature. The second is a very low heat conductivity, especially for dry, new-fallen snow. The heat conductivity of snow ranges from about .0001 to .0007 calories/cm-sec-°C. For comparison, the heat conductivity of copper is 1.0 calories/cm-sec-°C., some 10,000 times greater than that of snow. The third characteristic is the presence of water in the vapor and/or liquid states as well as the solid state. Vapor and liquid water play an important part in heat transfer within the snowcover.

The heat supply at the bottom of the snowcover is relatively minor. The internal heat of the earth provides a small but steady heat supply at the ground surface, and is sufficient to melt about 1 centimeter of ice each year. A larger amount of heat is stored in the surface layers of the earth each summer, and this heat will melt some of the winter snow as it is deposited. If cold weather precedes the first snowfall, some of this heat may already be dissipated by frost. In any case, an appreciable snowcover serves to insulate the ground surface from external heat exchanges, and the internal and stored heat, even though relatively small in quantity, is still sufficient to melt some snow throughout the winter. For this reason the base of the snowcover is almost always at 0°C., or 32°F., throughout the temperate zones.

Heat is both lost and gained in much larger quantities at the snow surface, and the temperature undergoes wide fluctuations below the freezing point. Because water cannot exist in a solid state at temperatures higher than the freezing point, the temperature of the snow surface, which is composed of particles of solid ice, can never be higher than 32°F., though a thermometer placed on the snow surface will often give a misleading value higher than 32°F. because of solar radiation. The principal media of heat transfer at the snow surface are heat conduction, radiation, condensation-evaporation-sublimation, and precipitation. Conduction, radiation, and vapor exchange may either add or subtract heat, while rainfall can only add it, as liquid water will always be at a temperature equal to or higher than that of ice.

The medium of heat exchange with the largest potential is the air. Heat may be conveyed to or removed from the snow surface in large quantities by the process known as *eddy conduction*, a transfer of heat accompanying turbulence; being dependent on the motion of air over the snow surface it does not occur with completely-calm air. Under this latter condition heat is transferred between snow and air only in very small amounts. When the air is warmer than the snow surface, heat is transferred to the snow, and as the difference in temperature increases, so does the amount of heat transferred. With air colder than the snow surface, heat flow is in the opposite direction. The turbulent transfer of heat depends on wind velocity—that is, the higher the wind velocity, the greater is the amount of heat transferred. The amount of snow that can be melted in a given period by a strong, warm wind, such as a Chinook wind, is much greater than can be melted by any other natural source, including solar radiation.

A great deal of energy arrives at the earth's surface as short-wave (visible) radiation from the sun, but only a small portion is available to snow because of its high reflectivity. Up to 90 per cent of the short-wave radiation arriving at the surface of freshly-fallen snow is turned back by reflection. This figure drops to about 60 per cent for wet spring snow, and may be even lower if there is any appreciable dirt on the surface.

In contrast to its behavior under short-wave radiation, snow is the most nearly-perfect absorbent of long-wave (infra-red) radiation in nature—or to put it another way, is the nearest approach to an ideal "black" substance. This means that snow is also an excellent radiator of infra-red, and thus can lose heat rapidly through this medium as well as gain it. When skies are clear, snow loses heat to space by long-wave radiation, the amount depending on the quantity of water vapor and carbon dioxide in the air, both of which have strong effects. Under overcast conditions snow will also lose heat by long-wave radiation to clouds if the cloud temperature is lower than that of the snow surface. Clouds of any appreciable thickness also behave as black bodies to infra-red, and if temperatures of cloud and snow surface are known, the amount of heat exchanged can be estimated. When the clouds are warmer than the snow surface, the process is reversed and the snow gains heat by long-wave radiation. This latter condition is most common in spring or summer when the air and clouds are warm, but the snow surface remains at 32°F.

The effects of long- and short-wave radiation add algebraically to produce the net radiation balance of the snow surface. The net balance is usually positive (snow gains heat) in the day and negative at night during clear weather. Occasionally, under conditions of clear skies at high altitudes in winter, when the sun angle is low, even at midday the outgoing long-wave radiation may exceed the short-wave radiation absorbed by the snow, which will actually be cooled while the sun is shining. Maximum positive radiation balance is not achieved on clear days, for then the outgoing infra-red radiation subtracts from the solar radiation available to the snow surface. The maximum amount of heat in the form of radiant energy is received by the snow under conditions when *both* infra-red and short-wave radiation are delivered *to* the snow surface. This usually occurs with a partly-overcast sky.

The behavior of water vapor as a medium of heat exchange at the snow surface is determined by the high heat of vaporization of water. The conversion of 1 gram of water from liquid to vapor without change in temperature requires 600 calories of heat. If water is converted directly from solid to vapor (sublimation), the heat of fusion must be added to this figure, giving a heat requirement of 680 calories per gram. It is thus seen that, even though the heat of fusion is large, the heat of vaporization or sublimation is very much larger. Accordingly, addition or subtraction of material at the snow surface through the medium of water vapor must always be accompanied by the exchange of large quantities of heat. This means, first, that evaporation can take place only if enough heat is available to supply the heat of vaporization. Heat in such quantities is not ordinarily available to the snow surface, and evaporation losses are always quite small. Significant amounts of evaporation can occur only when extremely-dry air with temperature well above that of the snow surface is accompanied by high winds, provided that the condition for evaporation described below is satisfied. A second corollary is that condensation of water vapor on a snow surface can be a large source of heat, for when condensation takes place, the heat of vaporization is given up to the snow. The transport of water vapor to or from the snow surface is governed by laws similar to those governing the turbulent transfer of heat, and increases with increasing wind velocity.

Whether evaporation or condensation occurs depends on a simple physical law. When the dew point (see Chapter 22) of the atmosphere is lower than the snow surface temperature, evaporation is possible. When the dew point is higher than the snow surface temperature, condensation can take place. If the air and snow surface temperatures are below freezing, the exchange takes place as sublimation. Conditions most frequently favor condensation in spring or summer, when air temperatures (and dew points) become higher, while the snow temperature remains at 32°F.

Rainfall rarely delivers more than a minor amount of heat to the snow surface. It takes 1 calorie of heat to raise the temperature of 1 gram of water 1°C. Each gram of rain which falls on a snow surface and is cooled to the freezing point gives up only 1 calorie for each degree Centigrade it is cooled. Since the heat of fusion of snow and ice is 80 calories per gram, it naturally follows that deluges of rain—rare in the high mountains—are needed to melt any significant amount. The heavy snow melt sometimes associated with rainstorms can usually be attributed to the accompanying warm wind and condensation.

The flow of heat within the snowcover is a complex phenomenon, due to the presence of all three phases of water. Part of the heat is transferred by molecular conduction, and part is transferred by circulation of air in the spaces between the snow grains. The air itself carries some heat, but the water vapor with it carries more. It has been estimated that in some environments up to half of the heat flow in snow is due to sublimation and diffusion of water vapor. Because of the high heat of sublimation of water, only small quantities of water vapor are required to transport appreciable heat in this manner. In any case, the total amount of heat transferred within the dry snowcover is quite small, due to its overall low conductivity. This picture is altered, however, when appreciable amounts of liquid water are present. The downward percolation of liquid water through a snowcover transports heat very rapidly, and a sudden thaw or rainfall which produces free water at the surface will quickly warm the whole snowcover to the freezing point. When water percolates into snow below the freezing point, the water refreezes and gives up its heat of fusion. Heat is thus transported through the snow by the physical penetration of water, circumventing the otherwise low conductivity of snow.

Special Forms and Features of Snow and Ice

Certain forms of falling or deposited snow have already been described and their origin explained; there are other special snow and ice forms of interest to the mountaineer.

The term *powder snow* has been so widely applied in the United States to light, fluffy, new-fallen snow that this usage has gained some measure of authority. However, powder snow is also more specifically defined as new snow which has undergone a certain degree of crystalline change, having lost some of its cohesion due to the interlocking of the snow crystal branches and arms—a state in which it can persist for an appreciable length of time only at fairly low temperatures. (The widespread phrase among skiers, "cold powder snow," has its basis in fact.) Such snow is loose and powdery, commonly affords good skiing, often betten than the original new snow at the time of deposition, and may form dry loose-snow avalanches.

After the advent of melting in early spring, a period of fair weather may be followed by the formation of coarse rounded crystals on the snow surface. When this *corn snow* thaws out each morning after the nightly freezing it offers an excellent skiing and stepkicking surface. These coarse crystals are formed from the alternate melting and freezing of the snow by the diurnal temperature changes during fair weather. The melting each day must be just sufficient to form some free water among the snow grains; if too much melting occurs part of the surface is ablated away, and the process must start afresh with another layer of snow the next day. Only when the same surface layer of snow is exposed to the alternate melting and refreezing does true corn snow develop. For this reason, corn snow formation is less frequent later in the spring and summer, when surface ablation is greater. A surface similar to corn snow is common on summer snowfields, or firn; but this is usually an ice layer exposed and disintegrated by ablation.

Rotten snow is a condition of snowcover, sometimes found in the spring, and characterized by a soft, wet snow in the lower layers of the snowcover which offers little support to the sometimes-firmer layers above. In its most pronounced forms it will not support even the weight of a man on skis. Snow conditions which promise good spring skiing early in the morning, while some strength remains in the diurnal crust, may later in the day deteriorate to rotten snow, the disappointed skier finding himself sinking in to his knees. This type of snow forms when layers of depth hoar in the lower part of the snowcover become wet and lose what little mechanical strength they originally possessed. Wet loose-snow or slab avalanches running clear to the ground frequently occur. Continental climates such as those of the Rockies are most productive of rotten snow formation, which is much less likely to occur in the more stable maritime snowcovers of the Pacific coastal ranges.

Crusts form in several ways. The simplest is the so-called *sun crust,* which hardens when water melted at the snow surface by solar radiation is refrozen and bonds the snow crystals together into a cohesive layer. This sequence of events can take place at any time of the year, on either snow or firn surfaces, whenever the radiation balance becomes positive during the day and causes melting, followed by a cooling of the snow surface at night to cause freezing. This cooling may be caused by heat loss from the snow surface to air below the freezing point, or it may occur as radiation cooling even when the air temperature is above freezing. In winter and early spring the thickness of a sun crust is usually determined by the thickness of the surface layer where free water is formed in otherwise dry snow. In later spring and summer (firn conditions) when free water is found throughout the snowcover, the sun crust thickness is determined by the amount of cooling at night.

This type of crust might better be included under the more general term *meltwater crust.* Melting due to warm air or condensation at the snow surface, followed by freezing conditions, produces a crust similar to that caused by the sun. The only difference is the source of heat.

In distinct contrast is the *wind crust* caused by mechanical action of the wind, often without the presence of meltwater. Once the surface snow layers are disturbed by the wind, age-hardening is initiated, and these layers become harder than the undisturbed ones underneath.

Furthermore, the snow crystals are broken and winnowed by wind transport, and the fragments are deposited compactly together when they come to rest, adding a further mechanical process of hardening. The hardening is compounded when the wind provides a source of heat as well as mechanical action, particularly through the medium of water vapor condensation. Even when there is not enough heat to cause melting, the warming of the disturbed surface layer, followed by cooling when the wind dies, provides additional metamorphic hardening.

Rime is the dull white dense deposit derived from freezing of droplets of liquid water on objects exposed to the wind. Rime deposits are always built up *toward* the direction from which the wind blows, and may form large feathery flakes, as well as a solid incrustation, but regular crystalline patterns are absent. This is in contrast to the distinctly crystalline nature of hoar deposits.

Hoarfrost, on the other hand, is formed by sublimation of water vapor from the atmosphere onto solid objects and has distinct crystalline shapes—blades, cups, and scrolls. When deposited on the snow surface, it is known as *surface hoar*, generally produced during a clear cold night when strong radiation and conduction losses can carry away the heat of sublimation from the snow or other surfaces. It is easily recognized by the fragile, feathery appearance of the crystals, which often reach a centimeter or more in length, and the brilliant sparkle of these crystals in sunlight. A heavy deposit of surface hoar makes a very fast and excellent skiing surface.

Crevasse hoar occurs within the snowcover in such enclosures as crevasses. Like surface hoar it is a product of sublimation, but because of a protected location and available free space, it can grow slowly over long periods of time, the crystals often attaining considerable size, sometimes a length of several centimeters. They may assume a cup or scroll shape similar to that of depth hoar, but on a larger scale.

Firnspiegel, or "firn mirror," is the thin layer of clear ice sometimes observed on snow surfaces in spring or summer. Its reflection is so highly specular that under suitable conditions of sunlight and slope angle it produces the brilliant sheen of "glacier fire." Firnspiegel forms when solar radiation can penetrate the surface snow layers and cause melting just *below* the surface at the same time that freezing conditions are prevailing *at* the surface. Once formed, it acts like a greenhouse, and can permit melting of the snow surface underneath while the transparent ice layer itself remains frozen at the surface. After a clear, cold night, miniature crevasse hoar crystals may be found growing from the underside of this thin ice layer into the hollows which were formed beneath it by melting on the previous day.

Verglas is a layer of thin, clear ice derived from liquid water freezing on a rock surface. A combination of a thaw to form the liquid water followed by a freeze is needed—most commonly encountered at higher elevations in the spring or summer. The water may come from melting snow or firn fields and flow down over the rock, from rain, or perhaps most commonly from the melting of a fresh fall of snow. Radiation cooling can cause the freezing, as well as chilling by air which is below the freezing point.

After melting has begun in spring, dendritic *drainage patterns* appear on snowfields, formed in snow—as on the ground—by the runoff of liquid water. However, the flow takes place *within* the snowcover, unlike the surface channels on the ground. As water is formed at the snow surface by melting it percolates downward until it encounters impervious layers (including perhaps an ice layer) which deflect its course, or highly-permeable layers which it can easily follow. Much of the water also reaches the earth beneath, and either flows along the surface or else penetrates farther and becomes groundwater. That water which flows along the layers within the snowcover tends to establish a dendritic pattern of channels just as does water flowing on soil. The reason the pattern so quickly becomes visible on the snow surface is that the flowing water locally accelerates the snow settlement around its channels, which in turn are soon outlined by depressions at the surface. The dirt which collects in these depressions absorbs solar radiation and accentuates them further by differential melting.

Suncups are depressions in the surface of summer firn, varying in depth from an inch to 2 feet or more. They never occur as isolated depressions, but always as an irregular pattern covering an entire snowfield. They form whenever weather conditions combine to accentuate irregularities in the snow surface. There must be motion of air to cause greater heat and mass transfer at points or ridges of the snow surface than at the hollows. The air must be dry enough to favor evaporation (dew point cooler than snow surface). There must be an additional source of external heat; usually this is solar radiation, but need not necessarily be so. Under these circumstances, more heat reaches the points than the hollows, but a larger proportion goes to cause evaporation than melt. Because evaporation of a given mass of snow demands 7½ times as much heat as melt, less mass is lost from the point or ridges as vapor than is lost from the hollows as meltwater. The hollows get deeper faster than the points melt away, and suncups form. Why suncups take the shape and size they do is still unexplained. Once formed, they are further enhanced by differential melting when dirt in the hollows absorbs extra solar radiation. Because the sun is not directly overhead (except in the tropical latitudes), the suncups melt faster on the

south sides of the ridges (in the northern hemisphere) and the whole
suncup pattern gradually migrates northward across its snowfield.
Warm, moist winds tend to destroy suncups by causing faster melt at
the high points and edges. A prolonged summer storm accompanied by
fog, wind, and rain will often erase a suncup pattern completely. They
immediately start to reform with the return of dry, fair weather.

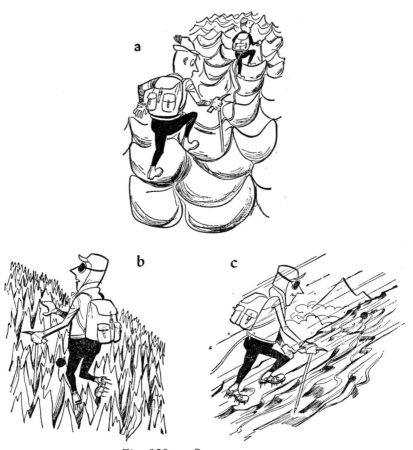

Fig. 126. a. Suncups.
         b. Nieve penitentes.
         c. Sastrugi.

Nieve penitentes (Spanish for "penitent snow") are the pillars produced when suncups are so pronounced that the cups intersect to leave
columns of snow standing between the hollows. They are peculiar to
snowfields at high altitudes, where radiation and atmospheric conditions conducive to suncup formation are particularly intense, and reach

their most striking development among the higher peaks of the Andes and Himalaya, where they may attain a height of several feet, with consequently-difficult travel. The columns often slant toward the midday sun.

The surface of dry snow may develop a variety of *erosional forms* when subjected to scouring by winds, minor examples being the small ripples and irregularities on winter snowcover. On high ridges and treeless arctic wastes, where the full sweep of the wind is unimpeded, these erosional features can attain considerable relief. Most characteristic are the wavelike forms, with a sharp prow directed toward the prevailing wind, known as *sastrugi,* from the Russian (singular: *sastruga*), or *skavler,* from the Norwegian. A field of sastrugi is difficult to travel

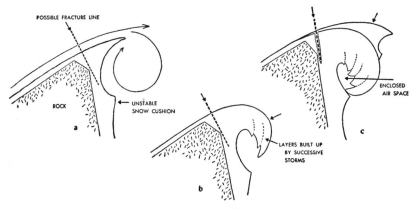

Fig. 127. Cornice development.
a. Young.
b. Middle.
c. Mature.

not only because of their depth, which may be as much as several feet, but because like wind crusts they also are usually very hard and unyielding. High winds over featureless snow plains also produce *dunes* similar to those found in desert sand, with the crescentic dune, or *barchan,* being most common.

Cornices are deposits of wind-drifted snow on the lee edge of ridges or other exposed terrain features. They offer a particular hazard to the mountain traveler because they often overhang to the lee, forming an unstable mass which may break off either from human disturbance or natural causes. Falling cornices, in themselves a large and dangerous mass of snow in motion, in addition are frequent causes of avalanches. Depending on wind and snow conditions, cornices vary from those soft and easily broken to structures extremely hard which remain solidly attached to the mountain throughout the winter. The stability of a cornice is best determined by test or inspection—there are too many complicating factors for advance prediction from consideration of snow and wind data, even if these were available. Probing with an ice ax or reversed ski pole may indicate whether the snow is solid, or weak and poorly compacted. Such probing can also help to locate the crack, if there is one, between a mature cornice and solid snow or bedrock. Where such a space—often hidden by surface drifting—has developed, even a very solid, hard cornice may be on the verge of detaching from the ridge, and great care is indicated. When the climber approaches the cornice from the windward the extent of its overhang and the danger it offers are often hard to judge; in the case of a mature cornice the probable line of fracture may be many feet back from the edge. Though, as with all snow phenomena, it is unwise to generalize too widely, a rather reliable rule is that the fracture line of a well-developed, unstable cornice is usually farther back from the lip than examination from the windward would lead an observer to expect.

Cornices are formed by drifting snow. During storms the precipitated snow furnishes material for cornice formation wherever appropriate eddies form to the lee of ridges. If a snowfield lies to the windward, additional material can be gathered by wind drift. Cornices form during fair weather as well, but here the only source of snow is that picked up to the windward and hence the presence of a source such as a snowfield or other accumulation area becomes essential. As a general, though not universal, rule, cornices formed during snow storms are softer than those produced by wind drift alone.

The Formation of Glaciers

Discussion to this point has been confined largely to the nature and behavior of a transient winter snowcover. Whenever climatic conditions during the melting season provide a supply of heat insufficient to remove completely the snow deposited during the winter, a certain part of the winter snowcover is carried over to the next season. If the climatic conditions leading to this annual carryover of snow are sustained for a long enough time, the successive annual increments will eventually form a glacier.

The process leading to the formation of glacier ice from snow is called *firnification,* during which snow is converted to *firn* (or *névé*) and firn to glacier ice. The exact point when firn turns into ice is clearly defined—it becomes ice when the pores become noncommunicating. To put it another way, firn becomes ice when the air spaces between the grains become sealed off from each other, so that the mass becomes airtight. The point at which snow becomes firn is not so easy to state, for this is purely an arbitrary division, and different authorities recognize the formation of firn on different bases. One definition describes firn as any snow with a density higher than 0.4 gram per cubic centimeter, regardless of its crystallographic structure. Firn is also defined as snow which has survived at least one season of ablation—i.e., snow which is carried over from one year to the next. The latter is probably a more convenient definition for the mountaineer, as the difference between snow and firn on this basis can be easily recognized without any special instruments. In terms of the processes involved, firn can be more generally defined as old snow in which destructive metamorphism of the original snow crystals is complete, any further changes leading to the formation of glacier ice.

The process of change, or metamorphism, observed in a newly-fallen snow continues throughout the time the water substance remains in a solid state. The wet, granular snow of spring is by no means an end product; changes continue to take place until it once more returns to the liquid state, whether it be in a few hours, or over a period of centuries. Diurnal melting and refreezing during spring and summer is the first step which carries old snow towards the formation of firn and eventually glacier ice. Once a snow layer has been carried over through a second winter, it is shielded from daily changes by the newer snow on top of it, but the melting and refreezing part of the metamorphic process continues on an annual basis with the alternate penetration of winter chill and percolating summer meltwater. Reinforcing this process are the changes effected by increasing pressure as subsequent burdens of snow are added each season. Together they gradually compact the snow, increase its density, reduce its pore volume, and lead to the formation of ice.

Part of the ice developed from layers of firn is formed by the refreezing of percolating meltwater each spring when the subsurface layers are still at temperatures below the freezing point. This refrozen meltwater is usually concentrated at certain levels within the snow to form discrete *ice layers*. Thus, by the time compaction and metamorphism have prepared the general body of a snow layer for conversion to ice, it may already contain irregular bodies of solid ice. Under certain subarctic conditions this refreezing of percolating meltwater is the predominant factor in converting snow into glacier ice.

The process most commonly encountered by climbers in the mountains is the one described above, but it does not apply in all cases. Under polar climatic conditions at high latitudes, the formation of glacier ice sometimes takes place without the presence of liquid water at any time. The metamorphism of snow through firn to ice is then controlled entirely by pressure and subfreezing temperature, with the melting and refreezing process entirely absent. Such glaciers are known as *polar glaciers,* where *dry firn* is produced by the process of *dry metamorphism.*

Once ice has been formed, metamorphism does not cease. Through crystallographic changes some of the ice grains continue to grow at the expense of their neighbors, and the average size of the ice crystals increases with age. The mechanical effects of ice flow in a moving glacier influence this growth, so that crystal size can serve only as a very relative indicator of ice age. In large glaciers, where the ice has undoubtedly spent centuries in its journey to the glacier terminus, crystals sometimes are found several inches to a foot or more in diameter—gigantic crystals which have grown from minute snow particles.

The climatic conditions which control the formation and preservation of glaciers—that is, the conditions which determine whether or not some winter snow will be left over at the end of each summer melting season—are complex in themselves, and are further complicated by the influence of topography. Recent studies have given some insight into the manner in which various weather factors influence glaciers, but the causes of the climatic changes which in turn affect these weather factors are obscure. Many theories have been advanced to explain the periods of glaciation which have occurred repeatedly throughout geologic time, but no single, positive explanation has yet been found. Even though factors which cause present-day glaciers to advance or retreat are not always clear, it is possible to discuss in a general manner how a glacier is formed and sustained.

The amount of snow deposited on the ground each year at any particular point on the earth's surface is determined by the climate and topography. Given a fixed climate and location, the amount of snow which would fall each year on a level surface varies with the altitude of that surface above sealevel. Generally, this amount of snow increases up to a certain elevation, and thence decreases with increasing altitude. Also, given the same climate and location, the amount of snow on a level surface which can be melted by the heat available each year varies with altitude, usually being maximum at sealevel and decreasing with height. For the given conditions, there will then be some particular altitude at which the snow which can be melted will equal the snow deposited. Above this altitude not all of the snow falling on a level surface each year will be melted away, and accumulation will result. If the altitude at which deposition and melting of snow are equal is postulated for each point over the earth's surface, it is possible to conceive of it as a surface in the form of a rough sphere surrounding the earth, being farthest above sealevel in the vicinity of the equator, and closest to sealevel near the poles, but varying considerably from point to point with local climatic conditions.

Over most of the earth this *cryosphere* is an imaginary surface, but wherever the real surface of the earth intersects it, it becomes real, and perpetual ice (glaciers) form. For a glacier to form where none existed before it is obvious that the level of the cryosphere must by some climatic change be depressed in elevation so that it will intersect an actual land mass and become real. It may be depressed by a decrease in the amount of heat available each year, by an increase in the amount of snow precipitated, or both.

It was pointed out in the previous discussion of the thermal properties of snow that there are several ways in which the heat supply can be altered. For instance, an increase in the average cloudiness reduces the amount of heat available from the sun. A decrease in the mean air temperature reduces the heat supply to the snow surface. More important, given the same air temperature, a reduction in the mean wind velocity also lowers the heat available from the air.

Snow accumulation, on the other hand, can be greatly altered by variations in the mean position of storm paths during the winter months. The prevailing direction of storm winds can ultimately determine which lee slopes will accumulate the greatest amount of snow. Increased snowfall goes along with the climatic changes brought about by the geological process of mountain building in the path of already-established storm tracks. This latter situation illustrates the earth's surface rising up to meet the cryosphere as it is depressed by climatic change.

To cite a specific example of such changes and their effects of glaciers: the general reactivation and advance of glaciers observed in western Washington State since 1945 appears to be due to a combination of increased winter precipitation and lowered mean annual temperatures. In this case the general trend of recession of alpine glaciers has been reversed; indeed in some places small cirque glaciers which had practically disappeared are now being reconstituted. Obviously the process can work both ways. An elevation of the cryosphere, or depression of the earth's surface, can lead to the recession or even elimination of glaciers.

One way to demonstrate the factors which affect glacier behavior is to follow the steps in the formation and development of an idealized glacier. The formation of a simple valley-type alpine glacier will serve as an illustration.

Consider a mountain in the northern hemisphere presently free from glaciation, and suppose a climatic change sufficient to cause snow to persist from year to year in a sheltered spot on a northern exposure. From the first, snow deposited on the mountainside will tend to flow valleyward in the slow motion of creep. As new layers of snow are added each year, the snow patch will grow in depth (and probably in extent) and the amount of snow in motion will increase. This creeping snow will tend to dislodge the soil or weathered rock beneath it, and the melting, refreezing, and flow of water around and under the snow patch during part of each year will add to the mechanical action of the snow patch on its surroundings. This small-scale process of erosion is known as *nivation,* and will eventually lead to the formation of a hollow where the winter snows can be deposited in deeper drifts. With the climate continuing to favor accumulation of snow each year, the snow patch will continue to grow, and as it becomes deeper its downslope flow will become more pronounced. When the depth approaches a hundred feet or so, the lower layers will be nearing the state of ice, and the increasing pressure of the many layers of firn will cause the plastic flow to accelerate.

In short, a glacier is born. With continued nourishment from heavy winter snows it flows toward the valley as a stream of ice. At some point in this descent of the mountainside it will reach an elevation low enough so that the melting each year will exceed the annual accumulation of snow. Then the excess heat supply left after each annual snowcover is melted away will melt some of the ice which has been carried down from above. Because ice has a much lower reflectivity for solar radiation than snow, it will absorb more of the available heat than snow.

Eventually the glacier will reach an even lower elevation where the supply of heat is sufficient to melt all the ice carried down from above. Until climatic conditions once more undergo a change, this will represent the lower limit of the glacier. The amount of snow gained on the upper reaches each year will equal the amount of ice melted away on the lower parts, and the glacier will have reached a state of equilibrium with its environment.

At the elevation on the surface of this idealized glacier where annual melting equals the annual snowfall, a feature will be developed known as the *firn limit.* This is the line across the glacier above which it gains material each year, and below which it loses material. Such a line is found on all real glaciers which descend from a region of accumulation to a region of ablation. In practice it is not usually a sharply-defined line, but rather a narrow, irregular zone whose position may vary from year to year, but whose average elevation remains more-or-less constant as long as the climate remains unchanged.

The elevation of the *regional snow line* is defined as the elevation above which annual accumulation exceeds annual ablation on a level surface. It thus corresponds to the position of the cryosphere at any given point. On a regional, rather than a point-to-point basis, however, the snow line obviously must be an average of wide fluctuations. In the first place, the idealized case of the definition, a level surface, is the exception rather than the rule in the mountains. In most places the annual snowfall is deposited on slopes whose orientation, and position in respect to other terrain masses, determine the amount of heat they receive, and the annual melting. Glacier formation and the persistence of snow patches from year to year occur on sheltered northern exposures well below the regional average of the snow line. On the other hand, southern exposures which receive the full benefit of solar radiation remain free of snow well above the regional average.

Because of these wide variations, describing the mean elevation of a regional snow line in any given mountainous area is often difficult. A more convenient indicator of the general level of glaciation in a given area may be the elevation of firn limits on existing glaciers, for it takes into account the effects of wind—drifting, exposure, etc. The firn limit is usually confined within relatively-narrow boundaries of elevation on any given glacier, and often exists at comparable elevations on several glaciers of a region. Even so, the firn limit elevations can be described only in general terms over any very large region.

The lowest firn limit elevations in the contiguous United States are found in the Olympic Mountains of western Washington. In the vicinity of the Mount Olympus massif, they presently lie between 4500 and 5500 feet. Eastward in the Cascade Range and the volcanoes of Washington, the firn limit elevations rise to between 6000 and 8000 feet, with considerable variations from north to south. Southward through Oregon and California the average level of the firn limits rises rapidly until in the Sierra Nevada they are found at 12,000 to 13,000 feet on a few tiny glacier remnants in the high sheltered cirques. Northward along the Pacific coast the firn limits descend rapidly to elevations of around 3000 and 4000 feet in southeast Alaska.

Only a few small glaciers exist today in the Rocky Mountains of the United States, although at one time these peaks were rather extensively glaciated. The concept of a firn limit can hardly be applied to the few scattered perennial snow patches found among the many 14,000-foot peaks of Colorado. In fact, in this area the regional snow line may properly be placed at elevations higher than the summits of the peaks. Farther north in the Rockies some true glaciation exists in the Wind River Range of Wyoming, where firn limits are found in the neighborhood of 12,000 feet. Near the Canadian border the peaks of Glacier National Park boast a few small glaciers with firn limits between 8000 and 9000 feet, but these glaciers owe their precarious existence at this elevation to heavy deposits of wind-drifted snow in certain localities. As in the Colorado Rockies, the regional snow line in this area is actually higher than the peaks. Still farther north, however, the Rocky Mountains of Canada support a much more extensive glaciation with firn limits no higher than 7000 to 9000 feet.

The regional snow line, and the firn limits on glaciers, over the earth as a whole vary more widely in altitude than the few examples from North America. In the tropical zones perpetual snow is able to exist only at elevations higher than all but the highest peaks of this continent while, at the other extreme, firn limits are found at sealevel in such places as northeast Greenland. The earthwide visible manifestations of the cryosphere are thus found to vary extensively with altitude, but even greater are the variations with time, illustrated by the great continental ice sheets of past ages.

A *temperate glacier* is one which is at the melting point of ice throughout its bulk. (The melting point decreases slightly under pressure, hence even a temperate glacier is a little colder at the bottom than at the surface.) During the winter, sub-freezing temperature causes the glacier to freeze at the surface. Penetration of this winter *cold wave* varies from a few feet to many dozens of feet, depending on climate and thickness of the insulating winter snowcover. All glaciers of the United States are temperate except those in northern Alaska. A *subpolar glacier* is at subfreezing temperature throughout its bulk except for a surface layer which experiences warming to the melting point during the summer. Its thermal regimen is thus just the opposite of a temperate glacier. A *high polar* glacier lies in a climate cold enough to prevent melt even in summer and thus is subfreezing the year around. Much of the Antarctic ice cap belongs to this category.

The *mass budget* of a glacier is the annual difference between accumulation and ablation of snow and ice. It is usually expressed in equivalent volumes of water, either for the glacier as a whole or for a unit area at some specific point on the glacier. If a glacier gains mass in the course of a year, it is said to have a positive budget; if it loses mass the budget is negative. In order for a glacier to grow and advance, it must experience a sustained period of positive mass budgets. The mass budget each year is determined by an intricate combination of weather and climate elements. In maritime climates with abundant snowfall, the mass budget is sensitive to temperature. In cold, polar climates where melting is slight or absent, variations in the usually-light precipitation are the dominating influence.

Glacier behavior varies all the way from stagnant masses with little motion to vigorously-flowing rivers of ice which annually transport large masses from higher to lower elevations. The concept of a glacier *activity index* is intuitively obvious in terms of the amount of mass which is added each year in the accumulation zone and the amount removed by melt in the ablation. The larger these quantities are the more mass must be transported by flow through the firn limit; and the greater their difference in elevation, the faster this flow must be. Formulated in physical terms, this activity index turns out to be the vertical gradient of specific mass budget. In other words, the faster accumulation increases with altitude (or ablation decreases), the more actively the glacier must flow to sustain its shape.

Temperate glaciers flow both by internal plastic deformation and by sliding on their beds. Velocity distribution is somewhat like that in a river, fastest at the center and surface and slower at the sides and bottom where bedrock creates a frictional drag. The basal sliding depends on plastic deformation to get the ice around large obstacles and *regelation* (melting and freezing) to surmount the small ones. Meltwater, including that involved in regelation, plays an important and not completely understood role. There seems to be some evidence, for example, that the velocity of glacier flow depends to some extent on the amount of meltwater produced at the surface. When the climate is sufficiently polar to cool the glacier below freezing clear down to its base, the flow of meltwater is cut off, regelation is blocked, and the glacier is frozen to its bed. Basal sliding is severely inhibited if not stopped entirely and the glacier is forced to flow by internal plastic deformation alone. Small polar glaciers present quite a striking difference in appearance from their temperate cousins; the former look much like flowing molasses, while the latter are rivers of broken ice.

Glaciers do not respond smoothly to changes in climate which alter their mass budgets. Often they tend to advance in spurts, overreaching new equilibrium positions and then stagnating in their lower reaches. One reason is that glaciers are unstable in zones of *compressive flow* which commonly occur below the firn limit. Compressive flow occurs when velocity decreases down-glacier and more mass is carried into a volume element on its uphill side than flows out on the downhill side (the difference is removed by ablation). In these circumstances a climate-induced thickening tends to cause the glacier to grow even thicker, while thinning causes the glacier to react by becoming even thinner. Another cause of erratic behavior is the development of *kinematic waves* in glacier ice. Suppose an excess of ice thickness develops in the accumulation zone. This may descend the glacier as a wave of thickening which travels at a velocity substantially greater than that of the ice flow. If the wave reaches the glacier terminus (diffusion tends to prevent this), the terminus may suddenly advance, sometimes overriding or invading a zone of stagnant ice. Large glaciers with valley ice streams of gentle gradient many miles long sometimes develop a *glacier surge*. A vast quantity of ice is suddenly displaced downvalley as much as several miles in a few months. Surface levels in upper parts of the stream may drop a hundred feet or more. Such large ice streams are known from a theoretical standpoint to be unstable, but the mechanism by which so much ice is moved so far so fast is still unclear.

Stability of the Snowcover

Like everything on the earth's surface, snow is continually under the influence of gravity. Because snow is composed of an irregular aggregate of independent particles, often mechanically weak, and is subject to constant change, it often yields to this influence. Upon a level surface this yielding is confined to settlement, or compaction. Upon an inclined surface, the effects of gravity may have results ranging from slow creep to a violent and destructive avalanche. The stability of snow determines its power to resist the force of gravity tending to carry it down a mountainside, and the correct estimation of this stability is essential to safe travel in the mountains, especially in winter.

It must be emphasized at this point that to attain familiarity with avalanche conditions there is no substitute for personal experience in the field. No mountaineer will become an expert by reading this or any other book—he must learn by first-hand experience the feel of snow under his skis, the resistance it offers to his ice ax, the instinct that warns of danger even when the "rules" say that the snow underfoot should be safe.

Here space permits only a cursory treatment of a subject deserving elaboration in a separate volume. For further details the reader is referred to publications dealing specifically with avalanches. (See Appendix 3.) It is possible in this chapter to present only a broad outline of conditions affecting snow stability, and their recognition, but a discussion of safe conduct through snow under hazardous circumstances will be found in Chapters 12 and 19.

This topic may be divided into two parts—stability of snow considered as an aggregate of individual particles, and stability of snow en masse. In terms of the active expressions of instability, avalanches may be divided into two major types: *loose snow* and *slab*. Each type may be further classified as *wet* or *dry*, depending on whether liquid water is present in the snow. Avalanches in motion may consist of snow sliding only on the ground, snow carried only through the air as a dust cloud, or a combination of the two.

Avalanche types are customarily classified according to conditions prevailing at the point of origin. Obviously, more than one kind of snow may be involved in an avalanche falling over a long slide path with a large difference of elevation. For instance, a slide might originate as a dry slab avalanche, and then assume the characteristics of a dry loose-snow avalanche once in motion. Such an occurrence is actually fairly common in the high mountains in winter. In the spring an avalanche originating in dry snow, either loose or slab, will often involve predominantly wet snow as it descends to lower elevations.

Regardless of the type of avalanche considered, the stability of the snow, the manner in which it changes, and the duration of any instability are all determined by the metamorphism of individual snow crystals. This metamorphism is controlled by the temperatures prevailing within the snowcover, and the temperatures are determined in turn by the processes of heat transfer described previously. Once the initial mechanical conditions have been established at the time of deposition, duration of any instability is controlled primarily by the snow temperature. If the mountaineer had to choose a single instrument to serve as a guide to snow stability on a winter expedition, that instrument might well be a thermometer.

LOOSE SNOW

Loose snow is defined as the condition wherein individual snow crystals are free to move in respect to one another. This condition can lead to instability, and in dry snow, to the commonly-observed powder snow avalanches of winter. Wet snow may also satisfy the same definition when the bond between individual particles of snow disappears.

Consider the behavior of a material such as dry sand which is composed of particles free to move in respect to one another. For any such material there is some angle of a sloping surface with the horizontal, above which the force of gravity acting parallel to the surface will exceed the cohesion of the individual particles. This angle is known as the *angle of repose* for each given material, and when a material is deposited on a slope with an angle greater than its angle of repose, it will tend to run off under the influence of gravity. If dry sand, for instance, is placed on a board at less than its angle of repose, it will be stable, and it is possible then to increase carefully the angle of the board with the horizontal beyond the critical angle for the sand without the sand sliding off. However, any slight disturbance of the sand in this position will cause it immediately to slide off or seek its angle of repose. When in this elevated but undisturbed position, it may be said to be in a condition of *unstable equilibrium*—any outside force acting on it will cause it to seek a new, and stable, position.

The behavior of loose snow is analogous to that of sand, but complicated by the fact that the cohesion between particles varies with snow type, manner of deposition, and with metamorphism. As new snow is deposited during a storm it may, especially if accompanied by wind, form a snow layer whose individual crystals are sufficiently well-bonded together so that they will never move in respect to one another under the influence of gravity, except for the slow movement of creep and settlement. Occasionally such conditions prevail that this inter-crystalline bond is low in the newly-deposited snow, as when the snow has low density and there is relative absence of wind. Such snow falling on slopes steeper than its natural angle of repose will tend to run off in loose-snow avalanches. Usually a slight bond will exist between the snow crystals sufficient to permit a certain amount of snow to build up an unstable equilibrium before it starts to slide. Very often, however, light fluffy new snow will run off very steep slopes, cliffs, etc., almost as fast as it falls. This actually has a stabilizing effect on slopes of lesser angle below, as the small sloughs running off the steep slopes dislodge the snow below before it can build up to any great depth. Occasionally the snow will be deposited in such a manner that a considerable depth may accumulate as an unstable layer before it is set in motion by some exterior disturbance. Then a loose-snow avalanche of great magnitude may occur, especially on long, steep slopes. *Wild snow* illustrates the most extreme case of this kind. This is new snow deposited under very calm, cold conditions, and its water content may be as low as 1 per cent. At the slightest disturbance it flows down the mountainside al-most like water, for wild snow represents deposition of material under extreme conditions of unstable equilibrium. Fortunately, true wild snow is quite rare, and is almost unknown in the coastal alpine zone of the United States.

Instability in loose snow may develop in other ways than by the deposition of new snow with little original cohesion between crystals. New snow frequently has considerable stability, due to the interlocking of snow crystal branches and arms. As metamorphism proceeds, these interlocking branches tend to disappear, and with them the inter-crystalline bonds. As a result a condition of unstable equilibrium is in-troduced in a snow layer which originally showed no inclination to ava-lanche. A slide may then be precipitated by some external disturbance, such as a lump of snow falling from a tree, or the metamorphism may simply proceed to the point where the snow can no longer support it-self on the slope. The latter is the frequent cause of a cycle of small loose-snow avalanches observed to run a day or two after a fall of new snow. However, this phenomenon is not to be expected after every snowfall. The introduction of instability in loose snow by metamor-phism depends on the original type of snow crystals. It most commonly

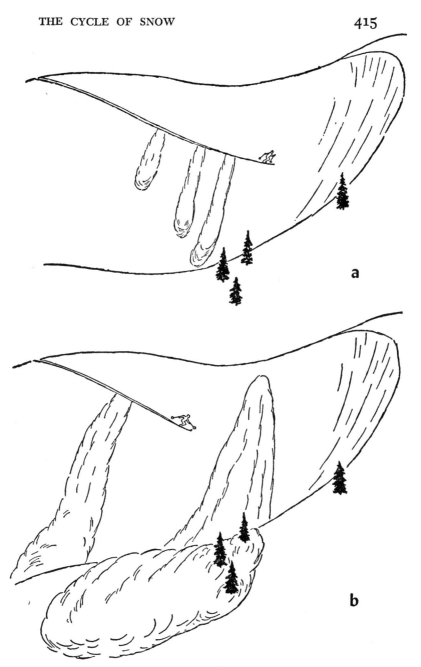

Fig. 128. Instability in loose snow.
      a. Minor or surface instability—harmless sloughs.
      b. Highly unstable—large quantities of snow involved.

occurs with stellar or dendritic crystals whose branches form a good initial bond, but one which can subsequently be weakened. With more granular types of snow, and with snow whose crystals carry any significant amount of rime, a period of decreasing stability during metamorphism is less likely to occur.

Wet loose-snow avalanches are common in the spring when significant amounts of melting take place at the snow surface. At this time of year metamorphism is usually well advanced, and the snow crystals have for the most part become rounded, isometric grains. Meltwater formed at the snow surface percolates downward and provides a lubricant between the individual snow grains, so that snow which has previously been stable is disposed to slide. Small wet loose-snow slides are common on southern exposures in spring, when the sun has reached sufficient elevation to provide a strong source of heat to the snow surface. During clear weather these slides are likely to occur only around midday or in the afternoon when the production of meltwater is at a maximum; each night the snow becomes stable as the surface freezes. Wet loose-snow slides of large and destructive proportions are more likely to occur during warm cloudy weather and wind or rain, when melting proceeds both day and night and large quantities of liquid water penetrate deep into the snowcover. Shallow snowcovers with a large proportion of depth hoar are particularly apt to produce wet loose-snow avalanches with the advent of melting conditions in the early spring.

Regardless of the type of loose-snow avalanche, the instability which produces it is usually of a transient nature. Frequently the processes which lead to the original instability can be counted on to carry the snow through to a more stable condition—for instance, by precipitating an avalanche in the case of newly-fallen snow, or by stabilizing the snow through settlement in the case of metamorphism, though the latter process may be quite slow if temperatures are very low (well below 0°F.). In any case, instability in loose snow is more easily detected than is that in slab avalanches. For a given snow condition where such instability exists, there will usually be a certain slope angle above which the snow can be set in motion by the mechanical disturbance of a ski or ice ax. The skier or climber has only to test the snow on sufficiently steep slopes to see whether or not it is in immediate danger of sliding.

SNOW SLABS

When the individual particles of the snowcover cohere sufficiently to behave as an aggregate, the development of instability takes on an entirely-different character. Most frequently snow which has lost its loose

Fig. 129. Instability in slabs.
a. Minor instability.
b. Grave instability.

nature and become a cohesive mass has increased in stability, for once the snow has gained mechanical strength it is able to resist for a time the force of gravity, instead of yielding to it immediately. However, this very cohesiveness bears within it the seeds of instability. Resistance in turn enables snow creep to build up tensions within certain snow layers, and when they finally break, the rupture may come with explosive suddenness.

Unlike the loose-snow avalanche, which begins at a point and involves more and more snow as it descends, the slab avalanche is characterized by an extensive area of snow starting to slide at the same time. The types of snow which may exhibit this characteristic when set in motion, ranging from soft, dry new snow through hard wind drifts to wet spring snow, are so varied that it is possible to apply the term *slab*, strictly speaking, only to the description of a type of instability, rather than to any particular type of snow.

A snow slab is a mechanical state which cannot be correlated with any specific physical appearance. The dull, chalky surface of certain types of wind-drifted snow (popularly called "wind slab") is not a universal indicator of unstable snow slabs—slab avalanches may and do develop in this type of snow, but many more develop in snow which is neither dull nor chalky in appearance. The action of the wind is a major factor in the formation of most slab avalanches, but wind is not a necessary condition. Under certain circumstances dangerous instability in a snow slab may develop through the action of metamorphism alone. Regardless of how a snow slab is developed, its hazard to the mountaineer is further increased if it is hidden under a subsequent snowfall. It must be emphasized here that there is no sure way in which an unstable snow slab can be distinguished from stable snow on the basis of physical appearance alone.

Whether or not a snow slab will actually become detached from the mountainside and descend as an avalanche depends on its adhesion to the underlying layer, the support it has at the bottom, and the strength with which it is attached to stable snow or fixed objects at the sides and top.

Gravity acting on the weight of the slab layer develops a component of force acting parallel to the slope on which it rests. This force has a shearing effect at the bottom of the slab where it rests on stable snow or earth. If the attachment of the slab to the underlying layer, or a weak snow layer in between, has a shear strength less than this force, then the basic condition for release of the slab is established. Whether or not it actually is released depends on the many complex variables involved in its support and attachment on the mountainside.

Both snow slabs and stable types of snow tend to flow down any incline with the slow movement of creep. The velocity of creep depends on the snow type, snow temperature, and slope angle. When a slab is anchored at the top and there is creep in its lower portions, the uneven motion develops a tension, and the snow undergoes elastic deformation. The amount of deformation depends on the snow type and its strength characteristics, and is actually quite small, but nevertheless, a snow slab in this condition is under tension just as much as a stretched rubber band. When the slab breaks off, the release of this tension causes it to fracture over an extended area, and a large body of snow is set in motion. It is the possibility of creep tension that gives the slab avalanche its dangerously-unpredictable character, and can cause an entire mountainside to erupt in an avalanche when only a small section of the slope is disturbed.

The uneven creep which produces tension may arise in other ways than from a slab anchored at its top, as discussed above. A common source of uneven creep is a slope with a convex profile, for the snow on the lower, steeper part will creep faster than the snow higher up. In contrast, differential creep on a concave slope produces a compressive force on the snow and is less likely to form an unstable slab. Snow which is drifted onto a slope so as to be thicker at the bottom than at the top will develop creep tension, for the deeper snow will creep faster at the surface than will the thinner layers. Layers within the snowcover consisting of different types of snow, or at different temperatures, will also creep at different rates and introduce tension.

When snow temperatures are near the freezing point, creep is rapid, and dangerous tensions in snow slabs may develop very quickly. However, at these temperatures snow is also able to relieve the creep tension by more rapid plastic deformation. The result is that slab avalanche danger can develop quickly under warm conditions, but the period of danger also passes quickly and the snow soon assumes a stable state. On the other hand, with low temperatures the creep process is retarded, but the snow can less easily relieve the tension by plastic flow. The consequence is persistence of unstable conditions over a long period of time at low temperatures (0°F. and lower).

In many cases a snow slab will develop an unstable condition, and then gradually return to stability through settlement and metamorphism if no outside force provides the trigger for its release at the critical moment. Avalanches do not "just happen." Though the degree of instability developed may be very high, in the last analysis something must actually set the snow in motion. In the case of snow slabs, this trigger may be any one of a number of effects, some of them complex.

The simplest triggering force is the mechanical breaking of a slab layer by a falling rock, a piece of cornice, or the weight of a skier. The weight of a new fall of snow can have the same effect, or a slide of new snow running on top of a slab may develop enough dynamic force to dislodge it. Metamorphism or penetrating meltwater can weaken the slab or its attachment to an underlying layer. Sudden changes in snow temperature can release slab avalanches by causing a rapid change in the creep process, which sets up force exceeding the mechanical strength of the snow. The support of a slab may be removed by the undercutting action of another avalanche running nearby. Sound waves of sufficient amplitude, such as the shock wave from an explosion, can release a delicately-poised slab, and it is theoretically possible that weaker disturbances, such as the sound of the human voice, could do the same, although such an extreme degree of instability must be very rare, if indeed it ever occurs.

There are three different types of slab avalanches against which the mountain traveler must guard. These are the *soft, hard,* and *wet* slabs.

Soft and hard slabs are usually found in dry snow conditions. The dividing line between them is more-or-less arbitrary. A convenient indicator is the resistance of the snow to a weighted ski. A man on skis will sink into the snow of a soft slab, but will stay on the surface of a hard slab.

Soft slabs are most frequently encountered during snow storms, when the snow is fresh and unconsolidated. At times the snow may appear so light and fluffy as to suggest the possibility of a loose-snow avalanche, but the characteristic fracture of a slab avalanche can sometimes be observed even when the snow is so soft a skier sinks to his knees. In these cases the avalanche usually assumes the appearance of a loose-snow slide once it is in motion, and no blocks or large segments of snow are found in the debris when it comes to rest. Soft slab avalanches form from a combination of wind and heavy snowfall, and usually run during or immediately after a storm. They sometimes form without regard to wind direction, and may be found on windward as well as lee slopes. This is the type of avalanche most frequently encountered in the coastal alpine zone of the United States, with its maritime climate and frequent falls of deep, heavy snow. Unstable conditions in soft slab do not usually persist as long as they do in hard slab, for there is greater scope for alterations which may be effected in the snow by metamorphism and settlement.

Hard slabs are the most dangerous and unpredictable of all unstable snow conditions. This unpredictability stems from the fact that they may persist in an unstable form for long periods of time, and from the high mechanical strength of the snow involved, which enables the slab to withstand the triggering action of weaker external forces. With soft slab, the weight of a ski or boot breaking through the snow is often sufficient to set an avalanche in motion. A hard slab, on the other hand, will often support the passage of several persons, appearing to be stable and safe, and then will suddenly break loose with the addition of only one more small triggering force. One case is on record in Switzerland of a slab avalanche being dislodged by the last 3 men of a 34-man military patrol which crossed a steep slope. A recent fatal avalanche accident in the Canadian Rockies involved a slope on which a number of people had been skiing all day just prior to the slide.

Hard slabs are the product of high winds and low temperatures. They are more commonly found above timberline, where the full sweep of storm winds is unimpeded and the higher altitudes bring persistent low temperatures in winter. High winds alone are sufficient to form hard slabs (wind slabs) on lee exposures, and dangerous conditions often develop even when no new snow falls. Their occurrence in the United States is most common in the Rocky Mountain regions, where high winter winds and sub-zero temperatures are common. In the coastal ranges, extensive hard slab formation from wind action alone is usually restricted to exposed areas of the higher peaks.

The snow of hard slabs has enough cohesion to preserve pieces of the slab as angular chunks and blocks as the slide descends the mountain, and the presence of such blocks in the debris serves as positive identification of a slab-type avalanche and of hard slab in particular. It must be pointed out that the line of demarcation between hard and soft slab is not always sharply drawn, and the mountaineer must bear clearly in mind that slab avalanches can occur in soft, light new snow, in hard windpacked snow, and in all the gradations between.

Strictly speaking, *wet slabs* are rather the product of structural changes in the snow than of the conditions prevailing at the time the snow was deposited. The snow which becomes part of wet slab avalanches is often deposited in stable layers, but some weaker layer within the snowcover develops which still has enough strength to support the overburden while dry. With the advent of melting conditions in the spring, water penetrates the snowcover, lowers the mechanical strength, and greatly reduces the shear strength of the weak layers. In addition, the free water itself provides a lubricating action. The instability leading to slab avalanche formation is thus introduced into a previously-stable snowcover. Such a phenomenon most frequently occurs in a snowcover which is poorly consolidated. Because percolating liquid water is refrozen when it reaches snow layers which are at temperatures below the freezing point, wet slab avalanches (and the same applies to wet loose snow) cannot form until the snow layers involved have become isothermal at 32°F. This provides the opportunity for a quantitative check on the development of wet slide conditions. If measurements with a thermometer show that sub-freezing temperatures exist within the snowcover, then the conclusion may reasonably be drawn that wet-snow avalanches are not likely to run, no matter how brightly the sun is shining. It must be remembered, however, as previously discussed, that the snowcover can be warmed up very quickly by percolating meltwater.

The formation of slab avalanche conditions by metamorphism of previously-stable snow in a dry, and therefore cold, snowcover is extremely difficult to discern in the field, and at times can be antici-pated only if a good record of previous snow, weather, and avalanche conditions is available. One example of how such conditions may develop will be cited here as an indication of the complexity of the problem. Consider a fall of light, dry snow deposited to an appreciable depth (say 3 feet) in the middle of winter. This fall of new snow may have some tendency to slide as a loose-snow avalanche at the time it is deposited, but it soon undergoes rapid settlement and becomes stable. If such a snowfall is on top of a deep and stable base of old snow, it may be expected to become incorporated as a stable part of that base and provide no further source of avalanche hazard. However, if it falls on a very shallow base—say on a slope which has been partly denuded of snow by previous avalanching—then an entirely-different situation can develop. If the period following its deposition is one of cold weather, a sufficiently-steep temperature gradient may be set up in this layer to initiate constructive metamorphism. (Such a gradient would not readily form where the new snow was on top of a deep base.) Constructive metamorphism then need not proceed to the formation of depth hoar, but only far enough to weaken the mechanical structure of the snow layer in question to the point where it could break loose as a slab avalanche. This might take place 1 or 2 weeks after it had been deposited as new, loose snow with no indication of any slab develop-ment.

From the foregoing paragraphs it can be seen that slab avalanches are complex in nature, and that analysis of the factors leading to their formation is sometimes difficult. Even more difficult is the quantitative evaluation of forces developed by creep tension. In fact it must now be apparent that the determination of avalanche hazard cannot be made by applying a fixed set of book rules, or by seeking a certain fixed sequence of physical events, or by external appearances alone. There are certain general principles for anticipating hazardous conditions and these are discussed in the next section, but, especially where slab avalanches are concerned, snow conditions must actually be tested in the field before reliable conclusions can be drawn, and even these must depend to a great extent on the personal experience of the observer.

Recognition of Instability in the Snowcover

The first and most common cause of avalanches is a heavy new fall of snow, and this is the first warning sign the mountain traveler heeds. As little as 6 or 8 inches of new snow may create a hazard, a foot or more should always be regarded with suspicion, and greater depths must always be treated with caution.

The total depth of snow existing on the ground affects the development of avalanche hazard. The deeper the snow, the more covered up are terrain irregularities, and the smoother the slide paths. With deep snows, fewer natural obstructions break the surface to hinder the release of avalanches, or reduce their size once in motion.

The rate at which new snow falls is an important factor. A 2- or 3-foot snowfall spread out over 3 or 4 days may produce little hazard, for settlement will often stabilize the snow faster than it builds up. On the other hand, only a foot of snow falling within a few hours may become very dangerous, for the stabilizing effects of settlement will not have had time to act. No hard-and-fast rule can be drawn, for conditions vary widely with the type of snow, but snowfall rates greater than 1 inch per hour can usually be regarded as a possible source of hazard.

With other factors equal, the development of unstable conditions will become much more likely as wind velocity increases. Wind is one of the prime agents in the formation of slab avalanches, and may build up dangerous conditions even when no snowfall occurs. In this case, hazardous areas are local and generally confined to high-angle lee slopes where heavy wind deposition of snow is taking place. This is not necessarily true when high winds accompany a heavy snowfall. In such cases slab avalanches sometimes may form without respect to exposure, and whole areas of a mountainside, both windward and lee, will become unstable.

The precipitation intensity, or rate at which water (in the form of snow) is deposited during a snowstorm, is an important key to snow stability, though it is more difficult to measure in the field. Very high rates of water deposition, accompanied by high winds for prolonged periods, are almost always followed by avalanche action. Qualitatively, heavy snowfalls of a dense or heavy type of snow (graupel, for instance) must always be suspected as a potential source of avalanche danger, particularly if winds are high. Quantitatively, observations of many storms have shown that $\frac{1}{10}$ of an inch of water per hour is about the critical rate of deposition if the snowfall lasts long enough to precipitate an inch or more of water. The greater the rate above this, the more likely it is that hazardous conditions develop.

Temperature is an important key to both development and duration of avalanche danger. Storms which begin with high temperatures and a damp, sticky type of snow which bonds well to the old snow surface, and then gradually turns to a drier type of snow with falling temperatures at the end, will be less likely to cause avalanching than will a storm which starts with a cold, dry type of snow and then warms up to produce a heavy, wet snow toward the end. In the latter case the light snow which fell first provides a poor bond between the old snow and the heavier snow which comes later. The lower the temperature after a storm or high wind, the longer will unstable conditions prevail. Hard slabs formed at low temperatures may remain dangerous for days, or even weeks, if the temperature remains well below 0°F. Clear cold weather early in the season when the snowcover is shallow will often lead to the formation of depth hoar within the snowcover. This is not always dangerous in itself, but provides a weak base which may fail to support a subsequent heavy snowfall.

An important clue to the formation of slab avalanches is the appearance of cracks in the snow underneath the foot or ski. This is particularly true of soft slabs forming during a storm. Local cracks around a ski formed by the breaking of the snow are not generally a sign of serious hazard. Cracks which run out ahead of foot or ski for several feet are a definite indication that slab conditions are forming. Whether or not a slide will actually occur on a given slope depends on many factors, such as the bond between snow layers, shape of the slope, etc., but an avalanche is always possible under these conditions, and caution is indicated. When cracks are observed to run out 30 or 40 feet ahead of skis in snow of any significant depth, it is time to return to safe terrain with all possible haste. Once snow has cracked without sliding, any tensions existing in the snow slab are relieved, and it will usually stabilize in place.

Regardless of how carefully snow conditions are studied and all the factors leading to instability considered, it is not possible to predict with any real certainty just when and if a given slope will avalanche. Nevertheless a mountaineer often finds it necessary to get the answer to this very question, as he may be about to cross a suspected slope where a miscalculation could be disastrous. If his estimation of the avalanche hazard can actually be put to test, he will be able to proceed with more confidence.

In Chapter 12 are described the tests ordinarily available to the climber. There always exists the possibility, especially with hard slabs, that the test procedures will fail to reveal a dangerous hazard. Such situations must always be borne in mind and a certain amount of judgment exercised whenever slab avalanche conditions are encountered. When selecting routes the wise mountaineer will allow sufficient margin of safety to compensate for errors in estimation of avalanche hazard, and when, on occasion, he deems it necessary to take calculated risks in crossing avalanche terrain, he will first assure himself that the risks are indeed calculated, and not foolhardy.

In conclusion it should be emphasized that a knowledge of theoretical considerations involved in avalanche formation will stand the climber in good stead, but that actual testing in the field must be the basis for practical decisions concerning avalanche hazard—with the reservation that the only completely-certain test of snow stability is the shock of high explosives.

The Higher Craft

This chapter has presented in very brief outline some of the characteristics of snow, and how these characteristics affect the formation of glaciers and the stability of the snowcover. The more serious student may continue his research by referring to the bibliographies published from time to time in alpine journals, which will serve as a guide to the extensive literature on snow and avalanches. For the skier or climber who would rather not delve into technical details there is still the best teacher of all—nature itself. An alert observation of snow in its many phases, coupled with at least a rudimentary comprehension of the processes which affect it, can develop within him a better understanding of an important part of his mountain environment, and with this understanding will come the making of a better mountaineer. Then will he learn what Geoffrey Winthrop Young meant when he wrote: "The higher craft of mountaineering begins above the line of perpetual snow."

22*

MOUNTAIN WEATHER

THE mountaineer travels over the rock and over the ice but he travels through the weather, of which Mark Twain said: "There is only one thing certain . . . there is going to be plenty of it . . ." Another famous comment is that of Charles Dudley Warner: "Everybody talks about the weather but nobody does anything about it." Warner's remark does not hold for mountaineers, who do at least a little by carrying tarps and tents and sweaters and parkas and maps and compasses. Nor is Mark Twain entirely right for often predictions can be made with some degree of probability.

The climber typically progresses through three stages of sophistication. As a novice he gives weather no advance thought at all, naively taking sunshine or storm as it comes. He will if brave (rash) have numerous narrow escapes from disaster. If cautious (timid) he will lose many a summit that could have been reached in perfect security. In the second or climax stage, experience has in some instances extended his definition of "climbable" weather and often he confidently continues upward in a downpour. At the same time he has in other instances restricted the definition, abandoning a big climb in brilliant sunshine with but a single cloud on the horizon. He tries to outguess the weather by studying current forecasts and records of past years, by sneaking around or between storms. The third or decadent stage is that of the "fair-weather climber" who has been so many times soaked to the skin and frozen to the bone, stood on so many summits gazing into fogscapes, that he will not leave home unless the sun is shining and the forecast favorable, will not leave his sleeping bag unless the stars have been bright all night, and will hastily retreat before the first cloud. He rarely gets wet anymore and rarely climbs a mountain.

It is not the intent here to summarize even briefly the present immature state of meteorogical science—which is advancing so rapidly textbooks are out of date before they are off the presses. The mountaineer in transition from Stage One to Stage Two should give direction to his awakening curiosity by reading a layman's introduction. (See Appendix 3.) Some such background of knowledge is assumed in the following treatment, which is concerned chiefly with the very special aberrations of weather in the mountains.

Origins of Weather

The status of the local atmosphere can be described as wet or dry, windy or calm, hot or cold, clear or cloudy, good or bad, promising or threatening, or any combination. The causes of these conditions, together constituting the weather, are quite simple in the abstract. However, weather is not made in the abstract, but on a spinning spheroid composed of solid and liquid matter in a thin envelope of gas, the whole revolving around a star.

Any gas such as air, when heated, expands, becomes lighter, and rises. When cooled it contracts, becomes heavier, and falls. Wind results both from these processes and also from nature's abhorrence of a vacuum: if in one neighborhood air contracts, the adjacent areas blow in more gas to fill up the space.

The earth's atmosphere is a mixture of gases including oxygen, nitrogen, carbon dioxide, and others. There are also suspended solids such as dust and smoke. There is also water in liquid state as fog, clouds, and rain, in solid state as snow, in gaseous state as vapor. The total amount of water vapor contained per unit volume is the *absolute humidity*. Warm air can hold more water vapor than cold air; therefore as air is heated it sucks up moisture, seeking to become full to capacity, or saturated. Its approach to capacity, expressed as a percentage, is the *relative humidity*. As air is cooled its capacity to hold water vapor decreases and the vapor condenses into such liquid or solid forms of water as fog, clouds, rain, snow, hoarfrost, rime, and so forth. The *dew point* is the temperature at which water vapor—ideally—condenses.

If the temperature of the atmosphere were constant there would be no weather—or rather, it would always be the same. The ultimate source of all weather thus is the sun. The visible and invisible solar radiation reaching the earth has a short wave length. Relatively little of this, only some 17%, is absorbed by the atmosphere. About 43% is reflected right back out into space, the remaining 40% being absorbed by the earth's surface and re-radiated as long-wave heat. Thus the atmosphere is warmed chiefly from the bottom up rather than the top down. The proportion of solar energy reflected to that absorbed and changed to heat varies with the surface. A forest absorbs about 95% of received energy, snow only 25%, water from 60% with a low sun to 96% with the sun overhead. A cloud may reflect as much as 75%, letting only 25% through to the ground.

Gravity is an obvious factor in weather by virtue of holding the atmosphere on the earth and giving it the weight that compresses lower layers. Weather is almost entirely confined to the *troposphere* which extends upward approximately to 40,000 feet. The stratosphere above is rarely anything but clear and cold.

Finally, motions of the earth assist in making weather. There are five of these. The earth moves with its galaxy in space and the solar system within the galaxy, neither motion having any known effect on weather. The earth's annual circuit of the sun, together with the tilt of the earth's axis with respect to its orbit, causes seasons. The daily rotation on its axis (with a slight wobble whose role currently is only a subject of speculation) causes days and nights and also prevailing winds.

Clouds

Clouds indicate what's going on in the atmosphere, always demonstrating that a layer or body of air has been cooled below its dew point so that some of its vapor has condensed into liquid or solid form. Clouds are defined by their appearance as belonging to the *cumulus family* with a billowing shape, or the *stratus family* with pronounced stratification. The two varieties are further classified by their altitude.

The *high clouds* or *cirrus,* composed usually of ice crystals, range roughly from 20,000 feet to 35,000 feet above the earth in the middle latitudes. The cirrus type which appears to consist of feathery wisps is sometimes called mare's tails. *Cirrocumulus,* more patchy and wave-like, forms the true mackerel sky. Unlike lower clouds it casts no shadow. *Cirrostratus* is the thin veil that gives the sky a filmy appearance without dimming the sun or moon though giving them a large-diameter halo.

The *middle clouds* extend from about 8000 to 20,000 feet. *Alto-cumulus,* denser than the high clouds it resembles, may obscure the sun and moon and if not produces a much smaller corona than the cirro-stratus. *Altostratus* is flatter, occurring sometimes in rifted sheets and other times as a dense veil that takes all the brightness from the sun and moon without producing a halo, perhaps causing them to appear to be behind ground glass. (When thickening, this cloud usually indicates rain within a few hours.)

The *low clouds* are those with bases ranging from the earth's surface to about 8000 feet. The *stratus cloud* (not to be confused with the more general stratus family) is a low uniform sheet that when thin makes a hazy day, thicker makes a dull heavy sky, and when quite dense may produce a drizzle but never anything more. *Stratocumulus* are billowing clouds confined to a single layer, characteristically sailing along in scattered or close formation, having dark flat bottoms and bright tufted upper edges. No rain comes from these, though they can quickly develop into the true rain cloud, the *nimbostratus,* dark and ragged with a bottom that may touch the ground, or if not can be identified from a distance by the sweeping vertical lines of the rain it discharges.

Towering clouds observe no altitude boundaries, basing themselves at any elevation from sealevel to 14,000 feet. The fair-weather *cumulus cloud* (as before not to be confused with the cumulus family) is formed in daytime by vertical rising of surface-warmed air and tends to disappear at night. Unlike the similar stratocumulus it can appear at virtually any altitude. This friendly cloud must be distrusted when it becomes overly picturesque for it can quickly evolve into the *cumulonimbus.* Even the latter may be harmless, perhaps fraying at the bottom and sending down a brief rain squall. However, development into a thunderhead can occur in a few minutes, producing torrential rains, snow, hail—and lightning. Violence of vertical motion thrusts the tops to a normal maximum of 35,000–40,000 feet in temperate latitudes —sometimes, rarely, as high as 75,000 feet, well into the stratosphere; even at much lower altitudes strong winds mold the billows into a dense flat cirrus layer, from its appearance and its consequences having an evil reputation among mountaineers as the "anvil," and among residents of the Great Plains as the breeder of tornadoes.

Clouds are an important source of information for the prediction of weather but not certainly reliable. Identical clouds are produced by a variety of causes—any of which at different times produces a variety of clouds. Moreover, identifying a cloud is not so simple as the preceding categories might seem to imply. Low clouds merge into middle and middle into high. Cumulus clouds, generally signs of good weather (unless they grow to cumulonimbus proportions), are difficult to distinguish from the stratocumulus which can change rapidly into nimbostratus. As will be further explained, observing the *sequence* of clouds is usually a necessary condition of interpreting their significance.

Large-Scale Weather: Air Masses

The global pattern of air currents is initiated by the proportionately-greater heating of the earth at the equator. Hot air surges constantly upward and outward from equatorial *doldrums* toward the poles, piling up around latitude 30° in the great high-pressure areas of the *horse latitudes* where the air finally cools and begins to descend. Some surges along the surface back to the equator. Since *in the northern hemisphere rotation of the earth deflects all winds to the right of their original direction,* the descending air with an original southerly direction blows ultimately from the northeast in the *trade winds.* Meanwhile some of the descending air moves north, again deflected rightward by rotation to produce the *prevailing westerlies* between latitudes 30° and 60°. A portion of the equator-heated air continues north at high altitude, cooling as it goes, at last sinking to the surface in the arctic regions and building high-pressure areas from which winds start south and are deflected into *polar easterlies.* The line of collision of these cold winds with the warmer westerlies in the vicinity of latitude 60° the *polar front,* is enormously fruitful of weather as the line of battle shifts up and down the hemisphere.

If there were no seasons and the earth's surface were homogeneous —all water or all desert or all forest—the story would be nearly finished. There would be permanent high-pressure areas at the horse latitudes and in the polar regions and a narrow zone of turbulent weather along the relatively-static polar front. However, the heating differential between seasons and between adjacent oceans and land masses injects giant interruptions of the prevailing air movements.

High-pressure areas, or *cells,* can occur on a local scale wherever air cools and sinks, but most of the very large ones, called *air masses,* are initiated in the arctic and then drift south. The paths they follow are complicated by many factors and at the present level of understanding seem almost random.

Within a high-pressure cell the air flows down and out from the center, being modified by the earth's rotation into a clockwise spiral, or anticyclone. Into the gaps between high-pressure cells air moves from all sides, and being deflected rightward by rotation sets up a counterclockwise spiral, a *low* or cyclone. Lows usually occur in troughs between highs.

The major source of air mass weather is a difference in temperature either between an air mass and the ground over which it moves or between two air masses which meet. Air moving over a surface warmer than itself becomes turbulent and unstable. However, within a high conditions tend to become more-or-less stabilized. Since a low consists of air from two separate highs, usually differing in temperature, the weather is generally more-or-less bad.

FRONTS

Assuming the theoretical case of a straight-line boundary between two masses, local conditions inevitably cause air from the colder mass periodically to surge under the warmer. The latter, in turn, must by a flanking movement rush in to fill the partial vacuum behind the advancing bulge of cold air. Thus a counterclockwise-spinning *low-pressure cell* is formed. On one side of the cell a bulge of warm air advances along a *warm front*. On the other side a bulge of cold air advances along a *cold front*. The two being parts of a rotating cell, a warm front is always followed by a cold front. However, since the masses are always drifting, a specific area may not be visited by both. There are great variations in scale: some lows, and thus fronts, cover dozens of the United States; others do not extend from one state line to the next. Having on the average twice the speed, the cold front normally overtakes the warm, producing an *occluded front*.

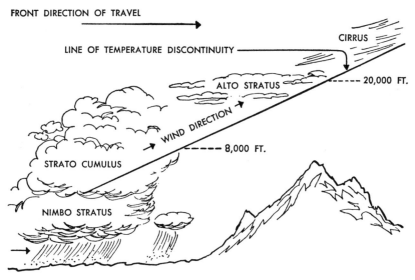

Fig. 130. Warm front.

An advancing warm mass rides up and over its rival, ground friction retarding retreat of cold air. Because of this long forward lean and a relatively-slow speed of about 15 miles per hour a *warm front* gives plentiful warning of its approach. The high frontal clouds appear perhaps hundreds of miles and 12–24 hours in advance, gradually succeeded by middle and low clouds.

The first signals are scattered wisps of cirrus, changing into cirrostratus and then into a leaden altostratus. The cloud level steadily descends, precipitation beginning from altostratus and continuing from nimbostratus.

When the barometer levels off or even rises slightly (altimeter drops slightly) the warm front has passed. Winds shift to the south or southwest, rain ceases, and perhaps fog envelops the area. The period between the warm front and the following cold front may range from a few minutes to as much as 24 hours. There may be time for a summit trip in generally cloudy, warm weather, but one must not be surprised if the cold front instantaneously succeeds the warm.

A *cold front* wedges under warmer air, ground friction slowing the under portion so that its upper part topples forward. This steep leading edge means a cold front gives little advance warning, but on the other hand has a relatively-narrow zone of turbulence. A cold front moves rapidly, an average of 20 miles per hour the year around but sometimes twice that speed in winter.

A swift cold front can come virtually unannounced, and the steepness of the leading edge with the consequent abrupt lifting of warm air can produce terrible violence seemingly from a clear sky. Scrambling along a sunny arete a party feels a sudden gust of cold wind from the south or southwest. The altimeter shows a sharp gain in elevation, meaning the air pressure is dropping. Glancing to the west or northwest (the most common but by no means invariable directions) they note altocumulus clouds—perhaps towering abruptly into cumulonimbus. If in addition there is stratus seeping swiftly up the valleys the prospect is very bad indeed. If lucky they feel a few spatters of rain, hear the rumbles of distant thunder, and watch black clouds pass by and vanish beyond the horizon. If unlucky they may be drenched by rain and swept by gales and blasted by lightning. When the front arrives over them the altimeter gives its highest reading (meaning the pressure is lowest), the rain continues in bursts, and also the wind—which however quickly shifts to west or north. The weather now improves rapidly, the winds steady, the temperature and altimeter drop. Cumulus or stratocumulus may persist for hours or days but without major threat. Good weather ordinarily follows for at least a few days—unless there is another cell spinning in on the heels of the first.

A swift cold front may be preceded by a *squall line* when both overtaken and overtaking air masses are moving rapidly in the same direction, thus retarding efforts of displaced warm air to rise out of the way. In such a case the front itself may be an area of relative peace while 100 to 200 miles in the van is a solid line of towering clouds. Some of the worst thunderstorms and tornadoes are thus born. The squall line at other times is feeble compared to the frontal storms. Scattered showers and rumbles of thunder in the morning may be followed by encouraging sunshine and perplexing clouds; assuming the front has passed a party continues upward, discovering its error when the front proper arrives.

When a warm front is overtaken by its pursuing cold front, producing an *occluded front,* the warm air mass is lifted bodily off the ground. Warm-front weather is closely followed by cold-front weather, the two sometimes mixing all together in a general hellish uproar. On the other hand, occlusion is a symptom that the low-pressure cell is fading away. An alarming display of clouds may have absolutely no evil consequences.

Stationary fronts are those which remain in one place. The weather is that of a warm front, not violently bad but just steadily miserable for hours or days at a time. On occasion a party will go despondently to bed seeing cirrus overhead and more ominous clouds in the distance, and be pleasantly surprised to arise in a clear morning—the front holding its position on the horizon, causing continuous despondency to climbers underneath it.

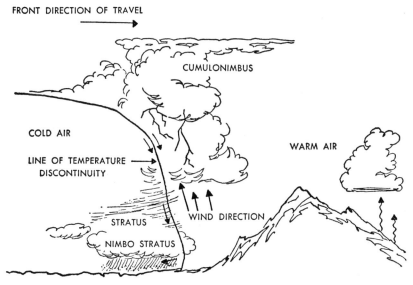

FRONT DIRECTION OF TRAVEL

CUMULONIMBUS

COLD AIR

LINE OF TEMPERATURE DISCONTINUITY

WARM AIR

STRATUS

WIND DIRECTION

NIMBO STRATUS

Fig. 131. Cold front.

Two air masses with identical characteristics of temperature and moisture in meeting merge together without any fuss. Rarely does this happen but often the difference is so small that the resulting *weak front* is noted only by meteorologists. Others with a bit more strength may fill mountaineers with foreboding but follow up the threat with only trivial scraps of weather or none at all.

Identification of a front is rarely easy. A warm front faster than average is quite similar in cloud symptoms to a cold front slower than average. Occlusions and local distortions further confuse the issue. In maritime mountain regions such as the Pacific Northwest fronts classically and unmistakably well-defined are uncommon.

UPPER-LEVEL LOWS

The primary weather producer in the Pacific Northwest during late spring and early summer—and sometimes troublesome throughout the summer—is the *upper-level low (cold low aloft* or *upper trough)*, a pool of cold air at 10,000 feet or higher which generates much cloudiness and considerable rain, particularly in the mountains. Systems of this type often exist without any indication of ground-surface fronts; in fact, the surface pressure frequently is high. They usually move very slowly, causing poor weather for days or even weeks at a time. Their locations are customarily mentioned by the Weather Bureau in its summaries, allowing the climber to plan accordingly; however, they tend to be capricious, behaving in a completely unexpected and unpredicted manner.

Small-Scale Weather: Mountains

Air mass weather sweeps over lowlands and mountains alike. The location and progress of large-scale masses are plotted by the U. S. Weather Bureau. Nowadays the best way to learn the overall situation in advance of a trip is by viewing a television report based on Weather Bureau data, a regular evening feature in most parts of the United States and often given so intelligibly in terms of highs, lows, and fronts that with a minimum of theoretical background anyone can quickly become a better-than-average amateur weather-guesser. Once removed from civilization an informed party can make some crude guesses about air mass movements by observation of clouds and winds.

AIR MASS DISTORTION

It is by no means true that all the bad weather comes from fronts. The meeting of air masses causes turbulence, but so also does the meeting of air with earth. An air mass moving over ground colder than itself is *stable;* being cooled at the bottom the bottom air is heavy and stays at the bottom. An air mass moving over ground warmer than itself is *unstable;* the bottom air is heated and rises through the colder upper layers, the resulting turbulence symptomized by cumulus-family clouds.

Local features such as mountains induce vertical currents that are quickly suppressed by a stable mass. The existing currents of an already-unstable mass are exaggerated. In lowland parks and patios the city population may be enjoying gracious living under blue skies dotted with pretty white cumulus billows while in a nearby mountain range climbing parties are suffering seventeen species of tempest: the foothills of the Cascades receive as much as five times the annual rainfall at sealevel several dozen miles distant.

A mountain range forms an obstacle in the path of an air mass, which thus must rise to cross. Atmospheric pressure decreases with altitude so that the mass expands. Any gas in expansion cools. Descending on the other side the air compresses, and again obeying the Gas Laws, warms. This *adiabatic* cooling and warming amounts to about 5½° F. per thousand feet of elevation gained or lost if the air is cloud-free; foggy or cloudy air warms (or cools) about 3° F. per thousand feet. The cooling on the windward slope may cause condensation of vapor into clouds and probably precipitation, a process that releases heat and thus subtracts from the effect of adiabatic cooling. On the lee slope the warming effect quickly dispels clouds. Quite frequently in a coastal range such as the Cascades an air mass moving east makes clouds and rains on the western slope while east of the divide the atmosphere is clear. The division often is dramatically abrupt, a few hundred feet marking the transition between drizzling fog and bright sunshine. Because of this leeward warming there is always on the average less cloudiness and less precipitation in the *rain shadow*. The Sequim prairie leeward of the Olympic Range has less than 15 inches of annual precipitation, compared with nearly 200 inches on Mount Olympus 25 miles away.

Another striking effect of adiabatic warming is the *Chinook wind* common on the east slopes of the Cascades and Rockies, where one moment the citizens of valley towns are ploughing through powder snow bundled up against the zero temperature and an hour later are sweltering as they wade through slush. There is on record a temperature rise of 43° in 15 minutes. In the Alps this wind is called the *foehn;* ski mountaineers on a high tour are stricken with terror by a sudden rush of warm air, knowing they are trapped on slopes that however solidly frozen will in minutes be roaring with avalanches.

Frontal movements are frequently distorted by mountains, particularly when the front is small in scale compared to the barrier. A cold front may be trapped against the windward slope and hang stationary there for days, perhaps being overtaken by a warm front which rides up and over the range.

The irregularity of a mountain range tends to break up a front, especially the narrow turbulence zone of a cold one. Instead of advancing in a solid line it may surge forward up a deep valley while held stationary by a high massif, this bulge perhaps being attacked by flanking air—little squalls breaking off and wandering about apparently at random. A party on one peak may experience lightning, hail, driving snow, pouring rain, and calm sunshine all within the space of an hour. On a nearby peak another party may spend the entire day undisturbed by so much as a drop of rain, using up all their camera film shooting the superb cloud structures.

Differential ground friction in the coiling mountain contours causes *mechanical turbulence* that obscures general weather patterns. At high altitudes air motion is more nearly normal; ground winds and low clouds therefore mean little compared to motion of upper clouds. A summit significantly higher than its neighbors thrusts up into this main-line air. For hundreds of miles around the atmosphere may be clear, yet 14,410-foot Mount Rainier be wearing a *cloud cap*. Just as a boulder jutting into a smoothly-flowing river sets up a series of waves downstream, so the windstream leeward of the peak dips up and down. If air is near the dew point even such small ripples produce a cloud banner that may stretch dozens of miles downwind, the frequent lenticular shape suggesting a wavelike motion. A cloud cap has an ugly look from below but it is not necessarily a storm, being sometimes

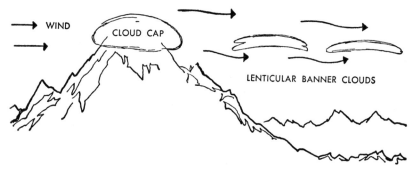

Fig. 132. Cloud cap.

merely a cold blowing fog. It is in any event a clue to upper air movements and usually is the first warning of instability and thus a change in the weather.

LOCAL WINDS AND CELLS

Processes that operate on global and continental dimensions have similar effects miniature in scale. *Convection* at the equator starts the atmosphere circulating; convection is also responsible for many local winds. On a coast, for instance, the land heats faster under sunlight than water—as air rises vertically over the land a horizontal sea breeze moves in to equalize pressure. At night, land cools faster, and a land breeze blows. A mountain (mainly without snowcover) warms faster in the daytime than a valley and cools more quickly at night, so that (without snowcover) the daytime breeze is upslope, the night breeze downslope.

Similarly, two adjacent valleys, one opening west to the afternoon sun, the other north to no sun at all, are unequally heated, and dense air from the cold valley spills over into the heated valley. Spillage always intensifies at low points in the barrier, which is why passes are drafty.

A *local low* may develop under a cumulonimbus, the violent updrafts sucking air from the surface, surrounding air rushing in with the typical counterclockwise spin. A good many of the busy squalls that rove around the mountains without any seeming relevance originate in this way.

A *heat low* is a subspecies native to any area warmed intensely relative to its surroundings. "Dust devils" are the smallest and most amusing of the family. There is no humor in their big cousins born over arid plains adjacent to mountain ranges, for commonly the resulting thunderheads drift over the summits. Lightning in the summer afternoon is almost axiomatic in the Tetons, and very frequent on the east slopes of the Cascades, adjacent to the Columbia Plateau. Hot, settled weather in the Puget Sound Trough inevitably sucks in moist air from the ocean (*on-shore flow*), with resulting breezes, clouds, rain, or even thunder. Lastly, a dry mountain range can itself be the villain, building over itself its own heat lows and thunderheads regularly every good afternoon.

FOG

A cloud riding against the ground is fog and fog launching into atmosphere is a cloud. A good many fogs are the lower extensions of clouds, generated by contact of two air masses. Others derive from air-to-ground contact.

Sea fog is familiar not only to beachwalkers but to those who climb in coastal ranges. When warm, moist air from the ocean is pushed or pulled over relatively-colder land there is fog. Stable air masses that move in from the Pacific bringing fair weather to the Northwest often bring fog to the coast that may push up valleys into the mountains. A heat low in the Puget Sound Trough can suck fog all the way into the Cascades.

Upslope or *adiabatic fog* is typically a "good-weather" fog indicating a stable air mass. In the maritime ranges of Western America it commonly forms in the evening, the upslope daytime winds continuing while the mountains rapidly cool. By seeing it come at night climbers can predict fine weather for tomorrow's climb even though by morning it resembles a leaden stratus.

Radiation or *ground fog* generates on ground cooled by radiation until air temperature descends to the dew point. A clear night sky expedites cooling, and stagnant air is ideal. Commonly ground fogs rise from moist surfaces such as snowfields and rain-soaked meadows on a clear night after a cloudy day. Though an obvious good-weather fog, it may pile deep enough in a high valley to darken the dawn.

Steam fog is more picturesque than meaningful. The usual source is cold air moving into a warm wet surface such as a lake and then sitting there. Surface-warmed humid air rises into colder air, moisture falls out constantly, forming a dense fog a few feet thick.

The oft-mentioned *dew point is not necessarily the condensation point.* Before fog or clouds can develop, the vapor must have preexisting particles upon which to condense. Usually there is enough dust in the atmosphere so that when the dew point is reached condensation instantly takes place, but very clean air may become super-cooled—cooled below the dew point without condensation. The sudden intrusion of foreign particles causes dramatically-rapid condensation. Falling rain may generate fog in previously-clear lower air. Surface features often provide nuclei for vapor. If the temperature is above freezing, *dew* forms on grass at night; below freezing, *frost.* Raindrops and snowflakes are microscopic at birth, merging during turbulence into droplets progressively larger, finally becoming heavy enough for gravity to overcome the buoyancy of air. A continued fog eventually initiates a descending mist, a "good-weather" rain that gets people and rock wet but is not to be feared: a party can always climb above it if the mountains are high enough.

LIGHTNING

The lightning of fronts and approaching desert lows often gives plentiful audio-visual warning. When a huge stratospheric anvil is seen and heard approaching it is indubitably time to go home right away. A distant rank of active black cumulus clouds tending suddenly to boil up and become noisy is another sure indication valleys are preferable to peaks. However, all too often an electrical storm is unpredictable, evidence being obscured by local clouds or mountains. A party climbing the west ridge of a peak may reach the summit in a dead heat with a thunderhead from the eastern desert, or may be on the very peak that is the birthplace of turbulence. There is an inevitable calculated risk. On an otherwise fine day a weak front may develop one sickly squall that staggers about aimlessly, discharging an infrequent bolt. The odds against its striking one peak among hundreds may be nearly infinitesimal, but one properly-aimed bolt, however puny, is too much.

An important aid in outguessing lightning is the fact light waves travel immensely faster than sound waves. Lightning is for all practical purposes seen instantaneously; the thunder arrives later, covering about 1100 feet per second or roughly 1 mile in 5 seconds. By counting at ordinary conversational speed "one thousand and one, one thousand

and two, etc.," distance of the bolt can be estimated. If a count starts at the flash and reaches five before the thunder, the strike was about a mile away. A long count is not of itself cause for confidence. One discharge may be 8 miles away, but 8 vertical miles at the top of a thunderhead, and the very next one may be at the bottom of the cloud, with no count at all. The general rule is that when the average length of count steadily decreases there is reason for concern.

Though not one of the principle perils of mountaineering, lightning and related electrical discharges have caused a number of serious—and

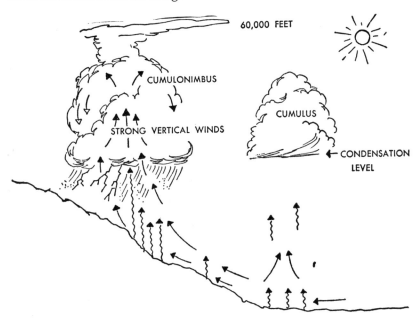

Fig. 133. Thunderstorm development.

mostly avoidable—accidents. The very nature of their sport places climbers on or near the most frequent targets: peaks and ridges help produce the vertical updrafts and raincloud conditions which generate lightning; the prominences serve to trigger the strokes. The climber therefore should understand the basic mechanisms involved and fix in his mind the fundamentals of evasive action.

For all practical purposes the hazards arc three: (1) a direct strike; (2) ground currents; and (3) in the immediate vicinity of a strike, induced currents.

Causes and Nature of Lightning

Electrical potential builds up in a cloud in somewhat the same manner one's body picks up a charge on a dry day. Scuffing the feet across a carpet separates positive and negative charges. The positive charges remain behind on the carpet; the body retains a surplus of negative charges which may amount to a potential difference of several thousand volts with respect to a nearby object, such as a door knob—and thus that sudden stinging "zap." The exact procedure by which the separation of charges develops is unknown. A vertical updraft caused by a mountain slope may sometimes be a factor, and the moving edge of a warm or cold front another. Whatever the mechanism, when *electrical pressures* (voltage differences) become great enough a discharge takes place between parts of a cloud, from one cloud to another, from earth to cloud, or from cloud to earth. The following discussion is confined to the latter case, which has most interest for climbers.

Air is normally a very poor conductor (good insulator) of electricity; trees, rock, or earth are better conductors, more so when wet; the human body is still better; and most metals are best of all. Lightning seeks the path of least total resistance between the cloud and earth—the shortest possible line through the air. Ordinarily the closest ground point is directly below the cloud, but a summit off to one side can be closer and become the bull's-eye.

Air ceases to be a good insulator when subjected to a sufficiently-high electrical pressure; it *ionizes* and thereupon loses its insulating quality and becomes a conductor. The ionizing breakdown around a conducting projection often gives off a crackling noise (notorious in the Alps as the "buzzing of the bees") caused by small sparks. The distinctive odor of ozone is usually noted. A bluish glow or *corona* (St. Elmo's Fire) may be seen. If a person's head is the projection, the hair (if any) crackles and stands on end. Corona discharges have often been observed when the nearest cloud seemed too far away to be at all relevant.

The sound or sight of corona does not necessarily indicate danger, but lacking more precise indication should be regarded as a warning, especially when thunderclouds are nearby. Additionally, any atmospheric activity symptomatic of commotion should stir suspicion. A sudden rush of cold air perhaps announces a strong cold front with possible lightning. A cloudburst of enormous raindrops or monster snowflakes or huge hail almost certainly means a cumulonimbus is overhead.

Personal Hazards and Protective Measures

Lightning is, of course, electricity, which is a stream of electrons. When the more than 100 billion billion electrons in an average bolt strike a peak or a tree they don't just lie there in a puddle, but immediately spread out in all directions. In the process considerable damage can result. Two factors determine the extent of human injury: the quantity of current, and the part of the body affected.

The worst threat is the passage of electricity *through* the body in a way to impair some vital function such as heart, brain, or breathing action. A current from one hand to the other through the heart and lungs, or from head to foot through virtually all organs, is most dangerous, even if relatively small; one can survive a larger current from one foot to the other through the legs.

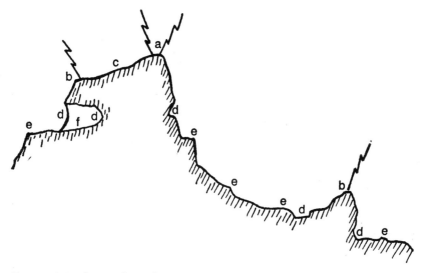

Fig. 134. Lightning hazard.
      a. Frequent strikes—extremely hazardous.
      b. Occasional strikes—hazardous.
      c. Preferable to a or b.
      d. Danger from ground currents.
      e. Relatively safe.
      f. Large cave. Relatively safe away from
         walls and entrance.

The climber faces other potential hazards: large currents can cause deep burns at points of entry and exit; a mild shock may momentarily startle him or set off muscular spasms, or he may move about in semiconsciousness, and in either case may fall off a cliff.

First thought should be given to avoiding areas which might be hit. The governing rule is to seek a location with nearby projections or masses which are somewhat closer than one's own head to any clouds which may drift by. In a forest the safest shelter is amid the shorter trees. The middle of a ridge is preferable to the ends; avoid shoulders.

Based on conclusions reached by engineers while developing lightning rods and other protective devices, the best spot is the vicinity of a prominent point, such as a rock spire. According to the engineers' theory, if one's line of sight to the top of a pinnacle or ridge is at an angle of 45 degrees or steeper, he should be completely safe from a direct strike: a conducting point will divert to itself any possible bolts within a cone-like zone of protection radiating downward at a 45-degree angle.

An important word of contrary advice must be emphasized. Other hazards, such as heavy ground currents or flying splinters from a shattered tree, decree that one should not be *too* close to the strike. Exactly what is a safe or dangerous distance is difficult to suggest. Since the terrain is a factor, results from studies of lightning rods cannot be directly related to other promontories; obviously there have been no high-voltage laboratory experiments involving human bodies on a pile of rocks. However, the available evidence indicates that a distance less than 60 feet is extremely dangerous, 100 feet is marginal, and more than 100 feet is relatively safe from the bolt, though ground currents remain a threat.

An electrical discharge at a strike point instantly radiates outward and downward, with the intensity of the flow, and consequently the danger to climbers, decreasing rapidly as the distance from the strike increases. On firm rock, especially when wet, the major path in most cases is along the surface. Lichen patches, cracks, or soil may hold moisture and thus also provide easy paths. High-voltage currents tend to jump across short gaps, as in a sparkplug, rather than take a longer path around.

Current flows because of a voltage difference between two points along its path. A person bridging two such points with some part of his body presents a second, and probably better, path for the current, some portion of which is therefore diverted through his body. The wider the span the greater is the voltage difference and the greater the flow through the body.

With this brief background, several precepts not previously covered can be listed:

1. Avoid moist areas, including crevices and gulleys.

2. Span as small a distance (occupy as little area) as possible. Keep the feet close together; keep the hands off the ground.

3. Sit, crouch, or stand on insulated objects if possible—a coiled rope or a sleeping bag, preferably dry.

4. Stay out of small depressions; choose instead a narrow slight rise. A small detached rock on a scree slope is excellent.

5. Stay away from overhangs and out of small caves. Large caves are

very good if one keeps clear of the walls and entrance. However, a cave might well be the lower terminus of a drainage crevice leading upward, and in such case should be avoided.

6. When on a ledge, crouch at the outer edge, hopefully at least 4 feet from the rock wall. If there is danger of falling off in event of a shock, tie in *crosswise* to the prospective flow of current. Make the tie short and avoid placing rope under the armpits.

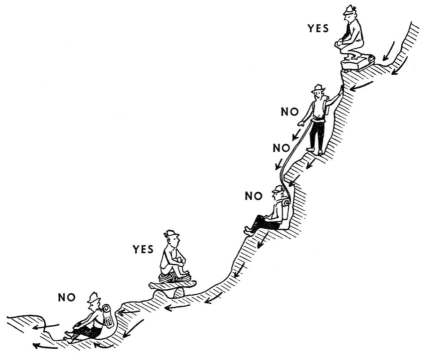

Fig. 135. Body position and location for relative safety from electrical ground currents. (Arrows indicate probable paths of flow.)

7. Rappelling when lightning is imminent should be avoided, but may be a valid calculated risk if it is the quickest way to escape a danger zone. Dry synthetic rope presents the minimum hazard.

8. Contrary to popular belief, metal objects do not attract lightning as such. However, in the immediate vicinity of a strike, metals in contact with one's person may augment the hazard from *induced currents*, the nature and mechanism of which lie beyond the limits of the present discussion. Induced currents usually are quite small, but when added to ground currents may mean the difference between life and death. Thus, it is best to set aside all metals, but to keep them

close by (don't worry about articles buried in the pack). A metal pack frame might well be positioned to provide a more attractive path for ground currents beside and past one's body. At distances greater than 100 feet from a possible strike there is no need to divest oneself of metal objects.

9. For first aid procedures when a companion is subjected to electrical shock, refer to Chapter 18.

FORECASTING

Meteorologists admit the science is young, and even with elaborate apparatus more often than not make predictions in terms of probability. A mountaineer can scarcely expect to do better. However, knowledge of the principles of weather-making combined with active curiosity and long experience allow a climber to narrow the range of possibilities. Consulting the Weather Bureau before a trip gives basic background about air mass movements and a general idea of what to watch for.

Once in the mountains evidence is confused. The meaning of clouds and winds is obscure, perhaps indicative of air mass weather, perhaps caused by purely local conditions. Weather signs, their causes previously discussed, have some limited value even in the mountains.

If the weather is clear it will generally remain so when: barometer remains steady or rises (altimeter drops); wind is steady and gentle from west or northwest; there are no clouds, or only scattered cumulus clouds in the afternoon; fogs burn off early in the day.

Precipitation may occur when: barometer drops (altimeter rises); a north wind shifts to west and then south; a south wind freshens while clouds move in from the west; a ring around the moon is succeeded in the morning by cirrus clouds that thicken and are followed by successively-lower clouds; the west is black; cumulus swells into cumulonimbus.

Clearing weather generally comes when: the barometer rises (altimeter drops); winds shift from south to west to north; cloud bases rise steadily.

The "habit of the locality" and the "habit of the season" often are helpful even to those without the least pretension to understanding air masses and gas laws. The monsoon of the Himalaya and the afternoon thunderstorm of the Tetons are familiar examples. A climber visiting an unfamiliar range does well to interrogate oldtimers about such matters lest he make drastic errors interpreting—for instance—Selkirk weather by Cascade lore.

Weather-guessing in the mountains is a chancy business at best. Even a climber who is also a professional meteorologist with years of local wisdom may after hours of shrewd observation and deep cerebration be able only to say: "Friends, it is now raining." A sound standard rule is always to hike into camp, and always to leave camp in the morning, however bad the conditions. High winds may be merely transfer of air from one valley to the next. Deep gloom and a drizzle may be nothing more than good-weather fog. Once high on the peak, but before the start of difficulties, is time to make the decision. By then the evidence ordinarily is clarified.

Climbers whose home hills have a great deal of assorted weather grow quickly bored in ranges more stable. The climbing environment has three layers—rock, snow, and weather—each of which contributes to the complexity and challenge. Without weather the sport would be less interesting.

APPENDIX 1

FOOD REQUIREMENTS
FOR CLIMBERS

Energy Expenditure in the Mountains

CLIMBING is one of the more strenuous human activities and demands a great deal more energy than the average everyday occupation. The increased food requirement can be calculated approximately by considering the body in its role as a machine.

In city or mountains or wherever, each individual expends a certain amount of energy merely breathing and circulating the blood and otherwise carrying on basic life processes. This *basal metabolism* uses about one "large" calorie per kilogram of body weight per hour, or approximately 1100 large calories per 100 pounds of body weight per day. (The "large" calorie is the unit of food calculations, equivalent to 1000 "small" calories—the latter being the amount of energy needed to raise a gram of water 1°C. in temperature. Throughout this discussion the calorie mentioned is the large one.) The rate of basal metabolism varies with height, age, sex, race, altitude, and other factors, but in relatively-insignificant degree. To find the energy requirements for a climb, the amount used to do external work is added to the basal rate.

The activities in Table 14 are those of "irreversible work," done against friction. Lifting the body to higher elevations is theoretically "reversible work," since the potential energy of the body is increased. Unfortunately the body is incapable of utilizing this potential energy on a descent (except in the undesirable way of falling) and indeed must work to climb down a mountain, though nowhere near so hard as in climbing up. The efficiency of the body in doing work over and above basal metabolism varies from 20 to 40 per cent. Assuming an average value of 30 per cent efficiency, the *energy needed to raise 100 pounds 1000 feet of elevation is about 110 calories.*

Table 14. Energy Rate Over and Above Basal Metabolism.

Activity	Calories Per Hour Per 100 Pounds of Body Weight
Walking 2 mph (on smooth level pavement)	45
Walking 3 mph (" " " ")	90
Walking 4 mph (" " " ")	160
Eating	20
Sitting quietly	20
Driving an automobile	40
Sawing wood	260
Swimming 2 mph	360
Rowing in race	730
Shivering	up to 220

Source: Carpenter, T. M., Tables, Factors, and Formulas for Computing Respiratory Exchange and Biological Transformations of Energy. Carnegie Institute, Washington, D. C., 1939.

The final factor in calculating energy requirements is the *specific dynamic action,* or "SDA." During metabolism from 6 to 10 per cent of the calorie content of food is released as heat, and thus is not available for doing work.

Table 15. Estimated Daily Energy Expenditure of 170-Pound Man at Office Job.

Activity	Calories Per Hour	Hours	Total
Basal metabolism (1100 x 1.7)			1870
Eating	34	1.5	50
Driving automobile	70	1.0	70
Working	90	8.0	720
Leisure and miscellaneous	40	5.5	220
Subtotal			2930
SDA (7% of subtotal)			200
Total			3130

Using such methods the energy expenditure on any proposed trip can be roughly calculated, and thus the food requirements. The "roughly" must be emphasized, since even professional nutritionists vary somewhat in their findings. The standard ration of the United States Army is 4500 calories for strenuous work, 3500 for garrison duty. R. W. Gerard, in *Food for Life*, University of Chicago Press, 1952,

Table 16. Estimated Energy Expenditure of 170-Pound Man Climbing Mount Olympus in Washington State.

To simplify calculation it is assumed the pack weighs uniformly 30 pounds throughout, making a constant total of 200 pounds. The walking energy rate from Table 14 is thus multiplied by a factor of 2. In addition it is multiplied by a factor of 1.5 to correct for rough trail. This factor may be several times larger for bushwhacking, boulder-hopping, snow-slogging, etc.

Activity	Calories Per Hour	Hours	Total
Day No. 1			
Basal metabolism			1870
Eating	34	1.5	50
Driving (Seattle to road end)	70	6	420
Hike from Jackson Guard Sta. to Elk Lake			
15 miles @ 3 mph	270	5	1350
1600 ft. elevation gain			350
Pack, unpack, make camp, etc.	100	3	300
Subtotal			4340
SDA			300
Total			4640
Day No. 2			
Basal metabolism			1870
Eating	34	1.5	50
Hike from Elk Lake to summit and return			
14 miles @ 2 mph	135	7	950
5400 ft. elevation gain			1190
Side trips, camp chores, etc.	100	6	600
Subtotal			4660
SDA			330
Total			4990
Day No. 3			
Basal metabolism			1870
Eating	34	1.5	50
Hike to car	270	5	1350
Driving	70	6	420
Pack, unpack, etc.	100	3	300
Subtotal			3990
SDA			280
Total			4270

estimates that general factory work requires about 3000 to 4000 calories daily. The Juneau Ice Field Research Project, in various reports published by the American Geographical Society, 1949–51, tells of several differing dietary experiments; on one trip it was later calculated that the average intake per man had been 4085 calories per day.

Composition of Foods

The three major food components are proteins, fats, and carbohydrates. Each provides energy, but also other essential values more-or-less understood at present. In addition the undigestible portion, the pure bulk, has a function. No less important are the trace quantities of vitamins and minerals needed for various vital body processes. All must be supplied in approximately the right amounts to maintain health of body and mind.

PROTEINS

Proteins are broken down in the digestive process into their constituent amino acids which are in turn recombined by the body to make new proteins, such as muscles and other body tissue. Animal proteins such as meat, milk, cheese, and eggs are called "complete" because they yield exactly the amino acids in the exactly-correct proportion the system requires. Cereals such as wheat and oats and legumes such as peas and beans yield varying amounts of amino acids, though their proteins are "incomplete," lacking several amino acids. However, the addition of a little milk or cheese renders vegetable proteins "complete," the combination supplying all essential amino acids.

Protein requirement per day is nearly constant regardless of activity. The body steadily renews itself, replacing old muscles. Hard work does not accelerate the process, which continues at the same rate during sedentary office work and violent manual labor. The recommended daily allowance is 70 grams of protein, at least half of it *complete*, distributed over the entire day. The body cannot utilize its entire daily requirement at any one meal; amino acids in excess of what can be immediately used, and "incomplete" groups of amino acids, are not stored. Having been rejected for tissue-building purposes they are converted into fuel or stored as fat.

FATS

Fats are used primarily for energy, but also supply the fat-soluble vitamins. In addition there are certain unsaturated fats with an imperfectly-understood but apparently-vital function. It is recommended that a minimum of 20 to 25 per cent of the total calories be supplied by fat. Major sources are meat fats, butter, margarine, cheese, egg yolks, and nuts.

CARBOHYDRATES

Carbohydrates supply nothing but energy but in a form so easily used that most nutritionists recommend their use for half the caloric intake. Carbohydrates include all sugars, starches, and celluloses, found in cereals, legumes, milk, vegetables, fruits, bakery goods, and candy. Only sugars and starches are digestible by man. Cellulose is digested by the browsing animals but in man passes through the system chemically unchanged, providing bulk, or roughage, in many people seemingly necessary for regular elimination.

VITAMINS

Vitamins yield enzymes which catalyze various chemical reactions and physiological processes. The quantities required are small, but when lacking, deficiency diseases result. Vitamins are broadly classified as to their solubility in fat or water, which determines their source. The principal fat-soluble vitamins are A, D, E, and K. The water-soluble vitamins include the B complex and C, found in cereals, vegetables, fruit, and meat both fresh and dehydrated. The fright-propaganda of proprietary drug manufacturers notwithstanding, any ordinary balanced diet supplies enough of all of these. However, body storage of water-soluble vitamins is slight, and though deficiency diseases such as scurvy and beriberi are unlikely to afflict a climbing party, the earlier symptoms of deficiency can occur, such as irritability and mental depression. Thus on any long trip with a diet possibly unbalanced, the carrying of vitamin pills should be considered.

MINERALS

The mineral parts of food include salts of calcium, phosphorus, iron, sodium, copper, chlorine, and a host of other elements, some of whose functions are unknown. All are water-soluble and thus provided by meats, vegetables, and fruits, and in sufficient amount by a balanced diet.

Metabolism

The mechanism of food usage by the body is extremely complex and not completely understood in detail. All food on digestion contributes to the common metabolic pool. The amino acids needed to build tissue are extracted, the remainder after a further digestive process being contributed to the fuel supply, which also includes the derivatives of carbohydrates and fat. Some of the fuel is used for immediate needs. Some is converted into glycogen, a starch that is stored in small quantities in the liver and muscles and converted to glucose for fuel on quick demand. The remainder is manufactured into body fat for long-term storage.

The end-products of food oxidation for energy are water and carbon dioxide and lactic acid. During hard work these accumulate while fuel dissipates, resulting in weariness. The function of rest is to allow blood and lungs to remove end-products and replenish oxygen and fuel.

Heat is a byproduct of work. Virtually all the energy of basal metabolism and specific dynamic action is converted ultimately to heat. Since the body is on the average only 30 per cent efficient in using its "work calories," the remaining 70 per cent are also converted to heat. Together these maintain body temperature. Excessive heat released by metabolism, SDA, and work is dispersed by perspiration. During inactivity in cold weather, metabolism and SDA may not supply enough heat; when the lower limit of the thermostat is touched the body sets the muscles to shivering.

CONDITIONING

During exercise the body improves its capacity for exercise. Metabolism becomes more efficient, the blood moving more rapidly to carry waste products away from the muscles and bring them new fuel. Glycogen storage is increased slightly, and also the speed of its conversion into energy. The harder a person works today the harder he can work tomorrow.

Before bursts of extreme and extraordinary exertion a simple life is best. How a person feels on a strenuous weekend climb depends partly on how hard he worked on the previous weekend—but also very largely on what he has been doing during the week. A well-balanced regular diet with steady moderate exercise and plenty of rest puts the system in finest tuning. Exotic foods and irregularity of meals and rest upset body chemistry and reduce physical performance for hours or days.

During the climb itself the only physiological requirements are energy and water. Theoretically, then, the most efficient diet during the period of heavy work is sugar and water—and indeed some mountaineers go hours at a time on fruit juice and candy. For various reasons cited herein fats and proteins are generally consumed in addition. Whatever the components, all meals immediately before and during a climb should either be small or be followed by a long rest. The blood cannot serve two masters, lungs and stomach; attempting to set a vigorous pace just after a feast causes rubbery legs or stomach upset or both.

FREQUENCY OF MEALS

Carbohydrates are most rapidly and efficiently converted into energy, and thus starches and sugars most immediately replenish the fuel supply. The rapidity of conversion, however, means that a diet high in carbohydrates requires frequent meals, as many as eight a day.

Proteins and fats are most slowly digested but release their energy over a longer period of time. An egg at breakfast contributes nothing to an energetic start but steadily helps the forenoon struggle. Similarly, peanut butter at noon powers the making of camp at sunset, and Goteborg at supper makes it possible to rise on the morrow. The body can adjust to very infrequent meals when the fat and protein content of the diet is high. Arctic explorers such as Vilhjalmur Stefansson consider one meal a day ample, and only two meals a week no excessive hardship.

Hunger pangs are symptomatic of an empty stomach, not of an empty energy reservoir, since there may still be ample body fat available. Even in the person of average weight this reserve is sufficient to sustain a high level of activitiy for several days; fasts as long as a month have been made without lasting body damage. During transition from a city diet high in bulk to a relatively-concentrated mountain diet it is well to endure mild hunger for a few days while the stomach shrinks; attempting to fill up on concentrated foods leads to obesity, or even illness. Extreme hunger is of course unpleasant, and to be avoided. A meal of carbohydrates passes entirely out of the stomach in 1 or 2 hours, while a meal high in fat remains as long as 6 or 7 hours. Bulk in the stomach gives a feeling of satisfaction; foods high in fat and protein "stick to the ribs."

From what has been said, obviously the optimum frequency of meals depends on the kind of food eaten. In addition there are great variations between individuals. Some people work best on almost constant intake of carbohydrates. Others attain top performance with one or two meals a day, high in fat and protein. Every climber should experimentally establish his own best frequency, and limits of variation. Most parties achieve the greatest happiness of the greatest number by planning only the main evening meal in common, letting adherents of the three-squares-per-day and the one-square-plus-constant-nibbles factions adjust the remainder of the diet to individual needs.

FOOD EFFICIENCY

On a short outing the ratio of calories to pounds scarcely merits consideration, since even with pure carbohydrates (with no water) 2½ pounds per day suffices, a weight relatively small compared to that of equipment. Most overloading of the commissary comes simply from carrying more food than necessary to satisfy energy requirements of the trip. Another key consideration is choosing foods low in water content, either naturally or through processing. The majority of mountains are quite liberally endowed with liquid resources, and it is pointless to backpack water long distances. Similar objections can be raised to hauling excess metal in the form of cans.

Table 17. Energy Values of Food.

	Calories Per Gram	Calories Per Pound
Protein	4.0	1800
Fat	9.0	4100
Carbohydrate	4.0	1800

As is apparent from Table 17, an increased proportion of fats in the diet is very desirable on long backpacking trips. A single pound of pure fat very nearly supplies the daily energy requirement, though such a menu is undesirable for various physical and psychological reasons. However, the case of pemmican is instructive, and a climber would do well to read the works of Vilhjalmur Stefansson, including *The Friendly Arctic*, Macmillan, New York, 1953, and *Fat of the Land*, Macmillan, New York, 1956. Pemmican was invented by the Plains Indian, and used by him on long hunting and war expeditions. Adopted by the early fur traders it made possible the economic penetration of the West, and by a later generation, exploration of the Arctic. Pemmican is composed of equal parts of dried, powdered, lean meat and rendered fat, and despite denunciations by experts who have proved by formula that a man living on pemmican will surely waste away and die in a few weeks, ample testimony to the contrary is provided by the history of the fur trade and Arctic exploration, which cites innumerable instances of men working hard and healthily and happily many months at a time on no other food than pemmican. During World War II, theory and experience conflicted in a "Pemmican War," the worst result of which was the production by the U.S. Army of a fruit-nut confection libelously labelled "pemmican." Genuine pemmican is expensive and rare, but with it the traditional limit of approximately 2 weeks for a backpack trip without relaying supplies could be extended to 4 weeks, the equivalent weight being half that of a conventional high-carbohydrate diet.

The virtues of pemmican appear only on a long trip, since like any other unfamiliar diet it requires a period of adjustment. In general it is best for a climber to eat in the mountains approximately the way he does in everyday living to avoid the unpleasantness of physiological conversion. The psychological values of food thus are particularly important on short outings. There is no physical necessity for hot meals, leafy vegetables, spices, and sweets, but if the craving for them is not satisfied morale suffers. This has been most strikingly demonstrated on high-altitude expeditions, leading recent Himalayan parties to synthesize from processed foods, at considerable trouble and expense, a diet approximating the one to which the members are accustomed at home. Even during a week in the Cascades it is usually worthwhile to carry a few such luxuries; the food value may be small, but the contribution to pleasure immense.

Table 18. Values of Representative Mountaineering Foods.

Food	Energy Value	Composition of Edible Portion		
	Calories per ounce	% Protein	% Carbohydrate	% Fat
DAIRY PRODUCTS				
Butter	203	0.6	0.4	81.0
Margarine	204	0.6	0.4	81.0
Whole milk	18	3.5	4.9	3.9
Whole buttermilk	10	3.6	5.1	0.1
Malted milk, dry powdered	116	14.7	70.8	8.3
Milk, dry skim	103	35.8	51.6	0.7
Milk, dry whole	142	26.4	38.2	27.5
Milk, evaporated, unsweetened	39	7.0	9.7	7.9
Milk, condensed, sweetened	91	8.1	54.3	8.7
Cheese, cheddar	113	25.0	2.1	32.2
Cheese, Swiss	105	27.5	1.7	28.0
Cheese, processed	105	23.2	1.9	30.0
FRUITS				
Orange	10	1.0	12.2	Insignifi
Banana	16	1.1	22.2	cant in
Apple, raw	13	trace	12.0	most
Apple, dried	78	1.0	71.8	
Apple, dehydrated	100	1.4	92.1	
Apricot, dried, sulphured	74	5.0	66.5	
Avocado, fresh	49	1.8	5.6	16.7
Date, dried	78	2.2	72.9	
Fig, dried	78	4.3	69.1	
Peach, dried, sulphured	74	3.1	68.3	
Prune, dried	64	2.1	67.4	
Raisin	82	2.5	77.4	

APPENDIX 2

MEALS FOR

SEMI-EXPEDITIONS

Breakfast

Weights accurate to ¼ ounce. Greater error in the dry measure.

	One Serving		Four Servings	
	Ounces	Cups	Ounces	Cups
CEREALS				
...at Chex	2 to 2.5	1 crushed	8 to 10	4
...enuts } combined	{ 2	{ ½	{ 8	{ 2
...enut Flakes	{ .75	{ ¼ crushed	{ 3	{ 1
	2.75		11	
...ermuesli (Familia)	3.5 to 4	¾ to 1	14 to 16	3 to 4
...ereal food including				
...s and fruit. No sugar				
...ded.)				
...an	2 to 2.5		8 to 10	
...germ	.25 to .5		1 to 2	
...y be added to all)				
...hole	.75	¼	3	¾
...be premixed)				
...white granulated	1	2 TBL	4	½ plus
...be premixed)				
...REALS				
...of Wheat	1.5 to 1.75	3½ to 4 TBL	6 to 7	¾ to 1
...k-cooking)				
...Hearts	1.4 to 1.75	¼ to ⅓	5.5 to 7	1 to 1⅓
...Ralston	1.4 to 1.75	¼ to ⅓	5.5 to 7	1 to 1⅓

Food	Energy Value	Composition of Edible Portion		
	Calories per ounce	% Protein	% Carbo-hydrate	% Fat
FRUIT JUICES				
Apple	13	0.1	11.9	Insignifi-
Applesauce, sweetened	26	0.2	23.8	cant in
Grape	19	0.2	16.6	all
Grapefruit, sweetened	15	0.5	12.8	
Orange	14	0.7	10.4	
Pineapple	16	0.4	13.5	
Prune	22	0.4	19.0	
Tomato	5	0.9	4.3	
Lemon juice concentrate, frozen, unsweetened	33	2.3	37.4	
Orange concentrate, canned	63	4.1	50.7	
Lemonade concentrate, frozen	55	0.2	51.1	
Fruit cocktail, canned, in syrup	22	0.4	19.5	
VEGETABLES, DEHYDRATED				
Cabbage	87	14.4	72.5	Insignifi-
Carrot	97	6.6	81.1	cant in
Potato	100	8.3	80.4	all
Sweet potato	107	4.2	90.0	
Tomato flakes	97	10.8	76.7	
NUTS				
Almond	170	18.6	19.5	57.7
Brazil	185	14.3	10.9	66.9
Cashew	159	17.2	29.3	45.7
Coconut, dried, sweetened	155	3.6	53.2	39.1
Peanut butter	167	27.8	17.2	49.4
Peanut, roasted	165	26.0	18.8	49.8
Pecan	195	9.2	14.6	71.2
Walnut	159	14.8	15.8	64.0
GRAIN PRODUCTS				
Breakfast Cereals				
Bran flakes, 40%	85	10.7	82.1	3.6
Cornflakes	109	7.9	85.3	Insignifi-
Oatmeal, uncooked	110	15.0	78.5	cant in
Rice, puffed	113	6.0	89.5	most
Farina, enriched, uncooked	103	11.4	77.0	
Wheat, puffed	103	15.0	78.5	
Wheat, shredded	104	9.9	79.9	
Wheat germ	102	26.5	47.0	10.3

Table 18 (cont.)

Food	Energy Value	Composition of Edible Portion		
	Calories per ounce	% Protein	% Carbohydrate	% Fat
Other Grains, (Uncooked)				
Barley, pearl	99	8.4	78.8	Insignificant in all
Macaroni	105	12.5	75.2	
Noodles, egg	110	12.8	72.0	
Spaghetti	105	12.5	75.2	
Rice, brown, raw	102	7.5	77.4	
Rice, white, raw	103	6.7	80.4	
Rice, precooked	105	7.5	82.5	
Pancake mix, wheat	101	8.6	75.7	
Pancake mix, buckwheat	93	10.5	70.3	
Baked Goods				
Bread				
Rye	69	9.1	52.1	
White	77	8.7	50.5	
Pumpernickel	70	9.1	53.1	
Whole wheat	69	10.5	47.7	
Boston brown	60	5.5	45.6	
Cooky, sugar	126	6.0	68.0	16.8
Doughnut	111	4.6	51.4	18.6
Fig bar	101	3.9	75.4	5.6
Triscuit	125	12.0	?	?
Rye wafer	98	13.0	76.3	1.2
Logan bread, moist	100	7.0	60.0	10.0
Logan bread, dry	112	8.0	67.0	12.0
MEAT, FISH, EGGS				
Beef				
Corned, canned	75	23.5	0.0	18.0
Dried, chipped	58	34.3	0.0	6.3
Hamburger, cooked	81	24.2	0.0	20.3
Pork				
Bacon, lean, cooked	173	30.4	3.2	52.0
Bacon, Canadian, cooked	79	27.6	0.3	17.5
Bacon, canned	194	8.5	1.0	71.5
Ham, smoked	87	23.0	0.0	30.6
Fish				
Salmon, canned	43	20.8	0.0	7.1
Sardines in oil, drained	47	24.0	0.0	11.1
Tuna, canned, drained	47	28.8	0.0	8.2
Processed Products				
Baked beans	35	6.1	19.0	2.6
Bologna	86	12.1	1.1	27.5
Chili con carne, without beans	57	10.3	5.8	14.8
Hash, corned beef with potato	51	8.8	10.7	11.3

Table 18 (cont.)

Food	Energy Value	Composition
	Calories per ounce	% Protein
Liverwurst	86	16.2
Luncheon meat, pork	83	15.0
Frankfurter	88	12.4
Vienna sausage	68	14.0
Bouillon cube	34	20.0
Eggs		
Egg, fresh	41	12.9
Egg, dried, whole	168	47.0
CANDIES AND SWEETS		
"Candy bar"	141	9.2
Candy, bulk (hard candy)	139	8.2
Candy, peanut	146	11.3
Chocolate, unsweetened	143	10.7
Chocolate, milk	147	7.7
Chocolate, sweet with almonds	151	9.3
Cocoa mix	111	9.4
Butterscotch	113	0.0
Caramel	113	4.0
Fudge, plain	113	2.
Peanut brittle	119	5
Honey, strained	86	0
Jam	77	0
Mincemeat	61	5
Molasses, cane	66	0
Sugar, brown	106	
Sugar, granulated	109	
Ice cream, plain	59	

Source: Adapted from Watt and Merrill, *Compos*
Prepared—Agriculture Handbook No. 8, U. S. D(
ington, D. C., revised December 1963. This han(
search data available, and is considered by exper
table lists several items for which information
Unfortunately, it has not been possible so far t
specially-packaged foods which nowadays cons⁺
the mountaineer diet.

	One Serving		Four Servings	
	Ounces	*Cups*	*Ounces*	*Cups*
Roman Meal (instant)	1.5 to 1.75	⅜ to ½	6 to 7	1½ to 2
Rolled oats (quick-cooking)	1.5 to 1.75	½ to ⅝	6 to 7	2 to 2½
Sugar, brown To be added to cooked cereal	1⅓	3½ TBL	5½	⅞
Powdered cream product OR	⅓	1½ TBL	1½	⅜
Whole milk To be added to cooked cereal	.75	2 TBL	3	½ plus
Margarine May be added in addition to or in place of milk	½ to 1	1 to 2 TBL	2 to 4	¼ to ½

FRUITS, sun-dried and vacuum-dried				
Raisins (sun)	1		4	
Date nuggets (vacuum)	1		4	
Apple nuggets (vacuum)	1 to 1.5		4 to 6	
Banana flakes (vacuum)	⅓ to ½		1⅓ to 2	
Mincemeat (sun)	1.5		6	
Apricot-raisin (sun)	1.5		6	
Prunes (sun or vacuum)	1 to 1.5		4	
Peaches (vacuum)	1		4	
Fruit cocktail (vacuum)	1 to 1.5		4 to 6	

These fruits may be mixed with cereals, hot or cold, or stewed separately with some sugar (⅔ to 1 ounce per serving) if desired. Cinnamon and nutmeg can be used to season fruits, also dried lemon peel or lemon crystals. Combining stewed fruits adds interest.

FRUITS, freeze-dried	⅔ to ¾			
Fruit cocktail				
Peach slices				
Apricot slices				
Strawberries				

STARCHES				
Pancakes (mix with milk and eggs)	2.5	½	10.5	2
Pilot biscuits	2 to 3	2 to 3 biscuits		
Logan bread	2 to 3			
Cinnamon-nut roll	2 to 3			
Margarine	1 to 2 (on breads and pancakes)			
Honey or jam	1⅓ to 3			

EGGS				
Omelets, freeze-dried	1 to 2	½ to 1 pkg.	4 to 8	2 to 4 pkgs.
Scrambled, freeze-dried	1.5 to 2		6 to 8	

	One Serving		Four Servings	
	Ounces	*Cups*	*Ounces*	*Cups*
MEATS				
Ham, freeze-dried	.5 to .8		2.25 to 3.25	3 to 4 tins
Prefried bacon	1.6	4 slices	6.5	1 tin
Corned beef	2 to 3		8 to 12	1 tin
Chopped meat product	2 to 3		7 to 12	1 tin
Bacon bar, dried	.75 to 1.5	¼ to ½ bar	3 to 6	1 to 2 bars
Meat food product bar, dried	.75 to 1.5	¼ to ½ bar	3 to 6	1 to 2 bars
Margarine for cooking eggs	.5 to 1 (less when meat fat available)			
BEVERAGES				
Milk, dry, skim	.75	⅓	3.2	1⅓
Milk, dry, whole (Kraft, Darigold, Milkman)	1	¼ to ⅓	4	1 to 1⅓
Cocoa, ground, with sugar	.75	⅛	2.75	½
Mix with milk	1.	¼	4.	1
	1.75		6.75	
Cocoa, premixed with milk	1.5	⅜	6	1½
Ovaltine, plain or chocolate	.75	¼	3	1
Mix with milk	1.	¼	4	1
	1.75		7	
Malt, plain or chocolate	.75	2½ TBL	3	⅔
Mix with milk	1.	¼	4	1
	1.75		7	
Breakfast Drink				
Carnation Instant Breakfast, variety of flavors.	.6 to 1.2	½ to 1 pkg.	3.75	3 pkgs.
Mix with milk	1.	¼	4.	1
	1.6		7.75	
Orange Breakfast Drink (Tang)	1.25	3 TBL	5	⅔
Jello	1.5	½ pkg.	6	2 pkgs.

Lunch

Amounts given in ounces per man-day.

MEAT—2	Deviled meats
Sausages	*Jerky—1*
Choose dry hard varieties that are well-cured.	*Meat bars, compressed*
	Bacon
Canned	Meat product
Tuna fish	*Chip beef*
Sardines	Cellophane-packaged types are
Corned beef	quite moist and don't keep long.

Table 18 (cont.)

Food	Energy Value	Composition of Edible Portion		
	Calories per ounce	% Protein	% Carbo-hydrate	% Fat
FRUIT JUICES				
Apple	13	0.1	11.9	Insignifi-
Applesauce, sweetened	26	0.2	23.8	cant in
Grape	19	0.2	16.6	all
Grapefruit, sweetened	15	0.5	12.8	
Orange	14	0.7	10.4	
Pineapple	16	0.4	13.5	
Prune	22	0.4	19.0	
Tomato	5	0.9	4.3	
Lemon juice concentrate, frozen, unsweetened	33	2.3	37.4	
Orange concentrate, canned	63	4.1	50.7	
Lemonade concentrate, frozen	55	0.2	51.1	
Fruit cocktail, canned, in syrup	22	0.4	19.5	
VEGETABLES, DEHYDRATED				
Cabbage	87	14.4	72.5	Insignifi-
Carrot	97	6.6	81.1	cant in
Potato	100	8.3	80.4	all
Sweet potato	107	4.2	90.0	
Tomato flakes	97	10.8	76.7	
NUTS				
Almond	170	18.6	19.5	57.7
Brazil	185	14.3	10.9	66.9
Cashew	159	17.2	29.3	45.7
Coconut, dried, sweetened	155	3.6	53.2	39.1
Peanut butter	167	27.8	17.2	49.4
Peanut, roasted	165	26.0	18.8	49.8
Pecan	195	9.2	14.6	71.2
Walnut	159	14.8	15.8	64.0
GRAIN PRODUCTS				
Breakfast Cereals				
Bran flakes, 40%	85	10.7	82.1	3.6
Cornflakes	109	7.9	85.3	Insignifi-
Oatmeal, uncooked	110	15.0	78.5	cant in
Rice, puffed	113	6.0	89.5	most
Farina, enriched, uncooked	103	11.4	77.0	
Wheat, puffed	103	15.0	78.5	
Wheat, shredded	104	9.9	79.9	
Wheat germ	102	26.5	47.0	10.3

Table 18 (cont.)

Food	Energy Value	Composition of Edible Portion		
	Calories per ounce	% Protein	% Carbo- hydrate	% Fat
Other Grains, (Uncooked)				
Barley, pearl	99	8.4	78.8	Insignifi-
Macaroni	105	12.5	75.2	cant in
Noodles, egg	110	12.8	72.0	all
Spaghetti	105	12.5	75.2	
Rice, brown, raw	102	7.5	77.4	
Rice, white, raw	103	6.7	80.4	
Rice, precooked	105	7.5	82.5	
Pancake mix, wheat	101	8.6	75.7	
Pancake mix, buckwheat	93	10.5	70.3	
Baked Goods				
Bread				
Rye	69	9.1	52.1	
White	77	8.7	50.5	
Pumpernickel	70	9.1	53.1	
Whole wheat	69	10.5	47.7	
Boston brown	60	5.5	45.6	
Cooky, sugar	126	6.0	68.0	16.8
Doughnut	111	4.6	51.4	18.6
Fig bar	101	3.9	75.4	5.6
Triscuit	125	12.0	?	?
Rye wafer	98	13.0	76.3	1.2
Logan bread, moist	100	7.0	60.0	10.0
Logan bread, dry	112	8.0	67.0	12.0
MEAT, FISH, EGGS				
Beef				
Corned, canned	75	23.5	0.0	18.0
Dried, chipped	58	34.3	0.0	6.3
Hamburger, cooked	81	24.2	0.0	20.3
Pork				
Bacon, lean, cooked	173	30.4	3.2	52.0
Bacon, Canadian, cooked	79	27.6	0.3	17.5
Bacon, canned	194	8.5	1.0	71.5
Ham, smoked	87	23.0	0.0	30.6
Fish				
Salmon, canned	43	20.8	0.0	7.1
Sardines in oil, drained	47	24.0	0.0	11.1
Tuna, canned, drained	47	28.8	0.0	8.2
Processed Products				
Baked beans	35	6.1	19.0	2.6
Bologna	86	12.1	1.1	27.5
Chili con carne, without beans	57	10.3	5.8	14.8
Hash, corned beef with potato	51	8.8	10.7	11.3

Table 18 (cont.)

Food	Energy Value	Composition of Edible Portion		
	Calories per ounce	% Protein	% Carbo- hydrate	% Fat
Liverwurst	86	16.2	1.8	25.6
Luncheon meat, pork	83	15.0	1.3	24.9
Frankfurter	88	12.4	1.6	27.2
Vienna sausage	68	14.0	0.3	19.8
Bouillon cube	34	20.0	5.0	3.0
Eggs				
Egg, fresh	41	12.9	0.9	11.5
Egg, dried, whole	168	47.0	4.1	41.2
CANDIES AND SWEETS				
"Candy bar"	141	9.2	59.6	25.3
Candy, bulk (hard candy)	139	8.2	64.2	22.5
Candy, peanut	146	11.3	60.5	22.2
Chocolate, unsweetened	143	10.7	28.9	53.0
Chocolate, milk	147	7.7	56.9	32.3
Chocolate, sweet with almonds	151	9.3	51.3	35.6
Cocoa mix	111	9.4	73.9	10.6
Butterscotch	113	0.0	94.8	3.4
Caramel	113	4.0	76.6	10.2
Fudge, plain	113	2.7	75.0	12.2
Peanut brittle	119	5.7	81.0	10.4
Honey, strained	86	0.3	82.3	0.0
Jam	77	0.6	70.0	0.1
Mincemeat	61	5.3	34.4	6.4
Molasses, cane	66	0.0	60.0	0.0
Sugar, brown	106	0.0	96.4	0.0
Sugar, granulated	109	0.0	99.5	0.0
Ice cream, plain	59	4.0	20.6	12.5

Source: Adapted from Watt and Merrill, *Composition of Foods, Raw, Processed, Prepared—Agriculture Handbook No. 8,* U. S. Department of Agriculture, Washington, D. C., revised December 1963. This handbook was compiled from all research data available, and is considered by experts to be authoritative. The above table lists several items for which information was derived from other sources. Unfortunately, it has not been possible so far to gain data on the values of the specially-packaged foods which nowadays constitute an important component of the mountaineer diet.

APPENDIX 2

MEALS FOR

SEMI-EXPEDITIONS

Breakfast

Weights accurate to ¼ ounce. Greater error in the dry measure.

	One Serving		Four Servings	
	Ounces	*Cups*	*Ounces*	*Cups*
COLD CEREALS				
Wheat Chex	2 to 2.5	1 crushed	8 to 10	4
Grapenuts } combined	{ 2	{ ½	{ 8	{ 2
Grapenut Flakes }	{ .75	{ ¼ crushed	{ 3	{ 1
	2.75		11	
Birchermuesli (Familia)	3.5 to 4	¾ to 1	14 to 16	3 to 4
(Cereal food including				
nuts and fruit. No sugar				
needed.)				
All-Bran	2 to 2.5		8 to 10	
Wheatgerm	.25 to .5		1 to 2	
(May be added to all)				
Milk, whole	.75	¼	3	¾
(Can be premixed)				
Sugar, white granulated	1	2 TBL	4	½ plus
(Can be premixed)				
HOT CEREALS				
Cream of Wheat	1.5 to 1.75	3½ to 4 TBL	6 to 7	¾ to 1
(quick-cooking)				
Wheat Hearts	1.4 to 1.75	¼ to ⅓	5.5 to 7	1 to 1⅓
Instant Ralston	1.4 to 1.75	¼ to ⅓	5.5 to 7	1 to 1⅓

	One Serving		*Four Servings*	
	Ounces	*Cups*	*Ounces*	*Cups*
Roman Meal (instant)	1.5 to 1.75	⅜ to ½	6 to 7	1½ to 2
Rolled oats (quick-cooking)	1.5 to 1.75	½ to ⅝	6 to 7	2 to 2½
Sugar, brown To be added to cooked cereal	1⅓	3½ TBL	5½	⅞
Powdered cream product OR	⅓	1½ TBL	1½	⅜
Whole milk To be added to cooked cereal	.75	2 TBL	3	½ plus
Margarine May be added in addition to or in place of milk	½ to 1	1 to 2 TBL	2 to 4	¼ to ½
FRUITS, sun-dried and vacuum-dried				
Raisins (sun)	1		4	
Date nuggets (vacuum)	1		4	
Apple nuggets (vacuum)	1 to 1.5		4 to 6	
Banana flakes (vacuum)	⅓ to ½		1⅓ to 2	
Mincemeat (sun)	1.5		6	
Apricot-raisin (sun)	1.5		6	
Prunes (sun or vacuum)	1 to 1.5		4	
Peaches (vacuum)	1		4	
Fruit cocktail (vacuum)	1 to 1.5		4 to 6	

These fruits may be mixed with cereals, hot or cold, or stewed separately with some sugar (⅔ to 1 ounce per serving) if desired. Cinnamon and nutmeg can be used to season fruits, also dried lemon peel or lemon crystals. Combining stewed fruits adds interest.

FRUITS, freeze-dried	⅔ to ¾			
Fruit cocktail				
Peach slices				
Apricot slices				
Strawberries				
STARCHES				
Pancakes (mix with milk and eggs)	2.5	½	10.5	2
Pilot biscuits	2 to 3	2 to 3 biscuits		
Logan bread	2 to 3			
Cinnamon-nut roll	2 to 3			
Margarine	1 to 2 (on breads and pancakes)			
Honey or jam	1⅓ to 3			
EGGS				
Omelets, freeze-dried	1 to 2	½ to 1 pkg.	4 to 8	2 to 4 pkgs.
Scrambled, freeze-dried	1.5 to 2		6 to 8	

	One Serving		Four Servings	
	Ounces	*Cups*	*Ounces*	*Cups*
MEATS				
Ham, freeze-dried	.5 to .8		2.25 to 3.25	3 to 4 tins
Prefried bacon	1.6	4 slices	6.5	1 tin
Corned beef	2 to 3		8 to 12	1 tin
Chopped meat product	2 to 3		7 to 12	1 tin
Bacon bar, dried	.75 to 1.5	¼ to ½ bar	3 to 6	1 to 2 bars
Meat food product bar, dried	.75 to 1.5	¼ to ½ bar	3 to 6	1 to 2 bars
Margarine for cooking eggs	.5 to 1 (less when meat fat available)			
BEVERAGES				
Milk, dry, skim	.75	⅓	3.2	1⅓
Milk, dry, whole (Kraft, Darigold, Milkman)	1	¼ to ⅓	4	1 to 1⅓
Cocoa, ground, with sugar	.75	⅛	2.75	½
Mix with milk	1.	¼	4.	1
	1.75		6.75	
Cocoa, premixed with milk	1.5	⅜	6	1½
Ovaltine, plain or chocolate	.75	¼	3	1
Mix with milk	1.	¼	4	1
	1.75		7	
Malt, plain or chocolate	.75	2½ TBL	3	⅔
Mix with milk	1.	¼	4	1
	1.75		7	
Breakfast Drink				
Carnation Instant Breakfast, variety of flavors.	.6 to 1.2	½ to 1 pkg.	3.75	3 pkgs.
Mix with milk	1.	¼	4.	1
	1.6		7.75	
Orange Breakfast Drink (Tang)	1.25	3 TBL	5	⅔
Jello	1.5	½ pkg.	6	2 pkgs.

Lunch

Amounts given in ounces per man-day.

MEAT—2
  Sausages
    Choose dry hard varieties that are well-cured.
  Canned
    Tuna fish
    Sardines
    Corned beef

Deviled meats
Jerky—1
Meat bars, compressed
  Bacon
  Meat product
Chip beef
  Cellophane-packaged types are quite moist and don't keep long.

CHEESE—2

Moist types are preferred for eating but keep less well than dry.

Moist
Monterey Jack
Kuminost (caraway)
Danish cheeses
Blue

Intermediate
Cheddars
Swiss
Edam

Dry—Keep very well
Provoloni
Romano
Kasseri

DRIED FRUIT—2 sundried, 1 to 1½ vacuum-dried

Raisins, dark or bleached
Dates, vacuum-dried or sun
Figs
Peaches, vacuum-dried or sun
Pears
Prunes, pitted, vacuum-dried or sun
Mincemeat, dried
Fruit cocktail, vacuum-dried
Apple nuggets, vacuum-dried
Apricots, vacuum-dried or sun

NUTS—2
Cashews
Mixed
Peanuts
Almonds
Pecans

CHOCOLATE OR CANDY BARS—2

Solid baking-type chocolate is preferred for its higher melting temperature.

Candy bars of most sorts
Candy-coated milk chocolate bits
Mint bar
Fudge
Caramels

HARD CANDY—1
Lifesavers
Sourballs

BREAD—3

Pumpernickle types
Choose the darkest and hardest breads for keeping and packing qualities.

Logan bread
Can up the weight and eliminate fruit and/or nuts in this lunch.

Cinnamon roll
Same note as Logan bread

Crackers—2
Rye crisp
Unleavened breads
Wheat Thins
Triscuits
Pilot biscuits

BEVERAGES
Premixed with sugar
Artificially-sweetened types
Citric powders plus sugar
Instant tea (sugar)
Powdered milk
Plain
Malted
Chocolate

Glops

OLD RELIABLES

Amounts per serving. Measure is ounces unless otherwise stated.

RICE-AND-MEAT

Rice, pre-cooked 2⅓ (⅔ cup dry measure)	*Soup* (Choose one) ½–¾ (¼–⅓ pkg.) Any quick-cooking vegetable soup—tomato vegetable, onion, tomato, etc.	*Meat* (Choose one) Tinned—4 Corned beef Roast beef Chopped pressed meat Sausage, bulk—4 Meat bars—½ to 2 Freeze-dried Hamburgers—1½ Beef patties—1⅓ Meat balls—1⅓	*Margarine*—1	*Cheese*—1 Cheddar

Comments About 9 total for tinned meat dinners. Add gravy mix for soup quantities greater than 4 people. May add milk powder.

CREAMED-STYLE RICE
(*Variation of above*)

Rice, pre-cooked 2⅓ (⅔ cup dry measure)	*Soup* Mushroom, leek, or chicken rice	*Meat* (Choose one) Tinned—4 Tuna Salmon Ham	*Margarine*—1	*Cheese*—1 Cheddar

Variations Freeze-dried mushrooms, particularly with mushroom soup.

		Meat (Choose one)	Margarine—1	Cheese—1	Comments
		Chipped beef—2 Freeze-dried Pork patties—1⅓ Ham—½ to ⅔ Shrimp—½ to 1 Chicken—½ to ⅔			Ala King: green peppers—2 TBL for 4; onions—¼ cup flakes Curry: 1 TBL for 4, dried onions, garlic powder

MACARONI AND MEAT

| Macaroni—2 5-to-7-minute varieties | Soup (Choose one) 1 pkg. for 3 or 4 servings Chicken noodle Tomato Cream soups: Mushroom Leek | Meat (Choose one) Tinned—4 Tuna Salmon Ham Chipped beef—2 Freeze-dried Pork patties—1⅓ Ham—½ to ⅔ Shrimp—½ to 1 Chicken—½ to ⅔ | Margarine—1 | Cheese—1 | Comments May add dried milk powder. Variations for creamed rice dinners suitable. Creole: with tomato soup add onions, green pepper. |

Glops (cont.)

OLD RELIABLES

Amounts per serving. *Measure is ounces unless otherwise stated.*

MACARONI-AND-CHEESE					
Macaroni—3	*Soup* Chicken Bouillon—1 cube or 1 tsp.	*Dried Milk* ¼ cup	*Margarine*—½	*Cheese*—3 Cheddar tsp.	*Seasoning* For 4: Onions—¼ cup Dry mustard—1 tsp. Oregano—½ tsp.
POTATO					
Potato, mashed—2	*Soup* (Choose one) Cream type for creamed dishes, any meat Onion or Vegetable with beef	*Meat* (Choose one) Tinned Roast beef Corned beef	*Margarine*—1	*Cheese*—1	*Milk* ⅓ cup for 4 With corned beef use Dry cabbage—¾ oz. (¾ cup) for 4 Onions—¼ oz. (¼ cup) for 4

SPECIALTIES

Amounts given in ounces for 4 servings.

SPANISH RICE	Ounces for 4	Comments
Spanish rice mix, precooked	12 (2 pkgs.)	
Tomato soup or tomato sauce		
mix	1 pkg.	
Meat (Choose one)		
Bacon bars	6(2 bars)	
Bulk sausage	16	
Shrimp—tinned	12	Heavy in water pack
freeze-dried	2	
Tuna, tinned	16	
Freeze-dried		
Hamburger	6.5	
Meat balls	4	More would be desirable—on
Beef patties	4	the order of 5 to 5⅓.
Margarine	4(1 cube)	
Parmesan cheese, grated	2	Optional

CHINESE RICE		
Rice	9⅓ (2⅔ cups)	
Chicken rice soup	1 pkg.	
Tuna	12	
and chicken, tinned, boned	4–5	
or freeze-dried chicken	6.5	
Margarine	4 (1 cube)	
Cashews, broken	4	

CHILI RICE		
Rice, precooked	9⅓ (2⅔ cups)	
Tomato soup or tomato sauce		
mix	1 pkg.	
Meat (Choose one)		
Compressed meat bars	6 to 8	
Roast beef, tinned	16	Add 4 oz. tin Vienna sausage
Chopped meat, tinned	16	to 12 oz. tin.
Bulk sausage	16	
Freeze-dried		
Hamburger	6.5	
Meat balls	4	More would be desirable.
Beef patties	4	More would be desirable.
Margarine	4 (1 cube)	
Cheese, cheddar type, grated	4	
Onions, dry	½ (¼ cup)	
Chili powder	1½ TBL	Those who like it hot will want more.

ALA

Ala	8 (1⅓ cups)	Slow cooking—15 minutes
Beef soup, beef noodle soup, or onion soup	1 pkg. and 1 bouillon cube	
Meat suggestions and amounts same as chili rice dinner above.		
Margarine	4 (1 cube)	
Cheese, cheddar	4	
Oregano	½ tsp.	

BEEF STEW

Potatoes, cubed, sliced, or diced	8	Slow—soak with vegetables.
Tomato *or* beef soup	1 pkg. and 1 bouillon cube	
Meat (Choose one)		
Roast beef, tinned	16	Add one 4-oz. can Vienna sausage to 12 oz. tin.
Freeze-dried		
Hamburger	6.5	
Meat balls	4	More is desirable—on order
Beef patties	4	of 5⅓ oz.
Margarine	4 (1 cube)	
Dried vegetables		
Carrots	1	Soak
Onions	¼ (¼ cup)	"
Celery	¼ cup	"
Green pepper	2 TBL	"
Parsley	1 TBL	
Mixed herbs	1 tsp. (½ tsp. marjoram, ½ tsp. thyme)	
Pepper	⅛ tsp.	

SPAGHETTI

Spaghetti, quick-cooking	8	
Tomato soup *or*	1 pkg.	Add chili powder—2 tsps., onions—¼ oz., and herbs.
Spaghetti mix with tomato	1 pkg.	Choose quick-cooking type—not too spicy.
Meat (Choose one)		
Freeze-dried		
Meat balls	4	Larger quantity desirable.
Beef patties	4	Larger quantity desirable.
Hamburger	6.5	

Roast beef, tinned	16 ⎱	Add one 4 oz. can Vienna
Chopped beef, tinned	16 ⎰	sausage to 12-oz. tin.
Bulk sausage	16	
Compressed meat bars	6 to 8	
Margarine	4 (1 cube)	
Parsley, dried	1 TBL	
Herbs	½ tsp. basil	
	½ tsp.	
	oregano	
	dash thyme	
Parmesan cheese, grated	2	

CURRY DINNER, BEEF

Rice, precooked	9⅓ (2⅔ cups)	
Beef bouillon	4 cubes or 4 tsps.	
Meat (Choose one)		
Roast beef, tinned	16	
Freeze-dried meats can be used but unspiced meats are preferred.	5 to 6	
Margarine	4 (1 cube)	
Raisins	3 (½ cup)	Soak fruits and vegetables.
Apples, dried sliced	2	
Green pepper	2 TBL	
Onion	½ (¼ cup)	
Lemon peel, dried	1 TBL	
Curry powder	1 TBL	
Marjoram	½ tsp.	Mix spices at home and pack-
Thyme	½ tsp.	age together.
Garlic powder	¼ tsp.	
Lemon crystals or citric acid crystals	½ tsp.	
Cornstarch	1 TBL	

CURRY DINNER, SHRIMP

Chicken bouillon	4 cubes or 4 tsps.	
Shrimp (Choose one)		
Canned	12	Heavy in water-pack.
Freeze-dried	4.5 (1 #2½ tin)	
Other ingredients the same as above.		
Coconut, dried	¼ cup	May be added to herbs and spices.

CHICKEN OR SHRIMP JAMBALAYA

Rice, precooked	9½ (2⅔ cups)	

Tomato soup	2¼ (1 pkg.) plus 1 chicken bouillon	
Meat (Choose one)		
Freeze-dried		
Chicken	6.5 (#2½ tin)	
Shrimp	4.5 (#2½ tin)	
Margarine	4	
Dried vegetables		
Onions	.25 (¼ cup)	Soak vegetables.
Green pepper	1 TBL	
Celery	2 tsp.	
Thyme	½ tsp.	
Cayenne	dash	
Parsley	1 tsp.	
Chili	½ tsp.	

HAM-YAM SURPRISE

Yams, dried, powdered	8
Cream of leek soup	2 (1 pkg.)
Cream gravy	1 (1 pkg.)
Ham, freeze-dried	2
Milk, powdered, whole	1
Margarine	4
Cheese, cheddar, grated	4
Cashews, broken	4
Raisins	2
Spices	
Nutmeg	½ tsp.
Cinnamon	½ tsp.

APPENDIX 3

SUPPLEMENTARY READING

The outpouring over the years of books on mountaineering might lead the innocent bystander to wonder how any time was left for climbing. No attempt has been made here to note all the writings known to be useful and interesting; bibliographies exist, and it is assumed the scholar will be able to find them by consulting libraries, particularly those of mountain clubs.

The following brief list contains two sorts of materials. Some are suggested because they have a different viewpoint from that of *Freedom*, and thus provide further insights into the relationship of men and mountains. Most, however, are recommended for their deeper or broader consideration of special subjects. In neither case do the editors say these are the only or even necessarily the best references, but merely that they effectively supplement *Freedom*.

General

Young, Geoffrey Winthrop, *Mountain Craft*. London, Methuen, 1920, 7th ed. revised, 1946.
Much of the technique is obsolete, but the spirit and style will never be. The classic exposition of how English greats played the game during the Silver Age.

Milner, D. Douglas, *Rock for Climbing*. London, Chapman and Hall, 1950.
Another basic handbook for philosophers. Excellent pictures.

Evans, Charles, *On Climbing*. London, Museum Press, 1955.
Anecdotes and essays by a modern great with credentials from firsts on Everest and Kanchenjunga to scrambles in Wales.

Rebuffat, Gaston, *On Snow and Rock*. New York, Oxford University Press, 1963.
Photos of the author in action doing contemporary advanced techniques, with text telling how and why he does it that way. The translation successfully transmits his Gallic élan.
(At last report, the Sydney Rockclimbing Club of Australia had in progress a full description of how the sport is practiced where the seasons and mountains are upsidedown.)

Part One: Approaching the Peaks

Brower, David R. (editor), *Going Light—With Backpack and Burro*. San Francisco, Sierra Club, latest edition 1958.

CHAPTER 1: EQUIPMENT

Cunningham and Hanson, *Lightweight Camping Equipment and How to Make It*. Ward, Colorado, 1959.
(The catalogues of outfitters specializing in mountain gear are indispensable guides to what is newest and best. In America, a dozen or more firms are now thriving; in Europe, hundreds.)

CHAPTER 3: ALPINE CUISINE

Mendenhall, Ruth Dyar, *Backpack Cookery*. Glendale, California, La Siesta Press, 1966.
Many valuable recipes and tips.

CHAPTER 5: NAVIGATION IN THE HILLS

Ratliff, Donald E., *Map, Compass, and Campfire*. Portland, Oregon, Binfords and Mort, 1964.
Simple exposition of how to use basic navigation tools.
Kjellstrom, Bjorn, *Be Expert with Map and Compass*. Silva.
Another of the same, adopted as the official guide of the Boy Scouts of America.

Part Two: Rock Climbing

Greenbank, Anthony, *Instructions in Rock Climbing*. London, Museum Press, 1963.
Wisdom from Britain, where cliffing still finds its purest form.

CHAPTER 9: ROPED CLIMBING

Smith, Phil D., *Knots for Mountaineering*. Twentynine Palms, California, Desert Trail, 1953, rev. 1960.
The more knots one knows the better. This handy little booklet—and the following one, equally good—offer them by the score.

Wheelock, Walter, *Ropes, Knots, and Slings for Climbers*. Glendale, California, La Siesta Press, 1960.

CHAPTER 10: BELAYING

Leonard, Richard M. et al, *Belaying the Leader*. San Francisco, Sierra Club, 1956. The fount of all modern belaying theory and practice. Unfortunately, the past decade has produced no comparable research effort, which is badly needed.

CHAPTER 11: PITONCRAFT AND RAPPELS

Word was received as this book went to press that Yvonne Chouinard, a master of Yosemite-style decimal rock climbing, is publishing the long-awaited full exposition of that sport.

Part Four: Safe Climbing
CHAPTER 17: CLIMBING DANGERS

Accidents in North American Mountaineering. New York, American Alpine Club, published annually.
Powerful object lessons. Required reading for all climbers, especially novices.

CHAPTER 18: FIRST AID

Wilkerson, James (editor), *Medicine for Mountaineering*. Seattle, The Mountaineers, 1967.
The first detailed exposition published in America of what to do *after* first aid and *before* the doctor comes—which may be a long period of time on expeditions.
Mountaineering First Aid. Seattle, The Mountaineers, 1968.
A miniaturized reprint of Chapter 18, designed to be carried in the first aid kit.

CHAPTER 19: MOUNTAIN RESCUE

Mariner, Wastl, *Mountain Rescue Techniques*. Vienna, Oesterreichischer Alpenverein, and Seattle, The Mountaineers and Mountain Rescue Council, 2nd ed. 1965.
The bible of mountain rescue groups throughout the world. This translation, by Otto Trott and Kurt Beam of Seattle, has been adopted by IKAR, the international rescue congress, as its official manual.
Field, Ernest K. (editor), *Mountain Search and Rescue Operations*. Grand Teton National Park, Wyoming, 1958.
Valuable manual on how to find lost people.

Part Five: The Climbing Environment
CHAPTER 20: MOUNTAIN GEOLOGY

Cloos, Hans, *Conversation with the Earth*. New York, Alfred A. Knopf, 1953.

Gilluly, James, Waters, A. C., and Woodford, A. O., *Principles of Geology*. San Francisco, W. H. Freeman and Co., 1951.

Milne, Lorus J. and Margery, *The Mountains*. New York, Life Nature Library, 1962.

Thornbury, W. D., *Principles of Geomorphology*. New York, John Wiley and Sons, 1954.

(See also the bibliography in *Routes and Rocks: Hiker's Guide to the North Cascades from Glacier Peak to Lake Chelan*.)

CHAPTER 21: THE CYCLE OF SNOW

Seligman, Gerald, *Snow Structures and Ski Fields*. London, 1936.
  Though written at a time when the subject was just beginning to be systematically studied, this remains the basic introduction.

LaChapelle, E. R., *The ABC of Avalanche Safety*. Boulder, Colorado, Highlander, 1961.
  A pocket summary by the author of Chapter 21.

Gallagher, Dale (editor), *The Snowy Torrents: Avalanche Accidents in the United States 1910–1966*. Alta, Utah, Avalanche Study Center, U.S. Forest Service, 1967.
  Detailed descriptions and analyses of some 60 life-involving avalanches and rescues. Further reports planned as additional information (which is solicited) is received.

CHAPTER 22: MOUNTAIN WEATHER

Cantzlaar, George L., *Your Guide to the Weather*. New York, Barnes and Noble, 1964.
  A concise introduction for the layman, as is the title below. Both demonstrate how little is known about the subject.

Zim, Herbert S., *Weather*. New York, Golden Press, 1960.

Journals and Clubs

A roster of North American mountaineering clubs and their publications is compiled and revised annually by Chicago Mountaineering Club, 2901 South Parkway, Chicago, Illinois 60616.

There is, in North America, only one mountaineering magazine published privately, and thus not subject to organizational strictures. The virtues and faults of a genuinely free press are here exemplified monthly, in what amounts to an on-going seminar in new equipment and techniques. For subscription information, write *Summit Magazine,* Big Bear Lake, California.

Accepted in recent years as an international point of reference has been *The Mountain World,* a book published biannually by the Swiss Foundation for Alpine Research.

See page xix in frontmatter for other
related books published by The Mountaineers.

*

INDEX